The Splendor of
Longing in the
Tale of Genji

Norma Field

The Splendor of

Longing in the

Tale of Genji

PRINCETON

UNIVERSITY

PRESS

Copyright © 1987 by Princeton University Press

Published by Princeton University Press, 41 William Street,
Princeton, New Jersey 08540
In the United Kingdom: Princeton University Press,
Oxford

All Rights Reserved

Library of Congress Cataloging in Publication Data will be
found on the last printed page of this book

ISBN 0-691-06691-4 (cloth)
01436-1 (pbk.)

Publication of this book has been aided by grants from the
Suntory Foundation and the Japan Foundation

This book has been composed in Linotron Electra

Princeton University Press books are printed on acid-free paper,
and meet the guidelines for permanence and durability
of the Committee on Production Guidelines for Book Longevity
of the Council on Library Resources

Printed in the United States of America

DESIGNED BY LAURY A. EGAN

3   5   7   9   10   8   6   4   2

For Rodger

Contents

Contents

Preface

IN PREPARING this book I have consulted a number of Japanese editions of the *Genji Monogatari*: chiefly, the Iwanami *Nihon Koten Bungaku Taikei* version, Shinchōsha's *Nihon Koten Bungaku Shūsei*, the *Kogetsushō*, Tamagami Takuya's *Genji Monogatari Hyōshaku*, and as the basic text, the Shōgakkan *Nihon Koten Bungaku Zenshū* edition. All the passages quoted from the *Genji* are my own translations (as are passages from other works unless indicated otherwise). Each is identified in the body of the text with its location in the Shōgakkan text followed by its location in the Seidensticker and Waley translations. Thus (3:206; S 405; W 461) means volume 3, page 206 in Shōgakkan, page 405 in the 1976 Seidensticker translation, and page 461 in the 1960 Modern Library Waley edition.

I imagine a number of uses for these correlations. First, the reader may wish to situate a particular passage in context. Second, the great differences in the three translations may provoke interest in their own right. I must caution the reader, however, that the particular element for which I am quoting a passage will often not appear in the Seidensticker or Waley versions. This is especially the case with character names or titles. I have, nevertheless, indicated the location of the passage in Seidensticker and Waley. This is also true when the omissions are more extensive. Only when a given incident or exchange is entirely missing do I mark its general location in brackets. This happens from time to time with the Waley translation. The celebrated omissions from Waley are of course a portion of the "Fireflies" chapter and the entire "Bell Cricket" chapter. A considerable section is also missing at the beginning of the second "New Herbs" chapter. Together with the writing of sequels or parodies, translation represents the most active form of reading. All translators have their own conception of the whole that governs the handling of the parts. I hope the reader will keep this in mind when reviewing my juxtapositions. Nevertheless, I cannot overestimate the extent to which I am indebted to both the Seidensticker and the Waley translations.

I have made certain decisions for the sake of consistency in helping the English-speaking reader to follow the text in either the Waley or the Seidensticker translation. I have used the Seidensticker chapter titles and listed Waley and Japanese equivalents in an appendix. I have also generally used the Seidensticker character names and given equivalents in the list of "Principal Characters." The reader may wish to supplement with the genealogical charts offered in the Waley translation as well as in Ivan Morris's *The World of the Shining Prince*. Better yet, the reader might follow in the venerable tradition of *Genji* scholarship and produce his or her own charts with the help of the descriptions in the list of "Principal Characters." Genealogies are one of the most valuable representations of the tale; it is best to have both charts that are specific to the context at hand and those that reveal more far-flung relationships.

This study began as a dissertation at Princeton University, and by now the list of those whom I would like to thank is considerable indeed. Work began during a two-year stay (1980-1982) in Tokyo, Japan, supported by Fulbright-Hays and Social Science Research Council grants. I wish to record my gratitude to the institutions that made possible this rich and happy period. My work in Japan was aided by the kindness of more people than I could possibly name. Nevertheless, I wish to thank Professors Akiyama Ken, Nakanishi Susumu, and Suzuki Hideo for their assistance in getting me started and their continued cordiality. To all the members of the Monogatari Kenkyūkai, my heartfelt thanks for sensible instruction, spirited exchange, and inexhaustible conviviality. Fujii Sadakazu, Takahashi Tōru, Kawazoe Fusae, and Kobayashi Masaaki have been generous with ideas and materials. To the indefatigably provocative Mitani Kuniaki my intellectual debt continues to be unbounded.

My years at Princeton were sustained by the warm encouragement of teachers and friends. My thanks to Andrew Plaks, Richard Bowring, and Ian Levy for diligently reading and commenting on my work, and to Earl Miner for his apparently unquenchable enthusiasm and willingness to prod, without which the project might never have been undertaken let alone completed. Lewis Cook of Cornell University gave generously of his powers of critical scrutiny. He may quarrel with much that remains but I am grateful for his efforts.

At the University of Chicago I found a wonderful community of friends and colleagues. My thanks go to students who have listened to and argued with me and, in particular, to my colleagues Harry Harootunian, Tetsuo Najita, and Bill Sibley whose enlivening exchange and encouragement have inspired new thought and energy. Karen Brazell and Thomas Rimer as readers for the Press offered a number of valuable suggestions. Cathie Brettschneider edited the manuscript with perspicacity and resolution. My thanks also for the friendship of Linn Freiwald and Maria Laghi, representatives of that fabled and exacting creature, the common reader. Finally, I wish for words with which to thank my patient family, both immediate and extended. I dedicate this book as a token of esteem and gratitude to my husband Rodger.

March 13, 1986

Principal Characters

THE FOLLOWING is a list of the principal characters referred to in the text. A variety of names are used in the *Tale of Genji* for any given character (the more significant the character, the more forms of reference). I have generally followed the designations in the Seidensticker translation and indicate the Waley and Japanese appellations in parentheses. For the latter I have generally used the principal listings in the genealogical charts at the end of each volume of the Shōgakkan edition. Where I have deviated from Seidensticker, I have so indicated with an * and listed the Seidensticker name first in parentheses. There are of course some variations in the Seidensticker and Waley translations as well. I have ignored slight variations of form and use "same" to indicate that the source uses the same name as the one listed immediately before it.

Akashi Empress / Akashi Princess (Crown Princess / Akashi Princess; Akashi no Chūgū). Genji's daughter by the Akashi Lady and therefore half sister of Yūgiri and, unknown to the world, the Reizei Emperor as well. Consort of the last emperor in the tale, a son of Suzaku. Mother of the First Princess and Niou among others.

Akashi Lady (Lady of Akashi; Akashi no Kimi). Daughter of the Akashi Priest and mother of the Akashi Princess by Genji.

Akashi Priest* (the old man; the ex- or old Governor; Akashi no Nyūdō). Former governor of Harima Province and father of the Akashi Lady. He is a cousin to the Kiritsubo Lady, Genji's mother.

Akikonomu (Lady Akikonomu; Akikonomu Chūgū). Daughter of the Rokujō Lady and a crown prince, dead before the beginning of the tale. Consort of the Reizei Emperor. Has no issue.

Aoi (Princess Aoi; Aoi no Ue). Daughter of a Minister of the Left and Princess Ōmiya, sister of Tō no Chūjō. Genji's first official wife and mother of Yūgiri.

Asagao, Princess* (Asagao; Princess Asagao; Asagao no Hime-gimi). Daughter of a brother of the Kiritsubo Emperor and therefore first cousin to Genji.

Bennokimi (same; Ben). Daughter of Kashiwagi's wet nurse; in attendance on the Uji princesses.

Eighth Prince (Hachi no Miya; same). Son of Kiritsubo Emperor, half brother of Genji. Father of the Uji princesses and Ukifune.

First Princess (same; Onna Ichi no Miya). Daughter of Akashi Empress and the last emperor in the tale. Sister of Niou. Kaoru, although married to her half sister the Second Princess, is ardently drawn to her.

Fujitsubo (Lady Fujitsubo; Fujitsubo Chūgū). Daughter of a "previous emperor" and consort of the Kiritsubo Emperor. Secretly bears Reizei Emperor by Genji.

Genji (Prince Genji; Genji). Eponymous hero. Son of the Kiritsubo Emperor and the Kiritsubo Lady. Father of Yūgiri, the Akashi Empress, and, unknown to the world, the Reizei Emperor. Officially married first to Aoi and later to the Third Princess.

Hana Chiru Sato* (Lady of the Orange Blossoms; Lady from the Village of Falling Flowers; Hana Chiru Sato). One of Genji's minor ladies, but installed in the Rokujōin. Entrusted with the care of young people, including Tamakazura, Yūgiri, and his daughter Rokunokimi.

Higekuro (Prince Higekuro; Higekuro Taishō). Married first to Murasaki's stepsister and later to Tamakazura.

Higekuro's Wife (Lady Makibashira; Higekuro no Kita no Kata). Daughter of Prince Hyōbu; Murasaki's stepsister. Replaced by Tamakazura as Higekuro's principal wife.

Hotaru, Prince (Prince Sochi; Hotaru no Miya). Genji's half brother and later husband of Higekuro's daughter Makibashira by his first wife.

Hyōbu, Prince (Prince Hyōbukyō; Hyōbukyō no Miya and later Shikibukyō no Miya). Brother of Fujitsubo and father of Murasaki and Higekuro's first wife.

Kaoru (same). Son of the Third Princess by Kashiwagi. Thought by the world to be Genji's son. As Genji's son, he becomes half brother to the Akashi Empress and therefore uncle to his close companion Prince Niou; as the Third Princess's son, he is Niou's cousin.

Kashiwagi (same). Son of Tō no Chūjō and half brother to Tamakazura. Married to Ochiba no Miya but loves the Third Princess and fathers Kaoru by her. Yūgiri's close companion.

Kiritsubo Emperor* (the Emperor; same; Kiritsuboin). Father of Genji. Brother of Princess Ōmiya (Tō no Chūjō's mother), Prince Hanazono (Princess Asagao's father), and the late crown prince who was the Lady Rokujō's husband.

Kiritsubo Lady* (a lady; same; Kiritsubo Kōi). Beloved of the Kiritsubo Emperor and mother of Genji. Daughter of a major counsellor who was a brother of the Akashi Priest.

Kokiden (same; Kokiden Nyōgo). Daughter of a Minister of the Right and sister of Oborozukiyo. Principal rival of the Kiritsubo Lady and Fujitsubo for the Kiritsubo Emperor's affections. Bears him the Suzaku Emperor.

Koremitsu (same). Genji's trusted attendant and companion on escapades, as with Yūgao.

Kumoinokari (Kumoi; Kumoi no Kari). Daughter of Tō no Chūjō. Wife of Genji's son Yūgiri.

Makibashira (the little girl; Makibashira). Daughter of Higekuro and his first wife. Wife of Prince Hotaru, Genji's half brother.

Minister of the Left (same; Sadaijin). Several characters hold this title. The principal one is husband of Princess Ōmiya and father of Genji's wife Aoi and his close companion Tō no Chūjō.

Minister of the Right (same; Udaijin). Several characters hold this title, of whom the principal one is father of Kokiden and Oborozukiyo and grandfather of the Suzaku Emperor.

Murasaki (same; Murasaki no Ue). Daughter of Prince Hyōbu by a minor lady; niece of Fujitsubo and beloved of Genji.

Nakanokimi (Kozeri; Naka no Kimi). Second daughter of the Eighth Prince and sister of Ōigimi and half sister of Ukifune. Established by Prince Niou in the Nijōin, the estate loved by Murasaki and originally belonging to the family of Genji's mother, the Kiritsubo Lady.

Niou, Prince (same; Niou no Miya). Son of the Akashi Empress and the last emperor in the tale. Close companion and rival of Kaoru, his cousin and uncle (see Kaoru, above). Makes Rokunokimi, one of Yūgiri's daughters, his official wife and keeps Nakanokimi at the Nijōin. Pursues her half sister Ukifune.

Oborozukiyo (Princess Oborozukiyo; Oborozukiyo no Kimi). Daughter of a Minister of the Right and sister to Kokiden. Beloved by the Suzaku Emperor but is herself drawn to Genji.

Ochiba no Miya* (Second Princess, 1; Princess Ochiba; Ochiba no Miya). Daughter of the Suzaku Emperor and wife of Kashiwagi, who is fatally drawn to her half sister the Third Princess. Pursued by Kashiwagi's friend Yūgiri after his death.

Ōigimi (Agemaki; Ōigimi). Eldest daughter of the Eighth Prince and sister of Nakanokimi, half sister of Ukifune. Loved by Kaoru.

Ōmi, Lady of (Lady from Ōmi; Ōmi no Kimi). Daughter of Tō no Chūjō by a lesser woman. Brought out from the provinces with hopes of providing competition to Tamakazura, then thought to be Genji's daughter.

Ōmiya, Princess (same; Ōmiya). Sister of the Kiritsubo Emperor and wife of a Minister of the Left. Mother of Tō no Chūjō and Aoi.

Reizei Emperor (Ryozen; Reizeiin). Son of Fujitsubo and Genji, but thought by the world to be the Kiritsubo Emperor's son. Akikonomu is his consort. He abdicates without issue, though a daughter is incongruously mentioned in "The Bamboo River."

Rokujō Lady (Lady Rokujo; Rokujō no Miyasudokoro). Daughter of a minister and widow of a crown prince, to whom she has borne Akikonomu. Once pursued by Genji. Possesses several of his ladies.

Rokunokimi (same). Daughter of Yūgiri and official wife of Niou.

Second Princess (same; Onna Ni no Miya). Daughter of the last emperor in the tale but not by the Akashi Empress. Wife of Kaoru, who is however drawn to her half sister the First Princess.

Suetsumuhana* (the Safflower Lady; Princess Suyetsumuhana; Suetsumuhana). Daughter of a dead Prince of Hitachi; befriended by Genji.

Suzaku Emperor (Suzaku; Suzakuin). Son of the Kiritsubo Emperor by Kokiden and half brother of Genji. Father of the emperor regnant at the end, whose consort is the Akashi Empress.

Tamakazura (same). Long-lost daughter of Yūgao and Tō no Chūjō and Kashiwagi's half sister. When discovered, Genji tries to claim her as his own daughter. Becomes Higekuro's wife.

Third Princess (Princess Nyosan; Onna San no Miya). Daughter of the Suzaku Emperor and sister of the last emperor in the tale. Married to Genji but has a son, Kaoru, by Kashiwagi.

Tō no Chūjō (same). Son of Princess Ōmiya and a Minister of the Left; brother of Aoi. Genji's companion and rival. Father of Kashiwagi, Tamakazura, and the Ōmi Lady among many other children.

Ukifune (same). Unrecognized daughter of the Eighth Prince by an attendant, related to the Prince's wife. Half sister of Ōigimi and Nakanokimi. Sought by both Kaoru and Niou.

Ukifune's Mother (same; Chūjō no Kimi). Attendant of the Eighth Prince; bears him Ukifune. Both are unwelcome in his house, and she subsequently marries the Governor of Hitachi.

Utsusemi* (Lady of the Locust Shell; Utsusemi; same). Wife of a provincial governor; pursued by the young Genji and later installed in a pavilion neighboring the Rokujōin.

Yokawa, Bishop of (Sozu; Yokawa no Sōzu). Priest who becomes entangled in the lives of Ukifune and Kaoru.

Yūgao* (Lady of the Evening Faces; Yugao; same). An undistinguished lady loved by both Genji and Tō no Chūjō, who fathers her daughter Tamakazura.

The Splendor of
Longing in the
Tale of Genji

Introduction

OUR CENTURY WANES, and the distance between us and the creation of Murasaki Shikibu's *Tale of Genji* will soon measure one thousand years. One thousand years: differences of culture or language fade before the sheer expanse of time. Yet such an expanse, like many-digited numbers, strikes most of us as meaningless. We are apt to be politely awed, as when shown a fossiled horn coral or told the number of light years between ourselves and the North Star, but for most of us the surprised reverence passes quickly. I do not know if most contemporary readers of the *Tale of Genji* in the West are struck by overwhelming differences (ranging from the provocative to the insurmountable) or by astounding similarities between their own lives and perceptions and those described in the novel. These reactions, of course, cannot be strictly exclusive, nor is it possible to conceive of some sort of ideal mean between them. It is difficult to possess in sufficient abundance the tact and imagination invariably required by distance and difference. The first task is to recognize them, which already involves the paradoxical operation of distinguishing that which one does not know. I shall begin this process by sketching the range of readings performed on the *Genji* over the centuries.

First, a word of caution. By now, in the Japanese literary tradition, the *Genji*'s place at the head of the canon is secure. It is so thoroughly implicated in a variety of arts that it is, simply put, taken for granted. It has provided inspiration as well as subject matter not only for subsequent prose fiction but also for poetry, drama, and the visual arts. It continues to be reproduced to this day—in multivolume editions, on cassette tape, and in comic book form.

One might say the book was a bestseller in its own time, but that is a ludicrous anachronism given the paucity of paper and of literate human beings. In her diary Murasaki Shikibu complains of unrevised drafts being stolen from her room in the course of her duties as an attendant to Empress Shōshi.[1] Perhaps

3

the better comparison would be to a popular serial, for the author's first audiences doubtless read the work in such pieces as they could get their hands on over the years of its composition. Somewhat more than half a century later, a young girl returning to the capital upon the expiration of her father's term as provincial vice-governor yearned so desperately for a copy of the *Genji* that she even made it the focus of her pilgrimage prayers. These were eventually answered, and the lucky adolescent, heedless of dream warnings to turn to scriptural study, abandoned herself to the pleasures of reading fiction. Like so many fiction readers she ardently hoped, in spite of her unpromising looks, to receive one day the attentions bestowed on the *Genji* heroines Yūgao and Ukifune. (That these two met spectacularly unhappy fates seems not to have given her pause; although her choices are naive, we must acknowledge the powerful stimulus the *Genji*, like so many good novels from different ages and cultures, afforded the reader's desire to "become a heroine.") Not until her thirties did she express serious regret over her choice of fiction over devotion. She recorded these matters in a sort of journal known as the *Sarashina Diary*. She is herself thought to have written several works of fiction. Remembered as Takasue's Daughter, she was the niece of a woman known as Michitsuna's Mother, whose diary is one of the oldest extant pieces of Japanese prose.[2]

The earliest recorded instances of scholarly attention to the *Genji* date from the late twelfth century. Much of the attention came from poets, the most celebrated of their age, who devoted impressive portions of their lives to copying and annotating texts. Their criticism often took the form of interlinear commentary. Enormous effort was expended in the production of chronologies and genealogies as guides to, or rather instances of, correct interpretation. According to the relentless trend of the medieval arts, these poets and their readings of the *Genji* formed themselves into rival factions such that points of pronunciation and allusions from historical, Chinese, or Buddhist sources became part of secret teachings transmitted within families. Today scholars recognize three large groups of texts, the Aobyōshi (the basis for most current annotated editions), the Kawachi, and "others."

Texts lacking a certain number of characteristics of the first two groups end up in the third.

It should not, of course, surprise us that there are numerous variants in texts of a work written nearly ten centuries ago, especially a work that was being circulated in draft form even as it was being written. There is no hope of ever possessing the "final" form of the novel as Murasaki Shikibu "originally" wrote it. Given these complications, as well as the scope of the work itself, it is understandable that critical endeavor over the centuries has tended toward the production of dictionaries, digests, and compilations of annotations (with traditions developing within categories, e.g., digests for poets, digests for painters). Perhaps the most important of the compilations is the *Kogetsushō* of 1673 by Kitamura Kigin, who was among other things a composer of verses in both the classical thirty-one-syllable *waka* form and the newer seventeen-syllable *haikai* form. The *Kogetsushō*, which has been periodically expanded and is still widely used, juxtaposes various critical notes, often vehemently opposed, as headnotes to a text of the *Genji*.[3] It affords wonderful access to the views of one's fellow readers over the centuries, and it was the text used by the redoubtable Arthur Waley for his translation.

Now we need to step back to Takasue's Daughter in order to pursue other themes in the history of readings of the *Genji*. There was something prophetic about her intoxicated fiction reading punctuated by dreams warning that her time would be better spent in the pursuit of holy truth. As if paying heed to these hints, there developed a tradition from the late twelfth century that Murasaki Shikibu was suffering in hell for the perpetration of lies and other vicious practices in her novel. Many prayers were offered for her soul. Praying for her salvation became a motif later pursued in the Noh as well as in other forms of theater. Almost contemporaneously, there circulated the view that the Bodhisattva of Mercy (Kannon) had taken the form of a woman, namely Murasaki Shikibu, to write this tale as an aid to salvation.

There were two ways that moralists of Confucian as well as Buddhist persuasion could recuperate the *Genji*—either as a cautionary tale or as an allegory. If Confucian scholars were favorably disposed, they propagated the view that the *Genji* could serve as a textbook for teaching desirable relationships between men and women, or between lord and servant; or as an example of the importance of the cultivation of the arts; or, as the warrior class became dominant through the thirteenth and fourteenth centuries, as a guide to etiquette. The elasticity of the work is attested to in subsequent centuries when it gained favor as a didactic book for young women. At the same time that various parodies were being written in newly popular fictional genres, there were such versions as one in which Genji fritters away his time in brothels so as to induce his father to shift his affections to a younger brother and make him heir.

Whereas the poet-readers, with their interest in minute motifs, inevitably contributed to a cannibalization of the work, the Buddhist and Confucian moralists, unpromising as they seem, had a salutary effect in directing attention to the work as a whole through their preoccupation with particular themes. Paradoxically, too, they contained the seeds of liberation from the literal-minded interpretation of truth: allegorical interpretations are of course based on presumptions of figuration, and didacticism did not require that a narrative be virtuous in itself in order to be useful.

The eighteenth and nineteenth centuries saw the emergence of a nativist strain of scholars opposed to foreign, specifically Confucian, interpretations of what they perceived as their distinctive cultural legacy. Among this group was one of the most significant readers the *Genji* has ever produced: Motoori Norinaga (1730-1801). Norinaga appealed to the prestige of Japanese poetry and claimed its affective powers for the *Genji* in an effort to free it from didactic readings. In addition to his philological expertise, Norinaga contributed to—we might also say imposed upon—the novel the possibility of an aesthetically unified reading such as had not existed since its beginnings. For modern readers, Norinaga's imprint remains ineradicable.

From the late nineteenth century on, the *Genji* has been dissected and reconstructed with a rich and bewildering variety of tools. It became the standard subject of experimentation for disciplines newly imported from the West. It was the site where such creatures as the modern subject were discovered. The *Genji* became, in a sense, a principal medium through which foreign intellectual perspectives were domesticated. Initially, the example of German philological studies was particularly prominent. The demands of positivism made themselves heard early and loudly. The emerging disciplines of sociology, psychology, and folklore, and the influence of Freudian and Marxist conceptions, all touched the study of the *Genji* sooner or later and with resounding vigor after the second World War. Today, given the accelerated pace of cultural commerce, a critical practice developed in Europe or America is absorbed into *Genji* studies within a year or two. It is worth observing that just as the legitimacy of Buddhist and Confucian interpretations was vigorously challenged by Norinaga, so murmurs and sometimes louder objections have been raised at the application of Western approaches to a national masterpiece—as if the *Genji* in the twentieth century could, any more than the culture of which it is a part, be cleansed of its history.

The modern history of the Japanese encounter with the West produced several consequences for the *Tale of Genji* that deserve mention. One is suggested in the observations of philologist and literary scholar Haga Yaichi (1867-1927) in a work published in 1898:

> To tell the truth, it is disheartening to be forced to cherish as our national literary masterpiece a work depicting such a decadent society. It certainly is disagreeable to think that it is being read in schools as a textbook.[4]

Upon the new sensibilities of many writers, the *Genji* registered as a musty and hopelessly unsophisticated embarrassment. What changed it all was the appearance of Arthur Waley's magnificent translation in six volumes from 1925-1933. Of course, it gave a moral boost to have the work recognized abroad (Waley's translation spawned a number of European-language translations) and it made one look at it anew; but of equal if not greater importance was the fact that in Waley the work could be read through in something resembling a reasonable amount of time—something no longer possible for most Japanese readers in the twentieth century. One of the surprising converts was the Naturalist writer Masamune Hakuchō (1879-1962), who purchased the translation in London and read it on the voyage home. The Waley translation provoked a flurry of comparisons with various European writers, the more plausible among them being Virginia Woolf and Marcel Proust, given Waley's Bloomsbury ties and above all the style he adopted for his translation. Such comparisons, and more particularly the translation of Proust into Japanese, stimulated new interest among Japanese writers such as Hori Tatsuo (1904-1953) who had previously been indifferent to if not contemptuous of the remote creation of their countrywoman.[5]

One of the more intriguing instances in the *Genji*'s international history is the French novelist Marguerite Yourcenar's parodic treatment of Genji's death, "Le Dernier Amour du Prince Genghi" in *Nouvelles Orientales*. As far as is known, Murasaki Shikibu never described Genji's death in her novel, even though an appropriate chapter title has existed since at least the end of the twelfth century. In her story Yourcenar has an aging "Genghi le Resplendissant," eyesight failing, reencounter without recognizing the docile and neglected "la dame-du-village-des-Fleurs-qui-tombent" (Hana Chiru Sato). Although the lady unnerves Genji by telling him that since his vows he has already been quite forgotten in the capital, she lavishes him with attention, and he takes keen pleasure in her company. After a nostalgic litany of his past loves, he says to her, "If only I had known you earlier in life! But it is right that one piece of fruit be preserved for late autumn." The lady is tortured by his omission of her name and pleads, does he not remember a certain "dame-du-village-des-Fleurs-qui-tombent"? But Genji is already dead.[6]

As it happens, Yourcenar was following in a tradition eight or more centuries old among *Genji* readers, that of filling in perceived gaps in the work. Most of these attempts have not survived, and those that have are themselves incomplete. Of the three main examples, one takes up the Uji story and unites Ukifune with her mother; another begins with Genji's last years and boldly takes us through the progeny of Kaoru and Niou; the

8

third, by none other than Motoori Norinaga, tells of the early days of Genji's love for the Rokujō Lady.[7]

Of course it is hardly a simple sense of deficiency that prompted these readers to produce their own narratives. Rather, one concludes that the *Genji* is a work with the property of inducing, on the one hand, such forms of reading as represented by the production of poems, plays, and scroll paintings and, on the other, various games such as the pairing of heroines to determine which ones behaved better on given occasions. These constitute a continuum rather than an opposition; the *Genji* provokes its readers into such engagements, both lighthearted and intent, and tantalizes them with its ellipses and shifting configurations. So in this century three Japanese writers of stature have translated the tale in its entirety into various versions of modern Japanese. They are the poet Yosano Akiko (1878-1942) and the novelists Tanizaki Jun'ichirō (1886-1965) and Enchi Fumiko (1905—). Akiko, one of the most successful practitioners of the traditional thirty-one-syllable verse form in the modern age, produced an astonishingly crisp *Genji*, published from 1912 to 1914, with a revised edition appearing in 1938-1939. Tanizaki's, by contrast, is richly stylized. His first version was published between 1936 and 1938, and two revised versions appeared after the war—interesting not only as a reflection of the stylistic evolution of a consummate artist but also as a record of what was and was not felt to be reproducible from an acknowledged national masterpiece under the conditions of prewar censorship. Enchi Fumiko's version of 1972-1973 includes a depiction of Genji's death. For all these artists, given the sheer length of the novel, the decision to translate it represents a powerful commitment, and though we can only guess at its significance for each of them, the labor surely had an effect on their own writing. Thus, the *Genji* continues to participate in the generation of Japanese letters.[8]

The reader may be wondering why such translations were conceived, let alone necessary. Earlier, in reference to the importance in Japan of Waley's English translation, I hinted at the difficulty of Murasaki Shikibu's variety of Heian Japanese. Most

Japanese today would be severely taxed to decipher even a few passages of Shikibu's text. They will invariably be familiar with certain selections favored by entrance examination compilers who reproduce them in mutilated form in a battery of cram books. This partially accounts for the need for modern translations, but it hardly exhausts the reasons for their proliferation or for the countless reading groups and lecture series usually directed at housewives who have gained some leisure time. The demand for the vicarious experience of heroinehood never disappears. There continues to be, in other words, a lively interest in this eleventh-century novel, and of course it is not confined to women. My dentist listens to a cassette recording of a modern-language version along with selections of Western classical music while he attends to his patients.

I fear that by now I may have overfilled the ground between Murasaki Shikibu's *Genji* and ourselves. Indeed, the plethora of aids interposing themselves between us and the work (without even mentioning our own helpful or blinding predilections) may drive us to seek refuge in a solipsistic protestant reading. It is not that indulgence in this particular fiction is altogether unhealthy. In fact, it is crucial to resupplying us as readers with a fresh vitality; but a different kind of care and patience are also wanted. The late John Gardner, recounting his literary vita in an essay called "Cartoons," had this to say about his encounter with medieval literature following his immersion in the New Criticism:

> The usual New Critical method, which is to stare and stare at the work until it becomes clear, was useless on this material, because again and again you found yourself staring at something that felt like a symbol or an allusion, or felt like maybe it ought to be some kind of joke but you couldn't see the humor. To figure out the poem you had to figure out the world it came from—read the books the poets knew, try to understand aesthetic principles abandoned and forgotten centuries ago. One had no choice but to become a sort of scholar.

The novelist Gardner found his efforts rewarded in this fashion:

I found in medieval culture and art . . . exactly what I
needed as an instrument for looking at my own time and
place. I of course never became for a moment a medieval
Christian believer, but medieval ideas and attitudes gave me
a means of triangulating, a place to stand.[9]

Now the book that follows upon this introduction is in part a
record of my own efforts to "become a sort of scholar" about the
Tale of Genji. Not being, alas, a novelist like Gardner, I cannot
put the results to the same end, but a "means of triangulating,
a place to stand" are precious possessions for any life. I should
add, as a sort of caveat, that I have spent the better part of the
last five years trying to read and understand the *Tale of Genji*—
a great extravagance on the one hand, and on the other too
niggardly even for a novitiate, as the reader may surmise from
my lightning-quick account of the history of *Genji* scholarship.
Perhaps it goes without saying, though I think it can never be
sufficiently acknowledged, that I have benefited incalculably
from Japanese scholarship, both from the abundance of its
knowledge and from its increasingly supple use of theory of varying provenance. (This is not, of course, to deny in any way the
enormous stimulus provided by contemporary studies of letters
in the West; rather, such distinctions become increasingly tenuous, especially from the Japanese point of view.)

In any case, I hope to share some of what I have gained, but
I shall not dwell on that here since it is part of the flesh and
blood of my text. Instead, let me offer a few words on a subject
that I rarely take up explicitly, something that might be called
the life and times of the author of the *Genji*.[10] Another name
for that interval in Japanese history between the late eighth and
the late twelfth centuries, most commonly known as the Heian
period, is the Fujiwara period. Strictly speaking, the latter is a
somewhat narrower designation, referring to the three centuries
following 894, when the Japanese decided to terminate embas-
sies to T'ang China (a medium that had served for two centuries
to bring in the artifacts of the dominant civilization literally by
the boatload). The Fujiwara period is a term of chronological
classification especially favored by art historians. It highlights, in

other words, that aspect of the Heian period that has widely been taken to be most characteristic—cultural splendor on a scale never to be reproduced and, intimately tied with this, the emergence of a sense of native identity.[11] Fujiwara is the name of the family of which the "northern branch" had consolidated power in its hands by the time the *Genji* was written. The northern branch was consistently successful in applying the principal strategy for political supremacy, which, succinctly put, consisted of ensuring that one of its daughters bear the next crown prince. At its smoothest, the system operated so that when the latter was still of a tender age, the emperor would be persuaded to abdicate, whereupon the grandfather of the new emperor would reign as regent.

Heian grandeur was supported by Fujiwara (i.e., private) wealth. There had been a time when attempts were made to put into practice the public, bureaucratic, Sinified version of state government. The Taika Reform of 645 had decreed state ownership and public distribution of rice land. The Heian period witnessed the rapid dissolution of this system: it was an age for large provincial estates held by absentee landowners. Land and emperor were privately controlled. Some of the medieval commentaries proposed an interpretation influential to this day—that the *Genji* was set during the reigns of Emperor Daigo (897-930) and his son Emperor Murakami (946-967), two idealized rulers who took an anachronistically active role in government. This reading has Murasaki Shikibu (so often thought to have written an apolitical novel) favoring imperial rule as an ideal over the politicized Fujiwara regency. I cannot imagine that she would have found so simple an opposition interesting. Her hero has the surname Genji (literally, he of the Gen, or Minamoto, clan). As a means of controlling the succession and presumably easing the strain on the public coffers, princes of the blood who stood outside the direct line of succession were given a surname (the other possibility was Heishi, or Taira) and made to join the ranks of the nonroyal upper aristocracy. Since the emperor had no surname, to be so endowed signaled that the bearer could not become emperor. Thus, the title *Tale of Genji* means a story about one who is barred from the supreme position in the land.[12] Genji's ambiguous political identity contrasts both with that of the uninspiring emperors in the tale and with that of his refreshingly grasping Fujiwara foil, Tō no Chūjō. Murasaki Shikibu was employed by the most powerful Fujiwara of all, Michinaga (966-1027), who was grandfather of not one but two emperors and close kin to four others. What were the terms of her employ? She was to add brilliance to the salon of Michinaga's daughter Shōshi, who, entered in the court of Emperor Ichijō (r. 986-1011) at the age of eleven, must have been a rather green competitor to Teishi, her senior by approximately one decade. Teishi's circle included Sei Shōnagon, the author of the other great Heian prose work, a collection of essays known as her *Pillow Book*.[13] Culture as embodied in the lady-in-waiting was a prized instrument of Heian politics. Shikibu came from a family of scholars and provincial governors, as did Sei Shōnagon. The early Heian poet Ise, the mid-Heian poet Ise no Tayū, the diarist Michitsuna's Mother and her niece Takasue's Daughter, the poet Izumi Shikibu, the poet and presumed compiler of the *Tale of Flowering Fortunes*, Akazome Emon, were all daughters and wives of provincial governors. Situated at the subtly humiliating fringes of the lower aristocracy, often entering court service, these women, whose dates of birth and death are unrecorded, were responsible for the flowering of Heian literature.[14] Being women, they wrote in Japanese and turned it into a supple medium suited for a variety of ends that men, hitherto confined to Chinese, were less apt to explore.

It is not that these women were altogether unacquainted with Chinese. Certainly, Murasaki Shikibu and Sei Shōnagon (though Shikibu sniffs at her rival's command of Chinese writing in her diary) were quite competent. One of the most memorable vignettes we have from Shikibu's life concerns her father's bitter disappointment over having a clever daughter who could make her way through the Confucian classics though his son had no such facility.[15]

The contemporary literary scholar Saigō Nobutsuna has suggested that the difference in quality of mind apparent in the writings of Murasaki Shikibu and Michitsuna's Mother has to do with the former's bilingualism.[16] I suppose what is meant by this is that acquaintance with another language and tradition afforded Shikibu a "means of triangulating, a place to stand." Bilingualism offered her access to a variety of genres: the *Tale of Genji* shows that its author had at her disposal the world as it was shaped by Buddhist and Confucian teachings, histories, fantastic tales, poetry, and diaries, both in Chinese and Japanese. From the lofty heights of the twentieth century we tend to take the multiplicity of genres for granted or, worse yet, to view them developmentally, according to the relentless march from the primitive to the sophisticated. A genre, first of all, represents a point of view, which is not an object available for the asking but a system of values to be cultivated and claimed.

If mere access to differing world views sufficed, there would be more novelists now as well as in the Heian period. I think the significance of bilingualism lies in metaphor: what distinguishes Murasaki Shikibu is her capacity to perceive one genre as a metaphor for another. It is a characteristic common to novelists, perhaps possessed on a grander scale by those who write encyclopedic novels, but what is important is the shared principle. Let me put it another way: the novel is the most supple instrument of thought ever devised. This also means that it is a fine tool for apprehending reality, however that reality is construed. What accounts for these extraordinary capabilities?

In the past I have relied on a reasoning that runs something as follows: fiction's distinguishing attribute is fictionality. Fictionality might be defined as "lacking in truthfulness," for which in turn a ready synonym is "falsehood." This series of associations makes possible the negative social assessment of the novel as well as the positive aesthetic one. The latter position, strongly put, asserts that the novel can do what it does because it floats free of truth. Because "truth" often overlaps with "reality," a more defiant assertion comes to hold that the novel has nothing to do with reality, indeed serves to wean us of such puerile notions.

Our own preoccupation with the linguistic constitution of reality is not merely heady but so compelling in its presumptions as to render it difficult to construe the world otherwise. Within that preoccupation, however, we must avoid plotting too hasty a trajectory from fiction to falsehood. Our linguistic, that is to say, our textual apprehension of the world does not direct us to equate fictionality with lack of truth. If the metonymic force of association thrusts us in that direction, we must hesitate before the equation itself. Above all, we must be alert to the political implications of the equation of fiction to falsehood—avoid, at the very least, the error of assuming it to be natural. It is, of course, of enormous consequence that the novel was early denied, and came to eschew, the legitimacy and authority essential to the existence of other genres and other disciplines, those that stand in the name of science, for example, or of religious faith. Although legitimacy and authority confer upon their holders precisely the power to determine truths, the novel's renunciation of these attributes is not identical to its being untruthful.[17] If we fail to keep this clearly in mind, we shall misapprehend the novel's capacity to discover uniquely tactful—that is to say, discreet, singular—connections between things. And we shall have deprived ourselves of this most exquisite instrument of thought.

A novel is lost if its reader refuses to think novelistically. This means in part that at a certain point every reader—and this point will be different for each reader and each reading—must gain some distance from inherited points of view (principles of theory, tools of the trade such as information on historical allusion, rules of etiquette, fashions in incense concoction) simply in order to make room for other perceptions. I realize that I am skirting perilously close to all the pitfalls of the intrinsic-extrinsic distinction dear to the old New Critics. Let me be more specific. In reading the *Genji*, I am continually struck by minute points of resonance, by extraordinarily complicated and unfamiliar configurations. In fact, a great deal of my book is an appeal to other readers of the *Genji* to *notice*, for example, a form of address, or the presence of a certain musical instrument. Now obviously, the points that I notice are determined by my other experiences in reading literature, by readings in other disciplines, by warnings from others about what one ought to notice in the *Genji* or other literary works, by what I have chanced to observe about tone of voice or gesture in domestic quarrels or supermarket lines, by how alert I am when reading a particular passage (for one must never underestimate the potency of the banal)—and by all the factors that have produced these circumstances. But to do my part as a reader in keeping the *Genji* alive beyond its thousandth year, I must always attempt to see in it something that I had not already known. This is the paradoxical responsibility of the reader: to replenish the strangeness of the novel by making connections with the familiar.

What is required is a dialectic between being "a sort of scholar" and a devoted reader of novels. Take, for example, the pervasive aestheticism of the Heian period. Much has been made of the refinement of Heian sensibilities—the excruciating devotion to details of color, scent, hand, or season. Now this can be interpreted in a number of ways, mostly overlapping, some contradictory. I will turn to this subject again at the conclusion of the book, but for now I would like to caution the reader to be attentive to these aesthetic matters as languages that are deployed throughout the tale. Certainly, from our own point of view, some of these interests seem precious at best and perniciously frivolous at worst. To put it another way, it has been repeatedly pointed out that the *Genji* works as a psychological novel; this is a view I subscribe to myself. Yet many readers, especially when they have been told this in advance, experience a certain disappointment and feel the characters are shallow and impenetrable when compared with those of the great European novels of the nineteenth and twentieth centuries. In part, I think this has to do with our equation of psychological depth with use of psychological language. Unless characters talk about themselves, either in dialogue or soliloquy, we think we do not really know them. There are of course *Genji* characters who behave in quite a familiar way in this respect, especially from the "New Herbs" chapter on, but others do not. We risk losing the latter unless we learn to follow the other languages—of dress, of calligraphy, of floral and musical preference, of incense concoction. This implies, of course, expenditure of effort to learn about these matters. We must be cautious, however, so as not to force the novel to conform to such expertise as we may have gained but rather to use it to help us apprehend that incense concoction, for instance, is one language among others within the novel. Usually we need to travel out of the novel to gain this sort of information, but having done so, we must return. I hope above all that this study will encourage new readers and old to turn and return to the *Tale of Genji.*

MY BOOK is organized around the heroines of the tale. They are points of convergence for the many languages constituting the work. The points themselves are not fixed but are constantly modified by each other—from which follows, necessarily, the continual transformation of whatever we perceive to be the totality of configurations. The eponymous hero, far from being the controlling center of the work, is as much constituted by his heroines as they are by him. Yet, for reasons to be seen, he is curiously absent by comparison to his ladies.

The discussion begins early in the hero's youth, at the point of entry of the first heroine, Fujitsubo, who replaces Genji's dead mother as his father's favorite.

Chapter 1

Three Heroines

and the Making

of the Hero

DICHOTOMIES AND SUBSTITUTION: FUJITSUBO

MOST OF THE CHARACTERS of the *Tale of Genji* are known to its readers by suggestive sobriquets such as "Evening Face" (Yūgao), "Village of the Falling Flowers" (Hana Chiru Sato), or "Evening Mist" (Yūgiri), which are culled from key poems associated with the characters within the text. Many of these names also serve as evocative chapter titles. It is not known to what extent the author or her earlier readers were responsible for these acts of naming, but convention now assigns the preponderance to the latter. The common designation of the characters within the novel is a version of official rank or place of residence, the particular choice being strategic to emphasis of tone or information.[1] In certain situations, however, the characters are starkly identified as "the man" or "the woman," or, with honorific suffix, "the gentleman" or "the lady." The situations are erotic, and these words signal that a climactic moment may be at hand. Of all the women pursued by the hero Genji, there are two who are never referred to in this fashion: they are Fujitsubo and Princess Asagao, the hero's stepmother and cousin, respectively.[2] The first is the object of Genji's lifelong attachment; the second, his staunchest resister. For reasons that are either not provided or have become invisible over the centuries, Princess

Asagao never permits herself a moment when the narrator could justifiably dub her a "woman." It is otherwise with Fujitsubo. During the one episode in which she incontrovertibly yields to the reckless young Genji, she is steadily referred to as "Her Highness" (1:305; S 98; W 95). Fujitsubo is never divested of her majesty.

The circumstances of this heroine's entry into the work are promisingly complex. She replaces the Kiritsubo Lady, Genji's poor dead mother, who, though but the daughter of a late major counsellor, had dominated the Emperor's affections and was consequently hounded to death by the jealous members of his household. It had been a mistake, reflects the Lady's grief-stricken mother, to have permitted her to enter court service in accordance with her late husband's immoderate ambitions. Some years later, the Emperor, who had remained inconsolable, hears of a young lady bearing a remarkable resemblance to Genji's mother. This is Fujitsubo, daughter of a figure known only as "the former Emperor." Her mother, mindful of her predecessor's fate, is reluctant to expose her daughter to such trials even though her higher station might shield her to some degree. Like so many mothers of literary heroines, however, this one dies at a critical point in her daughter's life. Sixteen-year-old Fujitsubo has no choice but to accede to her brother Prince Hyōbu's view that unprotected though she was, she would be better off at court than elsewhere.[3]

Fujitsubo is an instant success. Her uncanny resemblance to the dead lady wins the Emperor's undivided affection, which fortunately she can receive without fear of reprisal because of her own high birth. The problem, of course, is that she also attracts her stepson Genji, but five years her junior. The Kiritsubo Emperor, the most genial of cuckolds, personally attests to the new wife's resemblance to his young son's late mother and encourages their friendship. Of course, there are limits to their intimacy: once Genji is initiated and married, he is no longer permitted within Fujitsubo's curtains of state. Henceforth, their thoughts are conveyed in the notes of her koto and his flute.[4]

For some time Fujitsubo makes but fleeting appearances, and then only in Genji's thoughts, as he listens to his fellow young

men discuss the ideal woman, or overhears gossip about his carryings-on ("The Broom Tree"), or sits through a terrifying night
with the corpse of a lover ("Evening Faces"). It is not until the
fifth chapter ("Lavender") that Fujitsubo speaks in person, on
the occasion of an unexpected and, as will be seen, fateful meeting with Genji. Sometime thereafter, the narrator, in a moment
of unusual freedom with intimate detail, observes that Fujitsubo's ladies have been troubled when attending her at her bath.
This leads ineluctably to the day when Fujitsubo is compelled
to witness the Emperor's joy over the birth of a son he had not
fathered and over this new son's resemblance to an older favorite,
Genji. With the Emperor's passing in the tenth chapter ("The
Sacred Tree"), Fujitsubo is exposed to the vindictive passion of
another lady of the court, Kokiden, the principal victim of the
dead Emperor's devotion first to Genji's mother and then to herself. Not that Kokiden has been entirely robbed of her due, for
the Kiritsubo Emperor, in one of his more prudent moments,
had demoted Genji to commoner status and designated as heir
Suzaku, his son by Kokiden. Now it is Kokiden's season, for she
is the daughter of the supremely powerful Minister of the Right
as well as mother of the new Suzaku Emperor. There is still a
thorn in her side, however, for the late Emperor, in recompense
for having demoted his favorite son Genji, had decreed his supposed son by Fujitsubo (Reizei) crown prince at the time of Suzaku's ascension; moreover, he had promoted Fujitsubo to the
status of empress, which, of course, made her superior to Kokiden.

Even after the Emperor's death, the secret of her fleeting affair
with Genji weighs heavily upon Fujitsubo, and she finds but
slender protection in her title. To make matters worse, Genji
continues to prey upon her, thus increasing the risk of disastrous
exposure for their young son Reizei as well as themselves. Dark
thoughts invade her mind: "Even if I am spared Lady Ch'i's fate,
I will surely become the laughing stock of the court" (2:106; S
198; W 206-207). Lady Ch'i was a favorite consort of the Han
Emperor Kao-tsu, who had thought to put his son by her on the
throne after his death. Instead, his Empress captured Lady Ch'i,
cut off her hands and feet, gouged out her eyes, burnt her ears,

and forced down a burning potion that left her unable to speak.[5] Fujitsubo decides to relinquish her rank as empress and take religious vows. It is none too soon, for some of Genji's sins come home to roost, and, in a parallel gesture, he chooses retreat before exile is forced upon him.

Like everyone else in Genji's faction, Fujitsubo lies low during the years of Genji's seclusion in Suma and Akashi. Prosperity, though not tranquillity, comes with Genji's return to the capital and Suzaku's abdication. Now Fujitsubo, as the mother of the new Reizei Emperor, is granted the emoluments due to a retired emperor.[6] She uses her new-found power to scheme with Genji to secure Akikonomu, the late Rokujō Lady's daughter, as their son's consort even though she was coveted by the retired Suzaku Emperor. Then, having done everything in her means to assure the stability of her son Reizei's reign, she languishes to die at the age of thirty-seven ("A Rack of Cloud"). She returns once, wraith-like, to haunt Genji in chapter twenty ("The Morning Glory").

This is the explicit extent of Fujitsubo's role in the novel. It is surprisingly limited—as if, trapped in a secret relationship with Genji, she must be shrouded from our prying eyes, as if, being the incarnation of every ideal, she must be used sparingly. Even her poetry output is modest—twelve poems, of which ten are addressed to Genji.[7] Obviously, Fujitsubo's importance to the tale far exceeds her visible activity. It would not be hyperbolic to suggest that she embodies the principal dynamic forces of the work. They constitute dichotomies whose interrelationships and transformations are the source of abiding interest in the novel, a testimony to its author's passionately intellectual imagination. Let us begin with a description of Fujitsubo's manner during that fateful night with Genji in the "Lavender" chapter. She thinks of their previous (unrecounted) meetings.[8] Despite her resolve that there be no more, Genji had stolen in again: "she was so wretched, she looked as if she could endure no more, yet she was sensitive and sweet, though as reserved as ever, reflective, even intimidating . . ." (1:305; S 98; W 95). This is one of the most generous descriptions ever given of Fujitsubo. It comes embedded in a moderately long "sentence" beginning in Fujitsubo's mind and ending in Genji's, and it serves to illustrate the complexity of the author's mode of apprehending her characters as well as her penchant for piling one qualifying phrase upon another, with the result, in this instance, of producing a concrete representation of Fujitsubo's contradictory aspects.[9]

The dichotomies embodied by Fujitsubo may be variously generalized as sacred and profane, identical and similar, original and substitute, erotic and political, natural and cultural, arbitrary and motivated, mythic and fictive, otherworldly and this-worldly. Let us provisionally take "the sacred and the profane" to stand for the series (which, not being sacred, is of course expandable). These sets overlap, contradict, and undergo transformations in the course of the *Genji*. The complex relationship prevailing *between* the sets of terms may be described as one of "complementary bipolarity" with the precaution suggested by Andrew Plaks in his use of the term to describe the relation of "yin and yang" to other paired opposites:

> When we use the terms "yin" and "yang" as a shorthand for referring to this entire range of polar conceptualizations, we must be careful not to assume that all these paired concepts can theoretically be lined up in parallel fashion such that the two sets of poles form two logical categories of experience. In fact, the many sets of conceptual polarities, which serve as frames of reference for the perception of reality, are *overlapping* schemes not reducible to a final two-term analysis.[10]

Complementarity, however, is but one mode of relationship, and we ought to consider the choice of "sacred and profane" (or yin and yang) as the "shorthand" term for the series even, or especially, if it is one of convenience—that is, convention, tradition. We must, of course, also keep in mind the relation of the terms *within* each set.

Now, what is the function that "sacred and profane" is serving here as the representative polarity? I am of course borrowing from Mircea Eliade, for whom "the sacred and the profane" describe "two modes of being in the world."[11] The former is associated with origins, essences, timelessness, rituals, revela-

tions, and the inexplicable and therefore represents otherworld-
liness within this world; the latter, on the other hand, is bound
to the quotidian, the changing, and the rational and consequently is the very essence of this-worldliness.

To turn to the example at hand, the logic of Japanese imperial
rule is that mythic reality is embodied by the emperor, who represents a continuity from that time in the beginning when
heaven and earth were linked and divine rule was established in
the Middle Land of the Reed Plains, as Japan is called in the
early (eighth-century) chronicles. Through his participation in
court ritual, the emperor regularly interrupts the profane time of
ordinary mortals (who grow old and die) to restore the sacred
moment of creation. Naturally, it is his son who must succeed
him; necessarily, his women are exclusively his.[12] Of course, this
son and these women are at the heart of the problem: for the
emperor's sacred vitality is manifested in his multiple sexual relations, with the consequence that there is frequently, if not predictably, more than one son. The ready (and apparently digni-
fied) solution of designating the eldest as heir is all too
susceptible to being undermined by the rivalry of the sons and
their respective backers. The damning taint of manipulated
variation is not easily eradicated. The issue of succession, implicated in the political machinations revolving around women
(i.e., potential mothers), forever betrays the presence of the profane at the heart of divine rule.

Now, even from this schematic description, it should be possible to extract certain tensions in the relation within oppositional pairs. On the one hand, "sacred" and "profane" may be
said to stand in an oppositional complementarity; that is, it is
virtually commonsensical that without the profane, the sacred
could not be discerned, just as order requires chaos, or figure
ground. Now it is also apparent that much as figure needs
ground, ground is not on the same footing, so to speak, as figure.
Figure, in order to be figure, must constitute (and thereby de-
mote) its surroundings as ground; ground offers itself as mere
matter for the composition of figure.[13] *Within* the set "sacred
and profane" (and in the others as well) we can distinguish both
a symmetric, horizontal (complementary) opposition and an

asymmetric, vertical (supplementary) one. The former often masks the latter but cannot displace it, just as, conversely, depending upon our analytical desires, the latter may be made to subsume the former.

By this analogy, women as the bearers of future emperors serve as the incidental ground for the sacred (natural) phenomenon of the imperial succession. For the appearance of the sacred to be maintained, the manipulation of the women by their ambitious kinsfolk must be suppressed, that is to say, dissimulated as the education and cultivation of beloved daughters or sisters. When such daughters or sisters become the mothers of crown princes, then men who are by birth (by nature) excluded from the sacred realm of the emperor acquire a foothold therein—a metonymic link that may, perhaps, be made to serve as a metaphoric one. The distinctiveness of Fujitsubo is that she does not need to be transformed by "marriage" to an emperor or by delivery of an heir in order to partake of the sacred since she is born to that order. There is a certain redundancy, in other words, to her becoming an imperial consort. (Historically, of course, the choice of a princess of the blood as empress was inimical to the mechanism of the Fujiwara regency, which depended on the entry of a ministerial, commoner daughter into the emperor's household.) Countering this redundancy, however, is the lack implicit in Fujitsubo's entering the novel as a substitute.

Let us now shift our attention to the pair, "original and substitute." Both Genji and his father are initially drawn to Fujitsubo because of her resemblance to another. She stands at the head of an important list of heroines who recreate the image of another, original woman in the eyes of a male character. Of all such heroines Fujitsubo alone may have some inkling of this role because the Kiritsubo Emperor encouraged her to treat Genji kindly on account of her resemblance to his dead mother. I am tempted to call her an "original substitute," not only because she is the first, but also because, as the daughter of an emperor, she cannot realistically be said to be replacing Genji's mother who was merely the daughter of an ambitious major counsellor. Still, since the *Genji* never wastes such juxtapositions, we should hold this link in reserve.

As for the resemblance: to be like another is clearly not the same as being identical to that other. Indeed, it is the logic of resemblance that allows fiction to distinguish itself from myth, which is governed by the logic of identity whereby, for example, a deity known for destructive furor in one region turns out to be the same as a beneficent deity in another.[14] Now it is true that resemblance in the *Genji* is usually based on blood tie, which is purportedly natural and beyond human control and therefore a mythic element. Physical resemblance based on blood tie, however, is found not to guarantee moral similarity, let alone identity, as Genji learns in the case of the Third Princess, a hoped-for Fujitsubo substitute. What the tale shows repeatedly is that the confusion, created by desire, of resemblance and identity is a fertile one for fiction. It is crucial in the process of claiming— indeed, in inventing—the terrain of human psychology for literary exploration.

For our purposes, it is time to rephrase Eliade's description of the sacred and the profane as "two modes of being in fiction." Substitution, implying human agency, is a fictional mode par excellence. And fiction, at the same time that it is a term in that series of bipolarities within which it is locally opposed as falsehood to mythic (or, in a different perspective, historical) truth, also strives to transcend the series as a global mode of cognition. It is this property of fiction that operates to make of the *Genji* a novel. In this scheme, "sacred" and "profane" become whatever is interesting or banal according to the values of fiction, which may or may not coincide with those of "being in the world." Thus, a certain mythic yearning within fiction is indicated in the basing of resemblance on blood tie. And of course, the emperor, or rather the idea of the emperor, marks an ontological center, a point of origin in the *Genji*. A mother, on the other hand, is a personal point of origin, and Fujitsubo, being the daughter and consort of emperors, touches on both centers. Genji himself was driven from both, by his mother's death not long after his birth, and by his father's decision to remove him from the succession. The affair with Fujitsubo suggests a desire to recover lost centers of the self, a hunger for mythic dimensions of the self that is paradoxically expressed insofar as its object is a substitute figure. I should emphasize that it is the longing for mythic identity, not that identity itself, that is fictionally valuable. The ineffaceable distance between the actuality of Genji and the desired center is the territory of fiction.

When the boy Genji learns of Fujitsubo's unearthly resemblance to his dead mother, "his young heart is deeply moved" (1:120; S 16; W 17). Should their relationship be deemed to have been incestuous "in fact"? The question has been posed and answered variously, according to available concepts and prevailing ideology. Among modern readers, the late Oka Kazuo did not hesitate to write of Genji's "mother complex" (Oedipus is not honored in the Japanese phrasing). Fujii Sadakazu has undertaken a painstaking study of Heian marriage codes to show that the incest taboo is respected throughout the tale.[15] Surveying the complex of associations surrounding the word *tsumi* ("crime," "guilt," "pollution," "sin," etc.), which appears no fewer than 198 times in the course of the *Genji*, Nomura Seiichi casts doubt on the appropriateness of interpreting Fujitsubo as a tragic, guilty heroine.[16] One current tendency in Japanese scholarship is to transfer the guilt from the erotic to the political sphere, an odd mirroring of the shift in Fujitsubo's characterization within the tale itself. Thus, Genji and Fujitsubo are guilty not of violating the incest taboo but of disrupting the imperial succession.

Although scholarly efforts to provide a socio-historical context to incest are indisputably useful, the findings cannot be transported directly back into the novel to resolve its ambiguities. Such findings tend to be most helpful in providing a field that can set off the distinctiveness of the literary phenomenon in question. Political and erotic guilt, rather than being mutually exclusive, are mutually metaphoric, just as political and erotic concerns are shown to be interdependent throughout the tale. Indeed, incest provides an ideal ground for the play of the mutuality of the political and the erotic, as well as of the sacred and the profane, the mythic and the fictional.

To pursue this oscillating dynamic, we should return to the moment of the young Genji's demotion to commoner status. In arriving at this decision, his father relies on Indian and Korean as well as domestic modes of physiognomy. Only the Korean examination (which the Emperor cannot witness in person because of a decree against receiving foreigners) is recounted. Genji's mien is pronounced to be that of one who "should become the father of his nation and ascend to the peerless rank of monarch," but this accolade is balanced by a warning of dire consequences should he in fact attain such heights (1:116; S 14; W 15-16). This is the first of three prophecies about Genji's fate. The second, coming when Genji learns of Fujitsubo's pregnancy, elusively refers to an inconceivably extraordinary future along with the possibility of misfortune (1:308; S 100; W 96). The third, disclosed at the time of the birth of Genji's daughter, the future Akashi Empress, had predicted that of his three children, one would become emperor, another empress, and the least of them chancellor (2:275; S 273; W 287).

Now prophecies represent another, sacred world of transcendental knowledge potent enough to govern human relativity. But in the world of fiction it would be uninteresting for a prophecy to be merely, straightforwardly fulfilled. (It makes heroic action tedious, if not altogether superfluous.) This is where incest as transgressive love becomes indispensable. Genji takes the wife of his father the Emperor and fathers a son who will succeed to the throne. Through this private appropriation of the public, that which is profane in the historical ideology of the imperial system becomes a new fictional sacred. (The emperor, literarily speaking, is profane: he does not generate stories. The four emperors appearing in the *Genji* are granted few interesting moments.)

Violating the imperial succession is of course a political act, but it is also a sexual transgression as well, given the nature of emperorhood. Now for Genji to qualify as a fictional hero, he must be free of the taint of political desire, and there is no more powerful antidote for this than erotic desire. The pursuit of power is instantly transformed if it is the consequence, and not the cause, of passion, for we are accustomed to thinking of passion as irrational, irresistible, and therefore (God-) given. If the object of the passion is forbidden, so much the better (one who

27

would risk everything for love cannot be charged with mundane ambition). Fujitsubo as empress and as his father's wife, a stepmother, a metaphoric mother, is doubly forbidden to Genji. I should pause over this description of Fujitsubo as doubly forbidden. The first source of taboo, that she is the wife of an emperor, is unproblematic, both as a fact within the tale and as a matter of fictional value. The second, that she is the wife of the hero's father, is more complicated. The study on marriage taboos referred to earlier mentions an apparent prohibition against relations with one's stepmother, but Fujii dismisses it as inconsequential and accordingly concludes that the Genji-Fujitsubo affair only violates the purity of the imperial line. He does, however, detect a "taboo-like atmosphere" or "taboo as metaphor."[17] Now the *Tale of Genji* abounds in examples of metaphoric incest; where it is not actualized, it is, certainly, flirted with. In "New Herbs, Part Two," Kashiwagi, the son of Tō no Chūjō, Genji's closest companion and foil, violates the Third Princess, daughter of a retired emperor and Genji's wife. At the time, Genji is the father of the reigning emperor and is receiving the emoluments due to an ex-emperor. Kashiwagi is, accordingly, violating the pseudo-empress-wife of his pseudo-emperor-father. Mirroring this is Genji's biological son Yūgiri's visual violation of his stepmother Murasaki. Genji's own relationship with Murasaki begins as one of father and daughter; their backgrounds contain enough parallels to make them sibling-like as well. Genji poses as a father to two other women to whom he is erotically drawn, Akikonomu and Tamakazura, who are also the daughters of former lovers (the Rokujō Lady and Yūgao). It seems reasonable to conclude that Murasaki Shikibu was interested in exploring attachments that are problematic at least in part because of excessive proximity. Beyond offering the generic interest of forbidden love, the motif overlaps with the pursuit of origins/originals and substitutes: repossessing a dead lover through her daughter, or recovering one's own beginnings through union with a mother/sister. The pursuit is all the more tantalizing if there are fathers and brothers, actual or equivalent, lurking in the wings.[18]

It should be admitted that political ambition, even though unbecoming to heroes, can provide a fictional interest different from that of erotic anguish. And Genji is ambitious, as we shall see, but his political manipulations are usually masked, at times transparently, by erotic tension. Prophecy also contributes to this dissimulation. For instance, it is possible that Genji's violation of the imperial succession does not ultimately constitute a transgression, for according to a higher principle, he was born to rule, if not directly, then through his enthroned children. The aura of fate cleanses and sanctifies Genji's actions so that it seems indecent (if it should even occur to us) to regard them as calculated. So, as Genji works to consolidate his gains and ensure their transmission, it seems but the simple and satisfying fulfillment of fate. At the same time, the hint of the illicit as well as of political scheming precludes the sense of a naive realization of prophecy. Prophecy and action stand in a peculiar relation: each has the potential of rendering the other superfluous, yet each can legitimate the other. We will have further occasion to consider these matters, but for the moment, let us say that in the *Genji* prophecy can sanction but not predict.

We have been neglecting Fujitsubo. In the affair with Genji, Fujitsubo slips from the public, official realm into a private, erotic one. She struggles to abolish this private realm with Genji and more or less succeeds when she takes vows after the death of the Kiritsubo Emperor. Her object is to see her son safe on the throne. To this end, she must prevent Genji from repeating his follies, without, at the same time, making him so dejected as to take the tonsure himself, thus leaving their young son altogether unprotected. Once girded by her vows, Fujitsubo becomes more generous with her attentions, even speaking to him on occasion without intermediaries as was customary for highborn women. In time, upon Genji's return from his self-imposed exile, the two become political allies, acting in bold unison to establish the Reizei Emperor's reign on a secure footing. A marvelous economy develops in which the hidden, pent-up energy of erotic longing is converted into visible political performance. The reticent Fujitsubo turns verbose and even ruthless on occasion. When Genji reports to her of the retired Suzaku Emperor's desire to have the orphaned Akikonomu come to him, Fujitsubo coolly responds:

> Indeed, we are humbled by His Majesty's interest, and we must feel sorry for him, but let us make the Rokujō Lady's will our excuse and have her daughter enter [Reizei's] court. We can pretend to know nothing of his interest. In any case, he will no longer be concerned with such matters [i.e., women], now that he is devoting himself to his prayers, and I do not believe he will be deeply reproachful if you inform him of your plans.   (2:310; S 289; W 305)

Working by plan for a desired end is secular and unheroic, again because it is the absence of visible process that is associated with the divine. The program of action even for earthly heroes and heroines must be free of self-interest and calculation. (Here the values of fiction and "the world" coincide because both mimic myth, the principal source of heroic paradigms.) To place a daughter in an emperor's service and to bolster her position with cultural display (as in the Picture Contest in chapter seventeen) are appropriate forms of behavior for the scions of ministerial families (the northern branch of the Fujiwara clan being the prime historical example), but they are ironic both in Genji, son of an emperor and a fictional hero, and Fujitsubo, daughter of one emperor, wife of another, and a fictional heroine. But of course, Fujitsubo was introduced to the tale as a substitute for the daughter of an ambitious major counsellor who, like other aspiring men, put his daughter to the service of his dreams. While the Kiritsubo Lady was sacrificed to her dead father's ambitions, Fujitsubo is compelled to become politically ambitious herself—hardly the sense in which she was intended to substitute. In this sense Fujitsubo does indeed replace Genji's mother, and the absolute opposition between divine royalty and secular commoner is overcome. Yet, at the same time, when Fujitsubo and Genji effectively control the court upon the latter's return to the capital, there is an aura of archaic brother-sister rule, an impression retrospectively reinforced by the sororal aspect of the relationship of Murasaki (Fujitsubo's niece and surrogate) to Genji.[19]

If the figure of Fujitsubo contains powerful dichotomies in itself, it also serves to generate what might be called centripetal and centrifugal movements within the novel. Inasmuch as she is forbidden to him, Genji is driven to seeking substitutes elsewhere, and widely. There is of course Murasaki, and far in the future the unsatisfactory Third Princess. They are substitutes by direct descent and high pedigree, who belong to the central narrative, but there are others, the heroines of the subsidiary chapters that readers for centuries have been encouraged to read "adjacently" to the appropriate primary chapters. Utsusemi, Yūgao, and Suetsumuhana, coming from lower social backgrounds (except for Suetsumuhana, the destitute daughter of a long-dead prince), and lacking the sacred attributes that cloak Fujitsubo's story in secrecy, are the heroines of stories that are vividly, even realistically, detailed. Yet, even though these stories are open where Fujitsubo's is closed, they are not without elements of transgression or guilt, almost as if they were the intaglio versions of the Fujitsubo story.

Take the Yūgao episode. Genji falls in love with a nameless young woman of apparently modest circumstance and takes her away to a remote villa, where she dies suddenly and mysteriously. The conditions of Genji's guilt are ambiguous. As with his attachment to Fujitsubo, he is in the grips of an irresistible passion. Whereas the Fujitsubo affair produces a problematic birth, the Yūgao episode ends in death. Reizei's birth is accompanied by a mysterious dream (containing the second of the three prophecies) for Genji; Yūgao's death is evidently caused by a spirit visible to Genji alone. The secret of Reizei's conception is initially confined to Genji, Fujitsubo, and a lady-in-waiting, Ōmyōbu, who may have been the Empress's wet nurse's daughter, a sort of surrogate sister.[20] Similarly, Yūgao's corpse is secretly disposed of by Koremitsu, Genji's wet nurse's son.

One of the surrogate episodes generated by Fujitsubo's rejection of Genji deserves separate attention. Strictly speaking, neither Oborozukiyo nor her story can be described as "surrogate,"

since the lady is antithetical to Fujitsubo and her story constitutes an important development of the principal narrative. Genji
comes upon her accidentally after festivities at court one night
when he prowls about in frustration from his inability to gain
access to Fujitsubo's quarters. As luck would have it, Oborozukiyo is the daughter of the Minister of the Right and a sister of
Kokiden. Genji, young enough to brave what should have been
daunting risks, becomes a carefree hero, whose adventures are
pleasurable rather in the fashion of an Erroll Flynn movie—
something that can hardly be said of the Fujitsubo affair. The
Oborozukiyo entanglement is parodic in every way, and the fact
that it has such grave consequences is yet another instance of
Murasaki Shikibu's skillful wit. Oborozukiyo has been promised
to Suzaku, Genji's half brother and Crown Prince, soon to ascend the throne. In other words, Genji is once again usurping
imperial property.

The two are discovered in "The Sacred Tree," a beautifully
orchestrated chapter featuring the death of the Kiritsubo Emperor and Genji's intrusion into both Fujitsubo's and Oborozukiyo's chambers. The incident with Fujitsubo comes first. Since
her husband's death, she has been more strenuous than ever in
warding off Genji's attentions, but of course, neither prayer nor
barrier can stop him. On this occasion, when Fujitsubo per-
ceives his presence in her apartment, she is so distraught that
she falls ill; still Genji refuses to leave, and, as daybreak approaches, the faithful Ōmyōbu and her companion Ben can only
bundle him into a closet, shove his clothes in after him, and
leave him for an anxious day.[21] Fujitsubo's condition is worri-
some enough that her brother Prince Hyōbu is sent for, but by
nightfall, she is somewhat improved. Genji cautiously slips out
of the closet for one rapturous gaze. Predictably, he wants to be
seen as well as to see, and as the lady attempts to flee, he holds
her fast by the edge of her cloak and her hair. It is after this
encounter that Fujitsubo resolves to take vows.

Genji's meetings with Oborozukiyo are facilitated both by her
eager willingness to receive him and her stay at home from court
on grounds of indisposal. (Fujitsubo was similarly at her own
home when Reizei was conceived.) One night, Genji is unable

to make his retreat because of a thunderstorm. For once, he becomes feverish with anxiety lest he be discovered, and sure enough, the Minister of the Right comes in to check on his daughter's safety after the storm. Bits of stray clothing and writing catch the irascible father's eye. Both he and Suzaku had been aware of Oborozukiyo's dalliance and had tried to look the other way, but Genji's flagrancy is too much, especially for the Minister's daughter Kokiden, who brandishes dire threats.[22] It is in the face of this onslaught of hostility that Genji decides to withdraw to Suma (his surprising acumen is masked by the drama and sorrow of the moment). Thus, the great secret remains safe, but a smaller one, mimicking it, is revealed, and Genji submits to the consequences.

TRANSGRESSION, EXILE, AND THE DEVELOPMENT OF FICTION

It is, of course, the secret with Fujitsubo that gives weight to the exile (for exile it must be called, self-imposed or not, given the way it is realized in writing, embellished by numerous allusions to historically famous exiles). Genji's exile has been the subject of copious study. Whatever its relation to historical examples, it is one of the most literarily fruitful consequences of transgression, which is why it is taken up separately here. Genji's exile places him squarely in an ancient tradition of heroes who are expelled from their homes and compelled to wander. The accounts of their wanderings have come to be called *kishu ryūritan*, a term of recent origin (it is the folklorist Orikuchi Shinobu's) though the phenomenon it describes is doubtless as old as language. It might be translated literally as a "tale about the wanderings of one of noble blood," which I will abbreviate as the "noble exile," with exile referring both to the person and to the imposed journey and seclusion. Orikuchi's own definition is as follows:

> Among the epic poems handed down from generation to generation in ancient Japan, there are tales about frail and

delicate creatures, exalted beings resembling the offspring of gods, who wander from land to land. I have used the expression *kishu ryūritan* to designate their stories.[23]

In the classic pattern, a noble youth is compelled for various reasons to leave his homeland and wander abroad, where he is confronted by a series of tests from which he either emerges victorious or dies. It should be apparent why this pattern has been related to widely occurring tales and myths centering on initiation rites, whose core is the symbolic representation of death and rebirth.[24] In Japan the names that spring to mind are Ōkuninushi or Yamato Takeru from the archaic age, or the figure in *Tales of Ise* known only as "the man," the paradigmatic wandering hero in Heian literature. They are all compelled to travel to "other lands" where they are formed as heroes.[25]

As an early form in the development of prose fiction, the tale of the noble exile contains two warring impulses: the first is directed toward the evolution of long works with interconnected parts, the second toward short, episodic narratives with little or no connection between parts. Perhaps the first has to do with the biographical tendency implicit in the noble-exile tales.[26] The hero's birth, family circumstances, coming-of-age and ensuing vicissitudes are the principal elements of a life based on this pattern. However rudimentary, such a life represents a unit of thought and bears the promise of depth. Within the noble-exile narrative, however, the period of exile itself is often filled with various erotic attachments, leading to short, episodic amorous tales. Such episodes can be strung one after the other with no internal necessity for closure. What yokes these two tendencies so that they work together in the development of long, complex fictions? I would answer this by altering the form of the question, by suggesting that it is in the growth of the understanding of fiction itself as a mode of cognition (of which the novel remains to this day the most ambitious manifestation) that these two strands come together. It is fictionalization that unites the continuous (the biographical) and the discontinuous (the episodic). Let us turn to the example of the *Tales of Ise*, a work with many important significations, both formal and thematic, for the *Genji*, which it preceded by approximately one century.

The *Ise* consists of 125 brief passages each containing one or
two (occasionally more) *waka* poems. There are a number of
"runs" of passages treating the same subject, but connections
from one episode to another are frequently tenuous. What holds
the pieces together above all is the consistency of tone, form,
and content, particularly the repetition with slight variation of
the opening words ("Once, a man . . ."), whose cumulative impact gives elegiac force to the last episode, which begins, "Once,
a man fell ill and. . . ."[27] It is this last episode, recounting the
hero's death and evoking the first episode in which he had just
come of age, that gives this work the proportions, however modest, of a life. It may be added that Japanese readers have always
seen in the contours of "the man" the figure of the poet Ariwara
no Narihira (825-880), as celebrated for his good looks and supposed amorousness as for his bold, often elliptical verse. Narihira
was, moreover, the grandson of an emperor and an intimate of
a prince who was disappointed in his political ambitions. *Ise* does
not develop the hero's characterization beyond repeated display
of prodigious amorousness and poetic gifts. What transcends
mere repetition, giving him the suggestion of psychological continuity and retrospectively reinforcing the impression of a life, is
his commission of a grave transgression.

This is the subject of the third through the sixth sections, in
which the hero has an affair with a woman intended as an imperial consort, the future "Empress of the Second Ward." (There
are mild hints of the illicit in the first two episodes as well, the
first involving voyeurism, the second, an affair with a married
woman.) The hero is discovered, and the woman removed forever from his reach. The results are memorable moments in the
history of Japanese poetry and prose. The passage in the *Ise* begins as an indifferent account of events that turns into a remarkable expression of erotic despair:

> In the First Month of the following year, when the plum
> blossoms were at their height, he went back, driven by long-
> ing for the past. He stood and looked, sat and looked, but
> however he looked, he could find nothing to recall the past.
> Sobbing, he lay on the bare wooden floor and stayed until
> the moon sank in the west.   (*Ise* 4)

This passage appears in similar form as part of the preface to poem 747 ("Love, 5") in the *Kokinshū*, the first imperial anthology of Japanese verse, compiled in 905:

> The spring of the following year, when the plum blossoms were at their height, he went out on a night when the moon was lovely to that western wing, where he lay on the bare wooden floor until the moon sank in the sky. . . .[28]

The crucial difference is that the *Ise* attempts a dramatic expression of the hero's despair in the frustrated rhythm of "he stood and looked, sat and looked, but however he looked" (*tachite mi, ite mi, miredo*), whereas the preface in the poetic anthology is content with a dispassionate description.

The *Tales of Ise* belongs to a genre traditionally called the *uta monogatari*, loosely translatable as "poem tale." The unknown author of the *Mumyōzōshi*, a series of literary discussions written at the turn of the thirteenth century that contains the oldest extant consideration of the *monogatari* form of prose fiction, has a young female interlocutor distinguish the poem tales from "made-up tales," of which the *Genji* is the exemplar.[29] Although the implications of this contrast are not developed in this early instance of literary criticism, it is not difficult to disengage certain contemporary literary evaluations therein. I will have occasion to pursue the question of the relative values of poetry and fiction in Chapter 2, but let me emphasize for the moment that the compilation of the first imperial anthology in 905 conferred such prestige upon the thirty-one-syllable form of Japanese verse known as *waka* that it became a mode for the cognition and expression of truth, which one hesitates to qualify with the term "literary."

In a work such as the *Ise*, where the authorship of the core poems can be assigned to a historical personage, the truth value is doubled. There is, in fact, a persistent interest in situational specificity in the presentation of Japanese poetry, which manifests itself in prose statements indicating the occasion of composition, often with the names of other participating parties (the addressee of a poem, for example, or august figures commanding a particular composition). This is true of both official anthologies and personal collections. The phenomenon is at once consonant with, and subtly antithetical to, the essentialist/classificatory mode of presentation whereby poems are arranged according to the motifs of the seasons, love, travel, parting, and so forth.[30] Thus, while a poem may be said to be true because it is the expression in a brief, fixed form of a paradigmatic category of experience, it is also true because one can specify that it was composed by a real person on an actual occasion.

It is commonplace to argue for the expansion of the prose passages accompanying poetry in both the anthologies and the poem tales as a principal step in the development of prose fiction, but the impulse of the anthology preface to Narihira's poem, for example, is profoundly at odds with the workings of fiction. With the *Ise* hero's anguished standing and sitting, however, we detect something distinctive. I would like to describe it as a manifestation of the perception that the arrangement of words both as poetry and as prose can serve a larger category of cognition, namely, fiction. That, at least, is the retrospective evaluation of the *Ise* that the *Tale of Genji* encourages through its own uses of poetry, which is a topic to which we shall have more than one occasion to refer. The high praise long accorded the "style" of the *Ise* prose (so resistant to transmission in English) is a tacit recognition of this phenomenon—tacit insofar as the implications for the place of poetry in the hierarchy are not pursued.[31] To argue, for example, that the prose in the *Ise* is not subordinate to the poetry is in part to argue that good prose is poetic. Yet that is not sufficient to describe the process at work in the *Ise*, certainly not as Murasaki Shikibu read it. What happens in the fictionalization of the *Ise* is that both poetry as the short, fixed (and therefore precious) form of *waka* and prose as the reliable representation of the circumstances of the former's genesis are liberated from the requirements of historic actuality. What the *Genji* makes undeniable is that the invention of the novel as a particular use of prose alters the uses of poetry.

Now we should consider the more specific issue of the *Ise*'s thematic importance for the *Genji*. The poem that follows is one of the most celebrated in the Japanese canon:

Tsuki ya aranu   Is not the moon—
haru ya mukashi no   or the spring,
haru naranu   the spring of the past?
waga mi hitotsu wa   Alone I remain
moto no mi ni shite   my selfsame self.

The interpretation of this poem, thought to be characteristic of Narihira's elusiveness, has elicited considerable debate: should the questions of the first half be seen as rhetorical or literal (is the poet really wondering if the moon has changed)?[32] However that is answered, what is crucial is the assertion of dissonance between oneself and one's surroundings, especially the normally reliable elements of nature. Erotic despair, charged by the season, produces a radical sense of solitude for "the man."

Section 9 of the *Tales of Ise* describes the consequences of failed erotic transgression: "the man, finding himself needless in the world, thought, I shall not stay in the capital, let me travel East to seek a land where I might live. . . ." Thus begins the famous "Azuma Kudari," the journey to the eastern provinces that constitutes the hero's exile. If banishment has not been made explicit, it is at least clear that it has become exceedingly difficult for the hero to remain in the capital. Transgression followed by expulsion is a rich fictional motif because it contains the seeds of the psychology of alienation, as shown in the stunning "finding himself needless in the world" above. Add guilt to alienation, and we are at the threshold of the *Genji*: alienation and guilt can spawn and nurture long fictions because they imply connectedness and even causality; alienation and guilt are both the source and the consequence of the birth of consciousness. Like all travel, expulsion necessitates separation from the familiar, from the communal. The individual is born in solitude. Distinct characters—heroes—are forged in solitude. No doubt the development of the hero and the development of biography go hand-in-hand. The transgressive act stands outside, at the head of what may be a series of barely linked episodes, and casts a shadow over the whole—or rather, casts a shadow to create a whole.

The transgressions of many of the archaic heroes—a Susanoo

or a Yamato Takeru—are notable for their violence. Now it is also the case that the legendary heroes, both divine and human (e.g., Ōkuninushi or Emperor Nintoku), "wedded" the shamanic priestesses (usually daughters of clan chieftains) of each clan conquered in their journeys around the land. These women were tied to the land, to the guardian deities of the clan. Indeed, union with such a woman was the symbolic (and requisite) step signifying conquest. This pattern found a Heian reincarnation in the form of the amorous hero (such as "the man") and his exploits. From the point of view of the *Genji*, it is tempting to perceive a certain teleological shift of interest from the narratives of violent to those of erotic conquest. The propensity for the erotic to induce reflection is of course crucial to the development of interiority. We need only think of that pervasive Heian term, *monoomoi*, "thinking about things," the condition of constant longing (usually) produced by fruitless attachment. [33]

The emergence of the amorous hero in Heian writing is part of the evolution of the pursuit of erotic interests into art and finally play. [34] "Amorous" here refers to the difficult term *irogonomi*, which straddles the fence between love and eros but leans toward the latter. The appearance of the amorous hero marks the development of a sensibility that is rudimentary, if not altogether absent, in the rapaciousness of the early chronicles, but it also anticipates a potential loss through the refinement of erotic pursuit into virtuoso performance. Virtuosity is already detectable in the *Ise* hero or Genji, for that matter, and it comes to full flowering in Edo fiction. Virtuosity flirts with sterility and frivolity. The amorous tale is rescued from degeneration by coming under the shadow of transgression, which introduces values of light and darkness by marking one relationship as being more important than another. For its part, transgression finds an undepletable source of energy in erotic attachment. In the union of the noble exile and the amorous hero is to be found the seed of the Japanese novel.

As we have seen in the *Genji*, the series of episodes involving women of lower rank and narrower interest than the major heroines may be regarded as alternative, revealed versions of the hero's prohibited love for Fujitsubo. They are narratives that preserve and to some measure produce the central secret through their own unfolding—a procedure of importance since the erotic transgression in the *Genji* is potent because it remains secret. In the *Ise*, by contrast, the energy of transgression is diffused by discovery. A secret can shape a work. It marks out that which is important—indeed, makes it important, for the content of a secret is seldom precious in itself. Secrets create insiders and outsiders. Above all, secrets are important for their association with both sacredness and privacy.[35] The *Genji* never stoops to tempting its readers with suspense as to whether the secret of Reizei's conception will be discovered. (That sort of interest is deflected to the lighter Oborozukiyo affair.) Here as well as in the case of Kaoru, the protagonist of the next generation, the revelations are confined to the principals so that discovery is important only insofar as it influences their actions and thoughts.

Secrecy, in other words, is another of the effects of erotic transgression that serves the development of interiority. For example, despite the sparseness of portrayal, we are allowed telling glimpses into Fujitsubo's mind. Even as she is enraptured by Genji's dance in "An Autumn Excursion," she can only think "how much more splendid she would find him were it not for her frightfully inappropriate thoughts" (1:384; S 132; W 129). She can hardly respond when her husband presses her for comments on the performance. In the next chapter, "The Festival of the Cherry Blossoms," Fujitsubo has yet another opportunity to watch Genji distinguish himself, this time in the composition of Chinese verse as well as in dance. Even as she wonders at the hatred of the Crown Prince's mother (Kokiden) for this marvelous creature, she despairs of her own self that so wonders. Her anguish mounts with Reizei's birth: seeing his resemblance to Genji, we are told that she is troubled by her "demon of the soul" (*kokoro no oni* is the eloquent phrase)—what we know more plainly as "conscience" (1:398; S 139; W 136). Yet, as we have seen, the birth of the child transforms Fujitsubo's posture toward the secret into a severely practical one.

With Genji, too, guarding the secret becomes a paramount concern, with an added complication: his own worldly success is bound up in his son's succession to the throne. True, he is discomfited by his father's lavish affection in the face of his own treachery. Yet, even to introduce the word "treachery" rings false, for his passion for Fujitsubo is so overwhelming and so extraordinary as to be inexplicable, therefore silencing the potential censure of his readers. Passion is a cover whose extent lengthens to include Genji's self-interested efforts to protect the secret, his rejection of his son's wishes to step down, and his resolute insensitivity to the latter's longing for some admission of paternity. Indeed, Genji appears to keep the secret sealed from his own soul. One of the few descriptions of his own discomfiture occurs when his father so delights in the infant Reizei's resemblance to his older son that Genji feels himself "flushing—being frightened, awed, happy, and moved, all in rapid succession, so that he was on the verge of tears" (1:401; S 140; W 137). Then, he is struck by a sense of his own preciousness: the baby is so remarkable that if he, Genji, is indeed like him, then how truly extraordinary and invaluable he must be! Even in the chapters dealing with Genji's exile, the secret is treated obliquely.

It is only many years hence, when Genji learns of Kashiwagi's violation of his wife, that we find him wondering if his own father had actually known the truth but had kept silent. This illustrates the skill with which the secret is manipulated: for the public to learn the truth would be uninteresting, not to say destructive. For the Kiritsubo Emperor to learn it, at least on the pages of the tale, would foreclose on Genji's anguish decades later, an anguish that is heightened by our own ignorance as to the Kiritsubo Emperor's knowledge.

To take this point a bit further: it is precisely because of his presumed ignorance of the secret that the Kiritsubo Emperor is the most august of the unimpressive rulers in this tale. Cuckold that he is, he retains his dignity because he is not introspective, because he is not qualified by being developed in private terms. The contrast with Reizei is instructive, as is the further contrast between Reizei and Kaoru. When Reizei learns of his parentage, he seeks a solution in public terms, that is, by suggesting that he abdicate so that his true father, Genji, the rightful ruler, could succeed him. For Kaoru, in the last third of the tale, the same discovery results in the first full-blown identity crisis in Japanese literature. But of course, he is the son of a man who wills himself to death under the burden of guilt and revelation, in striking contrast to Genji. Although Genji is a fellow perpetrator of transgression, it is only when he is a victim too that he is shown to experience its consequences. We see, once again, that Genji's distinction as hero lies in his contradictory attributes: princely yet common, transgressor and transgressed, psychically closed yet momentarily revealed.

These contradictions have to do with the paradoxical nature of secrecy itself, which as stated earlier is associated with both sacredness and privacy. If secrecy, as it is used in the *Genji*, is a medium for the development of inner awareness, of a private self that can become the matter of fiction, it is at the same time a remnant of the mythical world. The issue of children from illicit love is the fictional equivalent of heavenly birth in myths. Transgression distinguishes the births of Reizei and Kaoru from other this-worldly births, and secrecy serves in lieu of mystery.[36] Secrecy serves to establish another world within the decidedly secular realm that is the domain of prose fiction. And, to the extent that the experience of the great secret of the tale is disclosed through Fujitsubo rather than Genji, he remains larger than life, a direct descendant of the archaic hero.

"Woman's body [like the cherry blossom] is another land."[37] The contrast drawn above between Genji and Fujitsubo should not domesticate her. The heroines of the tale represent various modes of otherness for the heroes, modes that also imply varieties of selfhood. Fujitsubo's particular otherness is captured in her refusal to become a "woman." Before we leave her, let us look at three boundary moments that situate her in a procedure characteristic of the tale.

After the brief but fateful meeting at Fujitsubo's own estate, she and Genji exchange the following poems:

(GENJI)

Mite mo mata   So rare the nights
au yo mare naru   of meeting
yume no uchi ni   that I would lose

42

yagate magiruru
waga mi to mo gana

myself
in this night's dream.

(Fujitsubo)

Yogatari ni
hito ya tsutaen
tagui naku
uki mi o samenu
yume ni nashite mo

They would talk about me still,
were I to dissolve
this self,
incomparably wretched,
in a never-ending dream.

(1:306; S 98; W 95)

Dreams, like spirit possession and prophecies, are signs of an other world. As such, however, they become aspects of the fictional reality of the *Genji*. The plurality of "aspects" needs emphasizing, since different dreams carry different nuances—that is, represent different kinds of internal distance. For example, there are several prophetic dreams in the *Genji* that seem to come from a remote and truly other world, such as the moon in the *Tale of the Bamboo Cutter* or the Palace of the Sea Dragon King, common in Asian legends.[38] Although the Genji-Fujitsubo relationship is repeatedly likened to dreams, the above exchange reveals the finely wrought tension between their respective conceptions of dreams. Genji's poem is youthful and self-indulgent; for him the dream represents an experience that cannot be admitted by the public, daylight world but one that is far more compelling than any offered by that reality. It is the attractive reality of night, the privileged time for earthly lovers that he would extend forever, thus nullifying the daylight world. Fujitsubo's dream would also be never-ending, not as sweet night but as dark death, the absolutely other. But even death cannot be trusted to shield her from the gossip of life.

What happens at Fujitsubo's actual death? As we have seen, in the years following the Kiritsubo Emperor's death, she manages to convert an erotic attachment into a private alliance. Having become a nun, she is able to maintain a private relationship on public terms. The tensions resurface, though in characteristically muted fashion, in Fujitsubo's last words, addressed to Genji:

Chapter 1

I have had many occasions over the years to think of how you have served the Emperor, just as the late Emperor requested at the time of his death, and I have sought opportunities to let you know of my gratitude. But I have tarried too long, and now it has come to nought.

(2:436; S 339; W 372)

On her deathbed Fujitsubo is all but reborn a romantic heroine. Genji is present at the deaths of Yūgao, Murasaki, and Fujitsubo. Yūgao's death is too horrifying to allow for grief, and Murasaki's is shared with the Akashi Empress. Fujitsubo's, however, is a private, elegiac moment (for the attendants do not count) in which, for the first time, she almost speaks her love. It anticipates the even more intimate death of Ōigimi in "Trefoil Knots" with Kaoru at her bedside.

Fujitsubo's actual passing is described as a "flame going out"—words echoing the Lotus Sutra. The private, romantic moment cedes immediately to the religious, and then to the public. Despite the doomed anxiety expressed in her "dream" poem, Fujitsubo is praised as saints are praised: "Even mountain priests who understood nothing mourned her loss" (2:438; S 340; W 373).

The scriptural evocation, followed by public mourning, seems to usher her safely, eternally to the land of the dead. On a snowy night in "The Morning Glory," Genji is reminded of the snow mountains Fujitsubo had built in her gardens one winter, and he is led to reminisce with Murasaki about her aunt and several other women. Of course he does not divulge their secret—he is only allowing himself the pleasure of giving modest expression to a continuing attachment by speaking of the lady in superlative terms. When he falls asleep, still thinking of Fujitsubo, she appears faintly to him in what might have been a dream (*yume to mo naku*, 2:485; S 359; W 397). (The Japanese locution identifies the phenomenon only with an attenuated denial of what it might be.) What is unmistakable is her displeasure: "You said you would not let a word of our secret out, but now my name is sullied and I can hide nowhere. I am ashamed, and in the midst of all my suffering, this is all the more painful" (ibid.).

Still on this side of salvation, Fujitsubo's spirit is free to complain for the first time. The reaction seems excessive, given the nature of Genji's comments. No doubt there is a tinge of hurt pride at being discussed with her successor, and as one of several women at that. It is an unsettling final image of an idealized heroine. Just as she had anticipated (prophesied), death does not remove her to a safe land.

THE ROKUJŌ LADY: PRIDE AND POSSESSION

The fictional possibilities of the spiritual realm receive their most sustained treatment in the character of the Rokujō Lady. As with Fujitsubo, but incomparably more dramatically, the Rokujō Lady's spirit, once free of the body, turns loquacious. Hers is arguably the most distinguished possessing spirit in a literary tradition rich in ghosts, and it is this manifestation of her character that is of abiding interest, even now when the darkness of Heian estates, so conducive to the play of spirits, has given way to well-lit rooms. Before we turn to her spirit, however, let us survey her earthly background.

The Rokujō Lady is the daughter of a minister, dead before the opening of the tale. (He is literally present, however, "in spirit.") This means that her father was a minister before the time of the Ministers of the Right and Left in the "Paulownia Court" chapter. The Rokujō Lady was married to a crown prince at the age of sixteen, bore him a daughter (the future Akikonomu), and was widowed at twenty. This Crown Prince was the Kiritsubo Emperor's brother. Their sister is Princess Ōmiya, wife of the Minister of the Left and mother of Aoi and Tō no Chūjō. Kokiden, daughter of the Minister of the Right, is a consort of the Kiritsubo Emperor and mother of the next crown prince, Suzaku. This complex of relationships might be described as a web spun by ministerial desire to be linked to the throne.

It must have been a proud and hopeful moment for the Rokujō Lady's family when she entered the Crown Prince's household. The pride and hopes were shattered with his premature death. Although the circumstances of the death are unstated, the view that he was a deposed crown prince, the victim of political rivalry, has become increasingly popular.[39] The reasons supporting this interpretation are that (1) it is unusual for both the positions of crown prince and empress to be vacant at the opening of the tale (the two normally go hand-in-hand); (2) the *Genji* itself incorporates the historical reality of deposed crown princes in the person of the Eighth Prince of the Uji chapters; and (3) most pertinently, the appearance of the spirits of both the Rokujō Lady and her father at Aoi's bedside carries a strong hint of grievance.

We first meet the Rokujō Lady as an unspecified lady of the Sixth Ward, a consummately elegant woman who, once ardently wooed by Genji, succumbed and is now condemned to suffer the effects of his cooling interest. She is introduced together with Yūgao, a young woman discovered by Genji on a visit to his sick nurse. (Readers will come to recognize such juxtaposition as a characteristic mode of argument in the *Genji*.) Yūgao appears to be of modest and therefore, to the still unworldly Genji, intriguing circumstances. Our views of Yūgao are interspersed with contrasting glimpses of the lady of the Sixth Ward. Yūgao, childlike and artless, is situated amidst the clatter of townsfolk at work, whereas the other lady, older than Genji and formidable in her refinement, inhabits a world admitting no hint of daily labor. Yūgao receives her name from the white gourd flowers garnishing her humble wall, "evening faces," which contrast with the morning glories (*asagao*, "morning faces") growing in the garden of the other lady. Unlike the morning glory, the evening face is unrefined by poetic associations when it is plucked by Genji (whereupon it will have to wait another two centuries before entering the poetic vocabulary).[40]

For all their differences, both women are shrouded in mystery. Do they meet in the deserted villa to which Genji removes Yūgao for the sake of an uninterrupted day or two? At the dank, dark villa, Genji and Yūgao banter about demons and fox spirits; that same night, Yūgao dies suddenly, evidently attacked by the apparition of a beautiful woman seen only by Genji. The episode is a brilliant synthesis of elements drawn from folk tales as well as from Chinese and Japanese poetry and fiction.[41] The thick gothic atmosphere invites the same sort of sustained speculation without resolution of a work like *The Turn of the Screw*. The attacking spirit is never identified with the lady of the Sixth Ward, and debate continues to this day as to whether it belongs to the Rokujō Lady.[42]

The apparition says to Genji: "Though I have admired you, you have neglected to visit me and keep this creature at your side to fuss over when there is nothing distinguished about her" (1:238; S 71; W 67). These words fit perfectly with what we already know and what we will learn of the Rokujō Lady. Indeed, just before this passage, Genji has been thinking of her, contrasting her haughty, demanding nature with the artless sweetness of the girl with whom he has stolen away. As we have already seen with Fujitsubo, and as we shall witness again, this is precisely the kind of offending stimulus that impels a spirit to leave its body. Indeed, in the hands of Murasaki Shikibu, the possessing spirit becomes a means of dramatizing the unspoken communication of troubled lovers' thoughts. It seems inefficient and uneconomical not to identify this murderous spirit with the Rokujō Lady, given that the *Genji* imposes on its readers a mode of reading in which no detail is left free (which also means that any one detail has various resonances). In contrast to later episodes, however, the crucial act of identification, both by the spirit and by Genji, is missing, and we must give this absence its due. In part it is a question of aesthetic tact: as Saigō Nobutsuna puts it, "If the Rokujō Lady were to hastily identify herself at this point, she would become a mere murderess who could arouse only a commonplace sort of interest."[43]

The Rokujō Lady's spirit makes its first incontrovertible appearance in the "Heartvine" chapter. The immediate cause is the famous carriage brawl taking place at the lustration ceremony of the new Priestess of the Kamo Shrine. Aoi, Genji's principal wife, is pregnant for the first time in the ten years of their marriage, and this, together with her customary aloofness, inclines her to stay away, but she is persuaded by her mother to go with the young women of her household: after all, Genji is to play a prominent part in the procession. The Rokujō Lady, whose own daughter has been appointed Priestess of Ise with the new reign, has been suffering more than ever from Genji's neglect and even contemplates accompanying her daughter to Ise. For the moment, however, she cannot resist the temptation of seeing Genji in his splendor, and so she goes quietly, hoping to escape notice. The excursion turns into a nightmare. After a shameless scuffle, her carriages are ignominiously shoved to the rear by Aoi's men. Genji, riding in the procession, pays solemn homage to his wife's carriage but casts not so much as a glance in her direction.

Thus the Rokujō Lady is humiliated at one of the great public ceremonies of Heian Japan. (The lustration ceremony takes place a few days before the Aoi Festival proper.) Within the novel it is, of course, Genji's presence that makes the occasion significant. Since accumulating superlatives is inadequate for describing his magnificence, unusual admirers are depicted instead:

> . . . even nuns who had turned their backs to the world were in the throngs, stumbling and rolling over. On any other day one would have said, "Look at them making fools of themselves," but today it was understandable. There were other dubious types, toothless jaws caved in, hair tucked into their robes, making spectacles of themselves as they raised their clasped hands to their foreheads when they caught sight of him.   (2:19; S 162; W 158)

Of course, the beautiful people are there as well. It is against this backdrop of a great communal celebration that two women are shown vicariously fighting over one man.[44]

The festival of the Kamo Shrine, called the Aoi Matsuri because the heartvine (*aoi*) was featured as an ornament, has a pronounced erotic cast. Verbally, *aoi* is ready-made for punning with *au*, to meet, as in lovers' trysts. If we turn to a description of the founding of the shrine, we learn that a crimson arrow came floating to Tamayorihime, the daughter of the founding deity, as she played in a shallow branch of the Kamo River. Tamayorihime placed it at her bedside, whereupon she conceived a son.[45]

On the day of the festival proper, Genji goes as a private spectator with Murasaki. He is offered a space for his carriage by the aging but lascivious Naishi with whom he had cavorted earlier

Naishi
⇕
Rokujō

in "Festival of the Leaves" (in a scene serving as yet another parodic version of Genji's secret violation of Fujitsubo).[46] Here, Naishi, who in the interest of decency should have forsaken flirtation long ago, becomes a caricaturized Rokujō Lady. Although the latter is never ludicrous, the implied comparison is hardly flattering.

Shortly after the lustration ceremony Aoi sickens. The altogether predictable diagnosis places the blame on malign spirits. Rumor identifies the culprits as the Rokujō Lady and her late father the Minister. Such reports necessarily distress the sensitive lady. Convinced as she is that no one has had more cause for brooding than she in the course of the years, she is now distraught as she has never been:

> After that small incident when she [Aoi] had humiliated her—treated her quite as if she did not exist—ever since the lustration day, she had been obsessed, and perhaps because of this, when she dozed off, she repeatedly dreamt of going off to where that lady was lying in beautiful state, where she would tug at her this way and that. Utterly unlike her usual self, she was violent and frightful in her single-mindedness, and she could see herself shaking the other lady. Ah, how odious it was! What they say is true, she thought, my soul forsakes my body and wanders forth.
>
> (2:30; S 167; W 163-64)

The Rokujō Lady's proud mind, so quick to detect injury, is doubly acute when it sees itself a shameful wrongdoer. It is even more difficult for such a spirit to wrong than to be wronged: or rather, wronging translates into a form of being wronged. The Lady removes herself from her own home, where her daughter is preparing for her priestly duties, and seeks refuge in a place where she can practice Buddhist rites.

As her condition approaches the crisis point, Aoi asks to speak to Genji. This is surprising in itself, but when he looks in on her behind her curtains, he is struck for the first time by her beauty and appeal: "Her white garments were set off by her long, luxuriant hair, pulled and bound to one side. At last, her eyes were sweet and bewitching" (2:32; S 168; W 165). Genji is moved to tears. "Her eyes, usually so distant and forbidding, looked up at his face and fixed it with their dull gaze; they began to fill with tears" (2:33; S 168; W 165). Genji seeks to comfort her, but his words are met with a gentle denial:

> No, that isn't it. They are making me suffer so, I just wanted to have them stop for a while. I never thought that I should visit you in this way. I see now it is true that the souls of those who brood wander forth. (Ibid.)

The affectionate voice continues with a poem:

Nageki wabi	My troubled soul
sora ni midaruru	wanders the skies
waga tama o	in sorrow:
musubi todomeyo	O bind my hem
shitagai no tsuma	and secure it within!

(Ibid.)

The last lines apparently refer to a folk belief according to which tying the lower inside corner of a robe would effect the return of the wearer's errant soul. *Tsuma*, the lower inside corner, is an attractive choice here since it doubles for "spouse": thus, the appeal is made to a secret (the corner of the inner fold is not visible) husband (2:33, n. 32). *Midaruru* (line 2), neutrally rendered here as "wanders," generally refers to disorder/disarray—of garments, the soul, the state; the quintessential source of such turbulence is erotic attachment. Tidy my garments, make me respectable again, stop this gaping wound in my soul (make me not love you any more, but don't, I would still love and be loved by you), appeals the spirit of the Rokujō Lady. The appeal far exceeds the capacities of the young man to whom it is made. Horrified and confused, he demands that the spirit identify herself even though he is anxious that no one else learn of this exchange.

We must keep in mind that the Rokujō Lady's spirit is speaking through Aoi's person. The above poem, for example, becomes altogether different if we read it as Aoi's. Of course, the Aoi familiar to Genji is not one to make appeals to her husband. In fact, she has the unflattering distinction of being the only one among Genji's ladies not to produce a single poem. She is consistently characterized as glacially perfect. Although there is a tempestuous streak to the Rokujō Lady, she, too, is customarily reserved. When Aoi's body houses Lady Rokujō's soul, when Lady Rokujō's soul inhabits Aoi's body, a new creature emerges far sweeter than either woman can comfortably be. The phenomenon of spirit possession is another form of juxtaposition, an instance of the continuous exploration of character formation. Aspects of one being can be combined with those of another to produce a new woman who embodies possibilities invisible in her sources.

Later, when Aoi delivers a son to the mounting frenzy of the exorcists, the Rokujō Lady becomes even more agitated:

> She had heard that the lady was in grave danger, but now she was safely delivered. . . . As she reflected upon how she had become estranged from herself, she noticed that the scent of poppy seeds permeated her robes, and try as she would to rid herself of it by washing her hair and her garments, the odor persisted.   (2:36-37; S 169; W 166)

Poppy seeds are used in the rites of exorcism, and their scent on her person confirms her suspicion of her spirit's mischief. Her misery only mounts, culminating in her spirit's killing Aoi while the men of her household are absent.

We should note the vividness with which the possession is described. It is not the realism of lurid detail, but its opposite: what other writer would have thought to juxtapose spirit possession with odors, shampoos, and laundry? Murasaki Shikibu harnesses the energy of foxes, ghosts, and demons to the task of creating the human psyche for fiction. The smell of the burnt poppy seeds is actual, but it obstinately resists removal by physical means. The external plague of ghosts is converted into the more intractable curse of inner demons.[47]

THE ELUSIVE SELF IN HEIAN JAPAN

The mid-Heian period (from the late tenth through the eleventh centuries) was the great age of spirit possession. Itinerant spirits in themselves were no novelty. Shamanic figures had long been distinguished for their ability to send their souls on distant missions, and lovers' souls were commonly thought to leave their bodies to travel to each other. As for vengeful spirits, the ninth century produced a paradigmatic example in the scholar-statesman Sugawara no Michizane, who died an unhappy death in exile. But it is somewhat later that spirits were set in motion with alarming frequency, wreaking havoc wherever they went. They did not necessarily belong to the dead; the spirits of the living (called *ikisudama*) were just as likely to forsake their bodies. The relatively sudden prominence of the word *mononoke* (spirit possession) suggests the presence of a new phenomenon. One study shows that apart from a mid-ninth-century history (the *Shoku Nihon Kōki*), in which the term is used twelve times without any explanation, *mononoke* must await such late tenth-century works as the *Tales of Yamato*, the *Tale of the Hollow Tree*, and the *Gossamer Years* before the phenomenon it designates sustains any description.[48] Note the genre spread: a poem tale, a fictional tale, and a woman's diary. The record is reached in the *Genji*, which has no fewer than fifty-three examples, seconded by the *Tale of Flowering Fortunes*, the historical tale written some four decades later, with seventeen examples.[49]

Mononoke is but one of a host of words prefixed by *mono* to proliferate in the Heian period. The etymology of *mono* is complex and obscure, involving as it does questions as to which Chinese characters were used to represent the sound of *mono* in early texts. In pre-Heian texts the characters now familiar as *oni* and *kami* ("demon" and "deity/spirit") were common, and it is thought that *mono* indicated the awesome and the fearful. The issue of the etymology of *mono* involves the contemporary status of ancestral souls, the distinction between malevolent and benevolent spirits (i.e., "them" vs. "us"), and finally, the range of ancient Japanese politico/religious history. It is possible that, by the time *mono* was attached to adjectives of sadness, fearfulness, and loneliness, or to verbs of thinking or knowing, these associations had been conflated and blurred so that *mono* as prefix only suggested the vague and the unspecifiable—which sounds like a secularized version of the ineffable.[50]

In the *Genji [Mono]gatari*, at any rate, it is possible to qualify the nature of the unspecifiable as anxiety. The author's evident interest in the *mononoke* reveals a sensitivity to a state of instability that caused people to experience themselves as other, which also implies heightened self-awareness. Indeed, the sudden proliferation of the *mono* prefix suggests that Heian life was permeated by the psyche. And, moreover, the most significant manifestation of this phenomenon was the destructive roving spirit. What accounts for this development?[51]

In an earlier age the soul (*tama/tamashii*) was a communal entity, to be distinguished from the heart-mind (*kokoro*), which was the physical site of individual vitality, emotions, sense-impressions, and so forth.[52] The *kokoro*, like other organs, died with the individual body, but the *tama* left the body to continue existing in other bodies. It is immediately apparent that the practice of ancestor worship, which is inherently communal, presumes such a phenomenon. It was only when the social character of the spirit weakened that it began to detach itself from the bodies of the living. Saigō Nobutsuna suggests that as the soul changed from a communal to an individual entity, a state of dissonance between body and soul was induced such that the soul was moved to vacate the body from time to time:

> Even though the mythical/communal estate that had been proper to the soul was disintegrating, it had yet to become an aspect of the self that human beings could fully possess. This, however, is a modern interpretation. From the archaic point of view, this was the point at which the soul became individualized, whereupon its ancient harmony with the body was tragically and irreversibly ruptured. It was the goal of Buddhism to rescue this soul by means of an afterlife.[53]

Any description of the nature and activities of the soul is an expression of the religious, psychological, and political beliefs of a given age. If indeed a new awareness of individual existence was emerging in the Heian period (if the evolution of the individual was in an accelerated state), it is not surprising that the soul (and therefore the body) was perceived differently. The rise of individualism is too large a topic to pursue here, but it is worth adding that Saigō singles out as a contributory force the Jōdo Buddhism so influential among Heian aristocrats. By emphasizing salvation—that is, the obliteration of the individual subject—Jōdo Buddhism had the effect of fostering the awareness of individual fate.

Contemplating with horror the activities of her spirit, the Rokujō Lady shudders to think how the world would judge her: "How wretched is my fate!" (*Sukuse no uki koto*, 2:30-31; S 167; W 164). *Ushi (uki)*, often used with *sukuse* ("karma," "fate"), suggests an active apprehension of one's fate as a particular and distinct entity, in contrast to, for example, the closely related *tsurashi*, which suggests more of a whine in the face of an imposition.[54] The Rokujō Lady's shudders always mingle wrath with horror. No religious rite can contain her rage. The "Heart-vine" chapter shows her oscillating between Shintō and Buddhist poles. (Despite the growing popularity of syncretism, Buddhism and Shintō were mutually repellent on some planes, each being unholy to the other. The Priestesses of the Ise Shrine had to forego Buddhist practices during their tenure but then made strenuous efforts to compensate for that period without the Buddhist Law.) How efficacious the Rokujō Lady's Buddhist rites are can be judged by the fact that it is from her house of retreat that her spirit flies to murder Aoi. After that incident, her inclination to accompany her daughter to Ise strengthens. When she eventually returns from Ise, it is to sicken and die.

If any one quality can be said to characterize the Rokujō Lady's behavior, it is excess. For all her refinement (but there again, she is overly refined), the Rokujō Lady is scandalous. Some time after Aoi's death, Genji arises from his lonely bed at dawn to find a letter from her containing the following poem:

Hito no yo o	Hearing of her sad life,
aware to kiku mo	my tears gather
tsuyukeki ni	like the dew on the
okururu sode o	chrysanthemum
omoi koso yare	I think of your sleeves,
	O one left behind.
	(2:44-45; S 173; W 170)

54

The message, on deep blue-gray paper (the color of mourning robes and nun's garb), is accompanied by a chrysanthemum just opening (*kiku*, line 2, is homophonous for "hear" and "chrysan-themum"). The hand, always superb, is especially fine. The Ro-kujō Lady is possibly the most celebrated calligrapher in the *Genji*. All this evidence of her taste is not lost on the young widower, yet having witnessed her spirit, he cannot accept the proffered sentiment. It is not the hint of hypocrisy in the message that offends, but the very elegance in which it is couched. More-over, the missive is timed to reach him in bed (though he is unable to sleep, as the sender has correctly guessed). Finally, there is the added rub that it is once again the Rokujō Lady who has taken the initiative. (Of her nine exchanges with Genji, an immodest seven are begun by her.)

If women usually showed more reserve in initiating exchanges of poems with men, mothers never accompanied their daughters to Ise. History records but one instance of a mother requesting permission to travel with a daughter who had been designated Priestess of that shrine. That request was denied.[55] Prior to their departure for Ise, the Rokujō Lady and her daughter make a customary call at the Palace. As she gets into her palanquin, the mother's thoughts turn to the past:

> Her father the minister had entertained the highest hopes for her and tended to her needs with the utmost care. But that had all come to nought, and now, an old woman, she was seeing the Palace again.   (2:85; S 189; W 196)

Ten years have lapsed since her husband's death, when she had last seen the Palace. For the Rokujō Lady, her talents and her sensibility—the best products of wealth and ambition—have be-come superfluous. She should have been empress.[56]

Instead, she has come to preside over the finest salon of the day. Widowed when young, she had remained aloof until Genji came along: but this part is forever shielded from us. Imagine the effect it had upon her to see Aoi, another minister's daugh-ter, flaunting her position as Genji's official wife and even bear-ing him a son. (It is equally easy to imagine how an undistin-guished creature like Yūgao would have excited her wrath.) The

Rokujō Lady's pride is a complex mixture of familial ambition and individual desire. Excessive energy, fueled by thwarted ambition, vain passion, and the knowledge of wasted talents makes of the Rokujō Lady a disturbingly memorable character. There is something majestic about the unprecedented move to Ise. Yet in that drama of willful self-abnegation, she is the prima donna, but whether of a tragedy or its parody is left artfully uncertain. There is the celebrated scene in which Genji comes calling at the temporary shrine for a final leave-taking. The Rokujō Lady is reluctant. She at length grants an audience to Genji who by then is ambivalent. They exchange verses—frosty and careful—yet her resolve weakens again. It is too late. In going to Ise, in becoming, in effect, the Priestess (for her image overshadows her daughter's), the Rokujō Lady compensates for, lives a negative version of, the life she would have had as empress. The Ise Priestess, often (but too vividly) translated as (Vestal) Virgin, is of course pledged to chastity, being the negative incarnation of royal consorts whose function it is to bear heirs. It is an appropriate role for the Rokujō Lady to play, especially given the hint of expulsion in the ancient darkness of the office: why should the guardian deity of the imperial family reside so far from the capial?[57] Another shadow in the image of the Rokujō Lady as a psuedo-Ise Priestess is the dreamy, seductive figure of the Priestess whose ephemeral meeting with "the man" is recounted in episode 69 of the *Tales of Ise*. The Rokujō Lady may transfer her unmanageable energies to Ise, but she can never dispel them in that troubled holy land.

She and her daughter remain in Ise for six years. During that time there is at least one exchange of letters with Genji in exile. Upon the Suzaku Emperor's abdication, mother and daughter return to the capital, and the Rokujō salon enjoys a brief revival. Genji does not visit, however, and it is only when she lies near death that the two meet again (meet, that is, with curtains and screens interposing). Genji pledges to look after the former Priestess—without improper sentiments, her mother bluntly stipulates. She dies soon after this interview.

Later, in Genji s palatial residence built in the neighborhood of the Rokujō Lady's estate, her daughter Akikonomu, who is by then empress, will have the place of honor in the "autumn" quarters situated on land inherited from her mother. For this reason, this residence, the Rokujōin, may be construed as a memorial edifice for the pacification of Lady Rokujō's soul:

> The spirit of the dead Rokujō Lady reposes at the "old estate in the Sixth Ward." This means, in one respect, that it has become the guardian spirit of the household. The blossoming fortunes of the "old estate in the Sixth Ward" undoubtedly console the guardian spirit. . . . The spirit, for its part, watches over the prosperity of the house and confers its blessings.[58]

This, however, is a "dangerous relationship," not only because the household must strenuously avoid the slightest hint of failure, as Fujii Sadakazu suggests in a continuation of the above passage, but because the Rokujō Lady is as demanding in death as in life.

The Rokujōin, with its seasonal quarters, each presided over by its own mistress, is, as we shall see, a private replica of the women's quarters (Kōkyū) in the Palace. As the principal consort of the crown prince, Lady Rokujō, had her husband lived, would in all likelihood have reigned supreme at the true Kōkyū. That her daughter as empress is honored both at the Palace and at the Rokujōin would seem to constitute fitting tribute, yet it is evidently offensive as well as insufficient. For Genji does not, after all, devote himself to prayers for the repose of the soul of a woman who has always required exclusive attention. And what, after all, are the women's quarters at the Palace and at the Rokujōin if not the breeding ground of the most intense rivalry conceivable among women? Since, for example, Yūgao's long-lost daughter is for a time the center of attraction, is the Rokujōin also a covert gesture of pacification dedicated to the Rokujō Lady's victim?

Some eighteen years after her death, the spirit of the Rokujō Lady strikes again. This time the victim is Murasaki, the most important of all of Genji's companions. Murasaki is vulnerable: despite her extraordinary fortitude, the shock of Genji's marriage to the Third Princess has shaken her to the core. She falls ill and is removed from the Rokujōin to the Nijōin, where she has always felt more at home. There Genji nurses her devotedly, but not without an anxious backward glance at the Third Princess. He eventually visits the Rokujōin where the Princess resides, and during his absence Murasaki apparently dies. (Genji was also away when Aoi succumbed.) Genji rushes back to mobilize exorcists in a frenzied effort to revive her. Miraculously enough, they are successful. The possessing spirit is transferred to a medium and insists,

I must speak to his lordship alone. The rest of you, leave. [To Genji] Because you have made me miserable these months with your rites, I thought to make you suffer as well, but now I see that you have worn yourself to the bone, risking your own life to save hers. . . . I appear in this dreadful form because of lingering sentiments from the past; I could not be indifferent to your sufferings. I had not intended to make myself known. (4:226; S 617; W 663)

Although Genji immediately indentifies the sobbing spirit with the one he had been horrified to witness at Aoi's beside, he still insists that it identify itself.

Weeping even more, the spirit replies with a poem:

Waga mi koso	I have a form
aranu sama nare	that I had not;
sore nagara	but you,
sora oboresuru	unchanged in appearance,
kimi wa kimi nari	feigning forgetfulness,
	are still the same you.
	(4:227; S 618; W 663)

For all the sobbing and flinging of hair, the spirit still has the vestiges of the Rokujō Lady's breeding and is therefore all the more eerie. Genji would silence her, but now her tongue is loosened:

I have been pleased and grateful as I have watched from the skies to see what you have done for Her Majesty. But perhaps because I have left the world of the living, I no longer experience as keenly the events that befall my daughter. My old sense of grievance has stayed obstinately with me. When I was alive, you held me beneath another and abandoned me; but now, worse still, you have described me as disagreeable and odious to that lady who is so dear to you. That has made me more bitter than anything else. I had hoped, now that I was dead, that you might have forgiven me, and that if others spoke ill of me, you would check them and defend me. And here I am, in this hideous state, having to be the source of such havoc. It is not that I hate her deeply. You are so protected and removed that I have not been able to come near. Even your voice reaches me but faintly. But now, pray for me that my sins may be lightened. These chants, these services, only bring me burning anguish, and it distresses me that I cannot hear the holy words. Tell Her Majesty of what I have spoken. Tell her, too, that in the course of her court services, she is never to stir the jealousy of another. Tell her that she must do penance for the sins accumulated while she was Priestess. How regrettable that was! (4:227-28; S 619; W 664)

This is one of the longest female speeches in the *Genji*. The immediate cause, as the spirit makes clear, is Genji's candid description of the lady as she was to Murasaki just before the latter fell ill. Ironically, but inevitably, he had passed from Aoi to the Rokujō Lady in that conversation:

There was never a moment for relaxing, one felt so constrained. She was too reserved for sharing the simple intimacies of morning and evening. One felt she would be contemptuous if one were to let down. And so, while I tried to maintain appearances, we drifted apart.
(4:200-201; S 608; W 652)

The last time Murasaki received such confidences, the angry spirit of Fujitsubo had appeared to Genji and charged him with betrayal. The Rokujō Lady is also indignant, and Murasaki is the perfect vehicle of her wrath. Yet she is not simply vindictive. She cherishes the opportunity to see Genji and to express her anguish.

Chapter 1

Although the spirit continues to hover near Murasaki's bedside with tearful plaints, there are no further dramatic appearances, and Murasaki makes a slow recovery. The next one to fall victim is the Third Princess who, unable to endure her existence after the birth of Kaoru, her son by Kashiwagi thought by the world to be Genji's, takes vows in spite of Genji's opposition. She continues to be weak, and one night, the spirit appears again:

> You see what I said? You were pleased to get the other one back, you thought you had been so clever that it annoyed me. I came here quietly and waited my chance. But now I'm leaving. (4:300; S 644; W 652)

The spirit bursts into laughter and vanishes from the tale. Subsequently, and only too predictably, we learn through her daughter that she continues to wander the skies, unable to find salvation. It is the raucous laughter that is unsettling here, coming as it does when a heavy quiet has descended on the tale. From the great "New Herbs" chapters onward, the writing has been turning steadily inward, with the protagonists brooding, speculating on each other's thoughts, willing illness and even death upon themselves. Whereas the Rokujō Lady's earlier appearances as a possessing spirit had offered flashes of psychological revelation when the surrounding tale was largely innocent of introspection, here her spirit turns demonlike and unrecuperably otherworldly.

Let us look back at her choice of victims. As we have seen, it is only after she has been formally supplanted by the Third Princess that Murasaki weakens, becoming susceptible to the preying spirit's attacks. On one plane, Murasaki and the Third Princess are in opposition, but this is clearly not their most significant configuration since the Third Princess also falls victim to the spirit. (Insofar as she is markedly inferior, however, the Third Princess cannot be analogous to Murasaki.) Like Murasaki, the Third Princess is Fujitsubo's niece; indeed, the blood tie is crucial to Genji's decision to make her his official wife. Fujitsubo herself is the daughter of a former emperor who cannot be situated on the genealogical charts. Now, although the Rokujō Lady's lineage also eludes literary genealogists, we do know that members of the Akashi family are conspicuously spared the attacks of her spirit. The Akashi Lady, both by temperament and accomplishment, resembles the Rokujō Lady, and the similarity is made explicit when Genji visits the younger woman for the first time. Akikonomu, the Rokujō Lady's daughter, has the important task of tying the cord of the ceremonial train at the coming-of-age of the Akashi Lady's daughter.

These points encourage the supposition that the Rokujō Lady is at the very least not ill-disposed toward the Akashi family and may even be related.[59] We recall that her father was a Minister in a generation preceding that of the Ministers of the Right and the Left holding office at the beginning of the tale. The Akashi Lady's father was also the son of an earlier minister, who was the brother of the Kiritsubo Lady's father, a major counsellor. Despite the sad fate of Genji's mother, the Kiritsubo-Akashi family's growing prosperity contrasts sharply with the declining fortunes of the line descended from the "former emperor": Fujitsubo, Murasaki, and the Third Princess.[60] Here again the economy of the erotic and of the political becomes evident: the Kiritsubo Lady suffered the erotic consequences of her father's political ambitions, but her descendants on the Akashi side, though never as interesting erotically, achieve political prosperity with the apparent blessings of the Rokujō Lady.

In this perspective the Rokujō Lady and Fujitsubo emerge as symmetrical figures. Fujitsubo never loses Genji's love, but the love is barely fulfilled, and moreover, it produces an ominous secret that burdens Genji's life just as the Rokujō Lady's curse does. Fujitsubo, as if to compensate for her hidden erotic self, becomes a powerful political figure, but her son Reizei abdicates without heirs (although a daughter is incongruously mentioned in "The Bamboo River"), and her nieces suffer private tragedies. And of course, Fujitsubo herself is never attacked by the Rokujō Lady, which not only accords with her absolute status but reinforces the symmetry, genealogical and otherwise, of their positions. I have described Fujitsubo, daughter of an unidentified emperor, as the "original substitute." Lady Rokujō, daughter of an unidentified minister, substitutes for no one. As possessing spirit, as bifurcated self, she achieves a concentration of being unreplicated by other heroines.

The force of her presence is such that there is a sense in which the victims of the Rokujō Lady come together, a sense in which they even become identified with their attacker. Like most victims of possessing spirits, Aoi, Murasaki, and the Third Princess are all in physically and psychologically weakened states when they are seized. The common cause of their condition may be crudely put as suffering induced by men, in this case, Genji. Though the circumstances are different in each case, all three are compelled to endure Genji's neglect, and in so doing each attains a certain crystallization of self. That moment is marked— made visible, as it were—by the Rokujō Lady, and in perverse fashion, she may be said to be speaking for them.[61]

Why is this cry heard by Genji alone? There is the obvious answer, namely, that he is the relevant party. But more important is the issue of the kind of hero he is, in distinction to the heroines his women are. As we had occasion to notice with Fujitsubo, Genji is seldom portrayed from within: he is internally invisible. As Saigō Nobutsuna puts it, the very epithet "Hikaru Genji," the "Shining Genji," has an archaic ring.[62] The interior occlusion and the archaicism go hand in hand, but in using the word *occlusion* I am suggesting that the archaicism is not innocent. Indeed, Genji's encounters with the possessing spirit may serve as moments of displaced intimations of his psyche. Because of the displacement, the confrontations between Genji and the spirit of the Rokujō Lady have the dramatic value of a confrontation between the archaic and the modern, or an archetypal ideal and its nameless, heterogeneous opposite. The Rokujō Lady as possessing spirit is a character of such force that she has left an indelible impression on readers' minds over the centuries. Hers is a "character" serving as a catalyst for the formation and disruption of other characters and configurations of characters. It is also the site of an enduring paradox: the possessing spirit heralds a new self—self as interiority—and reveals the division and discontinuity of that self at the very moment of its discovery.

Murasaki Shikibu, the creator of both Genji and Lady Rokujō, left behind a striking record of what we are pleased to call a modern consciousness. The evidence is everywhere in her tale, but there is an instance worth singling out from her personal poetry collection, known as the *Murasaki Shikibushū*.[63] Number 44, like several others, has a screen painting as its subject. The poem, together with its prose preface, runs as follows:

> Upon seeing a painting of a possessed woman in a hideous state: a young priest behind her binds down a former wife turned into a demon; the husband attacks the spirit by reading sutras:

Naki hito ni	He puts the blame
kagoto wa kakete	on one who is dead;
wazurō mo	but is not the suffering
ono ga kokoro no	caused by the demon
oni ni ya wa aranu	of his soul?

The key phrase is "demon of the soul," an entity that troubled Fujitsubo as well. (This phrase appears fifteen times in the *Genji*.) The husband in the poem, consistent with his times, can only transform his wife's memory into a literal demonic presence, returned to harm his new wife. The speaker of the poem, however, interprets the situation as the product of the husband's "guilt." This insight is taken a step further in the responding poem, number 45:

Kotowari ya	Of course:
kimi ga kokoro no	your soul being dark
yami nareba	you can clearly see
oni no kage to wa	the forms
shiruku miyuran	of demons.

Is the "demon of the soul" converted back into a physical demon, or denied altogether? In either case it is through the same principle that was used in the previous poem to the opposite effect, namely, that the state of the viewer's mind influences perception. The response is commonly supposed to have been composed by a friend, unidentified but presumably (for those who miss the ironic nature of the reversal) more sensible than Murasaki Shikibu. It is tantalizingly possible, however, that it was composed by Shikibu herself.[64]

Chapter 1

MEETING IN EXILE

The first time Genji is in the Akashi Lady's presence, he senses a resemblance to the Rokujō Lady. The perception is not without basis, as we have seen. There are parallels in family circumstance. If the Rokujō Lady is the daughter of a minister and the widow of a crown prince, the Akashi Lady is the granddaughter of a minister and the intended bride of a supreme partner. That partner, as it turns out, is Genji, a man who should have been crown prince. Going hand-in-hand with their marital attainments or prospects are the skills of the two women. Despite her provincial upbringing, the Akashi Lady is formidably accomplished, and it is perhaps that severity attaching to fruitless achievement that Genji detects in both women. But the similarities stop here. No one is less likely to manifest herself as a vengeful spirit than the Akashi Lady, even though her sensitivity to her own position is not a whit less acute than that of the Rokujō Lady.

The Akashi family is introduced to the tale early, in the "Lavender" chapter. Genji has left the capital for the mountains on a retreat to undergo cures for a malaria-like disease. Shortly before he espies the child Murasaki (it is the Akashi Lady's fate to be pitted always against Murasaki), he learns about the eccentric former governor of Harima from the conversation of a follower attempting to divert him. This attendant is himself the son of the present governor of Harima and therefore in a position to know about his father's predecessor, who will become familiar to us as the Akashi Priest. The Akashi Priest was the son of a minister who, unable to match his father's achievement, had risen only to the rank of middle captain in the bodyguards by middle age. Then, in an unusual move, he abandoned his career in the capital for a term as a provincial governor. At the conclusion of a not altogether distinguished performance, he chose to retire in the province. According to Genji's follower, he lived in remarkable luxury, not in the hills as one might think appropriate to a monk, but out in the open, close to the sea, the alleged reason being that excessive seclusion would be too taxing on his wife and daughter. As for this daughter, he had evidently broadcast the fact that his plans for her did not include a provincial governor as son-in-law, and that should he die without having realized his ambitions for her, she was to leap into the sea (as if she were the intended of the Sea Dragon King, jokes another of Genji's followers).

It is a peculiar vision indeed. First of all, the image of an elderly, monkish figure, living on the beach, not in a tumbledown hut but in palatial splendor: we picture the Akashi Priest's crooked, comical figure against the rays of the sun—so markedly absent from the image of the priestly figure as it has come down to us through the Middle Ages. (There is a reason for associating the sun with the Akashi Priest, as we shall see.) He is comical not simply for his exaggerated habits of speech or awkward gait but for his conspicuous success as well. He chose to be laughable but wealthy when he flung aside life in the capital for the provinces. It is well known that provincial governors had ample opportunity for amassing personal fortunes, which earned them the contempt of the less comfortably situated higher aristocracy.[65] Hence, the lavishly furnished structures that dot the shore and even the neighboring hillsides and above all, the well-stocked storehouses.

If this vision of plenty accords ill with priestly vows (although it should be pointed out that our eccentric is a "lay priest"), so does the scope of the old man's ambitions, focused upon the future of his daughter. It might be argued that in this he is no different from other fathers in the tale—the Kiritsubo Lady's father (who was the Akashi Priest's uncle), the Rokujō Lady's father, or that remarkably sane figure, Tō no Chūjō. (The Eighth Prince in the Uji chapters warns his daughters not to marry—a reversal of content but not of impulse.) The Akashi Priest, however, outdoes them all in the disparity of dreams to actual circumstances. By the time he meets Genji in the "Akashi" chapter, this odd figure has dedicated prayers and offerings to the gods of Sumiyoshi for eighteen years. Or, as he says in his own words,

I have had something in mind for her from the time she was little, and we have gone to that shrine every spring and autumn. During my six daily devotions in the morning and

in the evening, I have put aside my own hopes for salvation
to pray that my deepest wishes for her might be granted.

(2:235; S 256; W 267)

The peculiar yoking of this- and other-worldly modes also
characterizes Genji's relationship to the Akashi family. The circumstances of their meeting are marked by a concatenation of
apparently supernatural events. Genji has retreated to Suma,
where he has been leading a life dedicated to prayer and literary
pursuits, mostly Chinese. One spring day, after the visit of his
friend Tō no Chūjō, he holds a purification rite on the seashore
with an itinerant soothsayer presiding. At the climax of the ceremony, a boat bearing a life-size human figure to which all evils
have been transferred is set afloat. What is included in those
evils? The question of Genji's guilt, always tantalizingly vague,
surfaces in the poem he recites at this moment:

Yaorozu	The eight hundred myriad
kami mo aware to	gods
omouran	will surely pity me,
okaseru tsumi no	there being no especial
sore to nakereba	sin
	I have committed.
	(2:209; S 246; W 253-54)

The immediate effect of the rite is to stir up a storm and to
provoke the appearance of a strange figure in Genji's dreams who
inquires as to why he has failed to obey summons to court. Genji
takes this to be a message from the Sea Dragon King.

The tempest continues with extraordinary furor. Fearing that
they might perish, Genji and his men pray without pause, especially to the gods of Sumiyoshi. Just after the peak of the ter-
ror, the late Kiritsubo Emperor appears to Genji and bids him
obey the gods of Sumiyoshi and take a speedy boat away from
Suma. Genji wishes to prolong the conversation, but his father's
figure vanishes, leaving behind only the bright moon. The next
morning, the Akashi Priest, having been granted a miraculous
passage, lands in a small boat. He, too, has received divine instructions to bear Genji to safety. Genji is in no mood to resist.

A strange wind speeds their boat back to Akashi, where they debark as the sun rises. The Akashi Priest, as he gazes upon Genji, is moved to offer thanks to Sumiyoshi, for he feels as if he basked in the "light of the sun and the light of the moon" at once (2:224-25; S 252; W 261).

We are being flooded by mythologically significant images, whose import becomes clearer upon Genji's return to the capital from exile when he refers to himself as the "leech child" to his brother Suzaku. This is the child born from the heavenly couple Izanagi and Izanami's attempt at intercourse as it is told in the creation myths of the *Kojiki* and the *Nihon Shoki*. Because the female deity spoke first, a defective child issued who, unable to stand at the age of three, was sent out to sea.[66] Stripped of his titles, Genji spends three years by the sea at Suma and Akashi seeking refuge from the machinations of his stepmother Kokiden. Later, at their first meeting upon Genji's return to the capital, his brother Suzaku, weak but not evil, sighs over the years that have passed without music-making at the Palace. Genji is ungracious:

Watatsumi ni | The years have passed
shizumi urabure | since the leech child,
hiru no ko wa | unable to stand on its feet
ashidatazarishi | sank, forlorn
toshi wa henikeri | by the sea.
(2:263; S 270; W 282)

The leech child is the *hiru no ko*. Folkloric and mythological contexts, supported by homophonous links, make possible a series of associations between *hiru no ko* and "Hiruko," the masculine version of Hirume, another name for the sun goddess Amaterasu. (*Hiru* also means "day" or "noon.")[67] Since the deities of the sun and the moon were also born during the great procreation beginning with the unfortunate leech child's birth, it is possible to see him as a failed, or affirmatively, a potential celestial deity. The leech child is sent away on a "bird-rock-camphor-wood boat of Heaven."[68] Boats and voyages are important motifs of death and rebirth in archaic traditions; it can be no accident that Genji, having nearly lost his life in the terrible storm at Suma, reaches the haven of Akashi in the Priest's small boat.[69] Genji is the preternaturally gifted child of an improper union, who has suffered since birth from the ill will of his stepmother and her allies, whose father the Emperor had to cast him from the family and make him a commoner. The exile to Suma is a second expulsion, bringing with it physical threats to Genji's life. When Genji sends his effigy floating out to sea, he anticipates his own rebirth, whether by expelling the evil within or by rehearsing the voyage to safety. The gesture provokes the storm, to be sure, but the storm is necessary to moving him to Akashi. (It should be kept in mind that safety lies with his mother's kinsfolk, the Akashi family.) When the Akashi Priest feels the light of the sun and the moon upon him as Genji steps onto the Akashi shore, it is a signal that the crisis has passed and a new life dawning.

It is a signal not only for Genji but for the Akashi Priest as well. In the course of his public life he had deliberately forsaken prestige and recklessly staked everything on a miraculous recovery hinging on his daughter's marriage. The daughter is now twenty-two, rather past her prime by Heian standards. It had begun to seem that she would be forced to offer herself to the Sea Dragon King when fate so unexpectedly brought Genji to the shores of Akashi. No wonder the father feels justified in his eighteen years of zealous devotion to the Sumiyoshi cult. The cult embodies the mutuality of Genji's and the Akashi Priest's interests, for as we have seen, Genji and his men prayed repeatedly to those deities during the storms. The three deities of Sumiyoshi were created at the time of the god Izanagi's purification after defilement by the corpse of his wife Izanami, and the Sumiyoshi cult, together with a certain purification rite held in Naniwa, has ancient imperial associations. This, too, will be exploited some years hence.

More surprising, however, is the disclosure that the Akashi Priest had been determined to make Genji his son-in-law even before the storm. Those plans are revealed in a conversation with his wife near the end of the "Suma" chapter. She, sensible woman, argues that Genji already had many outstanding ladies in his household and that moreover, not content even with them, he had dared to lay hands on one of the Emperor's wives, and more than once at that. That was why he had ended up in Suma in the first place. Why would he waste a glance on country bumpkins like themselves? Irritated, her husband accuses her of not understanding him. (He does have his reasons, but they are not to be revealed for hundreds of pages, not until "New Herbs, Part Two.") In any case, continues his wife, why choose a man, however fine, who had been charged with a crime as a bridegroom for their daughter? Her husband snorts that this sort of thing always happened to outstanding men, whether in China or in their own land. Also to the point, he adds, is that this man was kin to him, being the grandson of his own uncle. Nothing could be more fitting (2:202-203; S 242; W 250).

This is the most matter-of-fact description given of Genji's exile. Through this homey exchange we learn the popular interpretation of recent events, that Genji had violated Oborozukiyo, and more than once, and that while this was serious, it was but an excessive example of general tendencies and would probably be excused in time. Of course we should allow for the excitement and pleasure of local folk at having a celebrity in their midst, but still, the absence of the anguish and the brooding surrounding the exile in the capital is striking. Most important, we learn that the secret with Fujitsubo remains sealed from the world. The Akashi Priest's wife is, to be sure, less sanguine than her husband about Genji's suitability for their daughter, but this may be attributed to her prudence as a mother. We should also note the statement of Genji's kinship to the Akashi family, a matter that is never made explicit by Genji himself. In "New Herbs, Part One," when Genji muses on the Priest's life, he merely refers to "that ancestor who was a minister" (4:120; S 578; W [640]). Perhaps out of deference, the Priest never alludes to the kinship in his conversations with Genji. Genji himself never forgets that the Akashi Lady is of inferior birth.

Nor, for that matter, does the lady herself. Even as her parents argue over the princely visitor, she thinks, "a noble person would never deign to recognize me, but it would be worse still to marry one more appropriate to my station. If I should outlive my parents, I must become a nun, or else, throw myself into the sea" (2:203; S 242; W 251). The phrase that repeatedly rises to the Akashi Lady's lips is *mi no hodo*, "station."[70] The glimpse that she has had of Genji, after all the years of rumor about his beauty, only makes her more despondent than ever.

It takes some time for Genji to make an overture to the young woman. It requires, first of all, music-making with her father, an accomplished performer on the thirteen-stringed koto and the lutelike biwa. Genji has brought with him a seven-stringed koto, the instrument of royalty. He learns that the daughter herself is an excellent musician and that moreover, her father intends her for him. Accordingly, Genji's misfortunes are cast by both men in a new interpretation, as part of his destiny to come to Akashi to meet this daughter.

Having learned of her cultivation, Genji takes pains, or so we are told, with his first letter to the lady, who lives in a house in the hills apart from her father. He chooses a walnut-colored paper from Korea for this poem:

Ochikochi mo	Mournfully I gaze
shiranu kumoi ni	into the sky,
nagamewabi	not knowing whether
kasumeshi yado no	it is near or far;
kozue o zo tou	I seek the treetops
	of the dwelling
	so suggestive with haze.

(2:238; S 258; W 268)

Kasumeshi means "hinted at," referring to the Priest's suggestion that his daughter would not be unreceptive, but it overlaps with *kasumi*, "haze," which fits innocuously with the other natural images in the poem. It may be because of her severe estimate of her own worth that the lady does not reply. It surely does not help, however, that Genji's poem is vacuous nonsense.[71] Given the Akashi lady's temperament, such a poem becomes one more indication of Genji's indifference. Her father, too eager, cannot compel her to write, so he responds in her stead. The lady's reticence alerts Genji. "This time," we are pointedly told, he chooses a thin, soft paper for the following poem:

Ibuseku mo	My heart is heavy,
kokoro ni mono o	and I brood,

nayamu kana
yayo ya ika ni to
tou hito mo nami

for no one asks,
"How do you do?"
(2:239; S 259; W 269)

Again the lady suffers a pang of unworthiness, but this time, she is moved to reply:

Omouran
kokoro no hodo ya
yayo ika ni
mada minu hito no
kiki ka nayaman

You say that you brood;
I wonder about a heart
that suffers
from rumors
of one yet unseen.
(2:239; S 259; W 270)

The first bond is formed; the Akashi Lady's poem is a fitting response, denying the gentleman's sentiments yet echoing his words. The suggestive "one yet unseen" must catch Genji's eye, but his only recorded thoughts are that neither hand nor manner is terribly inferior to the finest in the land. The intermittent exchange that begins has the effect of reminding him of life in the capital, and to underscore this, the tale breaks off with the Akashi story to recount various calamities in Kyoto, including the appearance of the Kiritsubo Emperor's spirit to his son Suzaku (a visitation that leaves the latter with an eye ailment). Akashi must always yield to the capital.

With these intimations of change, the Akashi story resumes. On a moonlit night in the Eighth Month, Genji dresses and mounts his horse to make his way to the house in the hills. Seeing the full moon, "his thoughts turn first to his beloved," and he is tempted to keep on riding all the way back to the capital and Murasaki:

Aki no yo no
tsukige no koma yo
waga kouru
kumoi o kakere
toki no ma mo min

O roan steed
race the moonlit sky
this autumn night
that I might see her
for whom I long
for but one brief moment.
(2:245; S 262; W 273)

Of course, Genji does not ride past, union with the Akashi woman being a matter of destiny. Not only has fate sent him specific indications, but in the tradition of the wandering hero, Genji must make an erotic conquest of the local shamanic priestess. Her father has made preparations for the first night. "The moon shone into her wooden door, which had been left slightly ajar" (2:246; S 262; W 273). The Priest's orchestration is oppressively perfect. This coy line, allegedly dubbed the finest in the *Genji* by the medieval poet Fujiwara no Teika, verges on parody and should evoke our sympathy for the young woman who must be so presented.[72] She, of course, is not ready to admit an intruder, and Genji grows irritated at being kept waiting (by such a creature).

When, however, curtain strings brush against her thirteen-stringed koto, conjuring for him a vision of the young woman playing the instrument at her leisure, he is roused. He addresses a poem:

Mutsugoto o
katari awasen
hito mo gana
uki yo no yume mo
nakaba samu ya to

Would there were one
with whom to exchange
 intimate whispers:
then might I
 begin to awaken
from this dreary world's dream.
(2:246; S 263; W 274)

Akenu yo ni
yagate madoeru
kokoro ni wa
izure o yume to
wakite kataran

How can my heart,
 which wanders
 in never-ending night,
recognize dreams
 and speak of them
 to you?
(2:247; S 263; W 274)

There is no intervening prose between Genji's poem and the Akashi Lady's response, delivered in a barely audible whisper. Although she claims to inhabit the world of night, her poem aches with anticipation. Consensus has it that the Akashi Lady is one of the finest poets in the tale. She condenses into this composition an overwhelming sense of moment as she hovers on the brink of yielding to Genji. In contrast to Genji's easy talk of intimacy, her poem is heavy with the timeless knowledge of young women and the particular sensibility of a Heian provincial governor's daughter that in a few moments life would be forever changed—a rather different perception of fate from the sort that has Genji and her father in its thrall.

Several months later, at the beginning of the new year, the Suzaku Emperor resolves to step down, and Genji is summoned back to the capital. He leaves his koto with the Akashi Lady, now bearing his child, with the promise that they will meet again before the middle string slackens.

By the time the child is born in Akashi, the Reizei Emperor has ascended to the throne and Genji promoted to a position just beneath the Ministers of the Right and Left. When he learns that the baby is a girl, Genji immediately recalls the words of the astrologer who prophesied that two of his children would become emperor and empress, and the third chancellor. That Reizei is already on the throne is proof enough to Genji that the child in Akashi is intended for an extraordinary career, and he speeds a nurse to Akashi to supervise the rearing of so precious a child (a task not to be left to country hands).

That fall Genji makes a pilgrimage to Sumiyoshi. It appears to be more than a journey of thanksgiving for deliverance from the perils of exile. The rites performed on that occasion, including a lustration ceremony at Naniwa, bear a provocative resemblance to the Yasoshima Festival, which is held at the beginning of a new reign. Moreover, Genji performs one rite that is the exclusive prerogative of the emperor.[73] These gestures prefigure Genji's promotion in "Wisteria Leaves," when he will receive the emoluments due a retired emperor. It is a lame though historically unprecedented gesture by his son Reizei, who would prefer to step down in favor of Genji once he learns the truth about his birth. At Sumiyoshi, Genji is already a shadow emperor.

The Sumiyoshi pilgrimage has an entirely different aspect as the occasion of a nonreunion with the Akashi Lady. As luck would have it, she has chosen the same time for her own semiannual visit to the shrine. Surprised by the bustle, she inquires and is shocked to learn of Genji's presence. His retinue is so extensive that she must forego making her own offerings. Genji, learning of her presence from his faithful servant Koremitsu, exchanges poems with her but does not meet her. For the Akashi Lady, the Sumiyoshi pilgrimage involves neither divine blessing nor imperial power but the recognition of inferior social class.

AT THE CAPITAL: THE AKASHI LADY AS URBAN ARISTOCRAT

Genji steps up his invitations to the lady to join him in the capital. He has, in fact, completed a new structure, the Eastern Pavilion, where mother and child could be comfortably accommodated. The Akashi Lady is genuinely attached to Genji: she had, as it were, fallen in love with him and had been grief-stricken to see him go. Why, then, the hesitation? It has of course to do with her status. In Akashi at least she enjoys territorial strength and the backing of her parents. Yet to remain there is to condemn her own daughter to share her miserable lot. The solution, that she should go with her mother and daughter to the mother's estate in Ōi, on the outskirts of the capital, is an exemplary display of Akashi family pride and shrewdness. The reactivation of the estate in Ōi signals the externalization of the urban aristocratic woman that had been held in reserve. Indeed, the new prominence of the lady's mother, in contrast to the father left behind in Akashi, emphasizes a hitherto dormant element in her makeup: the Ōi estate has been transmitted from her maternal grandfather, a prince. The plan is that there, on restored family grounds, she should await Genji's visits.

These anticipated arrangements reduplicate the relationship of Genji and his deceased principal wife Aoi, which conformed to the standard type of marriage practiced by the Heian aristocracy.[74] It was only when the woman was of lower status or had no protectors (such as a princess whose parents had died) that she lived in the man's house. Because this suggested kindness on the part of the man, it gradually became a desirable mode of existence for many women, including the variously romantic authors of the *Gossamer Years* and *As I Crossed the Bridge of Dreams.* When seen in this perspective, all the residents of the Eastern Pavilion as well as of the later, grander Rokujōin are the recipients of Genji's benefaction.[75]

The Akashi plan has its risks, since Genji could simply not visit, or visit at first but less and less frequently until all ties were suspended, as happened to the *Gossamer Years* diarist. But the family has a trump card in the new daughter. In fact, it is some time before Genji, hampered by increasing prominence as well as by Murasaki's watchful eye, can visit the Akashi women. They pass the days listening to the wind that reminds them of their seaside home and playing the koto left by Genji in Akashi. At long last, in response to the notes of the instrument, Genji appears. It is their first meeting in three years, and he and the Akashi Lady make music, exchange poems, and above all, talk about their daughter.

The inevitable next step is that Genji will claim the child, now that he has ascertained with his own eyes that she is not only unblemished but brimming with promise for the end he has in mind. (For all the fatefulness of their coming together, Genji's relationship with the Akashi family is decidedly instrumental—although it is also true that his deliberate, secularly promoted goals happen to coincide with the Priest's divinely supported ones.) He prepares the ground at home, suggesting to Murasaki that she might want to adopt the "leech child" (thus the motif migrates) spawned in Akashi. The childless Murasaki, who had been irritated by intimations of the Akashi Lady's existence, is pleased by the prospect of acquiring her child. The decision, however ineluctable, is naturally more difficult for the Akashi Lady. It is reached only after intense brooding (recorded in long interior monologues), consultation with the indispensable soothsayer, and finally, conversation with her mother, who makes the convincing argument that Genji himself was unable to become emperor because of his mother's inferior birth. At length, the Akashi Lady announces to Genji, "It would indeed be a shame for her future if she were to share the plight of a useless person like me; but on the other hand, I fear she might become a laughing-stock were she to mingle with the grand ladies" (2:420; S 332; W 364).

The separation takes place in winter, when the snow makes Ōi more desolate than ever. The scene is the most beautiful to be accorded the lady:

It was the morning after snow had darkened the skies. She was not one to come to the edge of the verandah, but today, brooding over past and future, she stared at the ice on the edge of the pond. Clad in layers of soft, white robes, her form as she gazed made her attendants think, this was how the very finest ladies must look. Wiping away her tears, she said pitifully, "How much more forlorn we shall be on days like this."   (2:422; S 333; W 365)

She appeals to the nurse who was sent to Akashi, who will now accompany the child to Murasaki's:

Yuki fukami	Though the sky be dark
yama no michi wa	and deep snow
harezu tomo	block the mountain path—
nao fumikayoe	make your way to me,
ato taezushite	write to me,
	never breaking off!
	(Ibid.)

The nurse replies:

Yukima naki	Even had I to visit
Yoshino no yama o	the mountains of Yoshino,
tazunete mo	where snow falls
kokoro no kayou	without pause,
ato taeme ya wa	the path between our hearts
	can never be blocked.
	(Ibid.)

The Akashi Lady is intelligent but plain. Her reflective nature is too austere to allow for romantic portrayal, but here, her creator treats her with unstinting generosity, matching her appearance to the stark beauty of the outdoors. It is in this passage that she is crystallized as the lady of winter, the role she will be formally assigned to play when she enters the Rokujōin.

The great compensation for her austerity is her gift of poetry, which surges forth at these moments. When Genji comes to take her daughter away, she initiates this exchange:

Sue tōki	The seedling pine,
futaba no matsu ni	now uprooted
hikiwakare	has so far to grow:
itsu ka kodakaki	when shall I see it
kage o mirubeki	a grand, shady tree?

Genji attempts to reassure her:

Oisomeshi	Its roots are deep:
ne mo fukakereba	let us,
Takekuma no	pines of Takekuma,
matsu ni komatsu no	gather our thousand years
chiyo o naraben	beside this sapling pine.
	(2:424; S 334; W 366)

The pines of Takekuma were thought to be twin, and Genji chooses them as a figure for himself and the Akashi Lady as the parents of the sapling tree. Despite her grief, the lady singles out the felicitous image of the long-lived pine for her daughter, an image that provides Genji with a rhetorical cover for the awkward moment.

An honorific is applied to the Akashi Lady as she bears the child in her arms to the waiting carriage. From the time of her departure from Akashi, she has been referred to as *onkata*, an appellation with some dignity. Now honorifics begin to adorn her actions: for her costly sacrifices she is offered linguistic compensation. (She will never be referred to as *ue*, however, which has long been Murasaki's prerogative.)[76] By having rejected entry into the Eastern Pavilion, she wins one of the four quarters in the utopian Rokujōin, even though it is the least of them, the northeastern "winter" section. At the same time, since she comes with her family resources, no doubt contributing to the sustenance of the entire establishment, she maintains a distinctly independent status.

The Akashi Lady's career continues to parallel Murasaki's, but always as its shadow. Genji's plans for his daughter proceed apace, and it is decided to enter her in the court of the Crown Prince (Suzaku's son) immediately after her coming-of-age ceremony at the age of eleven. It was of course to this end that he had taken the child from her mother.[77] He toys with the idea of inviting the Akashi Lady to the initiation but decides to forego it for fear of wagging tongues. Nothing should mar the precious creature's value at the dawn of her career. So, when she enters court, Murasaki is her attendant for the first three nights. The girl needs a trustworthy companion, but Murasaki cannot be spared forever, and so it is decided that her own mother should take her place. Mother and daughter are reunited for the first time in eight years. It is also the occasion for the first meeting between Murasaki and the Akashi Lady.

The Akashi Princess is a great success with the Crown Prince, and she soon conceives. When she returns to the Rokujōin, she is initially housed next to the Third Princess (who has taken up residence as Genji's official wife in the meanwhile), but as her time draws near, she is moved to her mother's winter quarters on the advice of the soothsayers. There she makes the acquaintance of her grandmother. She had scarcely known of the old nun's existence, for her own mother had told her little of her own background. At first she is repelled by the aging thing that darts to her bedside to chat about this or that with tears streaming from her eyes, but she is gradually drawn to her. And for the first time, she learns of the circumstances of her own birth. The thirteen-year-old is led to reflect,

> It is as she says. I had not been intended for so high a station, but polished by her ladyship [Murasaki], I have become one whom others do not regard unfavorably. Yet I thought myself without equal at court and grew proud. What the others must have been saying behind my back!
>
> (4:97; S 570; W 637)

Nothing has prepared us for such insight from this girl, although it is fitting in her mother's daughter. Indeed, there is a supreme justice to her backward glance at the gossips.

At court, the Akashi Princess occupies apartments in the Kiri-tsubo Court and accordingly is referred to as "Her Kiritsubo Highness" or simply "Kiritsubo" or "Shigeisha" (another name for those chambers). Her predecessor in those apartments was Genji's mother, who is also an ancestress. Pressed into court service by the ambitions of a dead father, that unfortunate lady was hounded to death by her rivals. Now Genji is furthering his ambitions through the young "Kiritsubo," doubly descended from the Kiritsubo Lady. The cornerstone of his program for her is the suppression of her background, which is partly a denial of his own past. Is it unwitting? Is Genji ignorant of his mother's fate? As far as we can see, he is barred, willfully or not, from insight into his own birth, and it is the Akashi family that places it in context.

A curious tension underlies the Akashi position, which is re-vealed when the old nun inserts a casual remark about Genji's mother's inferior mark while extolling him, or when she reveals her humble origins to her granddaughter while shedding tears of joy over her glory. The nun of course sees no contradiction be-tween her knowledge and her rapture. The deflationary effect is for us to enjoy, knowing as we do the mutuality of Genji-Akashi dependence. Genji requires Akashi fate and Akashi fortunes to achieve his ends. Of greatest interest to us is that neither he nor the Akashi family realizes the power of knowledge that the latter holds over the former.

Within her own sphere the Akashi Lady is acutely aware of the power of knowledge. When she comes upon her mother and daughter apparently absorbed in conversation, she is startled: her mother, in her nun's garb, is "tidy and refined, her eyes shining and swollen from weeping" (4:99; S 570; W 638; note again the author's penchant for juxtaposing contradictory attributes, often, as here, without the reassuring guidance of appropriate conjunc-tions). The lady senses instantly that her mother has been talking of the past: "No doubt she has been uttering nonsense about things that happened long ago" (ibid.). She had intended to keep these matters from her child until she had become empress, fear-ing that once her daughter learned of her lesser origins, she would be unable to carry herself with that unqualified air of superiority born of ignorance (or innocence) and required for the attainment of high positions. The enemy to be guarded against above all was "a sense of inferiority" (4:99; S 571; W 638). When, therefore, the Akashi Lady urges her daughter to take some food, she is lost in thought. The old nun, in the meanwhile, gazes with joy upon her grandchild though she is unable to restrain her tears: "Her face was smiling, her mouth gaping in unsightly display, but her eyes were wrinkled and wet from sobbing" (4:99-100; S 571; W 638). Her daughter signals with her eyes to stop the unseemly display, but the old woman, paying no heed, pours forth her emotions:

Oi no nami	The waves of old age
kai aru ura ni	rise in the worthy bay:
tachi idete	who shall reproach
shiotaruru ama o	this briny fisherwoman?
tare ka todomen	(Ibid.)

The old-fashioned composition is replete with puns and other figures that enable the nun to describe the culmination of a long and dramatic life: waves are of course wrinkles, "worthy" (*kai aru*) doubles for "having shellfish," "fisherwoman" (*ama*) for "nun," in this case one "briny" with salty tears. The lachrymose nun's granddaughter responds on paper:

Shiotaruru	With the briny fisher
ama no namiji no	for a guide,
shirube ni te	I would visit
tazune mo mibaya	the thatch-roofed hut
hama no tomaya o	on the beach.

The Akashi Lady finally surrenders to her own emotions:

Yo o sutete	Forsaking the world
Akashi no ura ni	to live in Akashi Bay,
sumu hito mo	he still must suffer
kokoro no yami wa	darkness of the heart
harukeshi mo seji	that knows no clearing.
	(Ibid.)

These three poems are a fine example of communal composition, known as *shōwa*. The Akashi Princess, grateful to her grandmother for her disclosures, repeats her self-deprecating image (briny fisherwoman/nun) but converts it into the venerable figure of a guide to the sacred though humble land of origins. The Akashi Lady, caught between the two, at first stands apart critically but finally abandons herself to the moment; she names the humble place and refers to the eccentric father who is still there. Her phrase "darkness of the heart" is one of many allusions in the *Genji* to a poem by Fujiwara no Kanesuke (877-933), Murasaki Shikibu's great-grandfather. The poem points out the obstacle that attachment to children poses to parental salvation. The parent in the Akashi Lady's poem is her father the Akashi Priest, but she herself is clearly implicated in the darkness of parental ambitions, as she waits, "expecting to see her own fate revealed" when her daughter gives birth (4:96; S 570; W 636). This is a memorable portrait of the Akashi family as a family in the brief moment before the birth that will be a public event and a manifestation of Genji's glory.

The young princess is safely delivered of a boy. Genji's supremacy is assured for yet another generation, even after the retirement of his childless son Reizei. Indeed, for the first time, Genji's position solidifies as a statesman in the Fujiwara mold, for prior to this birth, his official tie to Reizei had rested only on his being the foster father of Akikonomu (the Rokujō Lady's daughter and Reizei's consort), whereas now he has in all likelihood become the maternal grandfather of the next crown prince. This implies that the Akashi Princess will become empress, and thus the prophecy regarding Genji's fate will be fulfilled: one child an emperor, another an empress, and the third, chancellor (Yūgiri, in the meanwhile, has been making steady progress toward that goal).

True to the tradition of the amorous hero and the noble exile, Genji made an erotic conquest of the Akashi Lady during the trying years away from the capital. The union produced a daughter instrumental to the consolidation of his power throughout his lifetime and beyond. Now, although the episodic nature of the amorous hero tale gives way in the development of long, complicated fictions, there is one thing about its fragmentation that proves to be important to the emergence of the new (postarchaic?) hero. The episodic narratives show the essential pointlessness of the unions. Children, if they are ever mentioned, are inconsequential. If fictional heroes must not be interested in political self-aggrandizement, then it follows that they should not use their children toward such ends. Better yet that they have few or no children. It is only their foils (such as Tō no Chūjō) who procreate prolifically and are thus betrayed in their thirst for power.[78]

In order to protect Genji's status as hero from the threatening contagion of Akashi prosperity, certain maneuvers are necessary. The reader will recall how beautifully the transfer of the child was effected, with the focus on the Akashi Lady's grief in splendid snowy isolation. Then our interest was directed to the childless Murasaki's tenderness to the girl and, more recently, the affecting domestic drama played out among the three generations of Akashi women. These scenes and many others have deflected our attentions from Genji's unheroic aspects during the busy years following his return to the capital. I am not, of course, arguing that the only point of such scenes is to serve as smokescreens for Genji's ambitions. It is rather that every scene, every event, has more than one role to play, and that some roles are contradictory.

The Genji-Akashi tie comes into focus again with the arrival of a long last letter from the Akashi Priest to his daughter in response to news of the birth. It announces that since his life's goals have been realized, he is retiring into the mountains to meet his death. It also reveals, for the first time, the contents of a youthful dream that had governed the old man's life:

> In my right hand I held Mt. Sumeru, and from either side of the mountain the light of the sun and the light of the moon streamed down and shone upon the world. I stood below, hidden in the mountain's shadow and not lighted by the radiance. I let the mountain float upon the sea then took a small boat and began rowing westward.
>
> (4:106-107; S 573; W [640])

When the Akashi Lady was conceived shortly thereafter, the dreamer became convinced that despite his fallen circumstances, he was intended for extraordinary glory. After his own fashion

he took practical measures to ensure the fulfillment of the prophecy. When the daughter was born, he chose a provincial life for
its material advantages so that he could provide for her in the
requisite fashion. He embarked upon an existence of devotions
and pilgrimages. He steadfastly refused reasonable offers of marriage for his daughter, which led to a reputation of madness. It
did not matter, for the dream sustained him. No wonder he was
overjoyed when he heard of Genji's retreat to Suma. He did not
hesitate to recognize this event as a step in the fulfillment of the
prophecy.

What does this say for the prophecies regarding Genji's fate,
especially the one concerning his three children? Up to this
point we have followed Genji's rising star as the manifestation of
his own fate, but the revelation of this dream suggests that it was
but part of the fate of a crazed provincial governor, belonging in
turn to a larger fate encompassing Genji's undistinguished
mother as well.

By now I need not belabor the point that prophecy, whether
it concerns Genji or a mad priest, works as an intrafictional sacred force to undermine the role of calculation—in fact, madness reinforces the sense of the sacred. Still, with the juxtaposition of prophecies, and the juxtaposition of the supernatural with
the ultrapragmatic, we are forced to ask, what are prophecies?
what are miracles? and what is fate? For the Akashi Lady life
takes on a new clarity:

> It was because of his perverted mind, she had once thought,
> that he had insisted on troubling her with such an unsuit-
> able match. But it turned out to have been because of one
> insubstantial dream, in which he had placed all his faith,
> that he had borne himself so proudly.
>
> (4:111; S 575; W [640])

The lady is both saddened for her father and pleased for herself,
for she does not disbelieve the dream even as she recognizes that
it is "insubstantial."

Just as monarchs are created (through careful alliance) as
much as they are born, so fate is chosen and cultivated as much
as it is imposed. (It should go without saying that fate is more

chosen by some and more imposed upon others.) On the one hand the notion of arbitrariness touches on the divine (beyond human explanation or control) and on the other, the absurd (beyond human explanation or control). The juxtaposition of its incongruous instances—was Genji's success the fulfillment of his fortunes or of the Akashi Priest's dreams?—severely compromises the absoluteness of fate. If prophecy in the *Tale of Genji* functions as a theological device to mask mundane calculation, its theological stature is in turn undermined in the unfolding of the fiction. At the same time, we must bear in mind that this undermining does not dispel incongruities. The birth of the future crown prince presupposes the birth of the Akashi Princess, an event that required various acts of recognition of destiny by Genji and the Akashi Priest. In addition to, or perhaps in place of, destiny we could argue that Genji's success is assured by Akashi wealth. Yet at the very moment we believe we have put the suprarational in its place, we must remember that Akashi prosperity may work for Genji precisely because of that banal but magical relationship guaranteed by blood tie.

The Akashi Lady, perceiving her social inferiority as imposed by birth and therefore beyond her control (though never beyond her keenly critical spirit: she represents the interiorization of class), embraces the identity assigned her and turns it into something distinctive and useful. Thus, Murasaki plays the dominant role in the festivities surrounding the baby's birth, while she, on the other hand, fetches the bath water and busies herself with tasks not normally befalling the grandmother of a future crown prince.[79] She cautions her daughter to defer forever to Murasaki who has made all things possible with her painstaking education. For her forbearance the Akashi Lady is praised by all and criticized by none.

In his last letter the Akashi Priest instructs his family to make a pilgrimage to the Sumiyoshi Shrine to give thanks. Genji, having also seen the letter, decides, four years later, that the time has come for such a pilgrimage. His son Reizei has retired and his own grandson designated crown prince. Genji himself has enjoyed a position equivalent to that of a retired emperor for nearly a half dozen years. Predictably, it is a large retinue that sets out to Sumiyoshi, including Murasaki and the Akashi Princess in one carriage and the Akashi Lady with the old nun in another. Despite the Akashi presence, the pilgrimage is entirely Genji's affair. As always, the Akashi element in Genji's glitter is suppressed (for it is too perilously relevant), and the imperial ties between Genji and the Sumiyoshi gods subtly reasserted. It is interesting that the occasion produces poems by Genji, the old nun, the Akashi Princess, and Murasaki as well as one of her ladies, but none by the Akashi Lady herself.[80] Genji, longing for someone with whom he might share the sad memories of exile, resorts to an exchange with the old nun who, apparently dissatisfied with this expression of her own emotions, composes an additional poem to herself. Surely one would have expected to hear from her daughter as well on such an occasion as this, when, still ignored, she relives the past in the form of a pilgrimage she had made so often on her own and on her family's behalf.

The phrase *ukifune*, "floating," that is, drifting (homophonous with "miserable") "boat," the haunting symbol of life's uncertainties, appears in the *Genji* twice. All readers know its second use, by the young heroine who comes to bear the name "Ukifune," but fewer know that it originated with the severely practical Akashi Lady, who used it in an exchange with Genji shortly after giving up her child:

Isari seshi
kage wasurarenu
kagaribi wa
mi no ukifune ya
shitai kiniken

This flare, like the flares
of fishing boats
I cannot forget,
must belong to my own
vessel of sorrow
drifting back fondly.
(2:456; S 347; W 383)

Chapter 2

A Minor Heroine

and the Unmaking

of the Hero

MINOR CHAPTERS AND MINOR HEROINES

IN THE TWENTY-SECOND CHAPTER of the *Tale of Genji*, a
new, and yet not so new heroine emerges. Genji muses over her
paradoxical status:

Koiwataru	I, longing ceaselessly,
mi wa sore naredo	am still the same self,
tamakazura	but, jeweled garland,
ikanaru suji o	what line have you traced
tazune kitsuran	to find your way to me?
	(3:126; S 405; W 461)

Both chapter and heroine receive their names from this poem,
although the latter is never referred to as "Tamakazura" in the
Genji itself. It is, nevertheless, the name by which generations
of readers have known her. Genji's poem invites this gesture, for
tamakazura not only serves to introduce the word *suji*, "line,"
by virtue of a conventional association, but it is also personified
and therefore accentuated in its own right.[1] This is emblematic
of the character Tamakazura, who is made to serve both as figure
and ground. The use of "jeweled garland" also recalls an earlier
exchange between Suetsumuhana and her servant Jijū, in which
the phrase weaves together hair and constancy and relationship.

Genji's poem, raising the issue of his own identity and of Tamakazura's connection to him, anticipates the dynamic interchange between major and minor that informs the chapters we are about to examine. Indeed, it is the very distinction between major and minor chapters and characters that is at stake.

The chapters beginning with "The Jeweled Chaplet" and ending with "The Cypress Pillar" have been read as a group and called the "Ten Tamakazura Chapters" by generations of readers. In the heyday of scholarship dedicated to the reconstruction of the original *Genji*, these ten chapters were treated as a subgroup, a minor series inserted into a preexisting tale centered on Murasaki. Briefly put, the minor chapters (*narabi no maki*, literally, "adjacent chapters") are "The Broom Tree" plus the three chapters deriving from it (i.e., "The Shell of the Locust," "Evening Faces," and "The Safflower"); "The Wormwood Patch" and "The Gatehouse," which serve as sequels to "The Safflower" and "The Shell of the Locust," respectively; and the ten Tamakazura chapters. Depending on interpretational emphasis, various names are used for these combinations, such as "The Three Broom Tree Chapters" or "The Six Broom Tree Chapters" or "The Sixteen Broom Tree Chapters" (this designation includes the ten Tamakazura chapters). The major and minor chapters are often distinguished as the "Murasaki line" and the "Tamakazura line."[2] Now, in an age more skeptical of origins and original forms, the same features that led earlier scholars to view the ten chapters as a later, lesser addition are treated as thematic and structural issues pertaining to the work as a whole. The Tamakazura chapters, numbers twenty-two through thirty-one of the fifty-four, are located at the heart of the *Genji*. If they are minor, they are also subversive.

The heroine Tamakazura is first mentioned in conversation in "The Broom Tree," the second chapter, when she is just a child; she makes her final appearance as the anxious, widowed mother of grown children in "The Bamboo River," the forty-fourth chapter. In the case of truly minor characters, such longevity would serve as a reference for static continuity. Tamakazura's long novelistic life, however, is marked by contradictions. In "The Broom Tree," Tamakazura is the "wild carnation" (*nade-*

shiko), the child that blossoms from the young Tō no Chūjō's attachment to the elusive Yūgao. The wild carnation as *nade-shiko* initially suggests childlike sweetness: *naderu* means "to pat" or "to stroke," and *ko* is "child." The erotic possibilities become explicit when the wild carnation is called a *tokonatsu*, where *toko* is homophonous with "bed."³ Thus Tamakazura enters the *Genji*, a suggestively anonymous child in the shadow of her mother, herself a figure flitting about in a tale within a tale.

Yūgao's story is introduced in "The Broom Tree" by Tō no Chūjō, Genji's closest companion and lifelong foil, in an elegant locker-room discussion on the varieties of women available to young aristocrats. Because the conditions of Tamakazura's birth, like congenital defects, mark her throughout her life, it may be well to rehearse the pertinent features of "The Broom Tree."

That celebrated discussion of a rainy evening is opened by Tō no Chūjō as a lamentation on his amours. He begins ambitiously enough by positing three categories of women, but when pressed by a surprisingly shrewd Genji on the difference between appearance and reality, that is, on the distinction between the newly wealthy and the fallen wellborn, he flounders. The scion of the highest aristocracy must yield to the knowledge of a guards officer of the fifth rank who joins the pair together with another young man of similar rank. The guards officer embarks upon a thoughtful survey that is sociologically informed and even philosophically astute, likening the management of a household to that of the state. He expands his account by drawing on memories of tales recited by the serving women of his youth and by extended forays into the arts of painting, calligraphy, and cabinetmaking.⁴ He proceeds to illustrate his points from his own experiences, whereupon he is eagerly followed by Tō no Chūjō and the other young man. The anecdotes of the lower ranking youths are comical and even grotesque, with such odd figures as the finger-biting lady or the garlic eater. Tō no Chūjō's recounting of his Yūgao story is sweetly elegiac; its sequel, in Genji's hands, turns gothic.

Let us remember the quiet, insistent rain in the background; the use of fiction and other arts to illuminate the problem at hand, as well as the very activity of matching tales and women;

and finally, the introduction of bizarre figures who exceed the register of Heian sensibility. Let us also remember that it is a guards officer who expatiates while Genji simply listens, apparently falling asleep on one occasion. Genji's languor is affected. It serves to repress (for him) and conceal (from us) his agitation over his illicit relationship with Fujitsubo. Thus, in typical *Genji* fashion, this affair, the motive force in the major chapters, is made to slumber in the minor chapters. How effective this slumber is, how it fills with tension the background of the talk, can only be felt retrospectively.

The preoccupation with class that emerges from this discussion casts a long shadow over the entire work. It has several aspects, of which the fabrication of women, that is, of marriageable daughters, is the only one to be treated explicitly. The masculine aspects of the issue, the making of money and the acquisition of power, are carefully suppressed while Genji is alive—or more precisely, confined as a Fujiwara concern or permitted idiosyncratic expression through an oddity like the Akashi Priest. (The concept of class itself becomes central with the appearance of Ukifune in the Uji chapters.) Genji himself immediately translates the knowledge gained from the rainy night discussion into practice. He begins to venture into unaccustomed alleys and mugwort-filled gardens. There, he discovers new heroines: Utsusemi, Yūgao, and Suetsumuhana. Their stories illustrate the theories proposed in "The Broom Tree" and even span the range from the romantic to the comic. They initiate a dialectic with the stories of the women of the highest class in which they are embedded.[5]

The Yūgao story has already appeared in the discussions of Fujitsubo and Lady Rokujō in the first chapter, but we should touch on it again since it is the parent tale of the Tamakazura chapters. Mystery of identity (Tamakazura and Genji are both reluctant to disclose their names) is a distinctive feature of this story, where it serves to create an aura of game-playing that effectively leads to the gothic world of the haunted villa. Undisclosed identity and game-playing are also exploited in Tamakazura's story. Where her mother's story comes to a horrific surprise ending, Tamakazura's ends in a comedy of errors.

Chapter 2

From Genji's point of view, the Yūgao episode represents an excursion into foreign territory—foreign, it should be remembered, for its unaristocratic realism as well as its supernaturalism. To put it simply as an "excursion," however, would be to miss its significance, for if Suma and Akashi are a sacred other land in the classic tale of transgression and exile in the major chapters, then the worlds of Utsusemi, Yūgao, and Suetsumuhana constitute a profane other land. Genji trespasses on sacred terrain in his affair with Fujitsubo, but he is no less an interloper in Utsusemi's household or Yūgao's flimsy abode. (The case of Suetsumuhana, as usual, requires a separate word. With her, Genji is guilty of deliberate misinterpretation: he chooses to be lured by the romantic fiction of the princess-in-the-ruins and engages in sexual play with an inappropriate woman.)

Genji's ventures in these social and psychological other lands are internally motivated as an attempt to seek distraction from the forbidden love; but they also constitute a parallel narrative that serves at once to conceal and to betray the prohibited narrative. Surrogates cannot fail to evoke their originals. During those long hours with Yūgao's corpse, Genji's thoughts turn toward his "inappropriate" (ōkenashi, 1:243; S 73; W 69) desires—inappropriate in the sense of exceeding one's station, according to the first entry of a standard classical dictionary, the *Iwanami Kogo Jiten*. In the *Genji*, behavior deemed inappropriate in this sense is usually directed at members of the imperial family, and in any case, commentaries agree that the person in question is Fujitsubo.[6] Yūgao's corpse becomes a symbol for the absent Fujitsubo. The Rokujō Lady-like spirit interposes to cushion Genji from both the visible and the invisible signs of guilt.

This brings us back to the issue of Yūgao's unidentified possession. The scholarship devoted to distinguishing the major and minor narratives has it that the latter apparently acknowledges the events and characters of the former; the chapters concerning the major heroines, however, are ignorant of the doings of the minor. The ladies attacked by the spirit identified as the Rokujō Lady's are all her peers—Aoi, Murasaki, the Third Princess. In the case of Yūgao, as we have seen, the attacking spirit is unidentified. Perhaps it is appropriate that the Rokujō Lady's spirit not be named when possessing so inferior a creature as Yūgao. Perhaps too, on a different plane, the unidentified possession is a foreshadowing of the union of the two sets of narratives in the Tamakazura chapters.

It is interesting to note that many readers, beginning with the author of the mid-fourteenth-century commentary, the *Kakaishō*, posit the same historical model for the site of Yūgao's tragedy and the Rokujōin, the utopian manifestation of Genji's temporal supremacy. It is the Kawaranoin, the once magnificent estate of Minamoto no Tōru (822-895), born the son of Emperor Saga (r. 809-895) but demoted to commoner status, from which he eventually rose to the position of Minister of the Left.[7]

What these readers have done, in effect, is to join the major and minor lines of the tale in the structure of the Rokujōin. If the former is a classic transgression and exile story culminating in success, the latter is a parodic narrative of failure. Genji's escapades with Utsusemi and Suetsumuhana both have their comic aspects; although the Yūgao story discourages a comic interpretation, it is nonetheless more gothic than tragic. If Yūgao meets her death in the weed-choked villa of the "Kawaranoin," her daughter Tamakazura travels far from Tsukushi (in present-day Kyushu) to be trapped in its glorious version, the Rokujōin. The Rokujōin becomes the meeting ground of several varieties of otherness.

THE NOBLE EXILE AND THE STEPDAUGHTER

Yūgao's household, ignorant of her sudden death, attempt in vain to trace her after her mysterious disappearance. In the end, her nurse is forced to take the child Tamakazura along with her own family to Tsukushi when her husband is appointed to a post in the Dazaifu, the governmental outpost overseeing both the southern provinces and all continental contact. As seen from the Heian capital, Kyushu was the antipodes, and it requires no mean effort for the tale, which has just seen the construction of the Rokujōin, to incorporate such a world and to revive the Yūgao story, apparently closed seventeen chapters ago. True, there are certain bridges. The memory of Yūgao haunts the opening of the "Safflower" chapter (number six), and Yūgao's presence is invoked again to reintroduce her daughter in "Tamakazura," chapter twenty-one. Both chapters open with the claim that Genji's longing for Yūgao has gone unsated over the months and years. The association with Suetsumuhana is a succinct reminder of Tamakazura's fictional genealogy, that is, of her origins in the minor narrative, while the expression of unabated longing serves again to define the internal function of that tradition: to provide a substitute for the prohibited tale of the major narrative. For it is, after all, Fujitsubo for whom Genji's longing is never appeased. If Yūgao is but a minor surrogate (in contrast to Murasaki), and Suetsumuhana a surrogate for Yūgao, then how removed Tamakazura is from the center of the tale—so far removed that, as with the negation of a negation, she becomes crucially marginal and therefore essential.

Tsukushi is the nodal point for several kinds of otherness within the *Genji*. The first, once more through the useful Suetsumuhana, is that of the minor episodes. In "The Wormwood Patch" (chapter fifteen), Suetsumuhana's aunt, the vulgar wife of the assistant viceroy of the Dazaifu, attempts to drag her once superior but now destitute niece off to Tsukushi to serve as a governess for her own children. Suetsumuhana, like Tamakazura, is motherless, but her late father was Prince of Hitachi.[8] The obstinately unworldly Suetsumuhana resists to the end, but Jijū, her one faithful servant, is forced to leave her, for she is married to a relative of the assistant viceroy. It is in their parting exchange of poems that the word *tamakazura*, "jeweled garland," appears for the first time in the *Genji*.[9]

Suetsumuhana casts about for a parting token: her robes are stained from years of wear; she has no choice but to turn to her own locks, gathered over the years for compensatory use. Her hair is the poor creature's one beauty. (Plain heroines are often crowned by lovely hair, from the Lady of Ōmi, who will appear later, to Jo March of *Little Women*.) This is a gift of herself, a "spiritual gift."[10] It comes accompanied by this poem:

Tayumajiki   I had trusted this cord
suji o tanomishi   never to slacken;

tamakazura	but now, against all hope,
omoi no hoka ni	this jeweled strand
kakehanarenuru	will be torn asunder.

(2:331; S 297; W 315)

Jijū replies,

Tamakazura	Even though it break,
taete mo yamaji	I swear
yuku michi no	by the gods of travel,
tamuke no kami mo	this jeweled garland
kakete chikawan	shall always hold
	between us.

(2:332; S 297; W 316)

The "jeweled garland" is introduced as an emblem of sisterhood on the very eve of its loss. Sisterhood is a special kind of otherness in its implicit exclusion of men, which proves to be a theme of some importance throughout the work. We should not fail to note, moreover, that this is a sisterhood between mistress and servant, the humblest of surrogates, the furthest removed from the center, yet in the logic of the *Genji*, one to gain increasing prominence.[11]

Tsukushi is also associated with the Gosechi (festival) dancer who makes fleeting appearances throughout the early chapters and eventually finds her way to Genji's reminiscences in the last chapter of his life, "The Wizard." She goes to Tsukushi as the daughter of the assistant viceroy; on the family's return voyage to the capital, the party pauses to offer condolences to Genji at Suma. The "Tsukushi no Gosechi," as she is known, is not only associated with Genji's exile but occasions an explicit link between it and the exile of the statesman Sugawara no Michizane (2:197; S 239; W 248).

Indeed, the exile to Suma and Akashi is a part of the tale that has most inspired readers to seek historical models. In addition to Michizane, Ono no Takamura (802-852), Ariwara no Yukihira (818-893), or Minamoto no Takaakira (914-982) are among the most popular candidates. It is the example of Michizane, poet, scholar, and statesman, that is highlighted by the use of Tsukushi. Michizane was prized for his talents by Emperors Uda

(r. 887-897) and Daigo (r. 897-930), who apparently found him effective in restraining the growing influence of the Fujiwara family. Michizane evidently fell afoul of one of them, Tokihira (871-904), and was exiled to a post in the Dazaifu, whence he was never to return to the capital. After his death, a series of mishaps in the capital contributed to his becoming a hero and eventually a deity as well. Thus, the place name Tsukushi evokes a paradigmatic historical model of heroic transgression and exile.[12]

The example of Michizane, offering a combination of extraordinary gifts and integrity falsely impugned, is a polemically effective shadow hovering behind the exiled Genji. Now, Tamakazura too is sent out to Tsukushi. Hers may seem too slight a figure to bear such a shadow, yet such a bold yoking of a master statesman to a motherless young girl is only characteristic of the methods of Murasaki Shikibu, who, after all, accomplishes nothing less than the transposition of the politics of the state to the bedroom in the writing of the *Genji*. As we shall see, the particular example of Michizane is exploited further at the close of the Tamakazura cycle in "The Cypress Pillar" chapter, when Tamakazura is forced to play the role of a new wife and mother whose coming drives out the original wife and mother.

The juxtaposition of Tamakazura and Genji through Tsukushi and Michizane is reinforced by the image of the earliest castaway in Japanese letters, the leech child. This defective creature appeared in our discussions of Genji's exile in Chapter 1; he emerges again in the course of Genji's first interview with Tamakazura. When Genji entreats her to speak to him, to be familiar (for he is, after all, he insists, her father), she hesitates, then produces a remarkably bookish response for one of her background: "Unable to stand on my feet, I began to sink and could scarcely tell whether I lived or died" (3:125; S 404; W 461).[13] Both Genji and Tamakazura belong to the company of odd children, who, because of parental neglect or death, are forced to occupy temporarily the margins of life but are fated for a prominence unimaginable for their more fortunate peers.

Tamakazura's and Genji's shared condition is captured in the word *sasurai*, or "wandering." In the modest yet suggestive list of characters to whom this word is applied, Genji and Kaoru are the only men.[14] Since most of these characters do not stray far from home, it is clear that "wandering" concerns psychic displacement. A survey of early uses of the word distinguishes it from the related word *samayoi* in that the latter implies the possibility of return—preserves, in other words, the notion of origins—whereas *sasurai* lacks such a reassuring orientation.[15] Tamakazura returns from Tsukushi to the capital, but, as we shall see, this far from exhausts her "wanderings."

The travels of the child Tamakazura to Tsukushi and of the young woman Tamakazura back to the capital constitute a recognizable version in the tradition of the noble-youth-in-exile. The Tamakazura party's expedition to Tsukushi is accorded a brief, conventional treatment characterized by sorrowful poems and pitiful queries from the child as to whether they are rejoining her mother. The years in Tsukushi are passed over in silence until the nurse's husband dies shortly after the end of his term. He enjoins his sons to make the return of their young lady to her rightful domain their first duty in life. The family is hard pressed to respect these wishes, however, and in order to fend off inappropriate suitors (upstart locals), the nurse is obliged to resort to the ruse that the girl is mysteriously deformed and fit only to become a nun. This suffices to discourage all but one, a swarthy bureaucrat from Hizen, a poetaster and collector of exotic women: "Let her be blind or lame, I shall take her and devote myself to her," he announces (3:91; S 390; W 438). Two of the sons, more practical than their brother, are inclined to give in, for the poetaster's alliances in the region are extensive. The daughters, the old nurse, and the oldest son decide to sacrifice their own lives and choose flight to the capital as the sole means of saving their young lady. There follows a fantastic voyage on the high seas, complete with a chase by pirates, or worse yet (the escapees cannot determine the identity of their predator), the Hizen man.

The party manages to make its way to the capital but, predictably enough, finds itself in more precarious circumstances than ever. Only the hope of a miracle sustains them. After some six months at a house on the outskirts of the city, in the Ninth

Ward, Tamakazura is sent to pray, first at the Iwashimizu Hachi-
man Shrine, and then on foot to Hatsuse, a pilgrimage site
especially favored by women.[16] For her the object of pilgrimage
is reunion with her mother:

> What guilty deeds condemn me to a life of wandering in
> this world? O mother, even if you are lost to this world, if
> you pity me, take me to where you are. And if you are alive,
> let me have a glimpse of your face! (3:98; S 394; W 445)

At Hatsuse Tamakazura's prayers are answered after a fashion,
as prayers are in fiction. She is miraculously restored, not to her
mother but to her surrogate in the form of Ukon, her mother's
wet nurse's daughter. Ukon herself had been making pilgrimages
to Hatsuse in the hopes of being reunited with her lady's daughter.[17] In the course of hurried, intense conversations at Hatsuse,
Tamakazura's attendants propose various futures for their lady,
each tailored to the requirements of her own fantasy. The old
nurse, faithful to her original cause, wants her restored to her
father. The servant Sanjō would rather see her the wife of an
assistant viceroy. But Ukon, having been part of Genji's household since Yūgao's death, will have none of this. While watching the construction of the Rokujōin, she had naturally thought
of what her mistress might have been, and now that her daughter
has so miraculously been restored, her old dreams revive, and
she insists on placing Tamakazura at the lap of a man who at
once promises to be a father and a lover.

Tamakazura's "wandering" to Tsukushi and back is also the
occasion of an excursion by the work itself. We find ourselves in
the midst of a strange narrative, alien to what had come to seem
a world of the *Tale of Genji*. Once "The Jeweled Chaplet" is
seen as the logical extension of "The Shell of the Locust," "Evening Faces," and "The Safflower" chapters, the strangeness begins to sparkle. The Tsukushi story is high-spirited pastiche. Tamakazura, who is mysteriously untainted by her upbringing,
resembles the miraculously bestowed child of the old folk tales,
whose paradigmatic representative is the Heavenly Princess in
the *Tale of the Bamboo Cutter*. Tamakazura is extravagantly described as *kiyora* (3:86; S 389; W 437), "pure" and "radiant," an

adjective appropriate to the bloodless beauty of the Heavenly Princess, an adjective that, moreover, is generally reserved for royalty in the *Genji*. The *Tale of the Bamboo Cutter*'s own parodic spirit is echoed in the boorish Hizen man's courtship, which produces pseudo-etymological puns reminiscent of the older work such as *yobai* for "night-crawling" and "courtship" (3:90; S 390; W 439).[18]

To see Tamakazura's journey to Tsukushi and Genji's retreat to Suma and Akashi as versions of the noble-youth-in-exile tale is not to place them on equal footing. Like the episodes in the major and minor chapters, their relationship is asymmetric and charged with tension. Tamakazura's "exile" parodies Genji's exile and partially domesticates it, thereby challenging Genji's status as hero. In order to explore the further reaches of their relationship, it is necessary to cast the Tamakazura story as a version of the stepdaughter tale.

The stepdaughter tale enjoyed great popularity in the Heian period and circulated in both oral and written form. The genre has generally been understood as a female variant of the noble-exile tale and, correspondingly, as a female narrative of initiation.[19] One study lists the basic elements of the stepdaughter tale as follows: (1) courtship of the heroine and opposition by the stepmother; (2) cruel acts by the stepmother, resulting in the heroine's flight and/or confinement; (3) the appearance of one or more helpers, often in the form of animals or nuns and priests; (4) the suitor's search for the heroine with complications issuing from rival intervention and divine aid; (5) reunion and marriage; (6) birth of children; (7) punishment of the stepmother and her allies and rewarding of the helpers.[20] Since the standard heroine (as well as her reader) is almost of age, her stepmother's cruelty may be interpreted as an initiatory ordeal.[21] The stepdaughter heroines of folk tales are often forced to perform excessive or unusual domestic duties, but their sisters in Heian fiction are usually as well tended to by servants as their stepsiblings.[22] Instead, they are required to perfect certain skills, a process we shall see documented in the example of Tamakazura. It is not unreasonable to interpret the stepmothers' demands as a gesture intended to help prepare their daughters for the adult roles they must assume upon coming of age, when they will be confronted with marriage and motherhood. But the nagging question remains, why stepmothers? If some stepmothers, in an overzealous performance of their duties, attempt to kill their stepdaughters, it may be countered that marriage, the crucial event in female lives, signifies, as do all rites of initiation, symbolic death and the birth of a new self. The suitors' search constitutes their side of the initiatory ordeal. More often than not, with help from humble and divine sources, they are successful, and the stepdaughters are saved.

The critical point of the stepdaughter tale lies in the heroine's confinement, either imposed as punishment by the stepmother or self-imposed as a means of escaping her cruelty. The importance of confinement is revealed in the titles of many stepdaughter tales, such as the *Tale of Ochikubo* (a "sunken room") or the *Tale of Sumiyoshi* (a place name), a pre-*Genji* tale thought to have been influential in the conception of the Tamakazura chapters.[23] These titles designate the site of the heroine's confinement—that is, they reveal the secret within the tale. The motif of retreat and confinement has been associated with the practice of isolating young girls in special huts at the onset of menstruation.[24] Girls, upon becoming sexually available, must be hidden, but their very hiding distinguishes them, makes their secret transparent. This is important, of course: taboos can function only if they are known. The girl who attains puberty is temporarily taboo, and therefore sacred. Stepdaughter heroines are often marked by stigmas: physical deformities, humble garments, or ashes, from the familiar example of Cinderella. The stigma is a sign of their special state, an emblem of the sacred cause of their present suffering and, being temporary, of their future redemption—or fall—in marriage. From a practical point of view the stigma serves to protect its wearer from the more dire consequences of her stepmother's hatred and to ward off inappropriate suitors.[25]

The heroine's isolation and stigma curiously resemble the hero's transgression that drives him into exile. Perhaps the stepdaughter tale is indeed merely a female variant of the noble-exile tale. Because young women are less mobile than young men, retreat and confinement are substituted for dramatic travel with sexual conquests along the way (as in the *Ise*).[26] This view, however, leaves a crucial question unanswered: what is the feminine equivalent of the transgression motivating masculine exile? There is only one possibility: the condition of becoming sexually available. Sexual ripening constitutes the young heroine's transgression. Transgression against whom or what? It is easy, and not altogether incorrect, to answer, her stepmother: her stepmother as representative of all other women in the community, including her own mother—that is, women who have passed the age of sexual and literary interest. Once the heroine herself is rescued and married, she too will fall into banality (the quotidian and the profane) and out of narrative. Witness the Victorian novels that end with betrothal.

In the *Tale of Genji*, I believe we shall see how the mere variant of the stepdaughter tale challenges, subverts, and even subsumes the tale of the noble exile. In order to pursue this process, however, it is necessary to generalize by taking a step back and reemphasizing the fictionally sacred dimension of confinement whereby the symmetry of the narratives of the stepdaughter and the noble exile becomes apparent. Heroines, as well as heroes, are created in a state of isolation. The other land can be conceived of as sealed space, such as the section of bamboo in which the Heavenly Princess of the *Tale of the Bamboo Cutter* is discovered; the lacquered box that the Asian Rip Van Winkle, Urashima Tarō, brings back with him from the Sea Dragon's Palace; or even the fruits and vegetables in which folk heroes and heroines travel to the human world.[27] These images reshape our concept of the other land from that of an amorphous, unbounded "out there" to something enclosed, tangible, and portable—portable, that is, into our world. The other land as a site of confinement is also a privileged site, a concentrated space representing potential selfhood.

Tamakazura's early story follows the conventional outlines of the stepdaughter tale with certain strategic variations. Tsukushi as a site for retreat and confinement is excessively remote and thereby draws attention to itself. Although the Yūgao story hinted at the unpleasantness of Tō no Chūjō's official wife, there is no description of stepmother cruelty in Tamakazura's story. In its stead, there are economic and social perils: the circumstances of her nurse's family in Tsukushi and the pressures of local suitors. Indeed, the nurse's ruse of a deformity confers upon Tamakazura her first stigma, a stigma anticipating the more serious defect of possible rusticity. The child Tamakazura thinks of the voyage to Tsukushi as a journey in search of her mother, and the twenty years spent there suggest that hers could be called a "Tale of Tsukushi."[28] But the trip back to the capital is also conceived as a search for her mother, a search resolved neither by the wished-for reunion nor by marriage. In fact, the true site of confinement for Tamakazura becomes Genji's mansion, the Rokujōin, which she enters, in the eyes of the world, as his daughter.[29] Genji, of course, is interested in her as his dead lover's daughter. In addition to being a fictional father and a potential lover, he is also a sibling through the bond of exile and its surrounding circumstances. Thus the configurations of the Genji-Fujitsubo or the Genji-Murasaki relationships are mirrored with this secondary heroine. And finally, as the one who confines her in the Rokujōin, Genji is something of a stepmother.

To see the ways in which Genji plays this role, let us consider the following interpretation of the relationship between another young heroine, Snow White, and her stepmother, the Queen:

> For the Queen . . . is a plotter, a schemer, a witch, an artist, an impersonator, a woman of almost infinite creative energy, witty, wily, and self-absorbed as all artists traditionally are. On the other hand, in her absolute chastity, her frozen innocence, her sweet nullity, Snow White represents precisely the ideal of "contemplative purity": . . . an ideal that could quite literally kill the Queen. . . . Snow White is . . . childlike, docile, submissive, the heroine of a life that *has no story*. But the Queen, adult and demonic, plainly wants a life of "significant action," by definition an "unfeminine" life of stories and storytelling. . . . [30]

Of course, it is the Queen who interests us here. As background, we should recall that Genji has played a slightly androgynous, pseudo-parental role in the past, first with Murasaki and then with Akikonomu, entrusted to him by her dying mother, also a former lover. Genji urges Tamakazura to think of him as her mother, for whose death he is responsible. Now, in the description of the Queen above, the life of "significant action" is equated to an "unfeminine life of stories and storytelling"; but for Genji, the appearance of Tamakazura poses the life of "significant action" and the life of "stories and storytelling" as distinct alternatives—or rather, it reformulates the equation as that between a life of "significant action" and a distinctly *feminine* life of "stories and storytelling."

When Genji learns of Tamakazura's whereabouts from Ukon, he chooses to have her brought to the Rokujōin without passing on the news of her discovery to her father, Tō no Chūjō. He is excited by the prospect of adding to his family:

> I have been lonely, but here a child has come to me most unexpectedly. We shall devote ourselves to her, and she will become a seed of excitement to stir the hearts of our young gallants.　　　　　　　(3:116; S 403; W 456)

The principal occupants of the recently completed Rokujōin are Murasaki with her charge, the Akashi Princess; the Akashi Lady; Hana Chiru Sato; and Akikonomu. What is wanting is that all but indispensable ingredient in storytelling, an eligible young woman. The Akashi Princess is too young and has been destined since birth for the crown prince. Akikonomu is already empress, and Murasaki, Hana Chiru Sato, and the Akashi Lady are Genji's property of long standing. Tamakazura enters with a well-defined function: in order to embellish Genji's glory, she will be set to work at neither stitching nor cleaning but at playing the perfect young lady. By polishing her into the new ornament of the Rokujōin, Genji will generate new stories, new marriage plots.

This is the storytelling side of Tamakazura's potential use for Genji. As for the other, the possibility of significant action: by the time Tamakazura appears on the scene, Genji has already lived a life of significant action. The heady days of stealthy meetings with Fujitsubo and Oborozukiyo, of kidnapping Murasaki, and wandering in strange alleys, climaxed by the anguish of Suma and Akashi, are now remote. The secret of his transgression is safe, and moreover, now that he is the foster father of Empress Akikonomu, he has a public, legitimate relationship with the fruit of his sin, the Reizei Emperor. As chancellor and lord of the Rokujōin, he has attained the apogee of temporal success. By the same token, he has lost his claim to authenticity as a literary hero. Not only does Tamakazura offer the promise of vicarious rejuvenation by her ability to play the actress in the dramas he will produce; but as her mother's surrogate, she is the plausible object of new transgression. If Genji should violate the prohibition against sexual relations with both mother and daughter, he could recapture some of his youthful heroism.[31] By harboring a guilty secret, he could cultivate an internal other land, an identity opposed to the public self situated at the center of power and authority. He could, in other words, become interesting.

By virtue of Tamakazura's entry, the tale is blessed with a small secret, the fiction of her relationship to Genji. Tamakazura's story infuses Genji's with energy from various sources, not the least of which is the other land beyond the capital as well as the other land of the minor chapters. At the same time, the significance of Tamakazura as stepdaughter transcends such dichotomies: her story implicates all the other stepdaughters, or motherless daughters, of whom a casual listing would include Fujitsubo, Murasaki, Akikonomu, Suetsumuhana, Princess Asagao, the Third Princess, Ōigimi, and Nakanokimi. Finally, Tamakazura's potential can be gauged by the fact that she is entering a house that has no room for her.

In an apparent structural innovation, the *Tale of Sumiyoshi* (referred to earlier for its presumed influence upon the Tamakazura chapters) sandwiches a love story developed through seasonal poetry between sections describing the stepmother's cruelty and her final punishment. The Rokujōin is organized upon seasonal principles, and the Tamakazura chapters proceed along seasonal themes. In the case of the *Sumiyoshi*, it has been argued that the seasonal poetic section injects a note of lyricism into what is otherwise a crude tale of stepmother barbarism.[32] What is the significance of organization according to seasonal principles, both in the Rokujōin itself and in the Tamakazura chapters? We must begin with a structure and an incident preceding the construction of the Rokujōin.

THE EASTERN PAVILION AND THE BATTLE OF THE SEASONS

Structures are necessarily prominent in fictions whose characters are apt to be identified by their office (or by that of their male relatives, in the case of women) or by their residence. Dwellings represent a cosmos, and in the *Genji*, their political and erotic significations are richly developed. Initially and always, buildings are associated with women. In the very first chapter, when his father the Kiritsubo Emperor has his late mother's estate restored, Genji wishes it could house someone to his liking. He has recently been wedded to the impeccable Aoi but continues to be under Fujitsubo's spell. It is of course Fujitsubo that he would like to see installed at the Nijōin. This is an impossible fantasy, as Genji himself knows only too well. Instead, the Nijōin becomes the lifelong home of Fujitsubo's surrogate, her niece Murasaki.

Upon his return from exile, Genji begins work on a new structure on this estate, the building that will be known as the Eastern Pavilion (Nijō no Tōin). What are his motives? In "Channel Buoys," the first of the postexile chapters, the Suzaku Emperor abdicates hastily, and the Reizei Emperor ascends to the throne. Genji is given a supernumerary ministership and expected to run the affairs of the country. Pleading inadequacy to such responsibilities, he manages to foist them onto the aging shoulders of his father-in-law, the former Minister of the Left. His brother-in-law, Tō no Chūjō, also begins to prosper anew; he has been blessed with children, and one of them is being groomed to enter Reizei's court. Genji is envious. He has not forgotten the various women who languished during his absence, but given his new public importance, he can no longer flit about in the exercise of his sensibilities—hence the Eastern Pavilion, where he might house such creatures and have any future children cared for by

103

them. He has in mind such women as Hana Chiru Sato or the Gosechi dancer from Tsukushi.

Soon, in distant Akashi, a daughter is born. It is unthinkable to leave mother and child on that island, and with the Eastern Pavilion completed (in "The Wind in the Pines" chapter), Genji thinks of housing them in the eastern wing of that residence. Hana Chiru Sato has already taken up residence near the western wing, which has been made into offices. The northern wing, the traditional preserve of the principal wife, is particularly spacious so as to accommodate all those ladies with whom he has had brief encounters but to whom he has pledged eternal support. It has been thoughtfully designed with numerous partitions. The main hall is reserved for his own occasional visits. Thus, the Eastern Pavilion is an intermediate structure between an aristocratic half-way house and a harem. It is an erotic *vita* of Genji's youth and early manhood.

As we know, the Akashi Lady, who, with her daughter, first settles on family property in Ōi at the outskirts of the city, never moves into the Eastern Pavilion. She stays her ground until the Rokujōin is complete. Although the installation of the ladies in the Eastern Pavilion bears some relation to their psychic and material importance in Genji's mind, the structure lacks a powerful principle of organization. This is what distinguishes the Rokujōin, whose four quarters and respective occupants are each assigned to a particular season. To understand the evolution of this edifice, we should begin with the naming of Akikonomu (the "Autumn-Preferring One"), whose mother's estate provides part of the site for the Rokujōin, and who is in so many ways Tamakazura's precursor.

When the Suzaku emperor steps down from the throne in the "Channel Buoys" chapter, Akikonomu, in accordance with custom, leaves her position as Priestess of Ise and returns to the capital with her mother the Rokujō Lady. Their home enjoys a brief revival as a salon, but the Rokujō Lady soon falls ill and dies, leaving her daughter in Genji's care—not, however, without enjoining him from unbecoming impulses. Even as Genji silently protests, his glance is irresistibly drawn to an opening in the curtains (that mark of slight carelessness so fatal to many a Heian heroine), where he faintly makes out the form of the young daughter and finds it pleasing. Years ago, he had envied his half brother the Suzaku Emperor his opportunity to set eyes on her at the ceremony of her leave-taking for Ise. The Suzaku Emperor himself was much taken with her then, and now that she is orphaned he repeats an invitation to enter his household.

Genji, however, has other plans. In consultation with Fujitsubo, he decides to bring the young girl to the Nijōin and place her under Murasaki's supervision with the intent of entering her in Reizei's court. Need we add that Genji is a guardian of divided impulse? He desires his charge even as he plans her political use. In any case, with Fujitsubo's blessings, as we have seen, he conveniently ignores Suzaku's wishes and removes Akikonomu to the Nijōin from which she enters the service of Reizei, more than ten years her junior.[33] Akikonomu's supremacy in court, in the face of such rivals as Tō no Chūjō's daughter, must still be secured. This is accomplished by Fujitsubo's and Genji's skillful engineering of the Picture Contest.

It is during one of her subsequent visits "home" to the Nijōin that the incident occurs from which Akikonomu derives her name and which also serves as the clearest harbinger of the Rokujōin world. The chapter is "A Rack of Cloud," which opens with the winter transfer of the Akashi Princess from her mother to Murasaki. It is that same winter in which Fujitsubo dies.[34] The Reizei Emperor learns the secret of his birth and threatens to resign. Genji, still reeling from the shock of Fujitsubo's death, is panic-stricken lest their secret come to light. These are the circumstances in which the interview with Akikonomu takes place. The transition from guilty anxiety to judicious lasciviousness is economical and pointed. In one line we are reminded of Genji's constant longing for Fujitsubo (2:448; S 344; W 379); in the next, he is contemplating with satisfaction Akikonomu's performance in the Emperor's service (the word is *on'ushiromi*, a term normally reserved for the role played by maternal relatives of a young woman with prospects at court or of a crown prince or even an emperor).

During their meeting Genji and Akikonomu are separated only by a screen, for paternal Genji feels free to dispense with the usual intermediaries. His first words are discreetly scandalous: observing the signs of autumn in her garden, he remarks, "How the shrubs and grasses have loosened, their ties!" The emphatic *koso* in the original, buttressed by a poetic allusion (3:449, n. 20; S, 344; W 379), suggests that she, ungratefully enough, has remained unapproachable. He continues in this vein, his self-indulgence mounting until he beseeches Akikonomu for her understanding, even for her pity, for the difficult role he has had to play, tending to her interests and entering her in Reizei's service, all achieved only at great cost to his own feelings.[35]

Signs of discomfort from the other side of the screen become intense enough to give Genji pause. He shifts to play Akikonomu in another key, asking her to look after the Akashi Princess, to make the prosperity of his house her concern when he is gone. Then, he shifts again, or rather he combines his two previous themes in the genteel "battle of spring and autumn." The dispute he raises is a venerable one extending back to the courtly play of Chinese literati. Now elegant and temperate, Genji, declaring himself unable to choose, insists that Akikonomu disclose her preference for autumn or spring. Thinking that silence at all times would be overly dramatic, she voices a timid inclination toward autumn on the grounds that it was the season of her mother's death,[36] whereupon Genji casts neutrality to the winds and declares,

Kimi mo sawa	Then you must share
aware o kawase	your heart with me;
hito shirezu	I, who, unknown to others
wagami ni shimuru	have been pierced
aki no yūkaze	by autumn's evening winds.
	(2:453; S 346; W 381)

It is too much for Akikonomu. Sensing that she has slipped away, Genji has no choice but to take his leave as well. It is from this incident that Akikonomu takes her name and comes to preside over the autumn quarters of the Rokujōin and to engage in an elegant rivalry with Murasaki who, as a consequence of this episode (or so it is made to appear), is explicitly identified with spring and assigned to the spring quarters.[37]

What does it mean for Genji to demand that Akikonomu choose between spring and autumn? It implies, for one thing, that the seasons are his to offer. The gesture anticipates his coming reign as lord of nature in the Rokujōin. Underlying that role is the figure of the archetypal ruler, who is at once nature incarnate and thus lord of humanity and servant to humanity and therefore lord of nature. That is, he is to be worshiped for he embodies the necessary and hoped-for harmonious unfolding of the seasons; he is also to be constrained, for he is responsible for ensuring nature's fruitfulness.

Such concerns were reflected in the rituals of the Japanese court. For example, each year, in the eleventh month, just before the offering of the fruits of the new harvest (the Niinamesai), a festival was held in dedication to the pacification of souls (the Chinkonsai). Saigō Nobutsuna states that the ritual was originally called *tamafuri*, and following Orikuchi Shinobu, he argues that *furi* means to "make adhere," and that the object of the ancient rite was to fix the errant soul to the body and thus revive it.[38] That this rite nearly coincided with the winter solstice (the ritual-laden time all over the northern hemisphere) underscores the identification of temporal sovereign with nature itself: the earth, weak and dying, must be restored so that spring will visit again. The offering of the harvest fruits is at once a sign of gratitude for gifts received and prayers for their continuation.[39]

The identification of temporal sovereign with lord of cosmic nature is neither natural nor innocent but the result of a politico-historical process. Records of the construction of an imperial myth in Japan date from the seventh and eighth centuries. There are various traces of this process, such as the shift in imperial designation from *ōkimi* to *sumera mikoto*, or as we would read the same characters today, *tennō*.[40] The distinction is not absolute, since *ōkimi* itself was part of an effort to elevate the head of the Yamato clan above others by the distinguishing feature of lack of surname (*kabane*), but the heavenly element (the *sumera*) cannot be overlooked. Whereas earlier emperors were content to claim divine descent, Temmu (r. 672-686), for example, became himself a "very god" (*akitsukami*).⁴¹ The great seventh-century poet Hitomaro's poems not only reflect but contribute to this process, for his

> first recorded step as a poet is a step backward, a rhetorical evocation of the mythic world, in whose eternal time the descent of the first Emperor from the "fields of heaven" is identical to the enthronement of the latest sovereign at the palace in Asuka.⁴²

A crucial aspect of imperial rule is to be found in the development of ritual gestures and ritual language. These, in turn, are rhetorically mirrored—with distortions and inversions—in poetry and fiction.⁴³

When Genji poses the spring-autumn question to Akikonomu, he is repeating an imperial gesture from a much earlier age. The *Man'yōshū* is the oldest extant anthology of Japanese poetry, compiled sometime after the mid-eighth century. Poem number 16 in the *Man'yōshū* is preceded by a headnote stating that when the Emperor (Tenji, r. 668-671) ordered his Minister (Fujiwara no Kamatari, 614-669) to choose between the "brilliance of the ten thousand blossoms on the spring hillsides and the colors of the thousand leaves on the autumn hillsides,"⁴⁴ the Minister relegated the task to Princess Nukada (dates uncertain). No doubt this aesthetic exercise had been imported from China by a self-conscious Japanese court bent on cultural improvement. Princess Nukada, who proved herself more than equal to the occasion, concluded her poem with a resounding "But the autumn hills are for me," a personal declaration that bursts the bounds of ritual play. Her choice was to be seconded by generations of Japanese—in contrast to the Chinese, as Genji declares. Such a bias did not prevent the "battle of spring and autumn" from becoming a ritualized subject of poetry contests. Thus, in mimicking an imperial gesture, Genji is essentially engaging Akikonomu in a game. Her response, too, is personal, though in a sense different from Princess Nukada's, and it incites Genji to abandon the role of arbiter.

The rhetorical game of spring versus autumn prefigures the supremely rhetorical world of the Rokujōin, and the game-playing anticipates the fate of Tamakazura. The game substitutes for the erotic relationship that might have been—an incestuous and therefore disruptive and literarily fertile relationship. Akikonomu is Genji's foster daughter and the consort of his son, who is on the throne. As the daughter of a late crown prince, moreover, Akikonomu resembles a scaled-down Fujitsubo; she is, in every metaphoric respect, Genji's daughter, as Fujitsubo was his mother. Following the birth of her son by Genji and the death of her husband the Kiritsubo Emperor, Fujitsubo had to engage in the profane business of protecting her son's position, of ensuring his accession and a stable reign. A partially reluctant (or appealingly irresponsible) Genji eventually joined forces with her, as in the strategic maneuvering of Akikonomu's fate. Yet Fujitsubo died as his eternal love, all the more reason why Genji's overtures to Akikonomu, coming so soon after that death, may be hard to understand. It could be argued that the erotic is Genji's mode of bringing women into his sphere of influence and that therefore these gestures are consistent with the program jointly designed with Fujitsubo for Akikonomu and Reizei. (It is clearly in Genji's own interest to ensure the stability of his son's reign and to prevent the disclosure of the great secret.)[45]

For Genji to engage in an erotic relationship with Akikonomu, current empress and daughter of a former lover, would be to put that program in jeopardy and violate several taboos. It would, in short, bestow a new secret and a new (if not altogether fresh) sense of sacredness to the tale and its hero. And yet Genji retreats, perhaps because his son's recent threats of resignation compel him to be prudent. The retreat is realized through the ritualized aesthetic game of the spring-autumn debate.

It is interesting that ritualized play should be made to serve in lieu of sacred transgression, for games, like festivals, normally belong to the sphere of the sacred and signal the suspension of profane time. Here is Johan Huizinga linking the two in the perspective of play:

> Both [feast and play] proclaim a standstill to ordinary life. In both mirth and joy dominate, though not necessarily— for the feast too can be serious; both are limited as to time and place; both combine strict rules with genuine freedom.[46]

And, in the perspective of religion, Eliade discusses "Festival Time and the Structure of Festivals" as follows:

> The *time of origin* of a reality—that is, the time inaugurated by the first appearance of the reality—has a paradigmatic value and function; that is why man seeks to reactualize it periodically by means of appropriate rituals. . . . A festival always takes place in the original time. It is precisely the reintegration of this original and sacred time that differentiates man's behavior *during* the festival from his behavior *before* or *after* it. For in many cases the same acts are performed during the festival as during nonfestival periods.[47]

The "genuine freedom" in feast and play derives from the rule that ordinary rules do not apply. Social taboos and hierarchies are commonly suspended or reversed, dispelling the workaday world. Feast and play are theoretically democratic: theoretically, but only theoretically, because, for one, the context of the quotidian, the profane, can never be banished, and for another, feast and play are imposed modes of freedom. Feast and play, like myth, are always motivated.[48]

Within its immediate context, Genji's use of the courtly battle of the seasons is profane because of both its imperial implications and its ritualized aesthetic character. The management of nature, even if it is rhetorical, or precisely because it is rhetorical, is a sign of order and authority. As we shall see in discussing the seasonal books of the *Kokinshū* as a model for the structure of the Rokujōin, an imperial anthology of poetry is at once a verbal artifact and an expression of imperial authority. For literature, let us remember, the emperor can only be profanely sacred.[49] Princess Nukada's poem, with its passionate declaration (I am for autumn, I *am* autumn, and that matters), is a somewhat different matter. But when this personal choice of one or another season is exercised a countless number of times in poetry contests, it becomes less compelling. Once play becomes recognizable as such, once it is ritualized, it risks losing its privileged status as play.[50]

To say that literature has a propensity for altering if not inverting the sacred and profane values of the external world is to acknowledge that antireferentiality is one form that the perpetual literary search for the new takes. For ritual to be recognizable, it must involve repetition; hence, the literary use of ritual tends toward paradox. Genji contemplates for one critical moment the rupture of referential codes of taboo. Still, with Akikonomu being, after all, but a much reduced version of Fujitsubo, the transgression would pale beside the great secret of the first chapters; it would be an instance of mere repetition without an element of interesting variation. Genji can only sigh and withdraw. To say that the Rokujōin is founded on a failure to violate is to exaggerate only slightly.

THE ROKUJŌIN: PRELUDE

The Rokujōin is completed in "The Maiden" chapter, just before Tamakazura's arrival in the capital. As we have come to expect, the timing is strategic: Genji has staged a predictably brilliant campaign on Akikonomu's behalf. Eclipsing the other hopefuls, she becomes empress. With her appointment Genji himself is promoted to chancellor, the highest political office in the land. The Rokujōin at completion is modestly described only at the end of the chapter. It is divided into four *machi*, areas marked off by avenues and small roads, each to be occupied by one of Genji's principal ladies. Each residence has a garden devoted to one of the four seasons, and the ladies are housed each according to "her" season. With directional and astrological indications added, the structure can be summarized as follows:

Southeast—spring—dragon/snake—Murasaki
Southwest—autumn—sheep/monkey—Akikonomu
Northwest—winter—dog/wild boar—Lady of Akashi
Northeast—summer—cow/tiger—Hana Chiru Sato

Since place of residence customarily provides one form of appellation for women, all the designations above appear as names for the inmates of the Rokujōin. Thus, for example, Murasaki is "Mistress of the Dragon/Snake [quarters]," "Lady Spring," or "Lady of the South."[51]

Not surprisingly, the Rokujōin has inspired centuries of speculation as to its sources and significance. For simplicity's sake the theories may be classified as (1) religious/folklorical, (2) historical, and (3) rhetorical.[52] As for the first, structures conceived upon seasonal or directional axes abound in various traditions. Such expressions of the aspiration for wholeness and transcendence stem from a universal conception of sacred space, the *imago mundi*.[53] More specifically, there is an image of a dragon king's palace that finds its way into the *Tale of the Hollow Tree*, perhaps the most important domestic fictional predecessor to the *Genji*. The structure in the former is located by the sea, and although it is moved to the capital in the *Genji*, the aquatic feature is preserved through associations between the Akashi family and the Sea Dragon King. Akashi's position at the "dog/wild boar" corner is thought to draw upon an old folk belief centered on a diagonal axis from "dragon/snake" to "dog/wild boar."[54]

The principal historical source is the Kawaranoin, the ninth-century villa of Minamoto no Tōru. As mentioned in the Yūgao discussion, Tōru was born the son of an emperor but demoted to a Genji. To acquire a surname means that one has been removed from the succession, and perhaps that constituted a fact sufficient for the contemporary imagination to conjure up a tragic narrative. Does the construction of a grand, pseudo-palatial residence compensate? Strictly speaking, the Rokujōin mimics not the whole of the Imperial Palace but rather its inner, hidden quarters, housing the emperor's enormous female household, that section called the Kōkyū, the palace situated behind the outer, public structures.[55] The private part of the Palace (and the tale) is transparently concealed in the Rokujōin. At the same time, Genji's mansion is repeatedly compared to the Palace as a public structure: its ceremonies equal or outstrip imperial affairs.[56] Secrecy and invisibility are at issue here, too, for Genji becomes imperial by limiting his access to the public view: he confines himself in the Rokujōin as the emperors are (devoutly) imprisoned in the Palace. It comes as a surprise, being so much an announcement after the fact, when Genji is officially made the equivalent of a retired emperor in "Wisteria Leaves," the final chapter before the sun begins to set on the Rokujōin.

In the Tamakazura chapters the sun always keeps pace with the seasons. The sense in which the architecture of the Rokujōin and the patterning of these chapters are rhetorical is best expressed in Nomura Seiichi's observation that the Rokujōin represents an attempt to "spatialize, in prose, 'external' nature, which was transposed to the world of language in thirty-one syllables and regulated by the temporal order of the seasons in the *Kokinshū*."[57] Just as "nature" in the *Kokinshū* is hardly "natural," so the seasons in the Rokujōin are produced not only by the finest craftsmanship that taste and money can buy (as we recall, the presence of the warehouses on the grounds of the Akashi Lady's quarters was ever so discreetly mentioned), but by an imagination shaped by the rule of the calendar.[58] Then there are the four women, imprisoned or enshrined as the seasons themselves, elegant and altogether artful imitations of archaic priestesses. Of course, the heroines have had seasonal or botanical associations from the very beginning of the tale; but never have they been so rigidly confined within the circular order of nature.[59]

The first eight chapters of the ten in the Tamakazura group trace the passage of a year in the Rokujōin household. They are as follows:

1. The Jeweled Chaplet—flashback covering eighteen years, winter in the Rokujōin
2. The First Warbler—New Year's, early spring
3. Butterflies—spring
4. Fireflies—monsoon, early summer
5. Wild Carnations—summer
6. Flares—early autumn
7. The Typhoon—autumn
8. The Royal Outing—winter

* * *

9. Purple Trousers—autumn one year later
10. The Cypress Pillar—winter to fall

"Fireflies" and "Wild Carnations" divide the first eight chapters into nearly symmetrical halves. Chapters 1-3 trace the ascending curve of Genji's passion for Tamakazura. In chapters 6-8, he is no less intent, and Tamakazura herself is more susceptible, but consummation grows increasingly doubtful. "Purple Trousers" (9) is an intermediate chapter. The last, "Cypress Pillar," recapitulates the seasonal progression of the first eight chapters in rapid motion.

Both the architecture of the Rokujōin and the chapters that describe its glory adopt the arrangement of the seasonal books of the imperial anthologies of poetry. What are the implications? In the typical twenty-book arrangement of the imperial anthologies, the six books on the seasons (two each for the most important, spring and autumn) and the five on love each stand at the head of two ten-book divisions. They represent two competing though not equal systems of order. (In this they offer an analogy to the relationship between the narratives of the noble exile and the stepdaughter.) Following the authoritative example of the *Kokinshū*, the first imperial anthology of poetry, imperial anthologies begin with the seasons. The seasonal books and the love books may be contrasted in a number of ways (such as the relative freedom and informality of the latter), but these may provisionally be subsumed under the categories of circularity and linearity. This much said, however, it must also be granted that the course of a love affair in the five books of an imperial anthology is nearly as predictable as the unfolding of the seasons.[60] There is a beginning and an unmistakable (i.e., unhappy) end. The reliable repetition of this pattern has much to do with the formidable regulatory character of the imperial anthologies and with the naturalization of love: nature is made into a paradigm of order that not only sustains a poetry anthology and through it the imperial ideology but dictates the forms in which human experiences such as love can be intelligible in writing.[61]

I have already referred to the essential linking of the emperor to nature. Now I would like to consider the ambiguous uses of nature and the natural in the *Kokinshū*. Its justly celebrated Japanese Preface (which is no less a manifesto of Japanese poetry for its borrowings from Chinese poetics) begins with the statement, "The Japanese poem makes of the human heart its seeds, which grow into myriad leaves of words."[62] By the comparison to seeds and leaves, not only fleeting words but their formation into mere (Japanese, not venerable Chinese) verse is accorded the compelling substance of nature and natural processes. This is only fitting, of course, in a collection of words (an anthology of poetry) compiled by sovereign decree. The public, political character of the anthology both produces and requires the unrivaled persuasiveness (truthfulness) of things.[63] Hence the efforts to persuade us of the transparency prevailing between heart, word, and thing.

There is, however, another aspect that emerges from inspection of the uses of the phrase "leaves of words" in the *Kokinshū* (wherein there are twelve examples).[64] Here, there is a shift from nature as compelling substance and therefore repository and manifestation of truth, to nature as changeable and "leaves of words" (whether as gossip or pledges of love) as fugitive and unreliable. It is, of course, words in the service of love that bear the brunt of the notoriety—which is to underscore again the importance of love for fiction. Even nature and the Japanese poetry of imperial anthologies are vulnerable to the destabilizing presence of the topic of love. If, on the formal level, the linear narrative of love in the imperial anthologies takes on a certain circularity by virtue of repetition, so the seasons take on a linear aspect: spring signifies beginning and winter, end. Still, we must not lose sight of the fact that the context of the imperial anthology is all important. Even though the complexity of the relation between words and things (nature) is demonstrated in the aggressive rhetoricity of the *Kokinshū*, it is at the same time constrained by the genre.

To return the discussion to the topic of prose fiction, we might refer again to the love poetry in the *Tale of Sumiyoshi*, the early stepdaughter narrative. All the poems in the *Sumiyoshi* series, which are arranged by month, are composed by the hero and the heroine of the tale. In other examples of the genre, such as the sequence in the collection of the poet Ise (d. 939), the speakers are identified simply as "the man" or "the woman," and there is no indication as to whether they are to be seen as the same man or woman throughout.[65] In the case of the *Sumiyoshi* poetry, we should note the fusion of the seasons and love. If the

poetry indeed serves to introduce a note of lyricism into the un-
abashed barbarism of the stepdaughter tale, then it must be due
in no small part to the presence of the seasonal interest that
interrupts narrative teleology, much as erotic interest interrupts
brutal conquest in the accounts of the archaic heroes. In assign-
ing a consistent identity to the speakers of its poems, however,
the *Sumiyoshi* subordinates the circularity of the seasons to the
linearity of love. As I have suggested earlier, even rudimentary
characters imply finitude. The "significant action" whereby they
become the heroes and heroines of fiction is also finite and serves
to punctuate the repetitiveness of circularity.

In life and in ritual, what is important about seasonal circularity is reproductive predictability. We have noted that literary
heroes must be sparing of offspring: they share with the emperors
and their legendary ancestors sexual but not reproductive prodi-
gality. (Monogamy is antiludic and banal.) The young Genji is
free of the reproductive taint. If, however, there is an imperial
aura to Genji's image as lord of nature in the Rokujōin, it inevitably brings with it implications of the circular and the reproductive, which may serve as sacred emblems of myth in the lives
of the emperors but suggest profane sterility for fictional heroes.
The Heian emperor mimicked the sweeping journeys of his legendary ancestors within the confines of the women's quarters in
the Palace. In fact, his mini-journeys could only be made by day
since he was required to spend every night in one chamber, the
Seiryōden, with the sword and the jewels.[66] As might be expected, this enactment of myth-in-life had practical aspects. The
emperor's sexual activities were scrutinized because of the high
political stakes attached to their reproductive consequences. The
women with the most powerful backing were to be his most frequent partners, whether by day in their own quarters or by night
in the Seiryōden: the mother of the next crown prince would
come from among them. The Kiritsubo Emperor's attachment
to Genji's mother was scandalous because he should have been
more judicious in the distribution of his favors.

The issue of reproduction figures in a parodic fashion in the
Rokujōin in the person of Tamakazura, who enters as a false
child to compensate for the children Genji has not fathered. She

reinforces the sense of fictional sterility that fertile nature imposes in its circularity. And Genji, as much as Tamakazura and his other women, is trapped in the cyclical time of the chapters centered on the Rokujōin.

Spring in the Rokujōin

It should not surprise us that irregularities are detectable from the outset. For instance, although all the ladies are to move in together to start the clockwork, Murasaki and Hana Chiru Sato, always the docile one, come first. Akikonomu comes several days later with the deliberation appropriate to her status as empress. The Akashi Lady waits for a more than decent interval; her timing is strategic, at once suggesting deference to her betters and a sense of her own importance to the enterprise. The warehouses on the grounds of the winter quarters are stocked with Akashi goods for the sustenance of all quarters. And if Genji's prosperity presently rests on his position as foster father of the Empress, it will sooner or later depend on the little daughter born in Akashi.

Tamakazura enters the Rokujōin in the fall. She is housed with Hana Chiru Sato in the summer quarters. Toward the end of the year, Genji selects New Year's robes for the various ladies under his wing. Great care is taken in the matching of garment to wearer: a process to be seen in its dualistic implications, for if it suggests regard for the recipient's individuality, it must be kept in mind that it is Genji who has determined that identity. The selection takes place under Murasaki's watchful eyes, for it is a rare opportunity for her to gain insight into her various rivals. Genji's cynicism shows in his decision to include lesser items in Tamakazura's store, to allow for that preference of the inferior suggested by her country upbringing. Her principal gift is a bright red outer robe and another robe of the *yamabuki* combination, the color of "fallen leaves" on the outside, "red plum" or yellow on the inside. The *yamabuki* (kerria japonica) becomes Tamakazura's sign in the world of Genji's flora.

"Yamabuki" is also the combination of the tattered robes that Suetsumuhana bestows on Genji's messenger bearing her his

117

New Year's gift. She makes a brief appearance at the end of the chapter in what might be called a cautionary tale from Tamakazura's point of view. Earlier in the chapter, Suetsumuhana is remembered by Genji as a scandalous disappointment, whether as a consolation for Yūgao or a distraction from Fujitsubo. Now Genji is understandably anxious as to whether Tamakazura will prove a similar disappointment. Suetsumuhana, who makes her first appearance since "The Wormwood Patch" chapter, where she had made a rather pretty picture as one who had clung to Genji's memory during his exile, is stripped of her meager charms and made to appear her most ridiculous. As the narrator tartly observes, Suetsumuhana, as an occupant of the Eastern Pavilion, should be discreet and avoid undue familiarity with the residents of the Rokujōin. It is clear that Suetsumuhana consults a different guide to etiquette. Faithful to an outmoded decorum, rigid and innocent of tact, she chooses to play the part of a neglected lover in her response to Genji: how can she thank him for his gift when it comes unaccompanied by him? (Robes are a venerable erotic image: lovers spread them out with sleeves overlapping and sleep beneath them.) Genji uses the occasion to lecture Murasaki (who now has the Akashi Princess in her charge) on the principles of poetry composition and on the education of young ladies.

The passage gives us a glimpse of Genji as educator of women, a role to become increasingly significant in the course of the Tamakazura chapters.[67] It also sheds light on the relation between the Eastern Pavilion and the Rokujōin with Suetsumuhana serving as a representative of the former. Both belong to the minor chapters, and both express a negative value sexually and politically for Genji. Apart from her hair, Suetsumuhana has never satisfied the requirements for being recognized as female. In savage compensation, her creator has endowed her with an elongated, luminous nose. The women of the Rokujōin, by contrast, are either active sexual partners or actual sources of power for Genji. Genetically and generically, Tamakazura belongs more properly to the Eastern Pavilion. The mock erotic exchange between Genji and Suetsumuhana is slyly prophetic of the relationship to develop between Genji and Tamakazura in the Rokujōin.

The results of the clothing distribution are described in "The First Warbler." The chapter opens in spring, on the first day of the New Year: "On the morning when the year turned new, the sky was cloudless and gloriously serene . . . and even within humble fences, the grass was turning a fresh green amidst the snow" (3:137; S 409; W 467). It is the first spring to be celebrated in the Rokujōin, and the opening line plays with that relation between calendar and season so characteristic of a strain of Heian imagination. Its excesses are epitomized in the following poem from the *Kokinshū*, by Ariwara no Motokata (888-953):

Toshi no uchi ni	Spring has come
haru wa kinikeri	within the year!
hito tose o	Should this be called
kozo to ya iwan	last year
kotoshi to ya iwan	or this year?
	(KKS 1, "Spring, 1")

Although the poem's charms may escape modern sensibilities, its position at the head of the first imperial anthology of Japanese poetry demands a moment's pause. The lunar calendar required relatively frequent adjustments to keep the months synchronized with the seasons with which they were associated. The adjustments were made by inserting extra days or even months. This poem was composed when the First Month, the beginning of spring as well as of the year, came twice, so that spring could be greeted while it was still winter. In the *Genji* passage cited above, the coming of spring is of course felicitous: the weather is necessarily impeccable, for the occasion is celebrated above all through symbolic representation: the calendar, poetry, and court ritual. In "The First Warbler" it is Genji as chancellor whose tenure is being applauded by the well-regulated nature of the Rokujōin, which produces green within the humblest plots even as the previous year's snow lingers.

Spring is Murasaki's time, and her garden is likened to Buddha's paradise transported to earth.[68] Murasaki's ladies fuss over the New Year's cakes, making ribald wishes (echoing the fertility of spring) when Genji looks in on them. The first poems of the chapter are exchanged by Genji and Murasaki on the topic of the cakes, called "mirror cakes":

Usu gōri	Upon the mirroring lake
tokenuru ike no	whose thin ice
kagami ni wa	has melted away,
yo ni tagui naki	our forms, peerless in this
kage zo naraberu	world,
	are reflected side-by-side.
	(3:138; S 410; W 468)

The mirror cakes have become the reflecting surface of a lake from which the ice, appropriately enough, has melted away. Apart from the perfect aesthetic fit of conceits to place and moment, Genji's brimming confidence catches our attention, perhaps because such hubris is inevitably dangerous. Genji has just dressed for a round of calls and has stopped to look in on his first lady first. She responds,

Kumori naki	Upon the cloudless mirror
ike no kagami ni	of this lake
yorozuyo o	our forms will dwell,
sumubeki kage zo	clearly visible
shiruku miekeru	for ten thousand years.
	(Ibid.)

This is uncharacteristic optimism from Murasaki, though of course it is an optimism founded on reflections on a lake that is a mirror that is a rice cake.

After leaving Murasaki, Genji calls on the child known as the Akashi Princess. She makes an appropriate first stop because she is being raised by Murasaki and because she embodies Genji's hopes for the next generation. He is moved by a note sent by her true mother and supervises the writing of a response but does not proceed directly to the Akashi quarters, for this is not a spontaneous burst of visits he has undertaken.

Instead, he proceeds directly north, to Hana Chiru Sato's quarters, in "summer." He pushes aside her curtains, for he is, after all, her "husband," and she makes no attempt to hide herself. Quiet docility has been her trademark, and a play at excessive modesty would be vulgarly coquettish since she and Genji are no longer intimate. Genji's gaze is cruel. The robe he had sent her is subdued: without luster, without interest, as he had expected when he made a gift of it to her. It is the slight *ge ni*, "indeed," "after all" (3:141; S 411; W 469) that catches our breath as we take in Genji's unsentimental deliberation. The lady's hair, her most crucial feature, is thinning, and he wishes she would start using a switch. Genji takes this occasion to credit himself with extraordinary largesse for having been constant to such a one. The lady is out of season, but then, summer is never the season for love.[69]

Next Genji visits Tamakazura, who shares the summer quarters. (Her ambiguity is evoked by her domicile.) Her *yamabuki* robes complement her nicely; every part of her is resplendent. As if by contagion, however, her hair is a trifle thin at the edges, even though it is said that the effect is one of tidiness in her case. Tamakazura's beauty and sensible behavior are often subtly qualified in this fashion: it is her original stigma manifesting itself in different form.

Later in the day, Genji proceeds to the Akashi Lady's winter quarters in the northwest. He has a chance to study her furnishings before she appears, and he is impressed—by samples of her hand, her koto, her incense. The Akashi Lady's erotic appeal always comes from her furnishings and her skills. Here Genji is so taken that he is about to write a poem in response to one of her jottings when the lady herself appears. With a worried glance in Murasaki's direction, he decides to spend the night. A peculiar choice, perhaps, but everything is as it should be. Morning, the official time, begins in spring, the reigning season. Night ends in winter, relegated to the old year and the northwest corner, the only one of the four quarters burdened with the prosaic yet indispensable warehouses. Genji must pay tribute to them, and to the intelligence and taste they have made possible, as well as to their promise of future glory. It should come as no surprise that in this work, the lady most responsible for public power bides in the darkness of a winter night while she who basks in official daylight has but private and ephemeral sources of strength.

When the visitor-crowded days of a prosperous household during the New Year are over, Genji makes his way to the Eastern Pavilion. Poor Suetsumuhana. There is no end to her humiliation. When Genji comes calling, she is grotesquely referred to by her most formal title, Hitachi no Miya no Onkata, something to the effect of "the personage of the Prince of Hitachi" (3:147; S 413; W 473). Her caller's first unspoken observation is that her hair has not only thinned but turned gray and no longer able to bear scrutiny. Her robe, again as he had expected (*ge ni*), is unexciting, an effect coyly attributed to the wearer. Only that nose, *onhana*, with due but uncharitable honorific, is "gaily resplendent" (*[hana]yaka*, to get the pun), "unmistakable even in the mist," unlike other Heian blossoms so easily confused with the vapor (3:147; S 414; W 473). Genji sighs "in spite of himself" and draws the curtains upon her.

Next to be honored with a visit is Utsusemi. Since she took vows after the importunities of her stepson, she does not allow herself to be seen by Genji. We recall that she successfully resisted Genji's advances after a first accidental meeting in "The Broom Tree." For a woman, to be invisible is to reserve a modicum of power.

Genji's round of calls on his women has the appearance of a seigniorial survey of the grounds and, as such, is a mock courtship-in-exile. It brings to mind the rotation of women in the emperor's service, even to the favoring of those women with the most powerful backing. What does Genji do at each of his stops? The classic model, as in the *Ise*, calls for a reasonably dramatic encounter, an exchange of poems, and for closure, sexual union. In "The First Warbler" there is but the single ceremonial exchange between Genji and Murasaki, and the Akashi Lady alone "receives his favors." Mostly, Genji looks and sees.

There was a New Year's rite in the ancient court in which the emperor climbed a hilltop to survey his land. The second poem in the *Man'yōshū* has Emperor Jomei (r. 629-641) surveying his realm from the Kaguyama, a favorite site for this practice.[70] The ritual land survey probably began as a folk custom, not restricted to the beginning of the year, although it was thought that by looking in the direction of one's dwelling from an elevated point, one could augur what the year would bring.[71] The land survey, or *kunimi*, is one of the clearest examples illustrating the symbolic dimensions of the verb *miru*, "to see." Together with "hearing," "eating," and "knowing," "seeing" in archaic Japan signified possession. One scholar describes the essence of seeing as follows:

> The act of "seeing" is a means whereby one becomes fused with the life force of the [viewed] object and draws it into oneself. Hence [the expression of] possession or control can also take the form of this symbolic rite.[72]

Beyond the contexts of folk practice and court ritual, symbolic seeing manifests itself with remarkable flexibility and durability in the *Man'yōshū*, playing a part in poems of celebration, love, and mourning.[73]

The significance of seeing is also revealed in the form of voyeurism known as the *kaimami*, literally, "peeping over the fence." By the Heian period, the visibility of wellborn women was extremely restricted. For a woman to allow her face to be seen by a man was tantamount to accepting him as a lover. The romantic literary consequence was the *kaimami*, in which the unseen hero steals a glimpse of a lady through a gap in a fence or an opening in her curtains, a deed that could be termed visual rape. The woman, of course, is unaware of her exposure. The *kaimami* is the standard heroic approach to love. The *Ise* opens with a *kaimami*, and there are several celebrated examples in the *Genji*, such as the hero's first glimpse of the child Murasaki. On the other hand, "The Safflower" begins with eavesdropping rather than voyeurism. Suetsumuhana has been described to Genji as a gifted performer on the *kin no koto*, the instrument associated with princesses. Utsusemi also escapes being seen in advance. Perhaps this is the strategy developed in the *Genji* for the sake of the unlovely.[74] The normal result of the *kaimami* is for the hero to become enraptured by the stolen glimpse.

On his New Year's calls, Genji, being the master of the domain, takes his glimpses as his due. The women are pinned like butterflies beneath his cool gaze, and only the Akashi Lady, who is absent when he enters, and Utsusemi, shrouded by devotion, are spared. At the conclusion of his land-viewing poem, Emperor Jomei praises the land encompassed by his gaze, a praise that is also directed at himself as one identified with the land and its gods. The gesture is also one of propitiation, encouragement, and promise for continued good works in the year to come. Genji's tours of the Rokujōin and the Eastern Pavilion end with self-congratulation for his constant bounty.

The New Year's festivities at the Rokujōin end with the coming of singers from the Palace. They stop en route at the residence of the retired Suzaku Emperor, and when they arrive at the Rokujōin, they are elaborately feted. If we are inclined to boredom over such affairs, we should remember that Murasaki Shikibu never wastes details. The occasion provides an opportunity for Tamakazura to be introduced to Murasaki and the Akashi Princess. The ladies of the Rokujōin, like the spokes of a wheel, meet only at their center in Genji. To see Kokiden's name after so many pages have passed since its last mention (she is honored by the singers at her son's estate) is to be reminded of how the mighty have fallen. The Suzaku Emperor himself is pale but watchful. Above all, the singers' itinerary calls attention to Genji's imperial status: first the Palace, then the retired Emperor's residence, and finally, and therefore most prominently, the Rokujōin. In "The Cypress Pillar," the last of the Tamakazura chapters, the singers appear again, without, however, stopping at the Rokujōin.[75]

When spring by the calendar is a thing of the past, it flourishes miraculously in Murasaki's garden. The "Butterflies" chapter opens with another round in the spring-autumn debate. It is of course Murasaki's turn to be victorious, and Genji mounts a musical spectacle to show off her garden. He would like Akikonomu to see it in person, but her position makes that impossible. It hardly matters, since the occasion produces the players, that is, the amorous young men, that Genji has in mind for another drama. For if this lavish little event evens out the score in one aesthetic battle, it also marks the debut of Tamakazura. Her

flower, the *yamabuki*, blossoms profusely in Murasaki's gard
Akikonomu's ladies, who have been rowed over in dragon a...
phoenix boats, compose a series of poems, two of which feature
yamabuki. When Akikonomu, all too aware of defeat, makes a
characteristic retreat to religion with a reading of a sutra, Murasaki sends over eight girls, four dressed as birds carrying cherry
blossoms (her own emblem) and four dressed as butterflies carrying *yamabuki*. To this assault of secular splendor, Akikonomu
replies with a poem accusing Murasaki of erecting a barrier of
many-layered *yamabuki* between them. Tamakazura is passed
between her stepsisters before being launched upon the men.

FICTION AND COURTSHIP

The Tamakazura story begins in earnest after the spring festivities
are over. The letters pour in, giving Genji an opportunity to
lecture on the proper management of courtship by a young lady
and her attendants, in whose hands the success or failure of a
suit chiefly rests. The leading candidates are Prince Hotaru,
Genji's esthete brother; General Higekuro, uncle to the present
Crown Prince; and Kashiwagi, Tō no Chūjō's eldest son and
therefore Tamakazura's biological half brother. It is a deliciously
voyeuristic occasion for Genji. He can scrutinize letters that
would never have fallen into his hand without the lovely bait of
Tamakazura. Prince Hotaru, though close to Genji, has tended
to be secretive about affairs of the heart; Higekuro is a serious
man (a *mamebito*, an epithet also applied to Yūgiri and later to
Kaoru) and not normally associated with such pursuits. Kashiwagi is a special case: as the son of his great rival, he is also a
surrogate son to Genji, and he is naturally curious about the
young man. There is of course the interest of seeing him court
his own sister. Some day he will be enlightened on this score,
but until then, Genji will call the tune. For the reader, there is
a delectable pleasure in observing Genji study Kashiwagi's hand,
to store it in his memory for unanticipated use many years
hence. The irony is exquisite. For now, Genji intentionally engages Kashiwagi in an inappropriate courtship.

Chapter 2

Delivering his counsel to Ukon and Tamakazura, Genji oblig-
ingly urges the young woman, "think of me as that lady now
gone, treat me as your own mother" (3:173; S 426; W 487).
Tamakazura is not set to work sweeping the hearth but she is
forced to disguise her identity to entertain false suitors. They are
all false inasmuch as Genji soon reveals his own interest in her.
If it is unpleasant for Tamakazura to be courted by her own
brother (and conversely, to have to permit Yūgiri a greater intimacy than warranted), it is even more painful to be faced with
the attentions of her guardian, since there is no escaping them.
More than ever in her life, she is trapped, and her only recourse
is to fall ill.

Genji does not insist as he might have in his youth. After all,
there is the genuine problem of her identity: since the world
knows Tamakazura as his daughter, he cannot openly court her
himself. In order to do so (and thus invite complications with
Murasaki: in this Tamakazura anticipates the Third Princess), he
would have to reveal her identity to her true father, Tō no
Chūjō, and become his old friend and rival's son-in-law, thus
dragging the tale from banality to farce. His son Yūgiri has been
waging a long campaign for the same status, but Tō no Chūjō
nurses higher aspirations for his daughter Kumoinokari. Once
again, but on such different terms, Genji is subject to a passion
that must be kept secret from the world. And once again, he
seeks compensatory relief, this time by fanning the ardor of the
other suitors. Such pleasures reach their climax in the "Hotaru"
chapter.

By this time, Tamakazura can no longer be indifferent to all
her suitors. She is desperate to escape from Genji, and her desperation leads her to look not unfavorably on Prince Hotaru's
suit. One night, when he comes calling, Genji takes special
pains with the decor, much as a mother might, or a wise, trusted
servant. Upon his arrival, Tamakazura withdraws, receiving the
Prince's messages through an attendant, but Genji presses her to
move in closer. Uncertain of Genji's motives, Tamakazura fears
that she is cornered, and she is proved right. Genji releases a
swarm of fireflies he had prepared to light up her profile for his

brother's benefit. The sight is meant to plunge him into the agonies of passion.

In the *Tale of the Hollow Tree* an emperor uses fireflies to catch a glimpse of a lady he is interested in, and in the *Ise*, Minamoto no Itaru (the grandfather of the poet Shitagō, 911-983) releases fireflies into a lady's carriage in order to get a look at the occupants.[76] The *Genji* scene complicates the voyeurism, for the object is no longer a woman but a woman as she is being seen by another man. At the same time, through the elaborate preparations he has made for the presentation of Tamakazura, Genji has made himself part of the object, an extension of woman-as-target-of-vision. To wit, his own perfumes blend with the sophisticated incenses with which he has suffused the air, offering a pleasant surprise for the Prince, who had not expected so much. Here, however, we should principally retain the image of Genji as one who shows, the orchestrator of the deception, the producer of a scene apparently borrowed from other stages. (Later on, when his women are seen as Murasaki is by Yūgiri during the typhoon or upon her death, or the Third Princess by Kashiwagi during that fateful spring match of court football, he will not have staged the viewing.)

Shortly after this evening, Genji arranges for an equestrian archery event in Hana Chiru Sato's quarters. The leading courtiers are there, including some of Tamakazura's suitors, such as Prince Hotaru, and Yūgiri, who will become interested in her as soon as he discovers that she is not his sister. This time, Genji is arranging for the women, especially Tamakazura, to see. It is one of those occasions when women, on the dark side of the blinds, can look out onto the brighter world, themselves unseen except for the edges of the sleeves of their festival wear. Perhaps Genji means it to be an educational moment, a chance for Tamakazura to develop her skills of discrimination. At any rate, he himself steps out into the sunlight of midafternoon to ensure that the other men are measured against him. (He is evidently not quite ready to abandon altogether the part of actor; later, in "The Royal Outing," when he has nearly decided to enter Tamakazura in Reizei's court, he absents himself from the procession that she is sent to view.) The externally directed vision of the spectator cannot be expected to garner wisdom. Genji spends the night with Hana Chiru Sato in gentle conversation. The word used for this sort of talk is *monogatari*, the same word as that for "tale" in the *Tale of Genji*. It also suggests lovers' pillow talk,[77] but Genji and Hana Chiru Sato do not even occupy the same bed. Indeed, this fact is insisted upon, with the docile lady composing a poem, plaintive though not bitter, in which she compares herself to an iris growing on a bank where the grass is so withered that not even a pony will visit. What the talk does elicit is a statement from her that implicitly elevates Genji in comparison to both Prince Hotaru and another royal brother.

Immediately following this passage, the reading and writing of fiction—that is, *monogatari*—becomes the explicit subject of the narrative. This is what has come to be known as the *monogatari-ron*, often approximated as the art or the theory of fiction.[78] It is usually held to begin with the description of the Rokujōin ladies hard at work copying old tales and to end with the boldest of Genji's overtures to Tamakazura (3:202-206; S 436-38; W 500-502).[79] I would like to carve it out a bit more generously, with the following internal divisions:

1. The fireflies episode, in which Tamakazura is shown to Prince Hotaru.
2. The archery contest, which Tamakazura is permitted to see; the night of the contest, spent by Genji in talk with Hana Chiru Sato.
3. The Rokujōin ladies (especially Tamakazura) absorbed in reading and copying out old tales; Tamakazura trying to puzzle out her life with the aid of fiction but dissatisfied.
4. Genji holding forth on the uses and value of fiction with Tamakazura as his interlocutor.
5. Genji wooing Tamakazura by appealing to fiction to support his claims.
6. Genji discussing fiction with Murasaki, but this time being censorious and utilitarian.

Since (1) and (2) have already been discussed, let us begin with (3). The time is the Fifth Month, in the midst of the rainy season, a time of confinement, unpromising for love. It is, accordingly, a time for reading, writing, and talking: a time for tales. When the men swapped stories in "The Broom Tree," it was also to the background of falling rain. Then, a guards officer led the discussion while Genji listened, evidently dozing off for a time. Genji, in the throes of significant action, did not talk. Now, with no action to speak of, he has much to say.

The ladies of the Rokujōin rely upon their illustrated tales to while away an especially long rainy season. The Akashi Lady, gifted in these endeavors "too" (small words, like ants, bear surprising weight: this one emphasizes the talented lady's well-known sobriety—we do not associate her with frivolous fiction), prepares exquisite works for the daughter being reared by Murasaki. Tamakazura is "all the more" absorbed in these tales. "All the more" because given her background, she would be unaccustomed to such fanciful items (3:202, n. 4). But Tamakazura seeks more than diversion. She is in deadly earnest (even working up a sweat, as we shall see), wanting to comprehend her own peculiar life by finding one similar to it in fiction. She cannot. Only one episode, from the *Tale of Sumiyoshi*, reminds her of her own history; it recounts the heroine's narrow escape from rape by an accountant, an unappealing fellow nearly seventy years old. Tamakazura, who reads without being able to determine if what she reads is a true or false representation, compares the incident to her own escape from the Higo man. Of course, we cannot help detecting Genji's image as well.

Tamakazura finds herself in the midst of a marriage plot of classic proportions, complete with rival suitors (reminiscent of the five vying for the Heavenly Princess's hand in the *Tale of the Bamboo Cutter*, or the competition for Atemiya in the *Tale of the Hollow Tree*). This is overwhelming enough, of course, but the situation is all the more bewildering, for the plot has been hatched by Genji both as a direct means of resolving his own identity (should he take her for himself) and as a vicarious one (should he be content with watching others fight for her and finally, with rewarding one of them).

At the beginning of the chapter, Tamakazura finds herself ruing once again the loss of her mother. Now we are in a better position to understand why the stepdaughter (i.e., the motherless daughter) is the paradigmatic heroine: she has no recourse to a prior truth. Courtship is her great test, and even Tamakazura, albeit in rudimentary form, anticipates, from across the gulf of centuries and cultures, the "post-Austen" heroine's problems in choosing a suitor and therefore her own identity.[80] Without any worthy advisers, Tamakazura turns to fiction, a characteristic recourse for women even, and especially, in Heian Japan, where it was publicly held to be fit for their consumption alone. The *Sambō Ekotoba*, an illustrated collection of edifying Buddhist narratives compiled for the enlightenment of a princess (note the provision of pictures) by the scholar Minamoto no Tamenori in 984, observes in its Preface that fictional tales are

> but for the amusement of women. They flourish in greater profusion than the grasses upon the wooded graves of old, they are as numerous as the grains of sand upon the rocky strand. To creatures that lack the gift of speech they give words; to insentient objects they impart emotions. . . . Their words flow forth unchecked as the flotsam upon the sea; they are not rooted in truth. . . .[81]

It is the last observation, of course, that underlies all the others, the timeless source of damnation for all fiction: it is not rooted in truth.

Since it is that form of fiction called the *monogatari* that absorbs Tamakazura and attracts Genji's criticism, let us look at the associations of this term before proceeding further. The questions are even more intractable than in the case of the term *mononoke*, the possessing spirit, and I cannot attempt to mediate the differences within Japanese scholarship but will indicate some of the important strands:[82] the second element of the word, *katari*, is related to *katadori*, "modeling." *Katari* seems to have at its core the "representation" or "mimesis" not of a thing but of an event in time. *Mono*, by contrast, is an atemporal element. The yoking of the two in *monogatari* might be seen as being at once the substantiation of the fugitive and the mobilization of the static.[83] Adjacent to *katari* is *katarai*, which ranges in meaning from intimate talk to sexual intercourse, from confession to persuasion and deception. This sense of unanchored language use is reinforced by a genealogy of *mono* as spirit, especially the fearful ancestral guardian of a clan not one's own, and from there, that which is other, and eventually, lesser. *Monogatari* is even used in the *Genji* to describe the insubstantial "speech" of infants.[84]

So, Genji intrudes upon a Tamakazura earnestly engaged in the questions of fiction and life. Women, it seems to him, are born to be deceived, especially by those tales containing precious little truth (*makoto*). Worse yet, their addiction sets them to copying at the cost of letting their hair get matted in the heat of the summer rains. These rains, *samidare*, are juxtaposed to the locks' falling out of place (*kami midaruru*, 3:203; S 437; W 500), with *midare* inevitably adding a tinge of licentiousness to disorderly locks. The falsehood that Tamakazura is said to be unable to distinguish from truth (*makoto*) is called *itsuwari*. These forms of truth and falsehood may be diagnosed by the presence or absence of verbal consistency (or, in other words, whether or not they meet propositional requirements), whereas the falsehood designated by the term *soragoto* (suggesting emptiness) has an absoluteness independent of language.[85] Genji, in the very act of accusing women of susceptibility to deception, artfully and necessarily practices a kind of fiction himself: *itsuwari* in part designates rhetoricity.

Genji pursues the argument on a more conciliatory note: without such verbal fabrications, how could one while away the time? (It is useful that he should recognize pleasure as an end for fiction, and moreover gracious of him to make the statement general, but for the women who were the intended consumers of fiction, the vicarious life in duplicitous words was the true life.) He proposes two types (call them genres) of falsehoods (*itsuwaridomo*, plural): the realistic and the fantastic. Simply by pursuing this inquiry, he is according greater and greater legitimacy to the illegitimate. Perhaps he senses as much, for he suddenly leaps to the attack: surely these tales come from lips accustomed to uttering rank untruths—this time, *soragotodomo*.

Tamakazura does not let this pass. It is because he, Genji, is in the habit of fabricating (producing *itsuwari*)—witness her own lot—that he can make such claims. She, for one, had believed the tales to contain only true statements (*makoto*). Should we take this simply to be another indication of her naiveté? Perhaps, but we must also recognize what underlies her response. Is it not that she finds the events recounted in her stories more plausible, in light of her knowledge of life, than the parodic and even grotesque fiction Genji has imposed on her, to be daughter and lover at once? Trapped in Genji's fiction-in-life, she is inspired to champion lives-in-fiction. Which is also to say that she is pointing the finger at Genji's abuse of rhetoricity, at his attempt to translate it with impunity into life such that it becomes mere trickery.

Her prim earnestness leads Genji, still smiling, to embark on a full-scaled apology for fiction, corresponding to (4) above. The passage is a dense yet seamless combination of parody and earnest polemic. "From the age of the gods," opens Genji in a grand imitation of the *Kokinshū* Preface, and through it, Chinese poetics as well (3:204; S 437; W 501).[86] If Japanese poetry needed to borrow the authority of Chinese poetic practice to establish its credentials, then the *monogatari*, a twice-removed stepchild, must borrow on that borrowed authority. Next, in a distant echo of Aristotle, Genji asserts that histories tell but "part" of the story (*[kata]soba*, 3:204; S 437; W 501). In fact, it is fiction, to which he had just a moment before been willing to give but a "part of his heart" (*[kata]gokoro*, 3:203; S 437; W 501), that gives the details "correctly." The authoritative word is *michimichishiku*, "in accordance with the Way," used in "The Broom Tree" with reference to the "Three Histories and the Five Classics."[87] Not only is Confucianism, a model of propriety for both the conduct of the state and its recording (in history), stood on its head by Genji in the service of fiction, but he does so amidst the proliferating play of words.

The argument moves on to the motivating impulse behind the writing of *monogatari*, the famous argument that authors cannot bear not to transmit certain things, whether good or bad. This passage calls to mind the opening of the *Gossamer Years*, in which the diarist proclaims her need to write against the lies (*soragoto*) of fiction.[88] There is brash courage in her work, im-

passioned self-obsession relieved by bumbling insight and aesthetic vision that we must always be generous and intelligent
enough to applaud, for she was charting terra incognita with
untried tools: the recording of a woman's life in Japanese prose.
Nevertheless, Michitsuna's Mother must be counted an even
more naive reader of fiction than Tamakazura for being able to
discern only mere lies therein.

In addition to the diary, Genji's apology seeks once again to
borrow from the authority of poetry by mimicry. The *Kokinshū*
Preface's canonical description of the nature of Japanese poetry
suggests that it bursts forth like song according to whatever the
human subject sees or hears. I have cited the opening before,
but let me take it a few steps further:

> The Japanese poem makes of the human heart its seeds,
> which grow into myriad leaves of words. Living in a world
> abounding in events, human beings express what they hold
> in their hearts according to the things they see and hear.
> When we hear the warbler singing amidst the blossoms or
> the voice of the water-dwelling frog, we ask, what living
> thing has not its song?[89]

The Preface strategically simplifies that which it shows to be
complex. Spontaneity—the effect of transparent correspondence
between subject and object and language—is at once claimed
and achieved by the juxtaposition of human beings to warblers
and frogs. The *monogatari* comes from the sights one cannot tire
of seeing (that one cannot exhaust with the seeing), the sounds
that linger even when they have faded. There is simultaneously
a sense of comprehensiveness (the writer emphasizes the good or
the bad, depending on the desired effect upon the reader) and
inexhaustibility about fiction in Genji's description.

By contrast, that which is "bad" is never admitted by the ideo-
logues of *waka*, of poetry narrowly conceived as Japanese poetry. The presence of excess, the admission of evil as well as
good, the use of language that does not simply transmit "things
as they are"—these are the hallmarks of the land of fiction,
where truth is the absorbing consequence of a complicated fit
between subject, object, and language. The *Genji* as fiction may

be described as the history of a writer's wrestlings with, coming to costly possession of, all the languages in her life, oral and written, past and present, Chinese and Japanese, masculine and feminine, poetic, philosophical, and religious.

And so Genji observes, toward the end of his disquisition, that foreign or native, old or new, fictions cannot be dismissed as a pack of lies (*soragoto*). Fiction is a particular arrangement of words among other arrangements—histories, poetry, diaries, and even Buddhist parables, the last and most serious example adduced by Genji. As such, it might well seem a tissue of deceit, but when that tissue is scrutinized as to warp and woof, seen as a weaving as well as a thing woven (much as the thingness of *mono* is undone and reconstituted in the time of *katari*, or narrative), it becomes recognizable as both similar to and distinct from the other arrangements. It is similarity that Genji reveals in the extended comparisons of prose fiction with other forms of writing. Of course, what he seeks to borrow is the historical, political, and moral prestige of propositional knowledge such that he might clothe that naked stripling, experiential knowledge, in the form of prose fiction. In the very process, however, both by argument and especially by example, he deftly touches the more venerable discourses with the dread infection of rhetoricity. In effect, Genji demonstrates both the contingency of the authority accruing to any form of knowledge and the refractions occurring as any form of knowledge is expressed and produced in language. Where fiction parts company from its sister discourses lies in its impetuous embrace of these conditions, so that "the novel changes reality into fictions, makes lies into *effective truths*, and perilously calls attention to its own processes, and reverses them"[90] (emphasis mine). And to give it all enough fixity such that successive generations of readers may pursue this process for themselves, fluid *katari* is embodied in *mono*. We must not be deaf to the authorial *cri de coeur* in this passage, passionately claiming a distinctive truthfulness for the *monogatari*.

Having scaled these heights, Genji makes an abrupt descent, reducing fiction to an instrument of seduction. He parodies the Tamakazura who could not find her image among literary heroines: surely there is no fool like him in her tales. Enough of discretion: let them create a matchless *monogatari* in life. Tamakazura is unconvinced: they will only be feeding the gossips, she retorts. Genji presses his case, charging her with unfilial conduct and even invoking the Buddha to enjoin obedience. In the end he desists from any action bolder than stroking her hair.

The next scene shows us Genji with Murasaki who was also once his "daughter," having been abducted by him and confined to the Nijōin. Reared by her adoptive father to become an exemplary woman and an exemplary heroine, she, too, is caught in the spell of fiction fever. When Genji interrupts her, she sits rapt in an image that could have come from her own past, an illustration of a young girl in sound sleep. Interestingly enough, the passage, which had opened by respectfully referring to her as "Murasaki no Ue," shifts at this point and calls her a "woman." Why? Is it to remind us of Murasaki's now distant initiation by Genji, when she was transformed from daughter into lover in one unpleasant night? And thereby draw attention to the Genji who now plays at seduction, who makes a fiction of seduction? A Genji who is now the anxious father of a daughter for whom he has high hopes, whom he would therefore shield from fictions of seduction? Genji warns Murasaki to be careful about the selection of stories read to the little Princess. Properly used, fiction can serve a valuable didactic function, he cautions.

From the fireflies episode to this final scene, Genji has variously served as manipulator of and apologist for fiction. He has not, however, been an actor within—a state of affairs shown emblematically by his failing or electing not to perform as lover. This surely signals a change in the terms of herohood within the tale as a whole. For the amorous hero (in this case, Don Juan),

faithfulness is tantamount to an acceptance of the end, of *death*, whereas "falling in love" . . . constitutes precisely a new *birth*. The passage from one woman to another . . . is thus explained as the necessity of transcending death by the experience of rebirth.[91]

Genji, we should hasten to add, is not about to succumb to faithfulness. Rather, he stands at the threshold of another birth, but not simply another instance in the series experienced by the amorous hero. In this he has already been anticipated by the heroines, for whom "significant action" has long consisted of "stories and storytelling," of the investigation of the self in fiction. It remains to be seen not only whether Genji will cross the threshold, but how he will engage with the understanding growing within the *Genji* itself that "the self has been identified, in novels, with the feminine."[92]

VARIETIES OF CARNATION:
THE LADY OF ŌMI AND TAMAKAZURA

At the end of the "Fireflies" chapter, Tō no Chūjō has a dream auguring the discovery of a daughter. His circles have been rife with rumors of Genji's new daughter Tamakazura, and it is easy to imagine how they would whet his appetite to share in the limelight. The dream that announces the coming of a much-awaited child is a typical instance of communication from the sacred other world to the profane human one. Tō no Chūjō's dream, by both its circumstances and its absurd outcome, is a perfect parody. Desirous of a certain outcome, he dreams it and attains it. So much for the sacred plot in which dreams augur the coming of extraordinary children.

The Lady of Ōmi, the treasured child in question, is extraordinary enough, but before we see how, we should consider why her father is so eager to take her in. The question hovering behind this chapter is, "What purpose do daughters serve?" and its corollary, "How can they be made fit for this purpose?" For a man like Tō no Chūjō the single worthy destiny for a daughter is to bear a crown prince and become empress, thus assuring the success of her father's political career. To this end Tō no Chūjō has already been blessed with many daughters. Yet the results have failed to live up to his expectations. His oldest and most promising daughter has lost to Genji's adoptive daughter Akikonomu. Kumoinokari, on whom he had pinned great hopes, has been damaged by a puppy-love affair with Genji's son Yūgiri. He is still holding her in reserve, denying her hand to Yūgiri, but her worth remains in question. The Lady of Ōmi, a creature whose existence he had forgotten until the appearance of Tamakazura, turns out to be outrageously unfit—as well she might be, being a daughter by a lesser woman from the provinces. This is one of the ironic dimensions of the "miraculous" dream: the Lady of Ōmi is actually an ordinary, biological daughter, the natural consequence of a night quickly forgotten. Of course, the daughter Tō no Chūjō would like to have is Tamakazura, but he is ignorant of his own paternity—another parodic twist in the child-granting dream. Genji is not only a stepmother but a wicked fairy who steals the long-awaited beautiful child.

A look at the score card shows that for every one of Tō no Chūjō's disappointments, Genji has gained a point. For a man with only one natural daughter, Genji has done exceptionally well. He has defeated, damaged, or stolen his rival's daughters—all with apparent impunity. By falling in love with his adoptive daughters before putting them to use, he has even managed to keep his heroism largely intact. Compare him with Tō no Chūjō, who struts about, an irascible if fond parent, impatient with his daughters' inability to further his career: Genji dallies with Tamakazura in suggestively elegant settings.

The incidents in the "Wild Carnations" chapter read like textbook illustrations of things that can go wrong with daughters. The Lady of Ōmi is egregious, but she is not the only offending example. When Tō no Chūjō walks into his daugher Kumoinokari's quarters, he catches her napping with her ladies. Flushed with sleep, she is beautiful, but her father, recalling her indiscretions with Yūgiri, is appalled by her laxness.

Moving on to his new-found daughter's rooms, he finds her vigorously engaged in a game of backgammon. The ensuing exchange between minister and daughter, which produces such items as an "honorable chamber pot" (3:236; S 450; W 519), is unmatched in the entire *Genji*. The young woman is touchingly pleased to be united with her father after all these years; but it is not just enthusiasm that makes her speech objectionably rapid. She herself explains it as a congenital defect attributable to the presence of another hasty tongue on the premises when she was born. It is not only the pace of her speech but its semantic vigor that is objectionable. She has failed to master the art of rhetorical subtlety that makes life comfortable for Heian aristocrats.[93]

When it comes to poetry, her case is even more outrageous than that of poor Suetsumuhana with whom she has so much in common.[94] The latter offends with her excessive deference to outmoded composition books and a monothematic bent, an unfortunate predilection for Chinese robes as a sign of a lover's neglect. The Lady of Ōmi, writing to her half sister (the unimpeachable one in Reizei's court), produces the following:

Kusawakami	Since the grass is young
Hitachi no Ura no	at Point How-Do-You-Do
Ikagasaki	in Hitachi Bay,
ikaga aimin	how might I meet you,
Tago no uranami	waves of Tago Bay.

(3:240; S 452; W 452)

In order to convey her eagerness to meet her sister and demonstrate her worthiness as kin, the Lady of Ōmi produces an exuberant jumble of poetic place names from scattered regions. One of her sister's ladies gleefully answers,

Hitachi naru	O waves, arise,
Suruga no Umi no	in Suma Bay
Suma no Ura ni	of the Sea of Suruga
nami tachiideyo	in the province of Hitachi:
Hakozaki no matsu	the pines of Hakozaki are
	pining.

(3:242; S 453; W 523)

The Lady of Ōmi packs in three place names; her sister's attendant does her one better.[95]

The Lady of Ōmi is everything a heroine cannot be. Not only is her speech clamorous, her poetry scandalous, and her makeup vulgar, but she initiates a campaign on her own behalf to enter court service and horrifies her brothers by making an overture to Yūgiri. By failing to become a heroine, she demonstrates how heroines are made. She is perhaps the most extreme lesson offered by the *Genji* in the conventionality of convention. So much so that she ceases to be merely negative. She bursts through the curtains and screens of dark Heian rooms and airs them out with bracing country winds. She represents the intrusion of another world, another genre—a brief intrusion because such resounding laughter cannot be accommodated by the tale. (We must await Ukifune for a more acceptable and, finally, more serious alternative.)

Of course, the laughter is not entirely at the Lady of Ōmi's expense. It is enjoyable to see Tō no Chūjō reaping his rewards. He mutters about Kashiwagi—and not unjustly, for it is he who bears responsibility for the eruption of this creature into their decorous lives. The father's dream was quickly followed by the appearance of a candidate. Kashiwagi, the oldest son, was dispatched to verify paternity, just as he was busy pursuing his other half sister Tamakazura. Later, when he is disabused of that illusion, he will embark on the fatal pursuit of Genji's wife, the Third Princess. Shall we say that he is a bungler, one who unfailingly attaches himself to the wrong woman? A dream foretells the coming of a new sister. Since such dreams are meant to be believed, when a woman announces that she is his sister, Kashiwagi assents. Genji's mysterious new daughter is rumored to be beautiful and talented, the perfect object of pursuit by a young man like himself. Kashiwagi instantly joins the race. There are rumors that the retired Emperor wants to see his daughter married. A princess is ipso facto desirable; Kashiwagi sets his heart on attaining her and cannot desist even when she is given to another. (It should be admitted that Kashiwagi shadows Genji in all these attachments. Genji bungles in pursuing Suetsumuhana, and he is every bit the victim of the imperial delusion in wedding the Third Princess. The difference is that Genji is never portrayed either as a bungler or as a tragic hero.)

Thus unwittingly, Kashiwagi draws two half sisters into the same circle. Their sorority is exquisitely emphasized in the chapter title, "Wild Carnations," a reference to the flower that signified both Tō no Chūjō's erotic attachment to Yūgao and its fruit, Tamakazura, in the distant reaches of "The Broom Tree" chapter. The Lady of Ōmi and her mother are a parodic version of that pair. Indeed, the Lady of Ōmi's coming serves to put the finishing touches on Tamakazura as heroine. Every suspicion of

rusticity attaches to the joyously shrieking creature. Tamakazura
even takes music lessons from Genji (though hesitantly: *she* does
not forget where she was raised). The music-making both draws
her to Genji and intensifies her wish to meet her true father, an
acknowledged master on her chosen instrument, the *wagon*.
Tamakazura is sealed and stamped as a credible product for
the roles she must play. The Lady of Ōmi's coming revives the
issue of daughters as tools, an issue we might have forgotten with
respect to Tamakazura. The latter has certainly fulfilled Genji's
expectations of voyeuristic pleasure. He has yet to devise a
means of using her to practical advantage, and the project becomes increasingly difficult as his own attachment mounts. Mo-
mentary decisions to yield her to a Hotaru or a Higekuro always
give way in her presence. What, in fact, can he do with her?
Even were he to wed her formally, she would never become
Murasaki's equal. The older, more objective Genji has the mar-
gin of leisure to sympathize with such a plight, to acknowledge
that it would be better to have the exclusive love of a lesser man.
Yet he cannot bear the thought of her absence. He finally hits
upon the strategy of marrying her off but keeping her "at home."
In an age when it was customary for men of the upper aristocracy
to visit their wives at their fathers' homes (at least in the early
stages of marriage), Genji maintains three structures, the Nijōin,
the Rukojōin, and the Eastern Pavilion, in which to house all
his women. Now, as a "father," he thinks of turning the conventional form of marriage to his own advantage:

> Why not keep her here and see to her needs? I could steal
> over from time to time, chat with her and cheer myself.
> She is so unworldly now that it makes everything difficult.
> No matter if "the gatekeeper be strong," once she begins to
> understand things, I will no longer need to feel sorry for her
> and shall be able to persuade her of my feelings. Then,
> even if there are people about, it won't matter.
>   (3:227; S 446; W 514)

Genji's ardor is unmasked as naked desire. The allowance made
for Tamakazura's inexperience measures the distance he has trav-

eled since the rape of the young Murasaki, but the cool calculation is unsettling in a hero.

AUTUMN IN THE ROKUJŌIN

If the Rokujōin's humanly natural order was shown in harmonious operation in "The First Warbler," "The Typhoon" chapter, its opposite number, uses nature in the form of an autumn storm to unravel that order. In the last round of the spring-autumn contest, spring and Murasaki triumphed. Now it is Akikonomu's turn. What does it mean that this pious and retiring lady's moment should take such a disquieting form? Since her last victory occasioned no such disruption, it must be reasoned that something unsettling is wanted. There is unobtrusive mention of the anniversary of her father's death. We must remember that her father is thought to have been a deposed crown prince, the sort of man who could only have died in bitterness, and hence a fitting emblem of potential disorder. The unseating that takes place in this chapter is different in kind, however, from the removal of a crown prince. It is Yūgiri's usurping the power of vision from his father.

The chief target of Yūgiri's eyes is his stepmother Murasaki. If Genji's gaze during his New Year's calls was clinical, Yūgiri's is hungry. The chaos following the storm affords him his first glimpse of this fabled beauty. The scene invites comparison with Genji's first sight of the child Murasaki in "Lavender." Yūgiri, on his way to pay a courtesy call to his father, pauses before his and Murasaki's windswept residence without making his presence known:

> From above a small screen in the eastern gallery, he noticed a door left afar, and with nothing particular in mind, he looked in. He could see that there were many women about. Yūgiri stopped and stood without making a sound. Because the wind had been so violent, the screens had been folded and put to the side. He could see, his gaze unob-

structed, all the way to the verandah, where there sat a
person—ah, it had to be she. So noble and pure, her beauty
seemed to suffuse him. It was as if he were seeing, through
the haze of a spring dawn, a birch cherry blossoming in
wild profusion. Chagrin swept over him as he looked. She
radiated gentleness. There was no one like her. Her ladies
were struggling to hold down the blinds. All of a sudden
she laughed. It was wonderful. No doubt she could not bear
to leave the flowers to go indoors. Although her ladies were
all splendidly attired, each in her own fashion, he could
not find it in himself to transfer his gaze.

(3:256; S 458; W 528)

Yūgiri understands for the first time why, all his life, his father
has kept him at arm's length from his stepmother.

Twice more in this chapter, Yūgiri has intimations of Murasaki's presence: the following morning he hears snatches of his
father's bedroom talk, and later he catches a glimpse of her
sleeve as he waits in attendance upon his father. (Can we fathom
how momentous such occasions were, prodigal as we are with
our gestures and all but unthinking about our audibility and visibility? The sight of Murasaki in the aftermath of the storm stirs
Yūgiri to the core of his being; he will keep the memory carefully
locked for fourteen years, when her death will afford him one
more precious glimpse.) Genji, ever sensitive, guesses that his
son has seen.

The tranformed Yūgiri proceeds to study the other women in
his life: his grandmother and her sober household, or Hana
Chiru Sato, whose meager charms cause him to concur in his
father's estimate of his own generosity. Sent by his father to call
on Empress Akikonomu, he finds her garden in beautiful disarray. Akikonomu has sent out young girls to place insect cages
among the windblown grasses, thus producing a tableau from
the effects of disorder. It calls to mind the snow scene Fujitsubo
is said to have arranged (2:481-82; S 357; W 395). We learn that
just as the boy Genji was with Fujitsubo, so the child Yūgiri had
been permitted a degree of intimacy with Akikonomu and her
ladies.

Yūgiri witnesses one other scene that nearly rivals the glimpse of Murasaki for dramatic impact. One of his father's stops on his post-typhoon tour of inspection is of course at Tamakazura's. The new Yūgiri is bold: he lifts an obstructing curtain to catch his father in shockingly intimate pose with Tamakazura. Genji, who had so recently produced scenes from a love story featuring Tamakazura and another man for his own gratification, is now witnessed by his son as he acts in his own confused love story. Yūgiri being the proper young man that he is hesitates to form conclusions; but he is bewildered, for he has been taught to regard Tamakazura as his sister.

Transgressing on his father's domain, appraising it and ravishing it, Yūgiri comes of age. Seeing his father with Tamakazura enables Yūgiri to step out of the fictional cradle in which he had been kept. Now he can see for himself. And, able to see, he is enabled to speak—to formulate in language the images that define and control his father's women. Murasaki is the birch cherry in spring, Tamakazura the *yamabuki* at twilight, and the Akashi Princess, wisteria. Now, Yūgiri does not invent these associations. He draws from an established vocabulary and charges the selections with the energy of his awakened sensations. The selections are ratified by Genji in the second "New Herbs" chapter, when he looks in on his women as they hold a private musical fest with Yūgiri, who this time cannot see (4:183-84; S 602; W [649]). It is one indication of reversed authority that Genji adopts what might be called his son's world view.[96]

For all this, the symbolic character of Yūgiri's new-found power has conflicting implications. In the end, it is but metaphoric violation that takes place in the Tamakazura chapters. This is a reflection of the diminution in scale of external action in the Rokujōin world, an effect buttressed by the deliberately confining use of poetic order. Yūgiri only sees Murasaki, and the forbidden love he is actually pursuing is a mere minister's daughter. It must be stressed, however, that reduction in scale does not imply sterility. This outward diminution is preparatory to an increased interiority in the latter portions of the work.

If, moreover, the Rokujōin's significance is to be gauged rhetorically, then rhetorical disruption can be deemed fatal. It is characteristic of Murasaki Shikibu's economy that the same structure that supports sterile order is also used to produce fertile chaos. The autumn chapter comes at its appointed position, and the strong winds are characteristic of the season. And yet the tale appears to be modifying the poetic yoke to which it had submitted itself. Although autumn winds are a stock feature of Heian poetry, their destructive force is never so prominent as in this chapter. Indeed, the word *nowaki*, "typhoon," does not appear once in any of the first three imperial anthologies, the *Kokinshū*, the *Gosenshū*, and the *Shūishū*. Its history in the *Genji* itself is revealing: it first appears in the scenes following Genji's mother's death and again upon Murasaki's death.[97] The institution and the individual at stake here are of course the Rokujōin and Murasaki. The winds physically impair some of the Rokujōin structures. Murasaki's death is portended in a number of ways: she is losing to Akikonomu seasonally, as she will be at the time of her death; she is seen by Yūgiri, as she will be upon her death; and Genji's courtship of Tamakazura foreshadows his marriage to the Third Princess. (Like Tamakazura, the Third Princess was not intended to live at the Rokujōin; there is no room for her in the four-season design, and on that basis alone she constitutes a disruptive force.)

Perhaps Yūgiri's vision of his father with Tamakazura constitutes the event of the greatest immediate import. It implies the revelation of the deception at the heart of the poetic structure of the Rokujōin. As this deception is disclosed, time, cyclically arrested, inevitably resumes its forward motion.

TAMAKAZURA: THE STOLEN PRIZE

Following the intrusion of outdoor forces in "The Typhoon," "The Royal Outing" chapter sends the Rokujōin world, or specifically Tamakazura as its representative, outdoors to watch the Reizei Emperor's expedition to Oharano. Genji is conspicuously absent. Even as his appetite for Tamakazura mounts, he is forced to recognize that he cannot keep her for himself. Thinking he might repeat the Akikonomu solution and enter her in Reizei's court, he sends her out to have a look at his son. Tamakazura is permitted to see, but as before, under Genji's aegis. Nearly all her suitors are there, but the Emperor far outshines them and Tamakazura is smitten. This must qualify as a source of vicarious pleasure for Genji, for the Reizei Emperor is thought to resemble him perfectly.

As he prepares to relinquish her, Genji is obliged to give her an official identity. This necessitates a reconciliation with Tō no Chūjō, who is requested to preside at Tamakazura's coming-of-age ceremonies. As was the case with Akikonomu, Tamakazura is already in her early twenties and far too old for initiation by normal standards. In any case, once the ceremony is held, marriage is imminent, and Tamakazura finds herself more pressed than ever.

Taken as Tamakazura is with Reizei, entering his service will be awkward. Her half sister is already there, as well as Akikonomu, an adoptive sister. It is not altogether out of the question since, in her case, the position of Principal Handmaid is not to involve personal services.[98] In the meanwhile her true brother Kashiwagi has become fraternal, but Yūgiri, mindful of that shocking scene, attempts to court her. Prince Hotaru and a certain Higekuro continue to press ardent suit. She cannot of course trust Genji, and she does not know her true father well enough to confide in him. No wonder that she wishes, once again, for a mother to guide and protect her.

Just when it is decided that she should take the position at court, she falls into Higekuro's hands. This development is reported as a fait accompli in the startling opening to "The Cypress Pillar" chapter, where we are abruptly shown Genji counseling restraint to Higekuro in spreading news of his triumph. Genji of course had just reconciled himself to Tamakazura's going to Reizei and even given her an opportunity to look at and fall in love with him. How, then, did the solemn and unprepossessing Higekuro score his extraordinary coup? In that same opening passage, we find him paying homage to one Bennomoto as being the equal of the Buddah of Ishiyama Temple. Bennomoto is one of Tamakazura's attendants. Had he not won her over, Higekuro would never have had his way with Tamakazura—a dramatic instance of the power servants have over their mistresses' lives. We cannot imagine, for instance, that Ukon, who nursed other fantasies for Tamakazura, would have granted Higekuro access.

"The Cypress Pillar" comes as an appropriate if unexpected conclusion to the Tamakazura series: covering the space of one year, from winter to the following autumn, it serves as a rapid recapitulation and coda to the leisurely chapters from "The Jeweled Chaplet" through "The Royal Outing." It not only reexamines the themes of the Tamakazura series but reviews earlier concerns and anticipates future events.

Higekuro's conquest of Tamakazura echoes Genji's theft of Murasaki. Murasaki was a child, and therefore Genji's deed was a literal kidnapping, executed even as it had been decided that she should live with her father Prince Hyōbu. Tamakazura's story is an adult version of Murasaki's. What makes things interesting is that Higekuro's wife, whom Tamakazura displaces, is Murasaki's stepsister. She, too, is the daughter of Prince Hyōbu, only by his official wife, the woman who made life unpleasant for Murasaki's mother (much as Tō no Chūjō's official wife drove Yūgao into hiding). Prince Hyōbu and his wife have another daughter who, like Tō no Chūjō's, has suffered from Akikonomu's victory at court. Therefore, Prince Hyōbu's wife has reason enough to be ill-disposed toward Murasaki and Genji when "their" daughter Tamakazura drives her daughter from her husband Higekuro's house. The incensed mother indulges in indecorous ranting, in the fashion of that other stepmother, Kokiden, at the time she discovered Genji's carryings-on with her sister Oborozukiyo. From the storm of words unleashed by her stepmother, Murasaki emerges guilty for her stepsister's misfortune. The Prince, of a more pragmatic if not philosophical temper, attributes it to his own failure to side with Genji at the time of his exile.

This previously unemphasized relationship of Murasaki to her stepsister (known only as "Higekuro's wife") grows into something more than a byproduct of a jealous stepmother's rage, for Higekuro's wife's suffering foreshadows Murasaki's agony in the "New Herbs" chapters. "The Cypress Pillar" represents a particularly interesting moment in the relationship of the minor to the major chapters.

In the meanwhile, Higekuro grows anxious to remove his prize to his own house—for many reasons, not the least of which is that at the Rokujōin he is a literalist (one version of *mamebito*) in a palace of rhetoric. Although he intends a peaceful coexistence at his own estate, he fears that his official wife may be uncooperative, not only for the usual reasons but because she has been sickly and prone to spirit possession. Understandably enough, Higekuro is anxious lest a possession scene displease his already none-too-ardent bride.

One evening, as he prepares to leave to visit Tamakazura at the Rokujōin, he makes an unusual effort to reason with his wife. Perhaps conquest has loosened his tongue. The going is difficult, however, and he is anxious to get back to his lovely young bride before the threatening skies make it impossible. Because his wife is in one of her rare subdued moods, he finds it particularly awkward to make haste. Let us see how he maneuvers. As he weighs his departure, he thinks that

he would be conspicuous if he were to wander out under such skies, and that would be a shame for her [his wife]. If only she were smoldering with jealousy, he could meet fire with fire, but there she was, gentle and composed, claiming his pity. What could he do? He went out to the verandah, where the shutters were still raised, and gazed out.

His wife, who had been studying him, said, almost as if to encourage him, "How unfortunate that it should snow. How will you make your way, with the night growing late?" It was all over. There was no point in restraining him. Her evident resolve made her pitiful.

"How can I leave on a night like this," he began, then continued, "But still. . . . People do not yet know the depths of my feelings, they will start rumors, and the Ministers will get wind of them and that would be unfortunate. I should not break off my visits now, it would put her in a sad position. Calm yourself, and bear with me to the end.

Once I bring her over here we can be more at ease. When you are as you are now, all thought of dividing my affections disappears. I find you very touching indeed."

To which his wife replied, "Even if you stay, knowing that your thoughts are elsewhere makes it hard for me to endure. If you leave but think of me from time to time, then the ice might melt from my sleeve." Her manner was composed.[99]

She sent for the incense burner and bade her women perfume his sleeves. She herself was clad in everyday clothes from which the starch had worn off. Thin and frail, she was altogether woeful in her dejection. Her eyes, red and puffy from weeping, were not pleasing, but at moments like these when he found her genuinely pitiful, Higekuro could not fault her but chided his own heart for roving after all these months and years. And yet, his eagerness mounting, he sent for a small burner himself and began to perfume the insides of his sleeves. Sighing pointedly, he patted and tugged at his robes, now pleasantly soft. He was no match for the peerless Genji, but he cut a manly figure, and was even awe-inspiring, so little did he seem like a commoner.

His men could be heard muttering. "It seems to have stopped snowing. It must be getting late." They were trying to be discreet, but the sound of their coughs could only be meant to hasten him. "What have things come to," moaned Chūjō and Moku [women of the household], and they lay down whispering to each other. The lady herself was a sad and sweet figure as she leaned upon an armrest, evidently holding herself in, but suddenly she rose, snatched the big incense burner from under its cover, and before anyone knew what was happening, she approached his lordship from behind and poured the contents over him. For a moment he was stunned and helpless. His eyes and nose were filled with powdery ashes. He tried to brush himself off, but the air swirled with ashes, and he had no choice but to remove his robes.   (3:354-57; S 497-98; W 572-73)

When Genji takes the Third Princess as an official wife in "New Herbs, Part Two," he and Murasaki also have a long history as a couple behind them. Like Higekuro, Genji worries about seeming neglectful to the new bride's relations during the first nights of the marriage:

> For the first three days, he dutifully spent the night with the Princess. Over the years Murasaki had grown unaccustomed to such separations. Try as she did to steel herself, she could not help feeling forlorn. Lost to the world, she became ever more intent upon scenting Genji's robes. From without, she was as beautiful and sweet as ever.
>
> Why did I let myself be persuaded to let a stranger in, thought Genji. I have only my frivolity and faintheartedness to blame. . . . It never seems to have occurred to my brother to think of Yūgiri, who is so sensible despite his youth. So Genji berated himself. Turning tearful, he pleaded, "You will forgive me just one more night, won't you? It simply can't be helped. If I ever neglect you again, I shall be overcome with self-loathing. But even so . . . if His Majesty the retired Emperor were to hear rumors. . . ." His confusion and anguish were evident.
>
> Smiling faintly, Murasaki replied, "If you cannot decide on the proper thing to do, how am I to judge? What is to come of all this. . . ."
>
> She resisted his efforts to draw her into conversation. Genji lay down, chin in hand. She drew the ink stone to her and began to write.

Me ni chikaku	My world changes
utsureba kawaru	before my very eyes:
yo no naka o	I had trusted it
ikusue tōku	to endure
tanomikeru kana	into distant years.

He took the sheet, upon which she had scribbled old poems along with the new one. Though but a trifle, its point was not lost on him.

Inochi koso
tayu tomo tayume
sadamenaki
yo no tsune naranu
naka no chigiri o

Let life break off
   as it will—
our bond will endure,
   constant
in this fickle world.

Seeing that he tarried, Murasaki prompted him gently: "It will do me no credit for you to be late." Her heart nearly bursting, she watched as he left, clad in robes softened to just the right degree, his perfume incomparably wonderful.
. . .   (4:57-58; S 554-55; W 628)

Murasaki continues to feign good cheer as she passes the time chatting with her ladies. Some of them have been the recipients of Genji's favors, but now they rally about their mistress. Of course, Murasaki cannot indulge herself in their sympathy, any more than she can take consolation in the condolences coming from the other ladies of the Rokujōin. As the night wears on, she prepares to retire:

It was not her custom to keep late hours; her conscience told her she would be subject to criticism, and so she got into her bedclothes. Yes, these nights had been lonely, she could not deny it. Thinking back to the time when Genji was leaving for Suma, she remembered feeling that even if they were apart, if she could only hear that he was alive somewhere. . . . She had had no thoughts for herself then, only sorrow and despair for him. And now—she tried to console herself with the thought that if they had both lost their lives then, there would not even be cause for brooding now. A bitter wind chilled the night. She could not find a moment's respite in sleep, but not wanting her ladies to know, she held herself still until the strain was almost unbearable. Near morning she heard a mournful cock's crow.

She had not meant to be reproachful, but perhaps it was the turmoil in her heart: she appeared to Genji in his dreams. Startled, his thoughts rushing, he impatiently waited for the cock's cry. When it finally came, he hurried out, unmindful of the darkness outside.

(4:61-62; S 555-56; W 629-30)

It is on a snowy dawn that Genji makes his way back to Mura-saki's bedside.

The similarities and differences are apparent. Genji and Mu-rasaki write poems in the midst of extreme tension, whereas Higekuro and his wife's thoughts never become so formed. Her stepsister's fury is perfectly countered by Murasaki's restraint, but Genji cannot free himself of Murasaki any more than Higekuro can rid himself of the scent of the ashes. To appear in a dream is the closest Murasaki comes to being a possessing spirit. Her stepsister's attack on Higekuro is possibly the most secularized, psychological manifestation of the possessing spirit in the work.

Comparison with the likes of Higekuro is diminishing for Genji, as will be spelled out in the "New Herbs" chapters. In "The Cypress Pillar" chapter, however, it is the young Genji's shadow that haunts the pages. We recall that Tamakazura was already promised to the Reizei Emperor when Higekuro steals into her room. In the distant days of his youth, Genji spoiled a woman intended for Suzaku, then crown prince, and it was the disclosure of this theft that ostensibly necessitated his exile. The woman was Oborozukiyo, and she held the same office in court for which Tamakazura is intended. Lest the title alone be in-sufficient to evoke the link between the two women, Genji is made to reminisce over Oborozukiyo as he longs for the Tama-kazura now beyond his reach.

Tamakazura's marriage does not void the question of her court duties since they are not to include personal services. Higekuro finally gives his consent when he recognizes that the Palace can serve as a way station between the Rokujōin and his own man-sion. Once he succeeds in removing Tamakazura from Genji's hegemony, he will never return her.

Tamakazura and her ladies make a fine show of it at the Pal-ace. Higekuro is uncle to the current Crown Prince, which makes him third in power in the land, coming only after Genji and Tō no Chūjō. (His sister, the mother of the Crown Prince, is a bitter woman neglected by the Suzaku Emperor because of his attachment to Oborozukiyo.) He can see to it that Tamaka-zura is well equipped. He entertains the New Year's singers handsomely—the same singers who visited the Rokujōin during another New Year.

Chapter 2

While Higekuro busies himself chaperoning and chauffeuring Tamakazura, his wife prepares her own departure from his household. She will take her children, two sons and a daughter, Makibashira. Amidst the sorrowful commotion of a household being dismantled, she tells her children that she herself is prepared to face a life of wandering (*sasurai*, 3:363; S 499; W 576). Thus the motif of exile passes from Tamakazura to Higekuro's wife.[100] As it happens, Higekuro's wife will return to the home in which she grew up, where her own parents are still living. What is the meaning of characterizing this move as exile, apart from the banal though not invalid explanation that she is being displaced from her adult domain, the home of her husband? As we have seen, her father, Prince Hyōbu, reintroduced the topic of Genji's exile in attempting to explain the misfortunes brought to his own family by Genji and his family. (Prince Hyōbu's slow-moving mind helps to clarify certain points for the reader. In failing to side with Genji at the time of his exile, he miscalculated Genji's potential power; now, he fails to see that Higekuro's capture of Tamakazura is very much a defeat for Genji.) Exile is also an implicit presence in Genji's reminiscences of Oborozukiyo.

Sugawara no Michizane was perhaps the most prestigious historical figure associated with Genji's exile. Tamakazura was taken to Tsukushi, the site of Michizane's exile; and now, Makibashira, Higekuro's daughter, evokes Michizane in her farewell poem to the house in which she grew up:

Ima wa tote	The time has come
yado karenu tomo	when I must leave
narekitsuru	my home:
maki no hashira wa	but cypress pillar, my friend,
ware o wasuru na	I beg you
	never to forget me.
	(3:365; S 500; W 573)

The girl longs for one more glimpse of her father but must content herself with thrusting this poem into a crack in the pillar. To this poem that gives the girl and the chapter their names, her mother responds:

152

Nareki to wa	Even if the friendly cypress
omoiizu tomo	should remember us
nani ni yori	from time to time,
tachitomarubeki	on what ground should we
maki no hashira zo	stand
	to tarry in this house?
	(Ibid.)

Like her husband, Makibashira's mother is impatient with emotions born of figures.

Makibashira's poem is a girlish evocation of that famous poem allegedly composed by Michizane as he prepared to leave on his exile:

Kochi fukaba	Should an east wind blow
Nioi okoseyo	Send me your fragrance
Ume no hana	O blossoms of the plum:
Aruji nashi tote	Forget not the spring
Haru o wasuru na.	Because your master is
	gone.[101]

The *Ōkagami*, a so-called historical tale of the early eleventh century, records another poem composed by Michizane in the early stages of his journey to Tsukushi. It is addressed to his great patron, the retired Emperor Uda:

Kimi ga sumu	Journeying ever onward
Yado no kozue o	I looked back
Yukuyuku to	Until they disappeared—
Kakururu made mo	The treetops
Kaerimishi wa ya.	At the place where you
	dwell.[102]

Despite her severely practical attitude to her daughter's fancies, Higekuro's wife is not indifferent either: she cannot help

> looking back as the carriage was drawn out. Thinking that she would never see the house again, she became forlorn. Her gaze lingered over each treetop until it disappeared. It was not because it was the place "where you dwell," but

because it was where she herself had spent so many years
that she could not suppress her grief.

(3:366; S 501; W 577)

Thus, Michizane is summoned to the page.

In the Makibashira episode, Murasaki Shikibu rewrites the
story of the eminent statesman and man of letters as the tale of
an unappealing abandoned wife and her adolescent daughter.
Does the analogy domesticate Michizane or dignify Higekuro's
wife and daughter? Inevitably, it does both. If the Genji-Fujitsubo affair was a grand example illustrating the translation of the
political into the personal and vice versa, then this episode,
which is but a footnote to the story of Tamakazura, herself a
secondary character, shows Shikibu seizing on the least promising material to effect a similar exchange.

The Michizane motif draws together the various strands of this
chapter in a complex braid. While Higekuro's wife and daughter
abandon his estate, Tamakazura cannot help enjoying herself at
the Palace, so much so that Higekuro becomes desperate to re-
claim her. Genji, clinging to the vestiges of his influence, insists
on the observance of protocol. When Reizei arrives at her quarters, Tamakazura is more than ever struck by his resemblance to
Genji. He, for his part, is more than ceremonially taken with
her, although he confines himself to promoting her on the spot
and tarrying with her despite her husband's evident anxiety.
(How audacious Higekuro is, spending the night at the Palace,
thus announcing his proprietary interests in the woman, quite
undaunted by the prior claims of the Emperor. And yet there is
no hint of violation, for the world of the tale can no longer
sustain that sort of charged energy.) Tamakazura herself becomes
uneasy as she begins to detect a moral resemblance between
Genji and Reizei, and fearful of scandal, she calls on her true
father to extricate her. Reizei has no choice but to hand her over
to her father's men and her husband's hand carriage. Thus Tamakazura is transferred from the Rokujōin to the Palace to Higekuro's house. Hers is no forlorn exile, to be sure, but it is still
an enforced migration.

As Tamakazura is rushed off by Higekuro, the Reizei Emperor

rues the fate whereby he must lose a beauty on who he had prior claims. His wry reference to precedents has been taken since the fourteenth-century *Kakaishō* to indicate the story of Taira no Sadabumi (also known as Heichū, d. 923), a man who lost his lover to Fujiwara no Tokihira, the politician thought to have engineered Michizane's banishment.[103] Reizei bids a regretful farewell to Tamakazura with this poem, using, almost predictably, the image of the plum blossom.

Kokonoe ni	The plum blossom,
kasumi hedateba	barred from the Palace
ume no hana	by nine folds of haze,
tada ka bakari mo	will it not at least
nioi koji to ya	send along its scent?
	(3:380; S 507; W 584-85)

Tamakazura responds,

Ka bakari wa	Let the fragrance alone
kaze ni mo tsuteyo	float on the breeze,
hana no e ni	though I lack the scent
tachi narabubeki	to win me a place
nioi naku tomo	upon those flower-laden
	branches.
	(Ibid.)

Where Reizei makes Tamakazura into a plum blossom, Tamakazura turns the Palace into the site of beautiful plum trees whose fragrance she would like to catch though she must leave it for a humbler abode.

There is a more ominous image of fire and ashes associated with Michizane that peregrinates through the chapter. It is a familiar story that after Michizane's death in exile, a number of mishaps occurred in the capital that resulted in the posthumous restoration of his title and rank, and ultimately his deification. As we have seen (p. 147) Higekuro has fire on the mind even before the drama provoked by his wife, but at the time it makes no claim on our attention since fire is conventionally associated with love and jealousy. After the incident, Higekuro cannot go to Tamakazura's after all because not even a bath can rid him of

Chapter 2

the smell of ashes. Though his wife's unnerving behavior is clearly something he would like to keep secret, he sends the following poem to Tamakazura in lieu of a visit:

Kokoro sae
sora ni midareshi
yuki moyo ni
hitori saetsuru
katashiki no sode

As the snow
flew in the sky
so my heart
was in turmoil
while I lay alone
upon my chilled sleeve.
(3:358-59; S 498; W 574)

Hitori, "alone," is homophonous for "incense burner."

The next evening, he prepares to go again, although his robes have holes from the ashes and the burnt smell pervades his person. This time, it is the servant Moku who perfumes his sleeves, and as she does so, she ventures the following:

Hitori ite
kogaruru mune no
kurushiki ni
omoi amareru
honoo to zo mishi

Suffering alone
a smoldering heart,
her unquenchable thoughts
burst into flame.
(3:360; S 499; W 575)

Moku is startled by her own audacity. Although she is a not unattractive *meshūdo* (a servant who is intimate with her master), Higekuro is in no mood to lend her an ear:

Uki koto o
omoisawageba
samazama ni
kuyuru keburi zo
itodo tachisou

When I think
of that dreadful event,
it stirs coiling smoke
of horror and regret
within my heart.
(Ibid.)

The odor of smoke and the traces of ashes are hard to remove.

Retrospectively, we realize that ashes had found their way even to the Palace. The first poem the Reizei Emperor addressed to a shy Tamakazura at the Palace was

Nadote kaku
hai aigataki

Why did I stain
my heart

murasaki o
kokoro ni fukaku
omoisomeken

with thoughts of you
so resistant,
O purple-clad one.
(3:377; S 505; W 583)

The color of the Third Rank, to which he has promoted Tamakazura, is light purple. Ashes are used as a mordant in dyeing
fabrics purple (the color of relationship, as will be seen in the
next chapter, as well as of the Third Rank), and the depth of the
hue varies with the reaction of the dye to the mordant. "Hai
aigataki," rendered as "resistant," is more literally "difficult to
meet/combine with ashes." Reizei regrets being scorched by one
who cannot become his.

As for Genji, he of course suffers far more acutely than his
son. From time to time he manages to send messges through
Ukon. In the Third Month, when the *yamabuki* (Tamakazura's
flower) and the wisteria are at their height, Genji "deserts the
garden of spring" (3:385; S 508; W 587) and wanders off to Tamakazura's old quarters. There he silently composes a poem on
the *yamabuki*. This garden has plantings of Chinese bamboo;
the blossoms of the *yamabuki* remind him of faces, all bearing
the imprint of Tamakazura. (An infinitely sadder Genji will have
his loneliness magnified by blooming gardens after the death of
Murasaki.) The poem he actually sends off revives the parental
fiction. To a basket of duck eggs masquerading as oranges, he
attaches a brief note of reproach to Tamakazura for neglecting
her filial duties by her absence:

Onaji su ni
kaerishi kai no
mienu kana
ikanaru hito ka
te ni nigiruran

The duckling that hatched
within my nest
has alas, disappeared;
what kind of hand
cradles it now?
(3:386; S 509; W 588)

Higekuro, the serious one, will have none of this. A woman,
once married, seldom sees her true parents. How much more
tenuous are Genji's claims to visits! He will answer for his wife:

Sugakurete
kazu ni mo naranu

The duckling was forgotten
and ignored

kari no ko o   in its nest;
izukata ni ka wa   who would bother
torikakusubeki   to steal and hide it?

                             (3:387; S 509; W 588)

There is a pun on *kari no ko*, meaning both "duckling" and "temporary" or "surrogate" child. Upon the receipt of this reply, Genji wryly observes that he had never seen Higekuro indulge in such frivolities. One of the effects of falling in love has been to push the literalist to word play, though ironically (and appropriately), his conceits are directed at piercing Genji's fictions. Higekuro's gestures threaten the fictions-in-life in which Genji increasingly takes refuge in his middle age.

Tamakazura exits from Genji's life. There never was room for her in the Rokujōin; her birth in "The Broom Tree" chapter determined her fictional mode of existence to the end. Beginning as the daughter of a minister, she is destined to end as the wife and widow of another. There was the possibility of a transformation during her stay in the Rokujōin, a transformation that not only would have altered her but would have restored to Genji his mythic heroism. But Genji himself is no longer capable of heroic action. He cannot transform the banal fiction of paternity into the heroic one of incest. He cannot even transfer Tamakazura to his surrogate, his son, as he had his other fictional daughter Akikonomu. Even without Higekuro's interference, the Reizei solution would have been unsatisfactory, since it would have been disagreeable for Tō no Chūjō because of his older daughter and redundant for Genji because of Akikonomu. Not only is Genji's position for the present generation assured by Akikonomu, but it is also secure for the next through the Akashi Princess. If a child were to be born between Tamakazura and Reizei, it would only introduce confusion. Tamakazura is intractably superfluous. Put another way, Murasaki Shikibu has taken Genji as mythic hero as far as she can, and as far as she is interested in taking him. And the Rokujōin, which must remain for now a rhetorical and not a mythic structure, awaits the moment when it will become the stage for a drama of psychological realism.

Tamakazura's and the tale's failure to effect a transformation mark a crucial turning point, suggesting new possibilities as much as loss. When Tamakazura reappears in "New Herbs, Part One," it is to signal an end to the rhetorical glory of the Rokujōin. There, she offers the first of several feasts honoring Genji's fortieth year. For the normal man of such years youth is irrevocably past, and "new herbs" are offered as a symbol of regeneration. At forty, a man is overage to be the hero of a *monogatari*. This, coupled with the fact that linear time has been suspended in the Rokujōin, makes Tamakazura's gesture portentous.

Tamakazura herself appears in a role unbefitting a traditional stepdaughter-heroine. She is already the mother of two, and by "The Bamboo River" chapter she emerges as the widowed mother of three sons and two daughters who must struggle with distinctly unromantic issues such as family finances and profitable matches for her children. Unlike other heroines, Tamakazura neither dies nor takes vows. She is a functional character, bridging "The Broom Tree" world to the Rokujōin, and the Rokujōin to remote Uji. As a representative of the unknowing public within the tale, she touches upon its great secrets: in her youth she is moved by the stunning resemblance of the Reizei Emperor to Genji; in her middle age, she is struck by Kaoru's resemblance to her own late brother Kashiwagi. Beautiful yet sensible, utilitarian, and protean, Tamakazura, who is denied the grand gestures of negation, is doomed to live out her life as a stepchild in the kingdom of the *Genji*, never empowered to see, never permitted to become.

Chapter 3

A Substitute for

All Seasons

The Naming of a Heroine

"INUKI let my baby sparrow out—the one I was keeping in the incense-burner basket!" (1:280; S 87; W 84). Her cheeks flushed, thick hair waving to indignant steps, the heroine of the *Genji* makes her first appearance on the scene. It is a vivid entry: no other heroine begins her career with an outburst of speech. The angry Murasaki is lovely, and as Genji peers at her, he finds himself in tears. He soon understands why his gaze has been transfixed: it is because the child is strikingly like the woman "to whom his soul is dedicated," Fujitsubo (1:281; S 88; W 84). It is the miraculous resemblance once again, only this time it comes supported by blood tie: Genji's investigation quickly establishes that Murasaki is Fujitsubo's niece. The child's father, Prince Hyōbu, is Fujitsubo's brother, which makes Murasaki the granddaughter of the otherwise unidentified "previous Emperor." Is this link sufficiently powerful to achieve the transubstantiation (of niece into aunt, of copy into original, or metonymy into metaphor) so ardently desired by the hero, as his sudden tears reveal? We know the answer from the beginning, since we know that Murasaki Shikibu has chosen the world of fiction rather than that of myth, or more precisely, she has chosen to encase the latter within the former, with the consequence that one of her principal subjects is the ineluctable tragedy issuing from the confusion of the logic of resemblance with the logic of identity. This chapter focuses on the fate of one who is the object of this unhappy confusion.

The very name of the heroine is a beautiful but uncompromising statement of her essence: connectedness to another. In the first days of his acquaintance with the child who will come to be known as Murasaki, Genji utters the following poem to himself:

Te ni tsumite	When shall I pluck
itsushika mo min	and hold in my hand
murasaki no	the young field plant
ne ni kayoikeru	whose roots
nobe no wakakusa	join the roots
	of the *murasaki?*

(1:314; S 102; W 98)

The child has already been described as a "young plant" (*wakakusa*) by both her nun-grandmother and her nurse. Genji's poem draws on an anonymous *Kokinshū* poem:

Murasaki no	A single clump
hitomoto yue ni	of *murasaki*
Musashino no	makes all the grass
kusa wa minagara	of Musashino
aware to zo miru	dear to my heart.

(KKS 867, "Miscellaneous, 1")

The roots of the *murasaki*, which goes by the unpromising name of "gromwell" in English, were used for extracting medicines and a purplish dye. I have left it untranslated in the poems not only for the obvious disadvantages of the English name but also because there is no one word that will capture both plant and color. "Lavender" is an attractive possibility but limits us to the light blue end of the color. Purple, in its range from the palest of lavenders or pinks to the deepest red, almost black, blues occupied a special place in the extraordinary visual sensibilities of the Heian period. Here is how one writer describes it:

As for colors, with the development of dying techniques, they were able to produce over 110 hues and achieve the heights of splendor thanks to abundant financial resources, resulting in a golden age of color: both furnishings and clothing dazzled with gold and silver, with gems, with crimson and emerald, white and scarlet. Within this panoply of hues, it was purple that was idealized as the king of colors.[1]

It was fixed by code that only the highest ranking of the aristocracy could wear purple, the dark hues being restricted to princes of the blood of the fourth order or above and officials of the first rank, while medium hues could be worn by princes of the second to fifth rank and officials of the second and third ranks. It also connoted imperial rule, Buddhist law, and even the Taoist paradise.[2]

As suggested by the gradations of court rank, the precise nuance carried by purple was indicated by the depth of the hue: hence, its remarkable connotative range from awesome taboo to intimacy and affinity. For example, we just saw Reizei and Tamakazura exchanging poems using purple as a sign of both court rank and relationship. The anonymous poem from the *Kokinshū* that I have just cited is thought to be the source of the phrase *murasaki no yukari*, which refers to one who is related to the beloved or to the transfer of affection from the beloved to the kin.[3] The strength of the dye and its capacity to stain its surroundings was a metaphor for human relationships.

At any rate, the place name Musashino and the *murasaki* plant are repeatedly evoked to define the child Murasaki's position. Once Genji has succeeded in removing Murasaki to his own home, the Nijōin, he neglects all his other duties for two or three days to closet himself with her, for, as he scrawls on a piece of purple paper, he feels "reproachful when someone says 'Musashino' " (1:333; S 110; W 107). Another old poem, this time from the *Kokin Waka Rokujō* collection (compiled by an unknown editor late in the tenth century), makes this notion intelligible:

Shirane domo	Though I don't know the
Musashino to ieba	place,
kakotarenu	if someone says "Musashino,"
yoshiya sa koso wa	I sigh and complain—
murasaki no yue	it must be because
	of the *murasaki* plant.
	(*Zoku Kokka Taikan* 34353)

In this apparently rustic poem, the speaker professes such fondness for the *murasaki* plant that mere mention of Musashino, where it is presumably plentiful, stirs his heart. For Genji, the poem secures the association of Musashino and Murasaki, so that Musashino can be used to evoke Fujitsubo as well, since *fuji* is the wisteria. Just as the strong dye *murasaki* must be distinguished from the lighter hue of the wisteria, however, niece will have to be distinguished from aunt. Genji elaborates:

Ne wa minedo	Though I haven't seen its roots
aware to zo amou	dear to me is this plant,
Musashino no	kin to the one in Musashino,
tsuyu wakewaburu	the one I cannot visit,
kusa no yukari o	so thick is the dew.
	(1:330; S 110; W 107)

The terms are familiar to us by now, but what about the young Murasaki to whom this poem is addressed? Even if she were to know the *Kokin Rokujō* source of the phrase "when someone says 'Musashino,' " she cannot have any inkling of Genji's interest in Fujitsubo, and she may not even know of her own kinship to her. Moreover, the ten-year-old who still sleeps with her nurse until Genji separates them probably does not recognize the pun in his first line, *ne*, "roots," for "sleep" (*neru*). (There is a fine echoing of sound and sense in the two first lines of Genji's poem and of the *Kokin Rokujō* poem: "Shirane domo"—though I don't know—and "*Ne* wa mi*ne*do—though I haven't seen its roots.) Murasaki, coaxed to write something in response, valiantly produces her first poem in the tale:

Kakotsubeki	Not knowing why
yue o shiraneba	you should complain,
obotsukana	I am lost;
ikanaru kusa no	what plant might it be
yukari naruran	that I am kin to?
	(1:334; S 110: W 107)

A venerable poetic history is being brought to bear on Murasaki, a history that prefigures the fictional demands to be placed on her, still but a "young plant" or *wakakusa*. *Wakakusa* as an image for young women or girls appears very early in Japanese poetry. Since seedlings often sprout two leaves in the beginning, *wakakusa* is also an epithet for "husband" or "wife," or for a couple's first night together. The young plant is pure, tender, in need of protection—but also brimming with vitality and therefore nubile and seductive to the beholder. Genji's poem to Murasaki anticipates a day when the plant's roots will be revealed. It reminded a fifteenth-century reader, Ichijō Kanera, of the following poem from *Tales of Ise*:

Ura wakami	So new and tender,
neyoge ni miyuru	so good for sleeping
wakakusa o	is this young grass—
hito to musuban	ah, to think
koto o shi zo omou	of its being tied by another!
	(*Ise* 49)[4]

The poem plays on the conventions of travelers on the road gathering grass for pillows and of lovers pillowing each other with their arms. Here, the speaker is addressing his sister, who exclaims over her brother's "unexpected thoughts" in her response. It is provocative that Genji's poem on unseen roots (Murasaki) and an unvisited plant (Fujitsubo) should have reminded the poet Kanera of the *Ise* poem on brother-sister incest. He clearly had in mind the sum of the Fujitsubo story together with its Murasaki subplot: that is, he was reading as the *Genji* demands to be read—each part evoking the whole, with constant mutual modification. And, as this example shows, the "whole" includes not only the tale itself but also previous literature.

The reiteration of the place name Musashino brings to mind another *Ise* poem, this time from episode 12. There, a young man has abducted a young woman, and the two are in flight from the village authorities. The hero leaves his lover to hide in a grassy field, which the pursuers prepare to set on fire. The woman cries out,

Musashino wa	On this day,
kyō wa na yaki so	do not set fire
wakakusa no	to the fields of Musashino:

tsuma mo komoreri	my husband hides
ware mo komoreri	in the young grass
	and I am hiding, too.

(Ise 12)

This poem appears as KKS 17 in the spring section with Kasugano as the setting rather than Musashino. It is anonymous and was possibly a folk composition on the springtime custom of burning fields to stimulate new growth. The *Ise,* having already dwelt on the abduction of the young woman who was to become the "Empress of the Second Ward," skillfully transforms the light-hearted KKS poem through the prose context. The association of Musashino with *wakakusa* (here serving as an epithet for "husband") begins to show a dark side. Now, going back to Genji's first poem on the child Murasaki, we notice that *tsumite,* "pluck," contains *tsumi,* or "sin."[5]

We have traced the development of *murasaki* as a figure for kinship. *Murasaki* is also a fixed epithet, frequently used for the following words and names: (1) because it is a deep *(koshi)* hue, for the place name *Kodaka;* (2) because it is a noble and celebrated hue, for the place name Nadaka ("famous"); (3) because clouds (especially in Amida's paradise) and wisteria blossoms are purple, for these objects; and (4) because it is a beautiful, shining hue, for *niou,* "to gleam," or "to shine."[6] The first memorable use of *murasaki* in Japanese poetry occurs in poems 20 and 21 of the *Man'yōshū.* The first is by Princess Nukada, the poet who declared herself for autumn.[7]

Akane sasu	You go
murasaki no yuki	through the crimson-glowing
shime no yuki	*murasaki* fields,
nomori wa mizu ya	the royal fields—
kimi ga sode furu	won't the guardsman see you
	wave your sleeves at me?

The occasion, as the headnote tells us, is a hunt by Emperor Tenji (r. 668-671). The "you," to judge from the pairing of the poem with number 21, is the Crown Prince, Tenji's younger brother, who was to succeed him as Emperor Temmu (r. 672-

686). Nukada was first loved by Temmu and bore him a daughter, but she then became a consort to Tenji. The following poem is given as Temmu's reply:

Murasaki no	If you,
nioeru imo o	so beautiful in crimson glow,
nikuku araba	were odious to me,
hitozuma yue ni	why would I long for you,
ware koime ya mo	being the wife of another?

Was Nukada already in Tenji's service but still attached to Temmu at the time of these poems? There is no assurance that the poems were actually composed as a pair. Little does it matter. What counts is the association of *murasaki* with exquisite beauty and illicit love, an association supported by other names and words in three centuries of poetry.

CHILDHOOD AS A SYMBOLIC STATE

Murasaki's removal to the Nijōin takes place in the "Lavender" chapter in which Genji steals in on Fujitsubo and Reizei is conceived. The chapter oscillates between Fujitsubo and Murasaki. Genji, his longing only sharpened by the brief meeting with Fujitsubo, tries to console himself with thoughts of Murasaki. The child has returned to the city from the mountains where Genji first espied her. There, her maternal grandmother dies, leaving her with only her nurse Shōnagon and a small household. Her long-dead mother was the daughter of a major counsellor (as was Genji's mother) who had suffered at the hands of her husband's official wife (the unpleasant mother of Higekuro's first wife). Murasaki has been neglected. Genji visits her when she is still in mourning for her grandmother-nun. His interest in the child, while gratifying, had unsettled the nun. Now, it produces consternation in the nurse Shōnagon.

Murasaki, having heard of the arrival of a grand visitor, bounds in to see who it might be. Genji urges her to sit on his lap, whereupon she protests that she is sleepy. The nurse admonishes, "You see, it is as we have said. She knows nothing of

166

the ways of the world" (1:317; S 104; W 100). Nevertheless (given the divided impulses of attendants), she pushes the child toward Genji. (They are still separated by curtains.) Genji reaches in, to confirm with his hands what his eyes had captured in the mountains. He "feels garments with the starch worn soft, glossy hair falling over them, hair that he could tell was thick to the ends—ah, how lovely she would be!" (1:318; S 104; W 100). He grasps at her hand, but no, her child's reserve balks at this: "I said I was sleepy." Genji slips in: "I am the one you must look to from now on. Don't be so unfriendly." Under the pressure of the moment, the nurse's protective instincts come to the fore, and she verges on bluntness: "Really, sir, this is terrible. Whatever you say to her will surely have no effect." Genji's reply is almost as candid: "What do you think I would do, she's still a child. You must wait and see how remarkable my single-minded devotion is" (ibid.). Luckily for Genji, the onset of a furious storm makes the women grateful for a male presence.

Shortly thereafter, when Genji gets wind of Prince Hyōbu's plans to take his daughter into his own home, he stages a kidnapping, with the faithful Koremitsu assisting. Shōnagon comes, too, just as Ukon came with Yūgao. And just as Yūgao's people were left baffled by her disappearance, Prince Hyōbu can only imagine that his daughter was spirited away. He will learn of her whereabouts much later, presumably at the time of her coming-of-age ceremony (which is not described in the tale), just as Tō no Chūjō is told of Tamakazura's identity only at her belated initiation.

Murasaki's removal to the Nijōin places her in a constellation with certain other *Genji* heroines. The abduction of Yūgao, the kidnapping of Murasaki, the captivity of Tamakazura in the Rokujōin and in the Uji chapters, the removal of Ukifune to Uji by Kaoru, all share an informality of arrangement. Words such as "abduction" and "captivity" may have a hyperbolic ring since the victims rarely protest, but that is because they cannot, either from ignorance or from the knowledge that life offers them no suitable alternatives. A profound passivity characterizes these women at such junctures.

Of this group, Murasaki and Tamakazura begin as Genji's

167

"daughters." There is of course another fictional daughter, Aki-konomu. The critical difference in her case is that she was explicitly entrusted to Genji by her mother at the time of her death. Such a deed carries weight in the world of Heian fiction—it might best be described as a mythical quotation. This, together with other considerations (such as Genji's need to see her as Reizei's consort), distinguishes her treatment from that of the others. She enters first the Nijōin and then the Rokujōin with proper ceremony. Most of the women listed above are of lower status than Akikonomu, but Murasaki is the granddaughter of an emperor (to Akikonomu's being the daughter of a crown prince); the lack of ceremony with which Murasaki enters Genji's household, however, marks her for life.

Akikonomu's identity as the daughter of a former lover reminds us that Yūgao and Tamakazura are another such mother-daughter pair. This in turn brings out another shared characteristic, which is that these women are surrogates for other women in the eyes of their captor. They exemplify, each in her own way, the mechanism of substitution that is central to the workings of the novel. Every major character is in a sense a surrogate figure, the bearer of a false identity.

What distinguishes Murasaki from all the other heroines is that she is literally a child when she is spun into Genji's orbit. Despite his assertions, Genji's devotion is undeniably carnal from the beginning. There is no other attachment quite like this—tender, fervent, and displaced. In a subtle way it anticipates Kashiwagi's attachment to the Third Princess's cat, an adoration that carries the logic of substitution to what would be its parodic extreme were it not for the intensity verging on madness.

This cat, the only animal to have a part in the *Genji*, is the instrument whereby Kashiwagi gains his first and fatal glimpse of the Third Princess. Though he had been a candidate for her hand, he had lost (on grounds of his low rank), and by the time he sees her in the spring twilight she is Genji's official wife. As with Genji and Fujitsubo, so with Kashiwagi and the Third Princess: there is no reasonable surrender to harsh reality. Kashiwagi's first solution is to borrow the Princess's cat through her brother the Crown Prince, whereupon he proceeds to care for it, fondle it, and sleep with it. He is even moved to compose a poem:

Koiwaburu	You I have tamed
hito no katami to	as a token
tenaraseba	of my love;
nareyo nani tote	why do these notes
naku ne naruran	now issue
	from your throat?
	(4:150; S 589; W 648)

Note the obsessively alliterative *n*'s in the last two lines of the Japanese (4:150, n. 13). Kashiwagi's unusual behavior does not escape the eyes of his women attendants, who whisper among themselves about the curious state of affairs in which a "cat has begun to prosper in these quarters. He never showed such inclinations before" (4:150-51; S 590; W [649]). Many years earlier, Genji, musing over his relationship with Murasaki, recognizes that "even with one's own daughter, once she has attained this age, it wouldn't be possible to be so relaxed, to rise and sleep together without a second thought. This is indeed a peculiar attachment" (1:336; S 111; W 108). Of course, Genji with Murasaki is never so bizarre as Kashiwagi with the cat, but that is in part a measure of the distance traveled by the tale from the "Lavender" to the "New Herbs" chapters.

Genji provides the child Murasaki with playmates and dolls and looks after her lessons in calligraphy and music. To Murasaki, Genji must have been something of a fairy godmother. For Genji, however, the attachment from the beginning is to the woman Fujitsubo perceived in the child Murasaki. He waits some four years, until Murasaki is fourteen, before acting to realize that vision.[8] A fairly leisurely growing up, one might say, except that Murasaki has been portrayed as a child intent on her childhood. Back in the mountains of Kitayama, her grandmother rued her excessive innocence—her own daughter, Murasaki's mother, had "understood things" even though she was only ten when her father died. What would become of the child, so rapt in her dolls and pet sparrows, when she was no longer there to take care of her?

We have already seen Shōnagon remonstrating with Genji when he so brashly intruded behind Murasaki's curtains. A revealing exchange takes place between nurse and charge some time later, when both are comfortably ensconced in the Nijōin. Murasaki has just finished complaining to Genji about the latest misdeeds of that same Inuki who let her sparrow out. Shōnagon takes the opportunity to suggest to Murasaki:

"You must try to be a little more grown-up this year. Once they are past the age of ten, ladies put aside their dolls. You even have a husband—you should behave quietly and thoughtfully. But look at you now, you won't even sit still to have your hair done." Shōnagon wanted to shame Murasaki for being so preoccupied with her dolls. Murasaki thought to herself, so, I have a husband. The men these people mean when they talk about husbands are all ugly. But I have one that is handsome and young.

(1:394; S 137; W 134)

This revelation does not take her away from her dolls and her games. The members of the household are curious, but not nearly as much as they would have been had they known that Genji and Murasaki were sleeping as parent and child. Still, there are signs of impending change.

Just prior to Shōnagon's sermon, Genji is referred to as *oto-kogimi* (the "gentleman"), as if to emphasize the male aspect of his parenthood. Even Murasaki becomes a lady as she quotes from the fragment of a love poem to reproach Genji for his absence in "An Autumn Excursion," when he is preoccupied by his obligations to the court and to Aoi and above all by the birth of his secret son. Just after the carriage brawl between the Rokujō Lady and Aoi, Genji chooses Murasaki as his companion to go viewing the Kamo Festival from a carriage with blinds lowered.

Still, nothing happens until Aoi is dead. When Genji returns to the Nijōin and sees Murasaki for the first time after the long period of mourning, he is struck, in the lamplight, "by her profile, by her head, by how, in every detail, she had come to resemble that lady who consumed his heart" (2:61; S 180; W 178). Murasaki is no longer inappropriate as a partner, and Genji begins to make overtures, but she seems uncomprehending. They continue with their games, even as Genji fast approaches the limits of his restraint.

> He was not altogether easy about it. What could have happened? Their relationship was such that others had no way of knowing if the line had been crossed, but there came a day when the gentleman rose early but the lady showed no signs of stirring. (2:63; S 180; W 178)

Genji had been uneasy because whatever the strength of his desire, he could still anticipate that Murasaki would be surprised. There is a syntactic break, a near-awkwardness at the beginning of the above passage (marked by my division into two sentences), that is faithful to the rupture that Murasaki's sexual initiation represents. She is unprepared, and she does not resort to conventional gestures to conceal her shock.

When Genji pushes her writing box under her curtains, she does not even lift her head until later, when she is sure that no one is about. She notices a poem by her pillow. It is Genji's morning-after poem, usually delivered with some ceremony after the first night of a marriage:

Ayanaku mo	How have we passed
hedatekeru kana	night upon night,
yo o kasane	parted by these robes
sasuga ni nareshi	of nights so familiar.
yoru no koromo o	(2:64; S 180; W 179)

She does not answer. She "had never imagined that he had such ideas in his head. Now she felt humiliated to have trusted, without a moment's hesitation, a person with such odious thoughts" (ibid.). When Genji returns to look in on her (her puzzled ladies have reported that she is unwell), she hides her head under the covers. He pulls them back to discover a face beaded with sweat. She will not speak to him, and she continues to guard her silence even as he arranges for a modest marriage feast. She is still silent when, some time later, Genji prepares for her initiation ceremony.

In Chapter 2 we saw Tamakazura's abnormally late initiation

171

with the disclosure of her identity to her father. Murasaki's initiation, which is mentioned but never described, is an afterthought. (The correct order of initiation followed by marriage is reversed.) The wedding itself is so casual as to scar Murasaki for life. The Koremitsu who had been so useful in her kidnapping and in Yūgao's abduction is entrusted with the task of having special sweets secretly prepared. It is only when their containers are discovered that Murasaki's ladies realize what has happened. The bride, of course, does not understand that she now has a husband in fact. All of this reflects cruelly on Murasaki's social status (while giving her her particular fictional distinction). This is no solemn union of two families, as marriages properly were. Murasaki might as well not have existed in the eyes of the world. Earlier, when rumors of a new woman in the Nijōin first reached Aoi's household, her ladies whispered among themselves:

> Who could it be? Isn't it outrageous! Well, the fact that we don't even know who she is, not to mention the way he keeps her around at all times, proves that she can't be a refined or clever person. He probably saw her at court some time and made a big fuss about taking her in. He doesn't want any criticism for it, though—that's why he's hiding her. But what's this they say about her being so young and childlike? (1:406; S 142; W 139)

Murasaki is never Genji's official wife, the *kita no kata* (literally, "[the one] in the north," since the official wife usually occupied the northern wing of an estate). Interestingly enough, she is referred to as a *kita no kata* by the sociologically sensitive Higekuro and his wife in "The Cypress Pillar" (3:353-54; S 496; W 572). The latter is Murasaki's stepsister, and the issue of wifely status is much on her mind. Only in one other instance, at the time of the Akashi Princess's entry into the Crown Prince's household, is the term applied to Murasaki, but obliquely. It was the custom for the official wife to accompany daughters on such occasions, and Murasaki alone qualifies. Ironically enough, this occurs in "Wisteria Leaves," just before the emergence of the Third Princess as the universally acknowledged mistress of the Rokujōin.

Murasaki is not an official wife, nor is she a casual lover or a secondary wife (in the sense that, for example, the Akashi Lady or Hana Chiru Sato is). One might say that her identity depends on what she is not. She is not, first of all, Fujitsubo, the one for whom she is a substitute. The abiding importance of this is that she is linked to, but twice removed from, the centrality of being implied by the position of emperor as it is manipulated in the tale. Nor, on the other hand, is she a politically (that is, a profanely) useful wife: she produces neither a son (as did Aoi) nor, especially, a daughter (as did the Akashi Lady), and she has no powerful backers. These instances of not-being mean that there is virtually nothing Murasaki can offer Genji. From this emerges the attractive if tedious possibility of true love between Genji and Murasaki. At the same time, Murasaki's almost being the women listed above makes her not unlike Genji. Both are motherless children; both are preternaturally marked by physical, intellectual, and artistic gifts; and both are defined by a lack of fixed identity.[9] Surrogates are distinguished by their not-being, which signifies their fictional potential: since they are not identical to an original (and therefore powerful) model, they can become something new.[10] A principal character such as Murasaki retains the legacy of the original yet inevitably transmutes it.

Murasaki inherits Fujitsubo's extraordinary beauty, her refined bearing, and her aptitude for the arts. All this is useful but formulaic: the author asserts it without much elaboration, and we are willing to accept it on faith. The more interesting part of the *murasaki no yukari* legacy has to do with the illicit. Since Murasaki is Fujitsubo's substitute, the taint of the Genji-Fujitsubo relationship stigmatizes (marks as literarily interesting) the Genji-Murasaki relationship. The Genji-Fujitsubo relationship involves metaphoric incest. If we transpose the theme to Murasaki—and eventually to that other niece, the Third Princess—the claustrophobic, self-obsessed nature of Genji's principal attachments becomes clear. Murasaki's residence in the Nijōin, the estate Genji inherited from his mother, whom Fujitsubo reputedly resembles, expresses this succinctly.

Let us return to the fact of Murasaki's being a child. Her grandmother and her nurse are correct in diagnosing her as unworldly. *Yozukazu,* used pointedly by Shōnagon in the scene described above with a sleepy Murasaki, specifically means "not knowing the ways of men and women."[11] For the unworldly Murasaki her wedding night is the occasion of a betrayal both horrifying and humiliating. Radical purity—the innocence of a child that refuses to accommodate to conventional knowledge—distinguishes Murasaki throughout her life. Obviously, Murasaki grows in womanhood. Her purity and childlikeness are therefore symbolic as well as literal: as she matures, her literal inexperience becomes an acquired, and therefore all the more profound, innocence. Murasaki might well be called "unworldly" even on her deathbed. Violation of Murasaki therefore is a violation of a purity that is otherwordly, which violation of Fujitsubo is not.

IDEALIZED BANALITY AND ITS RUPTURE

There is, however, more to be understood about Murasaki before we witness her death. Despite its unpromising beginnings, Murasaki's marriage with Genji is happy. There are difficulties to be sure: notably, the long separation during the Suma-Akashi years and the threat of potential rivals. But essentially, with the exception of two ruptures (to be discussed later), the portrayal of Murasaki from the time of her marriage in "Aoi" through the pre-Rokujōin chapters and on through the Tamakazura chapters up to "Wakana" is idealized, static, and—uninteresting. Even her one flaw, jealousy, is reiterated mechanically and is therefore absorbed in the abstract idealization. (Genji always finds Murasaki's jealousy endearing and thereby trivializes it as an aspect of her *childishness,* in contrast to the symbolic *childlikeness* discussed above.) What is curious about this portrayal is that it comes, at least in the pre-Rokujōin chapters, in the midst of the greatest visible turbulence in the tale—the Kiritsubo Emperor's death, the reversals to Genji's faction, exile, then finally dramatic recovery. In "The Sacred Tree" chapter, for example, after a description of the baleful effects of the Kiritsubo Emperor's death on Genji and all those associated with him, there comes a passage on the remarkable good fortune of the lady in the western wing of the Nijōin, a good fortune that is the marvel of all the world. (This is a phenomenon that is later caricatured in the depiction of the Akashi Lady's mother.) Of course, there is one person who is agitated by Murasaki's happiness, and that is her stepmother—as if all this were taking place in a *monogatari*, observes the narrator coyly (2:95-96; S 194; W 201). Since things have turned bleak in the world of the tale, the description of such happiness has a jarring effect, precisely as if an episode from a benign, simple-minded sort of fiction had been inserted. The narrator's confirmation of this impression undercuts this effect.[12]

The story of the young Genji and Murasaki bears a fairy-tale-like outline. She is an orphan girl with nothing but herself to offer, he a handsome prince fallen on hard times. They are faithful to each other and are rewarded for their virtue. It stands to reason that such a relationship should flourish in inverse proportion to external circumstance.[13] Genji's public role is severely circumscribed after the Kiritsubo Emperor's death, which has a dampening effect on his private life as well. The result is that he is at home with Murasaki a great deal more than he might otherwise be. But more than common sense is at work in the production of many chapters in which Murasaki is distinguished only by domestic happiness. Domesticity is the caricatured manifestation of her purity, and in this sense, banality is to Murasaki as politicization is to Fujitsubo.

There are several elements that characterize Murasaki's brand of banality. The first has already been described as stereotyped jealousy. Prior to the "New Herbs" chapters, Murasaki has cause to brood over the Akashi Lady and Princess Asagao. She also knows well enough that Genji's paternal affections for Akikonomu and Tamakazura are not unmixed.

The second stereotyped feature is love of children, a quality that lends itself to exploitation then as now, particularly since Murasaki remains childless for life. Before leaving for Suma, Genji entrusts her with the management of his household. Murasaki is forced to grow up quickly, and true to expectation, she passes the test admirably. Having shown herself to be a capable partner in the operation of a large estate, she is next given the opportunity to raise a child, Genji's daughter by the Akashi Lady. Murasaki welcomes the project and finds the task so gratifying that even her resentment of the child's mother softens. (In just the sort of irony that her creator favors, Murasaki plays the role of stepmother.) Murasaki's devotion pays off in the Akashi Princess's brilliant success in the Crown Prince's court, an achievement that almost makes of Murasaki a political wife and mother. "Fondness of children" is a motif that is reiterated with the birth of grandchildren, especially the first and the third, Niou.[14]

The first rupture comes just as Genji's prestige and actual influence on the court are assured by the result of the Picture Contest (in chapter seventeen), and Murasaki's own position—fortified by the charge of an important daughter—seems unassailable. Fujitsubo's recent death, taking place in the same chapter as the adoption of the Akashi Princess, has been disruptive, but one might guess that with the death of her model, Murasaki's hold on Genji would become firmer than ever. In times of stress, however, Genji's bent is to compound his troubles. Before Suma, for example, desperation to see Fujitsubo (only intensified by fears that the affair might be exposed) drove him to initiate a flirtation with Oborozukiyo, a member of the enemy camp. In "New Herbs, Part One," after having broken Murasaki's heart and agitated himself by marrying the Third Princess, he scurries off to Oborozukiyo, recently liberated by the Suzaku Emperor's taking vows. Genji's psychic disarray following Fujitsubo's death soon finds a focus in the person of Princess Asagao, till then a decidedly minor character known for her refinement and sensible refusal to engage in anything but a correct if cordial epistolary relationship with Genji.

Why does this woman pose the most serious threat to Murasaki before the arrival of the Third Princess? For one thing, she is of high birth: her father, Prince Shikibu (not to be confused with Murasaki's father, Prince Hyōbu, who becomes Prince Shikibu upon the death of Princess Asagao's father), is the brother of the Kiritsubo Emperor (and therefore of Princess Ōmiya, the mother of Tō no Chūjō and Aoi as well). This makes her the granddaughter of an emperor, just like Murasaki, after all, but Asagao's superior standing in the eyes of the world is unquestionable. She is the sort of royal daughter who becomes Priestess of the Kamo Shrine, whereas Murasaki's existence is barely acknowledged by her own father.

In fact, it is because Princess Asagao has just resigned her priestly office following her father's death that Genji embarks upon his campaign to overcome her reticence.[15] It is not so much that he is erotically drawn to her (indeed, his poems are full of unmannerly speculation on her passing youth), but that her very resistance poses a challenge he cannot overlook. What alerts Murasaki to the state of affairs is Genji's furtiveness. In the past, as in the case of the Akashi Lady, he deflected her jealousy by keeping her abreast of his affairs. This time, he keeps to himself, writing letters or ostentatiously announcing the need to visit an aunt in mourning (at whose house Princess Asagao now resides). Murasaki, for her part, keeps her own counsel (she is usually quick to pout, in accordance with her "jealous" character), which in turn gives Genji an intimation of the depths of her anxiety. He seeks refuge in the usual banter about her childishness, but he nevertheless refers, at last, to his recent exchanges with the ex-Priestess of Kamo. This leads to the winter evening appraisal of women that culminates in Fujitsubo's appearance "as if" in his dreams.

Genji's remarks begin with superlative praise for Fujitsubo. He allows that his listener Murasaki resembles her in almost every respect except for a certain troublesome tendency to assert herself. He gives only cursory treatment to Princess Asagao. At this point Murasaki interjects, "But Oborozukiyo is surely outstanding for her cleverness and dignity. One wouldn't think to associate her with careless conduct, but it does seem that there were strange incidents, doesn't it" (2:483; S 358; W 396). This is the first indication that Murasaki has been aware of the Oborozukiyo incident. She is no mere child, given to petulant jealousy; it is actually she who is doing the evaluating in this exchange. Genji

177

tries to skirt the subject of Oborozukiyo by moving on to the Akashi Lady. In the end, a cold moon shines upon the couple's silence. Murasaki's thoughts may be gauged from her poem:

Kōritoji	Frozen,
ishima no mizu wa	the water between the rocks
yukinayami	is troubled in its passage;
sora sumu tsuki no	light from the clear moon,
kage zo nagaruru	sky-dwelling,
	flows on.

(2:484; S 359; W 397)

The poem's allegorical quality is secured by a series of puns: *yukinayami* ("having difficulty in movement") is close to *ikinayami* ("having difficulty in living"); *sumu* is both "clear" and "to dwell"; *nagaruru*, "to flow," approximates *nakaruru*, "to weep." The preceding conversation has brought home to Murasaki only too vividly her own hampered lot in contrast to Genji's freedom of action, action whose inevitable effect is to sadden if not threaten her.

Even as she recites this poem, however, Murasaki so reminds Genji of Fujitsubo that it seems as if his roving heart were reined home. That this is but speculation is emphasized by the narrator's *beshi*, "must be." Ironies crowd the scene, for "home" is evidently Murasaki as the repository of memories of Fujitsubo. As we know, when Genji falls asleep, his head filled with thoughts of the dead lady, she appears to charge him with betrayal of their secret. Murasaki interrupts his troubled sleep. Genji has no reply for her query, but this poem forms in his mind:

Tokete nenu	A lonely awakening
nezame sabishiki	from uneasy sleep
fuyu no yoru	on this winter's night:
musubōretsuru	how brief my dream
yume no mijikasa	so sadly formed.

(2:485; S 359; W 397)

This is the undelivered response to Murasaki's poem in which she likened herself to frozen water. *Tokete* is literally "melting."

178

The couple lie rigid and unintimate ("in unmelting sleep") so that slumber can bring no repose. The oneiric union that takes place is distressing and brief ("dreams," *yume*, are "tied"/ "formed" and "saddening," *musubōretsuru*). Adding to the still tension is Murasaki's proximity to, yet absolute exclusion from, the secret of the image informing her own identity.[16]

The Asagao episode takes place on the eve of the completion of the Rokujōin. The icy winter night yields to the sunlit world of the Rokujōin. There, Murasaki's idealization becomes more complex and powerful. If it is still her role to ensure the harmonious operation of the household, the household has not only grown more vast and elaborate, but it has acquired metaphysical properties as well. To keep pace with these developments, Murasaki is abstracted as "lady spring" and is even called by this name in the "Wild Carnation" and "Cypress Pillar" chapters. If spring stands at the head of the seasons, it is also but a member of an inexorably changing cycle: Murasaki may be first among the ladies of the Rokujōin, but like the others, her role in the pageantry is dictated by the demands of the artificial cosmic order. As we have seen, her very identification with spring in contrast to Akikonomu's with autumn has been imposed by Genji. As Lady Spring, Murasaki has no choice but to play the game of the seasons.

Genji rules this microcosm from the southeastern quarter, the residence of spring and Murasaki. We have already seen how Genji at the height of the Rokujōin years becomes a pseudo-emperor. Genji and Murasaki together, however, are more like a prince and princess (king and queen or emperor and empress are too adult, serious, and mundane) in an imaginary domain. The image, rather less parodically than the Genji-Fujitsubo pairing, tantalizes with overtones of brother-sister rule, from the shadowy reaches of archaic history.

The second rupture is of course the famous glimpse stolen by Yūgiri in the aftermath of the typhoon in the "Nowaki" chapter. As we have seen, the passage resonates on several levels, but its most immediate effect is to impart a physicality to Murasaki's beauty. If, up to now, we have given short shrift to the Rokujōin Murasaki, it is because there has been little to say. It has taken the rapture of sober Yūgiri to breathe life into Murasaki's abstract idealization. His hungry gaze invests radiant purity with a carnal dimension without impairing the purity. The passage is charged with the youth's hunger for the unattainable woman. Genji, in part because he literally possesses Murasaki, cannot convey her preciousness, the vitality of her perfections. Years later, when he echoes his son's assessment in "New Herbs, Part Two" at the time of the women's musical performance, he describes her in the following manner:

> Murasaki was dressed in what seemed to be a salmon-pink robe beneath a deep scarlet gown, upon which her abundant hair was gathered, giving her dignity in repose. Her size was exactly what was wanted, and her beauty seemed to spill over into the surroundings. If one were to liken her to a flower, it would be to the cherry, but even that would not suffice to describe her incomparable superiority.
>
> (4:184; S 602; W [649])

It is vital for our own pulses to quicken over Murasaki's beauty as we approach the "New Herbs" chapters, or else we cannot wince at the blow dealt therein. Yūgiri, a stepson, metaphorically violates his stepmother and makes her interesting as she had not been when she was violated as a child by his father. Now she is ready to become an adult heroine. Yūgiri's transgression of course mimics Genji's with Fujitsubo and anticipates Kashiwagi's with the Third Princess. Kashiwagi's obsessively dreamy violation of the Third Princess is the violation of another representative of the *murasaki no yukari*, a niece to Fujitsubo and cousin to Murasaki. That, of course, is a transgression against Genji, and Genji as victim is thus injected with a renewed literary interest.

THE GROWTH OF VISION

At first Murasaki makes light of the rumors that the retired Suzaku Emperor's third daughter is to come to the Rokujōin. She had agitated over the Princess Asagao affair, and nothing came of it. More recently, she had watched Genji become absorbed in the youthful Tamakazura but decided to hold her peace. This was a confident Murasaki who could see her form reflected beside Genji's for ten thousand years to come. When at last Genji apologetically discloses the truth of the rumors, she puts a brave and generous face on the situation: the poor Suzaku Emperor, aging and frail, to be burdened by such worries over his daughter. They are, after all, related—perhaps the Princess would be kind enough to be friendly with her (4:46; S 550; W 623). But in her heart the announcement is as unexpected and frightening as a blow from the heavens.

The appearance of the Third Princess is the spur that sends Murasaki on the lonely road to self-discovery. It is not, of course, that she literally learns that she has been a substitute for Fujitsubo, although it is clear from the above that she is informed about the blood tie. Her cousin's arrival prompts a new self-scrutiny. In spite of her resolve to be cordial, Murasaki finds herself thinking, "Why should anyone stand above me? Isn't it just that his lordship took care of me when I had no one else to count on?" (4:81; S 564; W 634).

Yet the reality is that Murasaki begins to be referred to unambiguously as *tai no ue* (mere) "lady of the wing." Thus far, she and Genji have occupied together the western wing of the southeastern quarters, but now the Third Princess is installed in the principal structure in the same quarters. Having learned that she is replaceable, exchangeable for a superior if similar model, Murasaki begins to make a host of other discoveries. Poems are an important aid in this process, especially in the form in which the writer jots down, in cursive style, his or her own poems along with those of others as they come to mind. In the *Genji*, of course, the selection is anything but random, and to engage in the exercise in itself connotes psychic turmoil. As we saw in the comparison with Higekuro's wife, Murasaki's jottings on the third night of the wedding serve as the sole explicit indication of her agony to Genji. Even as she thinks defiantly of her own status relative to that of the Third Princess, she finds that when she sits down, brush in hand, the poems that come to her are full of brooding—whereupon she must acknowledge that she, too, has things on her mind.

In retrospect it is not surprising either that Murasaki should become so preoccupied with knowing and understanding the secrets of life or that she should be adept at it. Throughout the long years of her marriage, she has been the repository of Genji's confidences—perhaps more accurately termed self-serving confessions. For the younger Murasaki such material was fodder for her jealousy, but it was also knowledge to be stored away for a more profound response in the fullness of time. In an age when it was hard for women, even (or especially) the highest born, to come upon firsthand knowledge, Murasaki husbanded every scrap of information that came her way. We saw her watching Genji select garments for all the women in his care at the beginning of the Tamakazura chapters. More directly, she sought out the acquaintance of these women, her presumed rivals. From "The First Warbler" through "New Herbs, Part One," four such first meetings are recorded: (1) with Tamakazura, on the occasion of the New Year's singers' visit; (2) with Akikonomu, at the Akashi Princess's coming-of-age ceremony; (3) with the Akashi Lady, when the Akashi Princess enters the Crown Prince's household; and (4) with the Third Princess, when the Akashi Princess returns to the Rokujōin for her lying-in. (Given that all these women occupied the same residence, what a degree of formality must have prevailed to require the passage of years and these special occasions for their meeting.) In each case, the initial meeting is followed by a sense of mutual good will, the exchange of letters, and in some cases continued correspondence. Of course, it is because of Murasaki's idealized character not only that these relationships should develop amicably but that they should develop at all. Murasaki also has a devoted following among her servants, including those who originally belonged to Genji's household, some of whom had been intimate with him.

Murasaki's poems offer a surprisingly revealing record of her internal journey. A conspicuous number contain the word *me* ("eye") or forms of the verb *miru*, "to see." They are as follows, in order of composition:

(1) Addressed to Genji before his departure for Suma:

Wakarete mo   Even if we part,
kage dani tomaru   if only your reflection

mono naraba	were to linger on,
kagami wo *mite* mo	I would console myself
nagusametemashi	by looking in the mirror.

                                    (2:165; S 224; W 234)

(2) Same as above:

Oshikaranu	I would trade my life,
inochi ni kaete	unregretted,
me no mae no	to postpone for minutes
wakare o shibashi	your departure
todometeshi kana	from before my eyes.

                                    (2:184; S 233; W 240)

(3) In a letter to Genji in Suma:

Urabito no	Compare
shio kumu sode ni	to the dripping sleeves
kurabe *miyo*	of the seaside dweller
namiji hedatsuru	these night clothes,
yoru no koromo o	parted by waves,
	from you.

                                    (2:184; S 233; W 243)

(4) Looking at Genji's exile paintings in preparation for the Picture Contest:

Hitori ite	Instead of grieving
nagekishi yori wa	by myself,
ama no sumu	I should have seen
kata o kakute zo	as you have drawn
mirubekarikeru	that beach
	where the divers dwell.

                                    (2:368; S 311; W 333)

(5) Replying to Akikonomu's triumphant autumn poem (sent with a pine tree planted in a miniature garden):

Kaze ni chiru	Flimsy are the scarlet leaves
momiji wa karoshi	that fly in the wind.
haru no iro o	Behold

iwane no matsu ni
kakete koso *mime*

the color of spring
in the pine upon the rock.
(3:76; S 386; W 432-33)

(6) Replying to Genji at the first New Year in the Rokujōin:

Kumori naki
ike no kagami ni
yorozuyo o
sumubeki kage zo
shiruku *miekere*

Upon the cloudless mirror
    of this lake,
our forms will shine
    clearly visible
for ten thousand years.
(3:138; S 410; 468)

(7) Sent to Akikonomu during the spring pageantries at the Rokujōin:

Hanazono no
kochō o sae ya
shita kusa ni
aki matsumushi wa
utoku *miruran*

Even the butterflies
of the flower garden
    must be resented
by the autumn-waiting cricket
lying low in the grass.
(4:58; S 555; W 482)

(8) A scribble to herself as Genji prepares to spend the night with the Third Princess:

Me ni chikaku
utsureba kawaru
yo no naka o
ikusue tōku
tanomikeru kana

The world changes
before my very eyes:
I had trusted it
    to endure
into distant years.
(4:58; S 555; W 628)

(9) Another such poem written after proposing a meeting with the Third Princess:

Mi ni chikaku
aki ya kinuran
miru mama ni

Can autumn
be drawing near?
    I watch:

aoba no yama mo   the green-leafed hills
utsuroinikeri   have already turned.

                                    (4:82; S 564; W 634)

(10) The first of a joint composition with Genji and the Akashi
Princess (now Empress) just before her death:

Oku to *miru*   No sooner do you see
hodo zo hakanaki   the dew settle on the *hagi*
tomo sureba   than troubled by the wind,
kaze ni midaruru   it trembles
hagi no uwa tsuyu   and falls.

                                    (4:491; S 717; W 731)

Thus, ten out of a total of twenty-three poems by Murasaki contain the word *me*, or forms of *miru* or miyu ("to be visible," i.e.,
"to appear"). The poems of the other heroines can be broken
down as follows: Fujitsubo, four out of twelve; the Rokujō Lady,
two out of eleven; the Akashi Lady, five out of twenty-two; Tamakazura, three out of twenty.

There are various kinds of seeing exemplified in Murasaki's
poems. There is a challenging tone to numbers 3 and 5 (in number 3 the "seeing" part of the verb is almost an auxiliary, but the
visual component is still active). Numbers 1 and 2, based on the
notion that to see is to have, express the sorrow of having to
relinquish both seeing and having. Number 4 takes this idea
further, though in a quite different vein: I should have seen for
myself, possessed the same experience that you have recorded in
your paintings. Number 6 rests (wishfully) secure in the notion
that for something to be visible means that it is real, and therefore durable. Numbers 8, 9, and 10 reflect a growing awareness
of the impotence of the watchful eye over the changes it observes. The rupture between seeing and having is decisive.

These poems are markers of Murasaki's psychological history.
"Seeing," "having," and "knowing" are mutually metaphoric,
and looking over the poems, one might say that Murasaki, whose
first composition is a query stemming from not knowing her
origins, has been engaged in a lifelong pursuit of seeing, having,

and knowing. What she comes to understand is that these activities and their objects are forever distinct. Murasaki, having led the most confined life among the heroines (the Sumiyoshi pilgrimage with Genji and the Akashi women in "New Herbs, Part Two" is an exceptional outing) wanders furthest internally. She is the noble traveler of the mind.

Let us trace the latter stages of her journey. In her book *Genji no Onnagimi* ("The Ladies of the Genji"), Shimizu Yoshiko titles the section on the post-"New Herbs" Murasaki, "A World Where Men Are Needless." The moment Genji announces his impending marriage to the Third Princess, Murasaki's heart begins to turn away from him. Of course, being an ideal heroine, she remains gentle, sweet, and constant. She helps in the wedding preparations and even assists Genji to dress to spend the night with another woman. (These gestures are probably as much for her own sake as for Genji's: the unthinkable has happened, and all that is left in her control is her own comportment.) There follows the excruciating night that she spends partly in labored conversation with her ladies, partly in feigning sleep to conceal her turmoil from them. When sleep comes at last, her soul departs and causes her to appear in Genji's dream (the closest she comes to being a possessing spirit). He comes scurrying home. The scene that follows must be read as one of a pair with the description of Murasaki's wedding night. Her ladies, no longer accustomed to such comings and goings, keep him waiting in the snow. When let in, he grumbles cheerfully about the cold, and in the same easy manner, pulls at Murasaki's bedclothes. She hastens to conceal a sleeve damp with tears: "Guileless, sweet, and yet unyielding—she put one to shame!" (4:62-63; S 556; W 630-31). Genji's awkwardness is muffled in the narrator's admiration. He who has just left the arms of another woman is rejected without a word and yet with grace.

Of course, the "other woman" is only a child. In fact, she is but a year or so older than Murasaki was when she was wedded to Genji. Her childishness has been emphasized as the source of continuing anxiety for her father the Suzaku Emperor as well as her attendants—a situation approximating Murasaki's two decades earlier. Yet where Murasaki was bright, lively, and independent, the Third Princess is an unusually passive (or even impassive) child. The contrast is reinforced by the presence of the slightly younger Akashi Princess when she returns to the Rokujōin to give birth. The Third Princess does not even know enough to be indignant over Genji's early departure. (Murasaki as a child may not have known what a "husband" was, but she could understand human attachment: in this light, even her jealousy becomes a sign of her superiority.) It is the Princess's nurse who must become exercised on her behalf, and it is under the direction of this same nurse that she manages to get off a response to Genji's morning-after-letter—the same response that an even younger Murasaki, in consultation with her own heart, refused to write. The reply comes when Genji is with Murasaki. He is mindful of her feelings and so does not wish to conceal it, but at the same time, the hand and the message are so woefully inadequate that he is vicariously humiliated. Murasaki tactfully averts her gaze. The Princess herself, barely visible beneath a mound of fine clothes, is quite unconcerned.[17] When Murasaki finally meets her, the conversation turns from illustrated romances to dolls.

This, then, is the creature who displaces Murasaki. At the time that Murasaki suggests a meeting with her, Genji relays the message in this manner:

> Tonight, the person living in the wing is going out to see the Shigeisha lady [the Akashi Princess]. She seems to want to take advantage of the occasion to make your acquaintance. Won't you consider permitting her a small audience? (4:80; S 564; W 633)

He goes on to recommend her company on the grounds of her youthfulness and suitability as a playmate. What is shocking here, first of all, is the manner of reference, with extremely humble forms used for Murasaki. Given the Third Princess's status, it is unthinkable for Genji to speak in other terms. A contrast is implied between intrinsic worth and outer form, linguistic as well as sartorial. Yet, such a contrast cannot overcome the unsettling effect of seeing Murasaki objectified in this fashion, so reduced in Genji's speech.

187

Chapter 3

THE STAGING OF DEATH

Murasaki, of course, does not know the terms in which Genji speaks of her to the Third Princess, nor does she need to. She has seen and felt enough to understand that her only salvation lies in withdrawal. Her refusal of Genji's advances on that snowy morning is symptomatic of a psychological retreat that she knows can most effectively be realized by taking vows. She begins to request Genji's permission from the time of the Reizei Emperor's abdication in "New Herbs, Part Two":

> These days I have been thinking about leaving behind my routine life and devoting myself quietly to my prayers. I feel as if I have reached the age where I can say, this is what the world amounts to. Please, you will permit this, won't you?   (4:159; S 592; W 649)

She is too tactful to be insistent. That would also be too ostentatious. Yet, she is painfully aware of her uncertain footing in the world, and the religious life continues to beckon:

> Even though she was not inferior to others, thanks to the attentions of one man, still, if the years were to accumulate, even his affections would surely wane. She would rather turn her back to the world now than be faced with that.
> (4:169; S 597; W 653)

In a long conversation with Genji after the musical evening with the Akashi mother and daughter and the Third Princess, Murasaki admits to being burdened by an unbearable sorrow;

> In truth, I do not feel that there is much time left to me. It distresses me to think of spending this year as I have all the others. If only you would permit me to do what I requested earlier.   (4:198-99; S 607-608; W 651)

Genji refuses, though he is not unconcerned since Murasaki is thirty-seven, a dangerous year for women according to folk belief. (This was the age of Fujitsubo at her death.) When in fact she almost dies under the spell of the Rokujō Lady's spirit, she presses her request once more, and a chastened Genji arranges for an abbreviated ceremony. This does not mean, however, that she can devote herself to the religious life. As she recovers a measure of health, she must content herself with preparing religious garments and articles for others—including, ironically, Oborozukiyo and the Third Princess. Why is she compelled to tarry?

> There was nothing more she wanted out of this world, nothing that concerned her that would disturb her devotions. Hers was not a life that she wished to prolong unduly—and yet, the prospect of turning her back on the pledges she had exchanged with Genji over the years, and to cause him pain was the source of a sorrow that she could share with none.
>
> (4:479; S 712; W 728)

Then why this tenacious pursuit of the religious life? Shaving the head or cutting off the better portion of one's hair—possibly the most dramatic aspect of taking vows—signals the renunciation of one's sexual being, which also symbolizes the cessation of social intercourse. It is, in short, a form of death in life. Now, the fictional world of the *Genji* offers a variety of motives for taking vows. There are those, such as the Rokujō Lady, who take the step on the threshold of death. For others, in similar spirit though somewhat more leisurely fashion, taking vows is the rite-of-passage in old age. After their vows, husband and wife no longer live as a couple (the Akashi Priest lives apart from his wife and daughter) and dedicate themselves to their prayers in the hopes of enhancing their next lives.

It is the case of those who take vows in early or middle age that is intriguing. With Fujitsubo, for example, it is precisely through the public renunciation of her womanhood that she is able to embark on a new life as a political being. Fujitsubo also falls into another category of *Genji* heroines who take vows unexpectedly in early life: they are those who have participated in illicit affairs.[18] Utsusemi, having spent one night with Genji, decides to become a nun many years later when pursued by her stepson. The Third Princess, having learned of Genji's knowledge of her affair with Kashiwagi and of Kaoru's true paternity, takes vows to escape from Genji's contemptuous lust. In the next generation, Ukifune, trapped between Kaoru and Niou, plunges into a river, then makes amends for being rescued by taking vows. It is clear that for these women, becoming a nun is an act of self-expression that can only take the form of denial. Sexual relations have governed their lives, and they resolutely turn their backs, usually in the face of variously interested opposition. No doubt there is an unarticulated desire to expend the energy of guilt in religious practice (a desire overlapping with concern for salvation), but the sheer need to announce a departure from the world of men is at least as strong.

Murasaki, for all her protective tactfulness toward Genji, repeats her wish to take this step because she knows everything she cares to know about this world, and at the same time (though she does not say this) she would like to spare herself the miseries she has yet to taste. Buddhism appeals by seeming to offer another world—which, to be sure, it does to everyone. But in Murasaki's case, her history reveals an insistent religious streak. She was discovered with her nun-grandmother and her bishop-granduncle by Genji while he was himself on a retreat in the mountains. Unacknowledged by her father and bereft of her mother, she was raised from early childhood in surroundings filled with incense and rosaries and the rhetoric of this-worldly despair (without compensatory hopefulness for an ameliorated future). When the adult Murasaki entered the Rokujōin, her garden was compared to the kingdom of the living Buddha—in other words, to the Pure Land of the Amida Buddha. Murasaki alone of the four principal ladies was actually called by the season to which she was assigned. Lady Spring was a paradisiacal figure. Just as the Rokujōin at its height was a secular replica (with its own literary privileges) of the Palace, so Murasaki's garden, where spring flourished long after it had yielded to summer elsewhere, was a Buddhist other world realized on earth. In the "Butterflies" chapter, as spring was celebrated in a rush of flowers, music, and poetry, Akikonomu sat apart in her autumn quarters. When the festivities were over in Murasaki's garden, Akikonomu presided over a solemn reading of a sutra. Murasaki, Lady Spring, a secular buddha incarnate, was juxtaposed with literal Buddhism.[19] Much later, in "New Herbs, Part One," both

Murasaki and Akikonomu made religious offerings part of their festivities honoring Genji's fortieth year. It was the spectacle organized by Murasaki on that occasion that invited comparison with the "true Paradise" (4:85; S 565; W [635]).

Not long after this comes the first of the requests for permission to retire from the world. Now, Murasaki is neither Lady Spring nor a buddha incarnate. As the decline of the Rokujōin sets in, she herself is shaken from the heights of her idealization. She has begun to pursue the Buddhist realm in search of a domain to call her own. Salvation for her is not a new life beyond death on a lotus petal but a death within this world.

The illness that strikes in the midst of her unsuccessful pursuit is of course a harbinger of physical death and a version of what she profoundly seeks. The immediate consequence is that she is removed from the Rokujōin to the Nijōin. This estate, where she was reared, which she guarded for three years during Genji's absence, has always felt more like home to her. (In fact, unlike Akikonomu or Tamakazura, she held her banquet for Genji's fortieth-year celebrations there rather than at the Rokujōin.) The Nijōin, of course, belonged to Genji's dead mother; it was restored for Genji by his father the Kiritsubo Emperor; and it stirred Genji's earliest fantasies—that he might house therein a lady exactly to his liking, namely, Fujitsubo. Here is one node in a network lively with tension: the Kiritsubo Lady's line is carried on by the Akashi family, and, as we have seen, this relatively modest clan attains a prosperity unknown to the descendants of the "former Emperor." In other words, Fujitsubo and the Kiritsubo/Akashi women do not mix: an intractable fact with serious implications for Genji's desires. In his search for surrogates, he would join together elements destined to be distinct from the beginning. Murasaki is not the realization of a fantasy but the substitute realization of a fantasy. Given this, as well as her lineage, it is not surprising that the spirit of the Rokujō Lady should follow her to the Nijōin and deliver a near-fatal blow. Murasaki's climactic illness in the Nijōin reveals her state of radical homelessness.

After her illness, Murasaki, still unable to persuade Genji to let her take vows, embarks on the last great undertaking of her life: to arrange for a ceremony much favored by Heian aristocrats, the Hoke Hakkō, in which the Lotus Sutra is recited over a period of four or five days. There are three other Hoke Hakkō recounted in the *Genji*. The first is sponsored by Fujitsubo following services for the first anniversary of the Kiritsubo Emperor's death. The second Hakkō is conducted by Genji upon his return from exile as a memorial service for his father, who, he has learned, is doing penance for unnamed transgressions. The third is Murasaki's in "The Rites," and the fourth is sponsored by the Akashi Empress in "The Drake Fly" to honor the memories of her father Genji and her adoptive mother Murasaki. She holds it in the Eighth Month, which is Murasaki's memorial month. Now, all three Lotus Sutra ceremonies other than Murasaki's have the character of memorial services. The Akashi Empress's service is unambiguously dedicated to the souls of her parents. Genji's is not only directed toward the repose of his father's soul but to the restoration of his own image as a public figure after the Suma-Akashi lapse. The implications of Fujitsubo's ceremony have already been discussed.

Whom does Murasaki's Hoke Hakkō memorialize? There is a Buddhist practice called *gyakushu*, which is, in effect, a funeral service performed in anticipation of one's own death.[20] Murasaki's Hoke Hakkō is nothing other than a staging of her own death.

> Over the years, she had had one thousand copies of the Lotus Sutra copied at her own behest, and now she hastened to have them dedicated. The ceremony was held at the Nijōin, which she regarded as her own residence.
>
> (4:481; S 713; W 728)

Note the emphasis on the personal nature of this enterprise.[21] Murasaki manages this elaborate affair largely on her own, with help from Yūgiri in the musical and choreographic arrangements. Indeed, Genji, who is not kept abreast of the details, is caught by surprise at the magnitude of the occasion, resplendent with the participation of everyone from the Emperor and the Empresses (the former Akashi Princess and the now "retired" Akikonomu) on down. It is spring in the Nijōin—which, of course, is different from spring in the Rokujōin. The old symbols are deployed again but to new ends. Even the Nijōin as "home" is now a stage for the renunciation of all homes.

The Lotus Sutra, of course, is distinguished for its consciousness (however attenuated) of the possibility of salvation for women. We have seen how, over the years, Murasaki developed a network of ties with other women, both her aristocratic rivals and her servants. That network is invoked during the ceremony. The silence of a pause during a ritual in which the celebrants chant while bearing offerings, water buckets, or firewood stirs pangs of loneliness in Murasaki. Using the young Niou as a messenger, she sends the following poem to the Akashi Lady:

Oshikaranu	A trifling thing
kono mi nagara mo	is my life;
kagiri tote	yet so sad
takigi tsukinan	the firewood, nearly gone,
koto no kanashiki	announcing the end.
	(4:483; S 714; W 729)

The image of the dying flame appears in the Lotus Sutra to describe Sakyamuni's death. The Akashi Lady responds:

Takigi koru	Cutting firewood—
omoi wa kyō o	a long life of devotion
hajime nite	to the Law eternal
kono yo ni negau	begins today.
nori zo harukeki	(Ibid.)

This poem is prefaced by the narrator's supposition that the Akashi Lady couched her reply in general terms because to have met pathos with pathos would have earned her criticism from future generations. (If the Akashi Lady represents her creator, as many readers have thought, then hers is a resolutely unflattering self-portrait.)

When the services are over, Murasaki sends a poem to Hana Chiru Sato:

Taenubeki	These rites, like my life
minori nagara zo	must come to an end.
tanomaruru	I count on our pledges

yoyo ni to musubu	to each other
naka no chigiri o	for worlds and worlds
	to come.

(4:485; S 715; W [729])

Hana Chiru Sato replies,

Musubioku	The pledges we make
chigiri wa taeji	will never be broken;
ōkata no	though all rites
nokori sukunaki	and lives
minori nari tomo	must near their end.

(Ibid.)

In both these poems there is a pun on *mi*, meaning "self" or "being" but doubling as an honorific for *nori*, "rites." Hana Chiru Sato's poem contains a difficult *ōkata no*, here translated as "all." Hana Chiru Sato could be saying, "As is true of everyone, your life and mine must come to an end." Or, she could be referring to herself: "Being older, I am the one with but few years left," that is, "you, Murasaki, should take heart." There is also the possibility that *ōkata* refers to religious rites, which yields the meaning that either all rites, including this one, or with the exception of this one, are "ordinary" (i.e., rites are only rites).[22] The possibilities are not mutually exclusive. What is unusual about this exchange is the emphasis on a personal bond that is more durable than Buddhist rites or Buddhist law (*minori* also means "holy law"). Moreover, this is a bond between two women: *chigiri* ("pledges") commonly refers to lovers' vows. Murasaki uses the occasion of an established religious ritual to make a personal plea to the Akashi Lady and Hana Chiru Sato. The latter responds in kind.

In any event, it is doubtful that Murasaki can be consoled by the words of her companions of "summer and winter."[23] The Murasaki who has attained a measure of knowledge is riddled with loneliness. She knows that all her erstwhile rivals must die some day, but she cannot help thinking, "I must go alone, and be the first to vanish" (4:485; S 715; W 730). The phrase she uses, *yukue shirazu*, is common in poetry and appears a number of times in the *Genji*. It is normally used to describe persons whose whereabouts are unknown and, occasionally, those whose well-being cannot be ascertained. Murasaki's use of the phrase to mean "death" is unique in the *Genji*.[24] Her *yukue shirazu*, "whereabouts unknown," is a radicalization of *sasurai*, or "wandering."

From spring to summer, Murasaki declines visibly. The coolness of autumn brings a slight relief, but it is too late. Her beloved foster daughter, the Akashi Empress, retires from the Palace to be with her. Murasaki no longer has the strength to go to the Empress, as protocol would require, so the Empress comes to her. One windy evening, Genji joins them and is delighted to find Murasaki sitting up, leaning against an armrest (no doubt out of respect for the Empress). Murasaki, for her part, is saddened to see him clinging to hope:

Oku to miru	No sooner do you see
hodo zo hakanaki	the dew settle on the *hagi*
tomo sureba	than troubled by the wind,
kaze ni midaruru	it trembles
hagi no uwa tsuyu	and falls.

(4:491; S 717; W 731)

A pun on *oku* joins the dew's settling with Murasaki's sitting up. Seeing the *hagi* plants in disarray in the windy garden, Genji understands Murasaki's poem:

Yaya mo seba	The dewdrops contend
kie o arasou	to hasten from this world;
tsuyu no yo ni	may there be no lapse
okure sakidatsu	between the first to go
hodo hezu mogana	and the last.

(Ibid.)

As Genji struggles with his tears, the Akashi Empress adds,

Akikaze ni	This world of dew cannot
shibashi tomaranu	withstand
tsuyu no yo no	the autumn wind

tare ka kusa ha no	for a moment:
ue to nomi min	who thinks this the plight
	of leaves and grasses alone?
	(Ibid.)

The three poems of this fine *shōwa* are joined by the common image of the dew, adopted from the garden before the poets' eyes, but its implications are handled differently by each. Murasaki, who has for some time seen death writ everywhere, finds it again in the natural spectacle being performed in her garden. For Genji, the thought of her dying becomes focused on his own loneliness, from which he longs to be spared by a swift death. The Akashi Empress echoes Genji's *tsuyu no yo* (a conventional phrase literally meaning "the world of dew," or life as evanescent as the dew) to produce a generalization. She is young, and a daughter, so this is as close as she can come to participating.

After the poems, Murasaki cannot remain seated and, fearful of being rude, asks the others to withdraw. She lies down and draws the curtains before her, but the Empress, unable to leave, takes her hand and gazes into her face, whereupon Murasaki fades "like the dew" (4:492; S 717; W 731).

Genji is in a stupor. Remembering the time she nearly died, he has the priests continue with their rites through the night. The next day, Yūgiri joins him. Genji now regrets that he had never granted her permission to take vows and suggests that at least the tonsure should be administered in hopes that it might help her in the next world. Yūgiri's answer is curious. First, he wonders if an evil spirit is not up to mischief again. Second, even though a day and a night of the holy life is said to confer blessings, he questions whether, "if the unspeakable has really taken place, merely cutting her hair would make the Buddha light her path in the next world, so utterly different from ours. Wouldn't it only be adding to our grief?" (4:494; S 718; W 732). Genji leaves everything up to him.

Yūgiri has never forgotten that glimpse stolen on another windy day fifteen years earlier. Although he has harbored no "inappropriate" thoughts, he has continually wondered when he might get another such glimpse or, better yet, a note of her voice. "I will never hear her voice, but when, if not now, will my wish to see her again, lifeless though she is, be granted?" He pretends to silence Murasaki's noisily weeping ladies and leans over to lift up a corner of her curtains. Within, Genji gazes by lamplight upon Murasaki's face. He sees (*miru miru*, emphatic but powerless) Yūgiri looking but does not stop him and instead remarks, "Nothing has changed, but as you see, it is all over." Yūgiri strains to see through his tears.

> Her hair fell to the side, abundant, but without a strand out
> of place, lustrous and incomparable. In the bright light her
> fair face seemed to shine. Her form, in innocent repose,
> undistracted by the gestures of life, was more beautiful than
> ever.   (4:495; S 718-19; W 732)

"Innocent" here stands for *nani gokoro nakute*—literally, "without a thought," hence "un-self-conscious." It is a phrase that was used to characterize the child Murasaki. When she burst in on Genji and was urged by Shōnagon to sit close to him, when she saw her new playmates at the Nijōin, when she told Genji that she did not know how to write well yet, it was all "un-self-consciously." So it was also (how little she knew!) when she opened Genji's morning-after letter. How ironic is the "undistracted by the gestures of life," how poignant the juxtaposition of Murasaki's innocence in childhood and in death.[25] Yūgiri's gesture is at once devotional and blasphemous: he adores a saint and desecrates a corpse.[26]

Murasaki dies on the fourteenth of the Eighth Month and is cremated on the fifteenth. That is a time when the moon is bright. (Genji thinks of the moon at Aoi's cremation, also in the Eighth Month.) It is also by the full moon of the Eighth Month that the Heavenly Princess, the heroine of the *Tale of the Bamboo Cutter*, ascends from the earth to heaven. Murasaki is radiantly beautiful in death, with the purity of childhood attributed to her once again. She resembles the Heavenly Princess enough to provide an effective contrast.[27] Plucked in the mountains by a shining prince (the Princess was discovered by a bamboo cutter in a shining bamboo), Murasaki is brought to dwell in the earthly capital. Her purity thrice violated (once in childhood by Genji, once in adulthood and then again in death by Yūgiri), she is irrevocably a creature of the earth. At the same time, however, she is homeless. The world of the *Genji* can in no way accommodate her ascent to the heavens any more than it could her predecessor Fujitsubo's. The moon is beautiful but inhospitable.

In Murasaki, we see that to be a surrogate is to be not only homeless but imprisoned in this world. The illicit gestures of men, in which they break the rules of this world in order to insert another within it, represent their attempt to construct a blissful earthly dwelling. As for the women entangled in this endeavor, Murasaki spoke for them all toward the close of her life:

> What can be more cramped and miserable than a woman's lot! She has to bury herself, pretending neither to understand feelings nor to notice the interesting things that happen from time to time. How is she to taste the fleeting pleasures of life, how comfort herself for its dreariness?
>
> (4:442; S 699; W 717)

THE HERO ALONE

The description of Murasaki's last year began with the Lotus Sutra reading in spring, moved on to her summer sufferings, and ended with her autumn death. The remainder of "The Rites" chapter belongs in spirit with the one to follow, "The Wizard," which recounts Genji's last year in the tale. It is in "The Rites" that characters begin to reappear one by one, and though some of them will live on into the Uji chapters, most of the adults take their last bows. Each returns with a portion of his or her burden of the past. The first of them, Tō no Chūjō, makes Murasaki's death the occasion for remembering the death of his sister and Genji's first official wife Aoi, the justification being that the two died in the same season. Tō no Chūjō sends Genji the following poem:

Inishie no
aki sae ima no
kokochi shite
nurenishi sode ni
tsuyu zo okisou

I feel
as if a bygone autumn
had returned:
on sleeves, then drenched,
dew settles anew.

(4:501; S 721; W 734)

Genji guesses that if he were to respond sincerely his old friend
and rival would find him fainthearted. He takes a studied refuge
in generalities:

Tsuyukesa wa
mukashi ima tomo
omooezu
ōkata aki no
yoru koso tsurakere

I cannot think
whether these are the dewdrops
of today
or days long gone;
autumn nights are always
the hardest to endure.

(Ibid.)

The next exchange is with Akikonomu. During her Lotus Sutra ceremony, Murasaki bade a poetic farewell to the ladies of
winter and summer. Akikonomu was apparently omitted, perhaps because Murasaki's death in autumn was a defeat that exceeded the plane of the battle of spring and autumn. The games
of the Rokujōin are played out. Akikonomu herself refers to the
rivalry in her condolence poem to Genji:

Karehatsuru
nobe o ushi to ya
naki hito no
aki ni kokoro o
todomezariken

Perhaps the one now gone
found the moors
withered to waste
distasteful, and so refused
her heart to autumn.

(4:503; S 721; W 734)

This year, Akikonomu adds, she can take no pleasure in the
season herself. Genji, though numb with grief, reads and rereads
her message. Here at last was one who understood, he thinks,
one with whom he could still exchange sentiments. But even as
he is distracted, he weeps:

Noborinishi
kumoi nagara mo
kaerimiyo
ware akihatenu
tsune naranu yo ni

Look back upon me
from even your cloudy peaks;
I, together with autumn
have finished
with this world.

(Ibid.)

Akikonomu might have wondered whether grief had caused Genji to mistake his addressee. Although *kumoi* ("cloudy peaks") is a conventional metaphor for the Palace, the opening lines seem to be a passionate invocation to Murasaki. *Akihatenu* is both "autumn is over" and "I have wearied of"—a use of homophony not altogether appropriate in a poem addressed to a former Empress and the lady of autumn. One has the impression that the logic of the Rokujōin spins on independently of the players'—especially Genji's—will. Akikonomu is still compelled to express herself in terms of the aesthetic rivalry. (Like a carrier who herself shows no symptoms, she bears the imprint of her mother the Rokujō Lady's apparent hostility to Murasaki.) Her attraction for Genji is automatically rekindled, yet the sorrow of Murasaki's death has so overwhelmed him that he babbles in response.

"The Wizard" chapter begins in spring, thus evoking the first spring of the Rokujōin, the spring of the incense contest ("A Branch of Plum"), and the previous spring, when Murasaki was alive to conduct her ceremony. Genji secludes himself from the vernal vitality outdoors. Only one caller, his brother Prince Hotaru, is admitted to his presence. The Prince has chiefly made his mark in the tale as an occasional *arbiter elegantiarum*, not as a superior to Genji but as his instrument. His role has been to provide reliable confirmation of Genji's values.[28] (Even as Tamakazura's suitor, he played a role assigned by Genji.) He presided over the incense contest and participated in the preparation of the Akashi Princess's initiation and entry into court. Harmony prevailed in the Rokujōin in part thanks to such aesthetic expressions of rivalry. Now Prince Hotaru has become an elegiac emblem of that life, and it is in this vein that he and Genji exchange poems, Genji addressing the Prince as spring, the Prince likening Genji to fragrance.

Other than the Prince, Genji sees no one but the women of his household. Since the end of "The Rites" chapter, he has been living in the women's quarters (whether in the Nijōin or the Rokujōin is unclear). Shunning the eyes of others, he has all but become a woman himself. In this, he was anticipated, though far more dramatically, by Kashiwagi, who began to fear the "eyes of heaven" after "seeing" the Third Princess and who walked to his deathbed after being "seen" by Genji. Cloistered women guarded their impoverished integrity (composed of chastity and ignorance) by keeping themselves invisible. Life was lived second- and thirdhand by highborn women, who heard the cuckoo's song through the reports of their attendants. Once they were seen (wedded or violated), however, they could begin to see, which could eventually lead, perhaps, to their choosing to renounce life. For Kashiwagi and Genji, the process is reversed. For men, being seen is the necessary consequence of success, of public splendor. Yet crises modify the terms of life so that seeing becomes uninviting and being seen terrifying.[29] It is as much as Genji can manage to gather his shattered self to take refuge in the private world of women—doubly private and nearly anonymous, since these are servants.

When not praying, Genji listens to them talk. Their conversation naturally tends toward the days when their lady was alive. Listening, Genji is made to relive that period, and to relive it from something resembling Murasaki's point of view. For example, when one of the women remarks on the falling snow (for the spring is still young), he remembers the chill of the morning when he was left waiting outside after the wedding night with the Third Princess. This time there is no dissembling in praise: Genji feels the painfulness of Murasaki's efforts to conceal the traces of her tears, and he longs "throughout the night" to see her once more, if only in his dreams (4:510; S 724; W 737).

Outside, the flowers bloom and birds visit according to their time. The Genji who avoids the eyes of others is no longer the Genji who manipulated nature into the art of the Rokujōin, the Genji who recreated his women as the flowers of that nature. Now he is adrift among the flowers of the garden. The birch cherry, the wisteria, the *yamabuki*, are all, if anything, more splendid than ever. Once these flowers evoked the forms of Mu-

rasaki, the Akashi Princess, and Tamakazura. The traces of the
association linger in the memory, but the flowers are now flowers. And the women have gone their separate ways. Spring no
longer wears a human face. Genji composes a series of poems
on the woman who once embodied the season.

One day, seeking distraction from his solitude, he makes one
of his rare visits to the quarters of the Third Princess. These are
his impressions of the former wife-turned-nun:

> She was reading sutras in front of a statue of the Buddha.
> Her understanding of the religious life was hardly profound,
> yet here she was, undistracted by regrets for the world,
> peacefully pursuing her devotions. Her wholeheartedness
> was enviable. It chagrined him to think that in vocation he
> lagged behind even this shallow woman.
>
> (4:517; S 727; W[738])

As a topic of conversation with this nun and former wife, Genji
settles on his sense of estrangement from the flowers because of
the passing of the wife who had dedicated herself to spring. He
finds the *yamabuki* "touching, for they bloom more brilliantly
than ever, apparently not knowing that she who planted them is
gone" (4:518; S 727; W 738). The nun replies, "Spring is a
stranger to my valley," quoting from a poem by Kiyohara no
Fukayabu (fl. 908-923):

Hikari naki	In this valley without light
tani ni wa	spring is a stranger:
haru mo yoso nareba	no need to brood
sakite toku chiru	over flowers
mono omoi mo nashi	that no sooner bloom
	than scatter.
	(KKS 967, "Miscellaneous, 2")

Stung by the rebuff, Genji struggles to conceal his tears. He
goes straight to the Akashi Lady's quarters. She is older, and a
woman disciplined to endure. He can count on her indulgence.
He proceeds to reflect on his life, touching gracefully on the
Suma-Akashi days. He rues his inability to be resolute and take
vows—something that he should have done long ago. But the
Akashi Lady is sagacious: even people of no importance have

difficulty renouncing the world. It would even be flighty of him, with such weighty responsibilities, to take so grave a measure in haste. No, he should wait until his grandchildren were grown and their positions assured. Genji wonders about the propriety of such calculation in matters of faith, but he is able to resume reminiscing, recalling his grief when Fujitsubo died. As he talks, Genji toys with the idea of spending the night there, but he thinks better of it and takes his leave. The Akashi Lady, now called "woman," is saddened. Genji manages to send off a poem in the early morning:

Naku naku mo	Crying, oh crying
kaerinishi kana	like the wild geese
kari no yo wa	I made my way home;
izuko mo tsui no	but this passing world
toko yo naranu ni	holds no resting place
	eternal.
	(4:522; S 728; W [739])

The poem hangs on a pun on *kari*, "passing" (literally, "temporary") and "wild geese." The birds make their way north just as the weeping Genji leaves the Akashi Lady's side for his own lonely bed. *Toko yo* (literally "eternal" or "other world" [of the dead]) contains *toko*, "bed." Wild geese are associated with the unchanging world of hermit-wizards (2:193, n. 23). Genji cannot guard his marital bed from change let alone fly off to a world where change is unadmitted.

Genji's poem is a difficult one for the Akashi Lady to respond to. This is what she does:

Kari ga ishi	Since the water has dried
nawashiro mizu no	from the field of seedling rice
taeshi yori	where the wild goose stayed,
utsurishi hana no	I never see the reflection
kage o dani mizu	of the flower
	once mirrored there.
	(Ibid.)

Here Genji is a wild goose whose beauty of form is represented by a reflected flower. Murasaki is the water upon which the image appears. Genji as both wild goose and flower is distracting, and therefore worth speculating about, coming from this poet. Murasaki, who searched in mirrors for Genji's image, is appropriately enough turned into the medium of reflection herself. She is the one who made Genji visible, and beautifully so, like a flower. (We have been accustomed to thinking of the Rokujōin as a place where Genji gathered women and made them flower beautifully.) His flowering was manifested in part by his visiting women other than herself, each incomparable in her own way. Thus, paradoxically, while the jealous Murasaki was alive, the Akashi Lady was able to see Genji from time to time, whereas now her life is parched of all such visits. She misses him. There is a split in the poem between the first three lines and the last two. Beyond whatever perceptions she may have about Murasaki's role, the Akashi Lady still finds Genji's presence magical and still yearns for him. After a characteristically practical pronouncement in conversation (asking Genji to concern himself with the welfare of his grandchildren, i.e., with Akashi progeny, thus verging on self-parody), the Akashi Lady discloses another self in verse.

Genji's visits to these two women provide concise sketches of the Rokujōin past and present. The bereaved Genji calls on them to mourn a former rival—as if, somehow, the governing contradictions of the Rokujōin had passed together with its glory. The surviving inhabitants are essentially unchanged.

Time passes. Summer robes arrive from Hana Chiru Sato. It had always been Murasaki's task to tend to Genji's apparel, so this gesture, like all others, carries a special poignance. The robes come with a poem in keeping with their giver's sweetly unassuming nature. Genji courteously frames a reply on the subject of human sorrow.

It is time for the Aoi Matsuri again. Genji comes upon a servant, Chūjō, taking a nap. A "Chūjō" appeared as early as the "Heartvine" chapter as a serving woman who received Genji's favors; during the Suma-Akashi exile she joined Murasaki's staff. There is no assurance that this is the same woman, and of course, it is just such indeterminate identity that characterizes the women of this status. Since Murasaki's death, Genji has kept even such women from his bed, even while cherishing their companionship anew. On this, the annual festival day of the

Kamo Shrines, Genji, not wanting his entire household to be shrouded in darkness with him, has suggested that the women attend from their own homes. (Many years ago, Princess Ōmiya urged her reluctant daughter Aoi to attend the same festival so as not to deprive her own attendants of a little merrymaking.) Chūjō has stayed behind; hence, the unexpected encounter. Earlier in the chapter, Genji likened her to a pine planted near her mistress's grave: she is, in other words, a modest substitute for Murasaki, and Genji is fond of her. Now, she awakens, flushed from sleep—a favorite feminine moment in Murasaki Shikibu's writings[30]—and there follows a detailed description of her garment, a staple topic of interest that had been abandoned since Murasaki's last illness.

Picking up a garland of heartvine, Genji inquires, in mock seriousness, what it is called. Chūjō replies shyly,

Samo koso wa	Well might you ask:
yorube no mizu ni	weeds crowd the water
mikusa ime	where the gods once alighted;
kyō no kazashi yo	even its name
na sae wasururu	you have forgotten,
	the garland for today.
	(4:524; S 729; W 740)

Yorube no mizu (1.2) refers to a vessel of water placed before a shrine altar. It was thought that the gods came to possess it and that accordingly it was possible to augur the future by looking into it. By "gods" Chūjō is of course referring to Genji and reproaching him for his neglect. Genji, acknowledging the justness of her words, replies,

Ōkata wa	Thoughts of the world
omoi suteteshi	I have cast behind;
yo nare domo	but still the heartvine
aoi wa nao ya	I might pluck
tsumi okasubeki	in sin.
	(Ibid.)

Just as in his first poem to Murasaki, there is a pun on *tsumi*, "to pick" (a plant) and "sin." Chūjō's poem is a rupture in a chapter filled with prayers, incense, and lugubrious talk, and Genji's response breaks with his spiritual if not his physical abstinence.

What we must not overlook, however, is the extent to which Genji's metamorphosis into an erotic god (as well as Chūjō's prompting) is governed by the calendar. All lives are, of course, regulated by the calendar in varying ways; and the life of a Heian aristocrat was bound by the mutual reinforcement of court ritual and folk customs and their refinement in poetic anthologies. What makes the role of the calendar, and especially the poetic calendar, particularly conspicuous here is that the tale has been stripped of all action and plot complications. Within the confines of his world of grief, Genji behaves as the seasons and the corresponding poetic conventions require. This is the Rokujōin with a vengeance, with its regulator now regulated.

The "entry" for the Fifth Month reinforces the emerging pattern. This is the season when time hangs heavily even in ordinary years. Yūgiri comes to pass the evening with his father. The moon bursts through the clouds to display the mandarin orange trees in bloom, and the stage is set for the cry of the cuckoo. While they wait, father and son carry on a conversation replete with appropriate poetic allusions. Needless to say, after a suitable interval, the fabled cry comes. "How did it know," asks Genji, echoing a line from a *Kokin Rokujō* poem:

Inishie no	When we talk of things
koto kataraeba	bygone,
hototogisu	the cuckoo—
ikani shirite ka	how did it know?
furu koe no suru	cries in a voice
	familiar of old.
	(*Zoku Kokka Taikan* 33650)

Genji continues with a poem of his own:

Naki hito o	O mountain cuckoo,
shinoburu yoi no	have you come
murasame ni	drenched in the rain
nurete ya kitsuru	of evening

yama hototogisu

as we mourn one
who is no more?
(4:527; S 731; W 741)

Yūgiri responds,

Hototogisu
kimi ni tsutenan
furusato no
hana tachibana wa
ima zo sakari to

O cuckoo,
let her know
that the blossoms
of the mandarin orange
at her home
are at their finest now.
(Ibid.)

This poem echoes, among others, the anonymous *Kokinshū* poem that established a lasting bond between the scent of the mandarin orange blossom and memories of the dead:

Satsuki matsu
hana tachibana no
ka o kageba
mukashi no hito no
sode no ka zo suru

May-awaiting
the mandarin orange blossom
bears in its scent
fragrance from the sleeve
of one bygone.
(KKS 39, "Summer")[31]

The passage closes with Yūgiri spending the night with his father and musing on his proximity to the marriage bed from which he was once guarded so vigilantly.

There are two more solitary compositions by Genji before the season changes to autumn. The poetic development of the spring and summer sections can be schematically represented as follows:

POETS	TOPICS (Seasonal or ceremonial motifs)
Spring	
1. Genji - Prince Hotaru	plum blossoms
2. Genji	lingering snow
3. Genji	plum blossoms, warbler

207

4. Genji	spring hedge (i.e., garden)
5. Genji - Akashi Lady	wild geese flying north

Summer

6. Genji - Hana Chiru Sato	summer robes, cicada
7. Genji - Chūjō	heartvine
8. Genji - Yūgiri	cuckoo, mandarin orange blossoms
9. Genji	insects (i.e., cicada)
10. Genji	fireflies

Most of the "topics" in these two sections are the natural objects that have acquired fixed seasonal associations in the history of Japanese poetry.[32] Number 4, in which Genji reflects on how Murasaki's garden, now in bloom, will in time go the way of its owner, contains no conventional seasonal items. As a measure of the poetic development of the chapter, this list is skeletal inasmuch as there are numerous such conventional items in the surrounding prose, which moreover is saturated with fragmentary quotations from other poems, Chinese as well as Japanese.[33]

In similar fashion the remainder of the chapter can be sketched as follows:

POETS	TOPICS (Seasonal or ceremonial motifs)

Autumn

11. Genji	Tanabata (the Star Festival)
12. Genji - Chūjō	Murasaki's first anniversary rites
13. Genji	chrysanthemums (on the ninth day of the Ninth Month)
14. Genji	wizards (i.e., wild geese)

Winter

15. Genji	Toyo no Akari no Sechie
16. Genji	mountain of death
17. Genji	sea grass (i.e., letters)
18. Genji - priest	snow, plum blossoms
19. Genji	end-of-the-year

The Tanabata Festival (number 11), on the seventh day of the Seventh Month, marks the annual reunion of the Herdsman (the star Altair) with the Weaver Maiden (Vega) via the Milky Way. Number 13 refers to the practice of washing oneself with floss moistened in chrysanthemum dew on the ninth day of the Ninth Month to protect against old age. The Toyo no Akari no Sechie (number 15) was one of the events of the great harvest festival at the Palace.

The brief descriptions I have just offered reflect the major difference between the spring/summer and autumn/winter sections: the replacement of natural objects in the former by ritual in the latter. Like natural objects, rituals have their seasonal associations, of course, but they have a pronounced social character as well. There are additional rites besides those appearing in the poems, and their cumulative effect is to bring into relief the image of Genji as a solitary onlooker. (Indeed, the majority of the poems in this section have no addressee.)[34]

Some of the poems deserve special comment. Number 17, for example, is

Ōzora o	O wizards
kayou maboroshi	crossing the great skies,
yume ni dani	seek out the soul
miekonu tama no	that will not appear
yukue tazuneyo	even to my dreams.
	(4:531; S 733; W [741])

In the spring, Genji wrote of the wild geese flying north in his exchange with the Akashi Lady (number 5). Now, he watches the geese return and likens them to wizards with magical powers to fly to the land of the dead. (Yūgiri demanded the same service of the cuckoo in his exchange with Genji in number 81.) In a great, arcing move, this poem reaches back to the poem composed by the Kiritsubo Emperor after the death of the Kiritsubo Lady:

Tazuneyuku	Would there were a wizard
maboroshi mogana	to seek her out,
tsute nite mo	that even through another
tama no arika o	I might learn

soko to shirubeki   the whereabouts
                                          of her soul.
                                          (1:111; S 12; W 14)

The mood of this poem is implicitly subjunctive, which already
separates it from the *Song of Everlasting Sorrow*, Po Chü-i's classic narrative poem whose bereaved monarch actually sends forth
two wizards, charged with the task of finding his beloved's soul.
They are successful and receive beautiful tokens to take back
with them. Genji goes beyond his father in the direction of secularized despair. He does this by reinvesting, metaphorically, the
conventional natural image of wild geese with the aura of the
magical only to emphasize the futility of such a gesture.

Perhaps in recognition of the finality of Murasaki's departure,
as well as in preparation for his own, Genji begins to dispose of
his letters. Those from Murasaki, especially those written to him
in Suma, stir the deepest memories. He has his closest attendants
shred them. In the end, he adds a poem to a note from Murasaki:

Kakitsumete   There is no point
miru mo kai nashi   in gathering them together
moshio gusa   just to look at—
onaji kumoi no   turn into smoke, O sea grasses
keburi to o nare   and join her
                                   in the sky.
                                   (4:534; S 734; W 742)

Sea grasses can be gathered together (*kakitsumete*, which is partially homophonous with *kaku*, "to write"). *Kai*, "point" (more
literally, "worth" or "benefit"), is homophonous with "sea-
shells." The letters, like sea grass, are gathered and burnt. When
the Heavenly Princess in the *Tale of the Bamboo Cutter* left the
earth for the moon, she left behind a grief-stricken emperor
(among other sorrowing mortals). She had shown him special
favor in addressing him a letter to accompany an elixir of im-
mortality. But the Emperor, finding the prospect of eternal life
chilling without the companionship of the Heavenly Princess,
instructed his attendants to take the letter together with the elixir

to be burnt at the top of the highest mountain in the land. There, at Fuji (homophonous with "immortal"), the smoke was to rise ceaselessly into the skies.[35] In "The Wizard," both hero and heroine are mortal.

The last exchange in the chapter takes place between Genji and a priest during year-end expiatory rites. As he serves the priest his wine, Genji recites,

Haru made no	I don't know
inochi mo shirazu	if life will last
yuki no uchi ni	until spring;
irozuku ume o	let us don today
kyō kazashiten	the plum
	that begins to color
	even in the snow.
	(4:535; S 734; W 743)

The priest replies,

Chiyo no haru	I pray this flower
mirubeki hana to	may see a thousand springs;
inori okite	as for myself
waga mi zo yuki to	I grow old
tomo ni furinuru	and droop
	with the snow.
	(Ibid.)

This exchange harkens back to the first poems in the chapter, the poems on the plum blossoms composed with Prince Hotaru and the solitary poem on spring snow by Genji. There, sorrow issued exclusively from Murasaki's passing. Now, one year later, it encompasses all human fate.

There are twenty-six poems in "The Wizard," quite a number for a short chapter. Poetry has acquired unprecedented prominence in the portrayal of the close of Genji's life. Is this in response to a new demand—is prose deemed to be inadequate to the task at hand? Since the question tends to be answered in the affirmative, it is worth pausing over the assumptions at stake. What follows is one of the more fully developed examples of the prose-ceding-to-poetry argument. In answer to his own question

of whether the tools of prose, like the life of the hero they seek
to present, have reached their limit and must now retreat, Fujii
Sadakazu responds:

> Of course, it is not that the methods of prose have retreated,
> but that the language of Japanese poetry is demanded by a
> plane that transcends the plane of prose. The essence of
> Japanese poetry is nothing other than expression in lan-
> guage. Japanese poetry is linguistic expression poetically
> condensed. We know many instances—they are the rule
> and not the exception—in places other than "The Wizard,"
> where poetry is used functionally. The distinctive character
> of the poetry in "The Wizard" is that it is not used func-
> tionally. Beginning with the spring "books" of this chapter,
> and continuing from the summer to the autumn "books," a
> heart-swelling grief permeates the scene. It is the fate of
> language to be required to depict this overwhelming grief.
> . . . In "The Wizard" chapter, the exposition of themes has
> been all but abandoned. When [the text] approaches a
> theme, the space of lyric poetry, that is, the space of poet-
> ically condensed language, is inserted into the work, and
> thus linguistic expression is realized.[36]

Fujii goes on to discuss the last poems in the chapter as showing
an elevation from "the plane of prose to the plane of language."
What had been a thematic "hesitation" (on Genji's part to take
vows) becomes an "essential 'wandering' " (ibid.).

No one would want to dispute the "condensation of language"
that characterizes Japanese poetry, or indeed any other form of
lyric poetry. Japanese poetry had a long and intensely developed
tradition by Murasaki Shikibu's time, and to judge from her
work, she was acutely aware of the possibilities for exploiting the
wealth accumulated by the tradition. It is doubtful, however,
that one of the greatest writers of prose fiction in history would
have equated language with poetry and accordingly have surrendered herself to the methods of the latter in a climactic chapter.
She labored in a world in which not only poetry but Buddhist
scriptures, histories, and Confucian texts had a proud authority

through the claim of priority, which seemingly conferred upon them the right to assert their equation with language, or at least with the legitimate use of language. The whole of the *Genji* might be seen as a splendid gesture to appropriate language for prose fiction, the putative latecomer, and thereby undermine the arrogant claim to exclusive legitimacy of the other genres. Rather than posit a dichotomy between the concentrated plenitude of poetry, with its adequacy to the expression of "essential" emotion, and the diffuse poverty of prose, quotidian in its discursiveness ("sacred" poetry versus "profane" prose), and without denying the differences of poetry and prose, it behooves us to understand the commingling of their methods in "The Wizard" and their complementary service to the fiction of the *Genji*.

To this end, it is provisionally useful to distinguish between the individual poems of "The Wizard" chapter and their effect as a whole, which is that of the seasonal sections of an imperial anthology of poetry. We have already touched, for example, on the conspicuous number of solitary compositions. The choice of partners in Genji's exchanges is also revealing. Indeed, each poem relies on other poems and on various prose passages in the *Genji* as well as on prior literature for the communication of its sense. No element is free-standing. The relation of the characters to their poems continues to be important. Each instance of the composition of a poem takes on a final, typical form in this chapter. Thus, Prince Hotaru is elegant and temperate. The Akashi Lady, though severely practical in conversation, expresses her never-satisfied yearning in her poem. Yūgiri exploits the medium of a poetry exchange to address Murasaki in an acceptable, aestheticized vein while furtively thinking about his parents' marriage bed. Also notable is the failure of Genji and the Third Princess to exchange poems.

This matter of "typical form" suggests a sense in which the prose of "The Wizard" has embraced the methods of poetry. That is, the prose contexts in which the poems are embedded are as focused and condensed as the poems with their seasonal or ritual topics. The difference is that while the seasonal and ritual objects have an extensive life beyond the *Genji*, the condensation in the prose takes place around the characters and

213

events of the tale (which is not to deny kinship to characters and events beyond the *Genji*; the difference of degree, however, is considerable). What we are witnessing in "The Wizard" is the *Genji*'s ritualization of its own past.

This also applies to the imposition of a seasonal, "poetic" order on the chapter as a whole. The poetic order in "The Wizard" is a pointed repetition with variation on the design of the Rokujōin and the structure of the Tamakazura chapters. (The Rokujōin and the Tamakazura chapters, in their turn, had borrowed the seasonal order of the imperial anthologies as a metaphor for order as such.) Once Genji, as the ruler of the Rokujōin and surrogate ruler of the cosmos, ensured the harmonious (the aesthetically pleasing) progression of the seasons. He was at the center of a golden cyclical time in which human and natural order were joined. The sunlit days of the Rokujōin were necessarily illusory and necessarily tainted from the first spring, but their potency in the imagination was absolute. By contrast, in "The Wizard" Genji is compelled, by poetic and by cosmic order, to trace the circumference of a circle that is closing without regard for his will. This noble hero's final journey is traced by the wheel of time.

And yet, even at this late hour, there is a sense in which he resists. It takes the form of inability to renounce the secular life. This nagging subject recurs throughout the chapter: with Murasaki gone, there is ostensibly nothing to hold him back. But he has become closer to the serving women who would be psychically if not materially destitute were he to abandon them; the Akashi Lady appeals on the behalf of the grandchildren; and there is always the need for a hero to adopt the priestly life in an ideal fashion, which seems improbable in the throes of grief. What does the religious vocation mean for Genji?

Early in the chapter he looks back upon his life and summarizes it, in a pronouncement similar to those he has made before, even as recently as "The Rites" chapter. He is addressing the serving women:

> In this world I have been born to a lofty position where it would seem that I could want for nothing; yet, the thought

has never left me that fate has dealt me more than my share
of things to regret.   (4:511; S 724; W [737])

Unparalleled glory and unparalleled sorrow—this is Genji's self-
proclaimed motif as a hero. The best-loved son of an emperor,
Genji from an early age gave intimations of unearthly gifts. After
the reverses culminating in the Suma-Akashi years, his life began
an unswerving ascent until, in "Wisteria Leaves," he was designated the equivalent of a retired emperor. Even, or especially
before, then he ruled over an earthly paradise that implicitly
diminished the Palace. On the other hand, as he increasingly
insists, his life was marked from the beginning by death, unsatisfied love, and betrayal. Kashiwagi's affair with the Third Princess produced the most bitter secret of all since it could be shared
with no one and, indeed, demanded the expression of joy over
the birth of Kaoru. Yet now, even when Murasaki has left him,
Genji still defers the gesture of renunciation.

The pluses and minuses on Genji's balance sheet show the
missing elements in his life, the loss of his mother and demotion
by his father to commoner status being early and obvious examples. The minuses record the failure of attempts to fill the
lack; the pluses, public successes that prove in the end to have
been inadequate compensation. Genji's lifelong pursuit of the
murasaki women—Fujitsubo, Murasaki, and the Third Princess,
a strong thread in the complicated weave of the tale—is an outstanding example of the former, in contrast to the Akashi connection, which belongs to the latter.

The contours of the lack at the center of Genji's life are metaphorically suggested and redefined in the course of the tale,
through all the events and characters confronted by him. The
recurrent motif of substitution attests to the potency of this lack,
as does the attraction of the illicit, which never ceases to whisper
the possibility of satisfaction. In this perspective, the symbol of
Genji's triumph, his attainment of a rank *equivalent* to that of a
retired emperor, is also the symbol of original and permanent
loss. Indeed, it is this enduring lack that makes Genji a hero,
that makes it possible for him to be written about for forty long
chapters.

The religious motif—to take vows or not—provides a bridge to the Uji chapters. Since "religion" is yet another mode of representing both the deficiency and a conventional solution, for Genji to take vows would be to nullify the deficiency by surrendering to it—a sure sign of his end as a hero. "The Wizard" manages to close Genji's life gently, without depriving him of his heroism and, more important, without simplifying the tale that comes before it by achieving consummate closure.

There is of course a price to be paid by Genji for being such a hero. A persistent concern of these essays has been the development of knowledge depicted in the course of the tale. It is this issue that underlies, for example, the preoccupation with vision. In contrast to the principal heroines, as well as to Kashiwagi and Kaoru, Genji is never seen in self-scrutiny. He is never psychologically revealed as they are—which of course brings us back to the question of what makes him a hero. Being closed, he benefits from the aura of secrecy and the grandeur of the archaic hero—the grandeur, without the excessive simplicity of mythic history. The subtleties by which he is everywhere surrounded in the novel make us interpret the fact that he does not examine himself as an indication of the unfathomable depths of that self.

Thus Genji cannot, must not, take vows on the pages of the tale. That he will eventually do so, and that death will follow soon after, are apparent. The slow agony of the seasons leading to Murasaki's death is accelerated by the poetic punctuations in "The Wizard." The chapter's haste grows increasingly evident. The prose becomes fragmentary, as if Genji's life can sustain only lists of events with appropriate verses. We are left suspended on the last day of the year, uncertain as to whether spring will quicken again when the calendar changes.

Chapter 4

Women Beyond

the Capital

UJI BEFORE THE UJI CHAPTERS

"THE LIGHT had passed, and none among his issue could cast a like shadow" (5:431; S 735; W 749). The beginning of the final section of the *Genji* opens with the declaration of an insurmountable loss. The hero is dead, the tale told out. And yet there is to come a magnificent set of chapters that for many readers over the centuries has constituted the finest part of the work. They are known collectively as the Ten Uji Chapters. The reader mindful of such details will observe that this popular designation of ten chapters conveniently conceals the problematic three chapters following "The Wizard," that poetic account of Genji's last year. "Irregularities" in diction, syntax, character appellation, or chronology have tempted scholars to the ready solution of multiple authorship. Those three chapters, designated as the Three Prince Niou Chapters, reintroduce as young men Kaoru and Niou, the two who must now attempt (in vain, as the opening has summarily declared) to fill Genji's shoes. The last chapter of this little set, "The Bamboo River," opens with this emblematic speculation:

> The following comes from the ramblings of old women who, removed from Genji's household, lingered on at the estate of the late chancellor [Higekuro]. It seems not to resemble the accounts given by Murasaki's people, but they say those are full of errors because they were told by older women inclined to confusion. Who is to be believed?
>
> (5:53; S 751; W 766)

217

With studied innocence the passage threatens the solidity of the
world that had us spellbound. It flashes before the reader the
possibility of other versions of what they have read, been seduced
by, and committed themselves to. The Prince Niou chapters are
evidently transitional, but the easy equation of the transitional
with the marginal reveals a pervasive discomfort with that which
strains the boundaries of preconceived, static notions of order. If
they are marginal, they are so as the very world that they prefigure, the world of Uji, which will at once amplify and refute the
world of the capital where the tale was born and nurtured.[1]

The city of Uji, now no more than a pleasant hour's train ride
from Kyoto, is bordered by hills on three sides and a lake on the
fourth: hence, the notion that its name derived from *uchi*, "inner." It was also "within" that known part of the cosmos that was
the Yamato state in the earlier days of Japanese history.[2] Few
things are more precarious than innerness: with the eventual settling of the previously migrant capital to the north (Heiankyō),
Uji found itself outside. This may account for another aspect
prominent in the play of place-name etymology associated with
the site, an aspect that first found expression in a poem by a
Priest Kisen (dates unknown). The poem, which was judged suitable for inclusion in the *Kokinshū*, is

Waga io wa	Serene is my dwelling,
miyako no tatsumi	southeast of the capital;
shika zo sumu	but people seem to think
yo o Ujiyama to	it's in the world-loathing
hito wa iunari	hills of Uji.
	(KKS 983, "Miscellaneous, 2")

Uji is made to coincide with *ushi*, "wearisome," "distasteful," or
"unsympathetic." Here the speaker is so smug about his isolation
from the world that he claims to have transcended the need even
to dismiss society as loathsome. The effects of punning, however, escape the poet's control, for it will not be the serenity
(from a play on *sumu*, "to dwell," and "to be clear," in line 3)[3]
of life in Uji that will be this poem's contribution to the legacy
of early Japanese literature but rather the gloominess of separation from the capital.

Now, the tension implicit in the two associations singled out here of inclusion and exclusion hint at the vicissitudes marking the site of Uji. The *Kojiki* and the *Nihon Shoki* recount a Lear-like scene enacted between Emperor Ōjin (r. 270-310, according to the *Nihon Shoki*) and his three sons.[4] The emperor asks his two older offspring whether an older or a younger son is the dearer. The literal-minded senior, Ōyama Mori no Mikoto, promptly replies in his own favor. The middle brother, Ōsazaki no Mikoto (later to become Emperor Nintoku), divining their father's wishes, pronounces in favor of the younger and is rewarded for his perspicacity by being assigned to assist the youngest, Uji no Waki Iratsuko, now designated crown prince, in governing the land. It should be understood that the young Waki Iratsuko has been superbly educated by the finest continental tutors his father could procure, and that he has already rewarded such care by boldly defying insults from the King of Koguryŏ (in northern Korea). He shows promise of becoming a saintly ruler, and indeed, accounts of his life are shrouded within a "Confucian veil."[5] The chagrined Ōyama Mori no Mikoto plots to kill Waki Iratsuko, who is forewarned by the piously astute Nintoku. Waki Iratsuko, disguised as a humble oarsman, strikes his unsuspecting brother and sends him tumbling into the rapid currents of the Uji River. The luckless Ōyama Mori disappears with the following poem:

Chihayaburu
Uji no watari ni
saotori ni
hayaken hito shi
waga moko ni kon

Here, at the ford
of raging Uji River:
let one who is quick
at the oar
come to my side![6]

The *Kojiki* and the *Nihon Shoki* have it that the virtuous Waki Iratsuko, recognizing that true wisdom resided with the older Nintoku, never took the throne but retired to Uji for three years, during which time he and Nintoku alternately refused the tribute that came to each as emperor. Finally, Waki Iratsuko, seeing the harm that was wrought upon the land by this confusion, put an end to his own life, whereupon Nintoku became undisputed ruler. No doubt this pretty story conceals an internecine feud; at any rate, the *Fudoki*, which—being a compilation of reports from the provinces—offers insight into visions other than that of the Yamato state, suggests that Waki Iratsuko actually did accede, that there was, for a time, such a personage as the "Uji Emperor."[7] Uji, then, is a tragic site of kingship almost gained but lost.

The ford in the drowning Ōyama Mori's poem represents another, less dramatic but not negligible aspect of the place: Uji as a crossroads for early travelers. With Ōmi to the northeast and Yamato to the south, Uji was witness to constant meetings and partings, and it is as such a confluence that it gains prominence in the poetry of the *Man'yōshū* as well as of the *Nihon Shoki* and the *Kojiki*. Toward the middle of the seventh century, the construction of a bridge over the river not only reinforced Uji's character as the locus of transient unions but gave rise to a host of new legends. Travel naturally craves divine good will. The Uji bridge came to have its own guardian deity whose identity was early established as female. She is known as *hashihime*, the "lady of the bridge." In the earlier legends the lady of the bridge is visited nightly by a male river deity, but in later accounts the principals become human, with the lady typically made to assume the character of a jealous wife whose husband is lost to a sea deity such as the Dragon King.[8] The most celebrated and potent formulation of the "lady of the bridge" before the *Genji* is to be found in this *Kokinshū* poem:

Samushiro ni	Alone again tonight
koromo katashiki	upon her straw mat
koyoi mo ya	will she spread her robe,
ware o matsuran	waiting for me,
Uji no hashihime	the lady of the Uji bridge.
	(KKS 689, "Love, 4")

"Spread alone/her robe" needs amplification: since lovers slept upon spread out robes, the sleeve of one overlapping a sleeve of the other, this bed is incomplete (*katashiki*, being a "partial spreading out"). Thus the place name Uji evokes the metamorphosis of a contented (or so we surmise if the god's nightly visits are regular) goddess into an angry human wife and finally a

220

woman forever waiting, in other words, from satisfaction through defiance to a frozen acceptance of permanent absence.

These oppositions acquire additional nuances in the Heian period. The increasingly powerful Fujiwara buried their dead in the hills of Uji and traveled by way of Uji to their tutelary shrine of Kasuga and the tutelary temple of Kōfukuji. Uji was also a necessary stopping place from the capital to Hatsuse, that pilgrimage site so important for women (to be visited, for example, by the *Genji* heroines Tamakazura and Ukifune). Such excursions often took on the coloring of pleasure trips, with the consequence that a number of villas were constructed. One of them belonged to Minamoto no Tōru, whose estate in the capital we recall was the common model for the haunted house where Yūgao died and the resplendent Rokujōin. In Murasaki Shikibu's time the estate belonged to her employer, the most celebrated Fujiwara, Michinaga. Michinaga's son had a temple built on the grounds, a part of which stands to this day as the graceful Byōdōin. The easy juxtaposition of devotion and pleasure—the proximity of the other shore of enlightenment (*higan*) to this one of worldly entrapment—is emblematic of Heian culture, which imagined the possibility of salvation while the flesh was still quick. Uji, in other words, was as much "in between" as it was "within" or "without"—geographically, historically, and spiritually.

Secrets, Fragrances, and Vocation: The Men of Uji

Uji is introduced into the world of the *Genji*—indeed, becomes the world of the *Genji*—in a chapter titled, pointedly enough, "The Lady at the Bridge." The opening signals another beginning:

> There was at that time an aging prince who had been quite forgotten by the world. With his mother coming from a distinguished family, he had enjoyed special esteem, but the reigns changed, and in the wake of certain events that left him humiliated, his supporters, bitter with disappoint-

ment, began to turn their backs upon the world, thus leaving the Prince with none to turn to publicly or privately.
(5:109; S 775; W 791)

His wife, the passage continues, was the daughter of a minister and as such keenly burdened by the vexation issuing from her princely husband's mysterious disgrace. The couple take consolation in their mutual constancy, though even that comfort proves short-lived since she dies giving birth to their second daughter. This passage, like virtually every element in the Uji chapters, compels comparison with the first opening. There, the daughter of an ambitious man (not quite a minister) is accorded unusual recognition by the Emperor, bears him a son, and dies amidst the furor caused by the inappropriate royal attachment. The son, of course, grows up to become the Shining Genji. The opening of the Uji story seems to be at once an enervated repetition with variation and an inexact negative of the first tale.

The ambiguities become focused shortly thereafter. The aging prince is known as the Eighth Prince: we learn that he is the eighth son of none other than the Kiritsubo Emperor and, accordingly, the younger brother of Genji.

When Reizei was Crown Prince, the Emperor Suzaku's scheming mother [Kokiden] planned that the Eighth Prince should succeed in the reign and busied herself with designs to increase the prosperity of her own family, with the result that the Prince became needlessly estranged from the others [Genji and Reizei]. And now, with the world in the hands of posterity, there was no way for him to mingle in society.   (5:117; S 779; W 795)

This passage seems innocent enough: the villain is still Kokiden. Yet these modest few lines hint at a history that was suppressed beneath the pathos of the Akashi Lady's yielding her daughter to Genji and Murasaki and the drama of the Picture Contest. Now we know that Genji's efforts to consolidate his power in the person of Reizei produced a specific and, moreover, innocuous victim in the person of the Eighth Prince. This hapless creature had lost both parents early in life and had been unable to acquire substantial learning—that is, familiarity with Chinese texts. Thus marked as unfit for rule, he was mercilessly squeezed between the designs of Kokiden and Genji. Inevitably, he became extraordinarily "refined and terribly gentle, like a woman" (5:116; S 779; W 795) and managed somehow to lose even his considerable inheritance from his father-in-law.

This could, of course, have been the fate of the young Genji had the Kiritsubo Emperor imprudently obeyed the dictates of his heart and designated this beloved son as his heir. That is one of the lessons of this passage. But there is in addition quite a different import to this discreet disclosure: for a moment it punctures, with the cool facts of the Shining One's political machinations, the mythic aura that the Genji story has acquired. The trace of the puncture is sealed over, however, and the aura soon enshrouds the fallen world of the Uji chapters once more. On yet another plane, this portrayal of the Eighth Prince belongs to the central myth of which the entire fiction of the *Genji* is a sustained exploration: namely, that to be fully human means to be emperor, to fill, that is, the idea of the emperor. (It is evident from the four emperors inhabiting this tale that the imperial regalia are powerless to render any individual adequate to the idea.)

Unlike the legendary Waki Iratsuko, the Eighth Prince retires to Uji only after a series of losses. Upon the death of his wife, he attends ineffectually to the raising of his two daughters, all the while seeking refuge in the reading of sutras. "In his mind" (*kokoro bakari ni*, more precisely "just in his heart-mind," 5:113; S 777; W 793)—a qualification the Prince and, as we shall see, other Uji characters are fond of making—he has already turned his back upon the world and become a *hijiri*, a lay ascetic.[9] His efforts at worldly renunciation are aided by a fire at his estate in the capital that forces him to take up domicile in a family villa in Uji, where he comes under the tutelage of a distinguished abbot. Late in life the Prince attempts to compensate for his schoolboy neglects.

We should pause over this minor detail of the fire. A celebrated image in the Lotus Sutra compares this world to a burning house from which we must hasten into the pure realm of enlightenment.[10] Doubtless reinforced by the actual prevalence of fires, the burning house becomes an obsessive symbol of false attachment in the religion-drenched climate of the late Heian and subsequent ages, with the *locus classicus* being the early thirteenth-century account by Kamo no Chōmei, who, after witnessing massive destruction, managed to confine his own life to a four-foot square hut.[11] The popular view that the Uji chapters are "medieval," that they constitute a bridge from the richly romantic Heian to the austere Kamakura and Muromachi periods, would treat the Eighth Prince's misfortunes piously. I prefer to see the Uji story as an instance of Murasaki Shikibu's keen ironic spirit parodying by anticipation the medieval ethos.

Another sufferer of the burning-house syndrome is Kaoru, the illegitimate offspring of Kashiwagi and Genji's wife (the Third Princess), known to the world as Genji's son. It is to this young man to whom we must now direct our attention. The Eighth Prince, after all, cannot generate a tale; his daughters are promising, but they still want a male protagonist. With characteristic economy Murasaki Shikibu makes an abbot the instrument of Kaoru's introduction into Uji. In spite of his vaunted unworldliness, this abbot appears to be an intimate of the retired Reizei Emperor. During one of his forays from the mountains to visit Reizei, Kaoru happens to be present—not altogether fortuitously, since Reizei (who knows himself to be illegitimate) has always sheltered Kaoru (who, though troubled, is still ignorant of the facts of his birth). The conversation turns to Reizei's putative brother, the Eighth Prince. The abbot expresses esteem for the eager religious scholar, who lately has shown "the resolve of a true saint." Reizei wonders, "But he hasn't changed his garb yet? Ah yes, I have heard the young people calling him the worldly saint or some such. Touching, indeed" (5:120; S 780; W 796).

It is the phrase "worldly saint" that causes Kaoru to prick up his ears, for he has thought of himself as one

> who, though knowing too well the futility of the world, performed his devotions but inconspicuously, all the while filled with a regret unknown to others: what could it be, this resolve of a mind at once worldly yet saintly?   (Ibid.)

The phrase "worldly saint," a concoction by Murasaki Shikibu,[12] is an oxymoronic sobriquet whose ironic implications (note the ambiguity of Reizei's observation that it is "touching") are missed by Kaoru, who, with characteristic laboriousness, spells out the paradox and determines to make himself worthy of such a title. Since it will reappear, it is worth observing that the word here translated as "resolve," *okite*, has a strong imperative nuance of "rule," "command," or even "law." It is also worth noting that the abbot provides an explanation for the worthy Prince's unusual situation, that is, the existence of two daughters he has thus far, though reluctantly, declined to abandon.

Kaoru's passionate curiosity about this remote figure stems from the fundamental doubt that has informed his life and resulted in his becoming a fervently religious youth who is nonetheless half-hearted in his devotional practices. From early childhood he had overheard things that clouded his mind, but there was no one he could question directly. His mother the Third Princess, still a youthful nun, he was especially reluctant to approach, for he had apprehended the discomfort it would cause her for him to have any inkling of his own history. Anxiety was his constant companion:

Obotsukana	O, uncertainty:
tare ni towamashi	whom might I ask
ikani shite	how I have come to be
hajime mo hate mo	one who knows of himself
shiranu wagami zo	neither beginning nor end?
	(5:18; S 737; W 752)

Kaoru's doubts can find expression in such a discreet poem, addressed to none, but his question must go unposed. Just before he utters this poem, his thoughts turn to one Zengyō Taishi, who had "sought for an answer within himself" (ibid.). This figure, known in some texts as Kui Taishi, is traditionally identified with the Buddha's son Rāhula. The young Rāhula, six years in his mother's womb, was born after Sakyamuni had taken vows. Understandably there were doubts about his paternity, but these were dramatically dispelled when the child recognized his father in a crowd of priests.[13] Kaoru's wistful choice of such a figure as another model for himself is revealing: Rāhula's father was the Buddha, Kaoru's a sinning commoner—"sinning" not so much in the Buddhist, theological sense, but in terms of the imperial order, which of course is thoroughly, even wickedly, secular vis-à-vis the Buddhist realm. And yet, as usual, the comparison folds back on itself, and we are reminded of Sakyamuni's worldly beginnings as a debauched prince. This several-faceted conflation of the sacred and the secular, as well as the solipsistic quality to Kaoru's formulation of the question of paternal identity, prognosticates his behavior in the course of the Uji chapters.

More than anything else, it is the burden of the unasked question that presses Kaoru forward on the lonely road to Uji. (Perhaps the mood is "medieval" here: Kaoru is something of a questing knight.) He does not expect to have his secret question answered; he does intend to find a companion, even a teacher, in the pursuit of the devotional existence he has determined is the only proper one for a youth harboring a secret question. As things unfold, ironically as usual, his question (still unvoiced) is answered and a teacher is found, but association with him and his household renders devotion impossible. Of course, we the readers have always known the answer to Kaoru's question. Whereas Genji's story unfolded in a world of prophecies and enigmatic dreams, Kaoru's is governed by testaments and memorials.[14] The shadow of the retrospective haunts the Uji chapters.

But let us not be overhasty. Herolike, Kaoru betakes himself on horseback to the Prince's isolated villa in Uji. He goes on horseback because he will not need to ford the river: in other words, the Prince lives on the capital side, that is, to the east of the Uji River. For the Heian Japanese, it is the West that is the true "other side" of salvation. Across the river from the Prince, Yūgiri maintains a splendid villa inherited from Genji. (This is the structure thought to have been modeled on Minamoto no Tōru's villa, later to become the Byōdōin Temple, the representative structure of Jōdo Buddhism.) The Prince's modest villa is divided into eastern and western halves. The two daughters, Ōigimi and Nakanokimi, occupy the eastern portion, and a Buddhist statue, the object of the Prince's worship, reposes in the west. The Prince actually lives in what might be considered an antechamber or even a closed-in verandah outside (to the west of) the Buddha's room. The Prince's "room" opens toward the mountains where his master the abbot's temple is situated; the Princesses, on the other hand, look out upon the noisily distracting river.[15] During his first visits to the Prince, Kaoru is acutely aware of the unseen Princesses just on the other side of the Buddha, but that will be the extent of his knowledge of them for three years.

Kaoru's journey to Uji that night is vividly described, as if in anticipation of the drama to follow. It is an autumn night. (In the Uji world, amputated version of the Rokujōin, the prevailing seasons are fall and winter.)

> As he rode along, the mists gathered, and he had to make his way through trees so thick that the path could no longer be seen. How chilly was the dew that fell from leaves tossed by the stormy wind! Through no one's fault but his own, he was soaked to the bone. And yet, unaccustomed as he was to such ventures, he felt at once forlorn and excited.
>
> (5:128; S 783; W 799-800)

Kaoru has strayed far from home, and as if his alienness needed emphasizing, his fragrance wafts through the night air to disturb the sleep of rough woodsmen.

Kaoru's fragrance and his anxiety are his twin identifying attributes. They are intimately entwined: the one is the paradoxical manifestation of the other. Kaoru's fragrance is charismatic and natural, unlike that of his putative nephew, cousin, and close companion Prince Niou, who spares no effort concocting perfumes in rivalry. (It should not be surprising that Niou is anxiety-free.) The pair are early identified as the "Fragrant Middle Captain" ("Kaoru Chūjō") and the "Perfumed Lord Hyōbu" ("Niou Hyōbu Kyō"; 5:22; S 740; W 754). Now, it is clear that Kaoru's fragrance is an echo of the possessing spirits, magical dreams, and prophecies of Genji's world. We have already seen that such forces serve contradictory purposes: they are literal (arbitrary) representatives of the supernatural world that undercut this-worldly (political, psychological, or sociological) patterns of logic, yet

227

they also demand to be read as political, psychological, or sociological signs that rationalize the supernatural. If the latter-day world of Uji is governed by wills and memorials rather than dreams and prophecies, what are we to make of Kaoru's fragrance?

Musing on the significance of Kaoru's name, which might be translated as "Fragrant," Fujii Sadakazu summarizes contemporary interpretations of this attribute as follows: (1) disorder of the sweat glands, (2) semen, and (3) the heavenly scent emitted by the decomposing corpses of Buddhist saints. The last is kin to the scent of incense used in religious ceremonies, the puff of white smoke that escapes from the box that Urashima Tarō, the Japanese Rip Van Winkle, brings back from the Dragon King's underwater palace. These are fragments of the other world that serve to create an other-worldly space within this world. Put another way, they translate a magical other-worldly time into a privileged this-worldly space.[16] The opposition implicit between the first two and the third is borne out by the divergent roles played by Kaoru's fragrance.

This opposition is articulated with another at work between Kaoru's name and Niou's. We should look at *niou* (verb)/*nioi* (substantive) first (Kaoru is profoundly derivative). Early in its history, *nioi* seems to have referred to a quality of light, particularly to the beauty emitted by redness.[17] Only gradually, no doubt by analogy with the diffusion of light, did this word come to be applied to scents. Thus, *nioi* is clearly related to *hikari*, "light," and to *kakayaku*, "to shine" or "to be radiant"—both terms associated with the divine from the earliest literature down through the *Genji*. Usage becomes somewhat broader in the *Genji* itself, where *niou/nioi* can refer to a beauty that is expansive and brilliant. The case is somewhat different with *kaoru/kaori*, which was never applied to humans before the *Genji*.[18] The origins of this word are disputed, but it seems to have been associated with that which sways (like seaweed) or trails in coils (like smoke, haze, or mist). The association with mist is especially pertinent since various forms of "mist" (*kiri*) appear thirty-five times in Genji's story (of which no fewer than thirteen pertain to the Kaoru-like Yūgiri) and twenty-one times in the far shorter Uji section. *Kaoru/kaori* in the *Genji* generally refers to a beauty more subdued and less susceptible to brilliant diffusion than that of *niou/nioi.*[19]

As character names in the Uji chapters, however, Kaoru and Niou principally, explicitly, designate olfactory effects. That is to say, there is a shift away from the mythic, visual dimensions of these words; and of course, such a shift is never simply etymological, or rather, the *Genji* is never content to leave etymological shifts unexploited. Indeed, the outlines of how such a shift might be accommodated in the reading being practiced here should already be apparent: the fall from the capital, the fall from quasi-imperial Genji, the fall from vision—with no fall being final, each reverberating back.[20] But we have yet to address the puzzling difference betweeen Kaoru's and Niou's perfumes. Why should Niou, who by name (the association with light) and by lineage (as the Emperor's son and likely candidate to become the next crown prince) is closer to mythical seeing and ruling, have to concoct his perfumes whereas brooding Kaoru, son of a mere commoner (whether Kashiwagi or Genji), is endowed with an unearthly fragrance?

An early passage describes Niou's efforts to better his rival as follows:

> He made it his task by day and by night to compound new perfumes. As for his garden, in spring he would gaze at the plum, in autumn, refuse his heart to the maiden flower so dear to the world and to the dewdrops on the lespedeza (beloved of the stag), but would rather dedicate himself to the age-banishing chrysanthemum, the fading purple trousers, or the uninteresting burnet until they were all frost-smitten. To such an extent were the objects of his interest determined by their fragrance that it almost seemed contrived.
>
> (5:21-22; S 740; W 754)

If this passage seems more than usually resistant to translation, it is because it is more than usually replete with allusion: it is constructed as a chain of fragments from familiar old poems.[21] This awkward stringing together is singularly effective in demonstrating how natural kingliness is created. Genji in the utopian

Rokujōin was able to affect the appearance of the natural ruler by adopting, both architecturally and matrimonially, the artificially cosmic plan of the seasonal books of the imperial anthologies of poetry. Here again, the words of poetry, a privileged form of play, are marshaled to elevate another form of play, thereby justifying the (mere) birthright of a prince. The select language of seasonal poetry masks the sources of sovereign power, but to a different effect from the embellishment of Genji in the Rokujōin. Here, the excessive, even mad, succession of phrases verges on the satirical.

It happens that this passage is preceded by a similar one about Kaoru and his fragrance, though the pastiche there is not quite as dense. Reading back from Niou, we understand that Kaoru's fragrance, too, is as much fabricated as it is natural; or, in other terms, that it is as much profane as it is sacred. If it is the achievement of fiction to make birth issuing from illicit union the equivalent of heavenly birth, then it is only "natural" that Kaoru should emit a heavenly fragrance. At the same time, we must bear in mind the *Genji*'s awareness of this state of affairs. The difference between being "equivalent to" and being "the same as" is not erased. That is why the perfume that trails Kaoru is at once motivated, parodic, and irreducibly strange.

We have left Kaoru cold but eager on his horse. As he draws closer to the villa, snatches of music float to his ear, notes so faint that he cannot at first make out the instrument. He realizes soon enough that the Prince's daughters are playing on their biwa and koto; they had of course never performed for him. He contrives, and succeeds, in capturing an unseen look at the two sisters: their forms, the one alluring, the other compelling, are alternately revealed and concealed by the misty moon. The scene has the effect of a visual quotation, both for Kaoru, who finds it just as it was described in the old tales he had heard recited, and for us, as the images of the young Genji or Yūgiri enraptured by their unsuspecting targets are superimposed upon Kaoru's. The Prince is away on retreat at the abbot's mountain temple. It is only to be expected that the fateful relationship between Kaoru and the Princesses should begin on this night.

In spite of impassioned declarations of a blameless interest,

Kaoru can make no headway with the retiring ladies, and his principal encounter that night is with an elderly woman in the household, one Bennokimi, who turns out to have been the daughter of his late father Kashiwagi's wet nurse, and as such, the sole surviving human who can answer Kaoru's unasked question. Just as his vision of the Princesses was unexpected and yet not surprising, so Bennokimi's halting disclosures are startling yet only too predictable to Kaoru's ears. His perturbation is such that he cuts her short, and some time elapses before he can allow her to unveil the full story, complete with crumbling remains of his parents' correspondence. These he peruses only in the privacy of his quarters in the capital.

Bennokimi is the female version of the night figures who receive and transmit secrets in the *Genji*: Fujitsubo's confessor who reveals his paternity to Reizei, or the Bishop of Yokawa who, later in the Uji chapters, will be responsible for letting the world know of Ukifune's survival after her supposed drowning. In contrast to the scene between Fujitsubo's priest and Reizei, here the facts of Kashiwagi's history are spelled out and rendered shabby by overexposure: we already know them, and Kaoru almost knows them. Uji is a world where things risk being laid bare, where the moldy secrets of the dead hold sway in the place of dramatic prophecies.

This is not to say that what there is to be laid bare isn't reasonably complex. The Eighth Prince, who had become Kaoru's guide in their joint pursuit of the religious life, dies after explicitly entrusting his daughters to his care in words suggesting marriage while at the same time enjoining Ōigimi, the elder sister, from disgracing the family by abandoning the mountain retreat. Kaoru, who has from the first been attracted to her, painstakingly reports on his Uji excursions to his libidinous double Niou, whose appetite is held in abeyance only by the logistical difficulties such a venture presents for one in his position. (He has been to Uji once, for a mid-journey pause at Yūgiri's villa across the river—Niou always moves with the capital. The Prince was still alive then, and his memories had been stirred by the music floating over the river. Niou took the opportunity to embark on an impatient correspondence with the ladies.) More destitute than ever, the sisters, Ōigimi in particular, are grateful for Kaoru's kindness but troubled by the peculiar intimacy forced upon them by economic dependence. For the moment, they cloak themselves in mourning.

Then one summer's day, with the heat unbearable in the capital, Kaoru fancies the cool of the riverside and promptly heads for the Prince's villa (note the proprietary confidence). He settles in the Prince's old quarters; through the thin partition he senses the movement of the Princesses retreating to their own room and swiftly stations himself before a hole noted earlier (observant Kaoru, attentive to more than the fine points of the sutras). At first, disappointment: the view is totally obstructed by a portable partition. But then the complicit wind threatens the blinds on the side facing the river, where Kaoru's men are strolling by, and an innocent attendant moves the partition to cover the apparent deficiency, thereby clearing the field for Kaoru's intent eye:

> First, one stood and appeared to be looking out over a partition at his attendants strolling along the river to catch the breeze. Her unlined robe, almost black, and reddish yellow trousers struck him as unexpectedly fresh and gay. It must be because of their wearer. A prayer sash hung casually over her shoulders, and a hand drawn into its sleeve concealed a rosary. Her form was slender and appealing; her hair, which might have fallen just short of the hem of an outer robe, gleamed in all its thickness without a trace of a tangle to its ends. Her sweet profile, her gay yet softly gentle manner—the First Princess would be like this, he thought, turning plaintive as he recalled the brief glimpse he had had of her.   (5:208-209; S 819-20; W 838)

This, of course, is Nakanokimi, the younger of the two sisters. She is consistently characterized as gay, and that quality transforms even her mourning attire: we should remember that she is clad almost entirely in black (the grey is so deep as to be virtually black), with the reddish-yellow trousers providing the merest if striking relief at the bottom. Nakanokimi has not been so crushed either by her bereavement or by her upbringing that she cannot exhibit a lively curiosity toward the visitors from the capital. That her profile should remind Kaoru of the First Princess is piquant, for the latter is Niou's sister, and together with him, a favorite grandchild of the dead Murasaki.

We have not seen Kaoru seeing the First Princess, but this reference, together with the apparent emotion attaching to it, immediately evokes the young Genji's disarray when he superimposed Fujitsubo's form upon the child Murasaki. Kaoru's vision places Nakanokimi in Murasaki's line (though it is no longer a question of blood tie); does it crown him as Genji's successor? Not without a twist, for Kaoru's eye is immediately riveted upon another form:

> The other one came out on her knees and said, "Aren't we quite unprotected on that side?" Her evident care, her vigilant attention suggested a profound thoughtfulness. Even more than with the first lady, the shape of her head and the sweep of her hair suggested exceptional elegance and refinement. "There are screens on the other side, too. He wouldn't rush over for a peek," ventured one of the carefree young women. "Ah, how unfortunate," she said, her retreat anxious but dignified. Cloaked in black lined and unlined robes of a similar combination as her sister's, she was softly graceful and sadly compelling. She seemed to have lost some hair, which was now pleasing and unoppressive. The ends were thin but what people describe as lustrous, like the feathers on a kingfisher's wing or a skein of silken thread. Her hand, which held a purple scroll with a sutra, was slighter than the other's—indeed, it was terribly thin. The other lady, the one who had been standing, now sat near the entry to the far room and looked in his direction with a smile suffused with charm.
>
> (5:209-10; S 820; W 838-39)

Notice that the older sister never stands; that she is enshrouded in more garments than the younger; that her hair (an abundance of which being the sine qua non of the Heian beauty) is thinning. To judge from her hand, she is bordering on emaciation;

her age is also suggested by the implied contrast with the heedless young woman. Note, too, that every one of these attributes is turned into a virtue by Kaoru.

The implications of this peeping scene in contrast to the others can be understood only in light of future developments, but there are still other points to be observed now. The first is that Kaoru is peculiarly incorporated into the scene: the attendant, in her denial, ironically describes precisely what this most refined and priggish of aristocrats is up to. Kaoru the viewer is also transfixed by the gaze of the viewed, of both Ōigimi and Nakanokimi. He becomes, in a sense, the hole in the partition.[22]

Now, if Kaoru's gaze succeeds in fixing Nakanokimi in the Murasaki genealogy, does it similarly direct our understanding of Ōigimi? The proud reserve that is never so harsh or crude as to seem aloof is evocative of a Fujitsubo or an Utsusemi. Yet it is also possible to detect reverberations with Kaoru's mother, the Third Princess.[23] After pouring over his parents' correspondence, a distressed Kaoru had called upon his mother. Incongruously youthful in her sober nun's garb (we recall that she took vows shortly after Kaoru's birth), she looked at him without knowing that she now saw a son who knew. Instead, what roused her to self-consciousness was that like Ōigimi, she had been reading a sutra, which she hastened to conceal. (A woman would not want to seem intellectually—let alone morally—pretentious before a man, even if he were her son.)

If the Third Princess and Ōigimi are related to each other, it is as an intaglio to a cameo. The Third Princess, a princess of the blood, is literarily uninteresting and comes to life only through Kashiwagi's illicit attachment.[24] (Correspondingly, it is this destructive passion that transforms Kashiwagi from a merely ambitious youth into a tragic hero.) Ōigimi, as the daughter of the unfortunate Eighth Prince, lost to the wilds of Uji, is a princess of the blood twice removed. Where the Third Princess, passive and virtually speechless, must live a long life of renunciation after her crisis, Ōigimi is born to a renunciation to be realized in language and sufficiently potent to forestall crisis forever.

Thus Kaoru's summer gaze is overcast with the fleeting shadow of incest: fleeting, of course, because the scene is but a quotation of the heady taboo-breaking of the past. What exceeds mere quotation is the division of the viewer's attention, though uneven, between two objects: for we leave the hole with Naka-nokimi's smiling image on our retinas.

SISTERHOOD IN UJI: ŌIGIMI, THE FIRSTBORN

The pulse of the Uji story quickens in the "Trefoil Knots" chapter, which opens with preparations for the first anniversary rites for the Eighth Prince. Kaoru and the abbot (who did not allow the Prince to be reunited with his daughters before his death—he had impediments enough to his salvation—who finds occasion to remind the Princesses of their father's munificence to the monastery) have taken charge of the affair; they both call at the villa on the day the Princesses are to shed their mourning robes: "It was a time when they were murmuring to each other, 'and so time passes,' in the midst of a tangle of threads for the sacred incense" (5:213; S 821; W 840). The threads are of the traditional Buddhist five colors, to be used for tying with deco-rative knots packets of sacred incense (*myōkō*, the same word used to describe Kaoru's fragrance), and they are in a state of disorder (*hikimidarite*, with the by now familiar *midari* carrying nuances of political and psychological disorder as well as physical disarray). The sisters are referring to an undistinguished poem from the last of the books in the "Love" section (a part of the imperial anthologies invariably devoted to the sad aftermath of attachment) of the *Kokinshū* (number 806) in which a dreary, unwished-for life is likened by a pun to thread being spun and woven. Kaoru seizes on the thread motif with a soulful "let me thread my tears as jewels," an allusion to a poem by the poet Ise on the occasion of the death of the Emperor Uda's consort On-shi.[25] Ise, one of Uda's lovers, fancied the voices mourning the Empress as a thread upon which tears were jewels to be strung.

From within their screens the sisters recognize and appreciate the allusion but hesitate to respond for fear of seeming knowing; instead, they silently recall a travel poem by another Heian poet, Ki no Tsurayuki:

Chapter 4

Ito ni yoru	Since our paths
mono naranaku ni	cannot be entwined
wakareji no	as one cord,
kokorobosoku mo	how frail they seem,
omooyuru kana	parting at the crossroads.

(KKS 415, "Travel")[26]

The unspoken allusion is not lost on Kaoru, who boldly combines all the threads on the table, so to speak, into

Agemaki ni	Let us tie our pledges
nagaki chigiri o	for a bond enduring
musubikome	in a knot
onaji tokoro ni	where our strands
yori mo awanan	shall always join.

(5:214; S 822; W 840-41)

The "knot" (*agemaki*) in question is of the elaborate sort used in religious and domestic ornamentation; it also refers to a style of coiffure worn by young girls. The word figures prominently in a song (*saibara*) with lines such as "we slept apart/but I rolled over."[27] Whether Ōigimi would have permitted herself to recognize such an allusion is a tantalizing question, but she evidently finds the poem as unwelcome as all other intimations from Kaoru:

Nuki mo aezu	If tears are jewels
moroki namida no	they shatter
tama no o ni	and cannot be strung:
nagaki chigiri o	how shall I tie
ikaga musuban	a bond enduring?

(5:214; S 823; W 841)

It is worth lingering over this artful tangle of threads, some of which are dyed in the familiar colors of the religious and the secular, to which the talented interlocutors add the hue of history. (Although "they" has been used in the description of the Princesses, there is little doubt that it is the older, Ōigimi, who offers the meager utterances from the other side of the screens. A country princess she may be, but she is every bit as adroit as

236

Kaoru in verbal sparring and, indeed, demonstrates that she is a fit partner for him.) Kaoru introduces the jewel/tears into the exchange through reference to the celebrated Ise. The injection of Ise (a woman who mourns a dead mistress who was the consort of a man by whom she herself has a son) is complicated in itself, but when Ise is joined by Tsurayuki in the next allusion, Kaoru and Ōigimi together recreate a pairing that appeared in "The Paulownia Court," the very first chapter in the *Genji* (5:214, n. 5). The occasion was the visit by Myōbu, the bereaved Kiritsubo Emperor's emissary, to the house of the Kiritsubo Lady's mother, Genji's grandmother. The messenger describes to the grieving mother how the Emperor, inconsolable after her daughter's death, has absorbed himself in illustrations of the "Song of Everlasting Sorrow" as well as of poems by Ise and Tsurayuki (1:109; S 10-11; W 13). Thus Ōigimi and Kaoru subtly cooperate to reintroduce that ill-fated love. Kaoru's own poem shows him at what we will retrospectively recognize as his most ardent; Ōigimi, in turn, delivers a characteristically prim slap by ignoring the immediate allusion and skipping back to an earlier one, but she does not rebuff Kaoru altogether since she repeats one line from his poem, which happens to be about pledges of an enduring bond.

The threads of exchange are snipped by Ōigimi's poem; Kaoru goes off whimpering to Bennokimi. Having filled her capacious ears with plaints about the sisters' resistance both to him and to Niou as bridegrooms, he tarries, "wishing to spend the night in gentle conversation" with the older daughter (5:222; S 825; W 844). Though Ōigimi finds his presence bothersome in the modestly proportioned house, she cannot treat him as summarily as she would, for "compared to most men," his was "an unusually sympathetic heart-mind" (ibid.). As long as Kaoru behaves as a soulful *castrato*, he appeals to Ōigimi as no other man besides her father.

Tonight, intelligent creature that she is, she places herself in her late father's chapel and has the Buddha's lamp lit full. She attempts to have Kaoru's side (beyond a screen in addition to the regular partition) brightly lit as well, but he refuses, pleading indisposal, which, he fears, might mar his deportment. Indeed,

having sent his men off to the verandah with food and drink he
promptly sees fit to lie down. Ōigimi's women, despite her strenuous objections, also sidle away. (Addled as they seem, they have
a keen understanding of their self-interest: like other women staff-
ing the households of fallen princesses—a Suetsumuhana or a
Princess Asagao—they know that their own fortunes depend on
their mistresses' erotic acquiescence to prosperous aristocrats.[28] It
should be added that Ōigimi herself is acutely aware of Kaoru's
economic favors, which constitute the unacknowledged component of his "sympathetic" nature.) Given the circumstances,
even Kaoru finds it ridiculous to be restrained by a "barrier of
flimsy things," but he maintains his "feeling and interesting"
conversation (5:223; S 826; W 844-45). Ōigimi's courage begins
to fade with the waning glow of the Buddha's lamp, and she
pleads indisposal on her own part as a prelude to retreat. Even
Kaoru is moved to act. The partition proves flimsy indeed. Horrified and indignant, Ōigimi charges, "So this is what you meant
by being 'without barriers' " (5:224; S 826; W 845), referring to
Kaoru's wish that they might speak "without barriers." Kaoru is
prepared:

> "If you still refuse to understand what I mean when I speak
> of a heart that erects no barriers, I will make you see. You
> say you find me shocking, but what could you be thinking
> of? Let me make my vows before the Buddha himself. Oh,
> do not be so afraid. I have only wanted to respect your
> wishes. The world would never guess what a fool I have
> been all this time," he said. Her hair was falling upon her
> face; he brushed it back, and as he gazed in the teasing
> flickering of the light, he saw that she was lovely and in-
> triguing, just as he had imagined.   (Ibid.)

Long ago, in another word-laden encounter, Genji stroked
Tamakazura's hair and called himself a peerless fool. Here, the
older Ōigimi's chagrin is hardly to be compared with Tamakazura's. She is reduced to tears. Kaoru, watching her, is overtaken
by a kaleidoscope of sensations: first, with the realization that he
has made his way to her so easily, fear that others might do
likewise in so inconsequential a dwelling; then, annoyance with

himself for having wasted so much time; but finally, seeing her distress, a sense that "it should not come about thus, he should wait until her heart softened of itself." Ōigimi berates herself for having trusted him with such extraordinary intimacy, but her deepest despair stems from "the lack of feeling that made you bring to light these unpropitious sleeves" (5:225; S 827; W 846). She refers to the fact that she is still in mourning robes. At the heart of this act of seeing (*miarawashitamō*, literally, "look and make appear" and therefore, "disclose," "uncover") lies the revelation of death on the person of the lady.

Kaoru, earnest fellow that he is, admits that she is quite justified on this score. Given the length of their acquaintance, however, why should she insist on formalities? He proceeds to recount in unfortunate detail the course of his attachment, beginning with that first "seeing" by moonlight. The net effect of his words is that Ōigimi is more than ever horrified with both her own hitherto unsuspected exposure and the course of his inclinations—when he had seemed so serious.

Perhaps his passion is stimulated by his torrent of words: Kaoru, who is not after all entirely witless, draws a screen to separate them from the statue of the Buddha, then lies down casually beside her. We seem to be approaching a climax again, but wait: a fatal scent pervades the air. It is the "sacred incense" (*myōkō*) from the altar, "bothersome to one who, more than most, lent his thoughts to the Buddha" (5:226; S 828; W 846-47). His timing was, after all, ill-considered, he convinces himself. He will wait until she has emerged from mourning. The two pass the time in quiet conversation.

At daybreak come the usual signs announcing the time of parting to a couple: the neighing of horses, the sound of men delicately clearing their throats, and light entering through the cracks of shutters. Kaoru opens them, and Ōigimi, referred to as "woman" just as this erotic encounter approaches its end, sidles out as well. Together, as if to mime the classic lovers' stance, they admire the pathos of the early morn, complete with brightly glistening dew. Taking heart, Kaoru pleads, "If only we could go on like this, simply appreciating, with one heart, as we do now, the moon and the flowers, and pass the time exchanging tales about this inconstant world. . . ." Ōigimi, no longer afraid, replies, "If it weren't so shameful, if we could speak through barriers of things, there would truly be no barrier to our hearts" (5:227-28; S 828; W 847-48). Kaoru "the visitor" (*marōto*), as he is often called in the Uji chapters, departs after an exchange of poems.

To refer to Kaoru as "the visitor" is to mark him as a hero, as a noble young man who travels far from home to die or to return triumphant. We expect action from such a figure, but instead we follow the exquisite tracing of nonaction. This night is perhaps the finest of the series that includes such specimens as the night Yūgiri spent pressed against the closet where Ochiba no Miya (the widow of Kaoru's father Kashiwagi) had taken refuge, or of the day young Genji watched Fujitsubo from a closet. What distinguishes it from earlier scenes is that here, there is no external impediment (no "barriers of things," as Ōigimi would put it) to Kaoru's having his way.[29] Vision, having humiliatingly exposed the presence of death in this erotic confrontation, must yield to verbal exchange. Vision, as directed by one such as Kaoru upon one such as Ōigimi, cannot lead to union even in fantasy; rather, it implacably produces separation in a psychic field where sense and sensibility are distinct. And yet it is precisely in such a field that a woman like Ōigimi can become erotic, can be called a "woman" and participate in the iconic stance of lovers who, faced with the hateful dawn, sublimate the separation in the language of poetry. That is why this scene, and others like it, stop short of wholehearted parody.

When Ōigimi is alone with her thoughts at last, she acknowledges for the first time that in fact, her father might have permitted marriage with Kaoru. Heretofore she had defended her refusal as consistent with her late father's wishes:

Disgrace neither your late mother nor me with thoughtless behavior. Do not permit yourselves to be seduced by words to drift away from this mountain village without reliable support. Rather, only think of yourselves as fated to a lot unlike that of the rest of the world and resign yourselves to living out your time here. (5:176-77; S 806; W 822-23)

The Prince who had lost his chance to be supremely human as emperor apparently condemned his daughters to live out their lives unwedded—as if, with his own failure, the sole usefulness of women had been canceled out from his world. "Apparently," of course, because he was at the same time pressing them upon Kaoru. Ōigimi now lets us know that her father had also endorsed Kaoru to them, but, she persists, "I myself will continue as I am." Much has been written about the power of the Eighth Prince's "will,"[30] but we must not let the latter blind us to the strength of his daughter's "will." The Eighth Prince's ambiguities are paltry compared with Genji's, but they are converted into a forceful unity by his daughter, who finds her own will by vicariously asserting his.

Mere resistance seems insufficient to the aging twenty-five-year-old; it is her sister, at the peak of her womanly beauty, who should be married. And how would she not look after her, once she was united with Kaoru! As for herself: had Kaoru been an ordinary person, she might have yielded to him, but with his superior manner (literally, "his hard-to-be-seen-by manner") she would find it too humiliating to be intimate with him. In short, it is neither marriage in principle nor Kaoru in particular that she finds objectionable, but the state of her own flesh. Despite her protestations that she finds Kaoru reprehensible, despite the fact of her already-having-been-seen (though imperfectly, in the vagaries of flickering lamplight), and in the cloak of death at that, she is neither repelled nor resigned. Indeed, Ōigimi is coming to life as she exercises her imagination in the pursuit of death-in-life.

Such moments cost dearly, however, and perhaps out of longing for creature comfort, she crawls tearfully into Nakanokimi's bed. The younger sister is happy to feel her older sister come in and touchingly spreads her own bedclothes over her. But then, she detects that "unmistakable" fragrance (5:231; S 829-30; W 849). Overshadowed by her powerful sister, Nakanokimi is usually closed to us, but here we learn that she had been hearing the servants' whisperings, and now the migrant scent seals her suspicions. Overcome by vicarious chagrin, Nakanokimi can only turn over and feign sleep so as to prevent conversation.

Ōigimi, for her part, is not one to miss such signs; knowledge of her sister's knowledge makes her miserable.

The misery is not sufficient, however, to cause her to change her mind. Kaoru's patience grows shorter; anticipating the sisters' emergence from deep mourning late in the Eighth Month, he wishes to visit immediately, for with the Ninth Month being taboo for marriage, he knows no peace of mind. Ōigimi hints to her sister that her father's strictures apply only to her, and that she should consider marriage. Nakanokimi feels both indignant and abandoned. By now we are accustomed to heroes who seek and create substitutes to fulfill their desires; now, a heroine proposes a substitute for herself. We might be reminded of the Akashi Lady, who willingly participated in the commerce of her daughter (now much esteemed as the Akashi Empress, in large part due to her mother's yielding her to Murasaki). In her case, however, we watched the workings of a disciplined will sacrificing private emotions for the glory of the line. How shrunken is the place for such considerations as the "glory of the line" in Uji. What is left for Ōigimi to preserve is her pride, and all that remains for her pride to protect is the privacy (the secret) of her aging flesh. Woman's flesh, that most public of commodities in the functioning of the Fujiwara regency, is turned into the last refuge of the private self. Not, however, that this is acknowledged by that self. For the metaphysically inclined Ōigimi, the body, like other material things (such as partitions and screens) is subsidiary, serving to protect that pure essence called *kokoro*—heart-mind-spirit.

Accordingly, when Bennokimi comes to plead Kaoru's cause (he is on the scene; the other servants are obviously determined to help him, and with their opprobrious lack of subtlety, urge their mistresses to brighter colors), Ōigimi discloses her intent to commend Nakanokimi to his care in her stead. She puts her case this way: "If he is truly faithful to the past [i.e., to the Prince's wishes], let him think of us as one. Sharing the same flesh (*mi*), I will have yielded to her everything in my heart (*kokoro*), and thus I will surely be disposed to see him" (5:238; S 833; W 853). An extraordinary vision, this: shrouded and thus invisible in her sister's body, Ōigimi will be able to see (possess)

Kaoru's and conclude a marriage of true minds. Small wonder that Bennokimi goes away sympathetic but doubtful.

That night every fiber of Ōigimi is alert. The eager servants can do nothing about the awkward fact that the sisters sleep together. At the first hint of Kaoru's approach, Ōigimi rises and swiftly "crawls to conceal herself" (5:242; S 834; W 854). She is filled with pity (guilt?) for her sister; she would prefer that they hide together, but she has no choice. So, trembling, she watches. Kaoru, now repeatedly called "the visitor," lifts up a corner of the curtain with a "practiced look,"[31] outer garments already removed, and slips in. At first, when he makes out only one form, Kaoru delightedly assumes that Ōigimi has decided to yield to him. But as his eyes become better adjusted, he realizes that "this one was slightly more beautiful and fresh in her charm" (5:243; S 834; W 855) just as Ōigimi had always argued and feared. As Nakanokimi awakens, Kaoru pities her and resents the hidden sister, but at the same time, he cannot find it in himself to

> cast this one off as an utter stranger; yet it would cause him chagrin to give the lie to his pledges: I won't let her [Ōigimi] think me shallow. Let me get through this pass, and if inescapable fate so deems and I am united with this one, she will not seem entirely different. (Ibid.)

As he had done with her sister, he passes the night by drawing from his apparently inexhaustible store of gentle conversation. In the meanwhile the old servants, confident that their plans had succeeded at last (although they do wonder why Nakanokimi should be tarrying with the couple), grin their toothless grins and fall asleep with loud snores. As the autumn night draws to a close, Kaoru finds himself unsatisfied, as every good lover should; he cautions Nakanokimi against imitating the painful manner of her sister, and he leaves with pledges of an enduring bond.

As for Nakanokimi, what is she to think when Bennokimi comes to her wondering "where Nakanokimi might be" (5:245; S 835; W 856)? When Ōigimi emerges at last from her hiding

place, she is described as a cricket in the wall, a daring appropriation from the *Book of Rites*, which juxtaposes the activities
of such modest creatures with those of the Sovereign in its pre-
scriptive description of the seasons.[32] The sisters have no words
to exchange.

In reflecting upon this remarkable scene, we might first recall
that night a very young Genji found himself lying with a robustly
vulgar Nokibanoogi instead of her stepmother, the plain and
modest Utsusemi (in "The Shell of the Locust"). He certainly
did not pass the night in gentle conversation. More important,
Utsusemi (who in strength of will is not dissimilar to Ōigimi)
was neither forced to nor chose to watch. Indeed, the tarrying
Ōigimi obliquely recalls the middle-aged Genji using the light
of fireflies to display Tamakazura's lovely profile to his brother
Prince Hotaru. This unprecedented example of female voyeurism comes tinged with sadness. When Murasaki toward the end
of her life began to "see" with her mind's eye, she invoked new
bonds with the women about her. Ōigimi's seeing can only strain
her ties with the sister whose flesh she claims to share. If the
notion of two sisters constituting the single object of one man's
desire wears a mythic aura,[33] then that aura is destroyed from
within in a procedure typical of the *Genji*. On the one hand,
Ōigimi's very deliberateness is utterly unmythic. On the other,
Kaoru's reponse betrays the undermining of a mythic procedure
internal to the *Genji*, that of pseudo-incestuous substitution.
Kaoru stealing a glimpse of the two might possibly arouse a thrill
of anticipation, but Kaoru comfortably oscillating between the
sisters as he lies with the wrong one is a radically different hero
inhabiting an altered fictional space.

Upon his return to the capital after leaving Nakanokimi,
Kaoru, as ever scrupulous about form, promptly writes to Uji.
He has contrived to find a branch with half its leaves green (ignorant of the season), the other half properly crimson. It accom-
panies the following poem:

Onaji e o	O mountain goddess
wakite somekeru	who have dyed
yamahime ni	one branch as two:

izure ka fukaki   let me ask
iro to towaba ya   which hue is the deeper.

                               (5:247; S 836; W 857)

"Mountain goddess" here stands for *yamahime*, close kin to *hashihime*, "lady of the bridge." Whether it refers to Ōigimi or Nakanokimi is necessarily unclear, but it is unmistakably the former who bears responsibility for the confusion. And it is Ōigimi whom Kaoru means to address as a goddess, just as he had referred to her as "lady of the bridge" in one of his first poems to her (5:141-42; S 790; W 806), doubtless without grasping the import of such gestures. The second instance brings out the fatefulness of the first: through such rhetorical play, Kaoru names Ōigimi as irrevocably other, as eternally inaccessible to him.

If Kaoru and Ōigimi cannot become husband and wife after the fashion of ordinary mortals, they do bear a semblance to special siblings. We think again of Genji and Murasaki as a fictional version of the archaic diarchy. Kaoru and Ōigimi are still another fictional version: condemned to an exclusively private realm, they attempt to constitute their erotic selves through the substitution of others—"others" who happen to be their doubles, a sister in Ōigimi's case and a nephew/cousin in Kaoru's.[34]

To wit: Kaoru determines that the only way he can combat Ōigimi's plan to unite him with her sister is to offer the latter to Niou. Niou is happy to cooperate, and with the assistance of the now thoroughly confused servants, the venture succeeds beautifully—at least for Niou. Another autumn morning dawns upon Kaoru and Ōigimi after a night spent together yet resolutely apart (even though he managed to clutch at her sleeve for a while). Thoroughly irritated, Kaoru coughs in summons to his more satisfied companion, who of course fails to emerge. As usual, Kaoru is left to reflect:

Shirube seshi   I was the guide,
ware ya kaeri   yet now I wander,
madoubeki   heavy hearted
kokoro mo yukanu   on this path
akegure no michi   in the darkness of dawn.

                               (5:257; S 841; W 862)

The "path in the darkness of dawn" belongs to a rich network woven about the word *akegure*, that time of darkness before night yields to day. It is a time for dreams and wandering, a time shared by Genji and Fujitsubo, Kashiwagi and the Third Princess, and Yūgiri and the dead Murasaki. Add Kaoru and Ōigimi to this list and certain patterns emerge. The dream in which Genji longed to lose himself was "incomparably wretched" and "never-ending" for Fujitsubo.[35] *Akegure* has a special prominence in the Kashiwagi-Third Princess affair, where it is variously described as a time when the sky cannot even be made out (Kashiwagi), or when one wishes to dissolve oneself into the sky (the Third Princess; 4:219-20; S 615; W 660). *Akegure*, however, is not reserved for illicit couples alone. Since it is applied to Murasaki's loneliness, both when she is abandoned by Genji for the Third Princess and when death stares her in the face, it juxtaposes different orders of individual crises for mutual reinterpretation. Furthermore, the adulterer Kashiwagi is made to wander in the same darkness as the betrayed Murasaki.[36]

That time of day when one's being is uprooted left tangible consequences for Genji and Fujitsubo, as well as for Kashiwagi and the Third Princess, in the forms of the Reizei Emperor and Kaoru; for Yūgiri it ended in doomed desire. The recurrence of *akegure* with Kaoru has the frustrated ring of the quotation of a quotation: not only is Kaoru thwarted in the fulfillment of both desire and vocation, but he is condemned to mimicking the posture of pursuit.

Yet it will not do simply to point to the absences of Uji as the negative version of the plenitude of the capital and its story, especially since that story itself taught us the fabrication of originals through substitution. (That story, being past, however, always threatens to assume mythic proportions.) It will also not do to be duped by the dolorousness of Uji as *ushi*. The motif of the "night unspent together" is essentially comical, and moreover, within the continuous explorations of the *Genji*, it heralds new presences and new potencies. As suggested above, Kaoru and Ōigimi constitute themselves through substitution, and with Niou and Nakanokimi now occupied with each other, the more

sober pair are left to come together in their own fashion. As
Ōigimi will retort to Kaoru when he presses a certain claim to
intimacy,

Hedate naki	Though our hearts
kokoro bakari wa	admit no barrier
kayou tomo	in their communion,
nareshi sode to wa	you cannot suggest
kakeji to zo omou	our sleeves are worn.
	(5:265; S 844; W 866)

Worn sleeves here would mean the communion of lovers' bodies;
sleeves can be unworn thanks to material barriers, the best guarantee of spiritual exchange: in brief, used hearts, pure bodies.

Once set in motion, the parallel relationships trace their separate destinies. Niou, with considerable difficulty, manages to
demonstrate his sincerity by visiting Nakanokimi on three successive nights, thereby instituting a marriage between them, a
marriage that, however, is unknown in and unacknowledgeable
by the capital. The predictable occurs sooner rather than later,
and Nakanokimi's new-found pleasure turns to keen grief. The
chagrin of neglect is even more acute for her sister, however,
and her health begins to decline together with her always-sub-
dued spirits.

The decline turns steep after an autumn visit by Kaoru and
Niou, engineered by the former for the sisters' benefit. Niou, a
potential crown prince, is under strict surveillance since rumors
of an inappropriate attachment in Uji have made his mother the
Empress more than usually anxious about her philandering son.
Twinges of responsibility prompt Kaoru to arrange a quasi-offi-
cial visit to Uji for Niou. He settles upon that most acceptable
of activities, an excursion for admiring the beauties proffered by
the season, in this case, the autumn foliage of Uji. The large
party settles at Yūgiri's villa on the other side of the river and
proceeds to make music and compose poems. Even the fish are
attracted to Prince Niou,[37] now ensconced as lord of the mountains and streams in the season of plenty. And this is the han-
diwork of the unlordly Kaoru, who has succeeded in bringing to

247

the unruly nature of Uji the order of the capital—aesthetic paraphernalia necessary for the reaffirmation, indeed the rendering visible, of cosmic order.

Yet this success is the other side of his failure to achieve his goal in arranging the expedition in the first place. It was his intention that Niou should slip away at an opportune moment (to that end he had had the sisters hard at work scrubbing), but of course such a moment never comes. The order so easily, so naturally, assumed by Niou cannot be transplanted to the truncated world on the other side of the river. Kaoru, child of ambiguity (sacred through illicit birth), yearns for ready reconciliations, pairing off, for instance, Niou with Nakanokimi, himself with Ōigimi, and through it all, believing that he can be both "lay" and "holy." But his Midas touch accentuates schisms everywhere.

The apparent cause of Ōigimi's decline and eventual death, at least as explained by Bennokimi, is her refusal to eat, coinciding with rumors of Niou's impending marriage to the daughter of Yūgiri, now the leading statesman of the land. Learning of her indisposition, Kaoru pays a visit and is even admitted close to her bedside (since the earlier misadventures, the servants believe them to be intimate). Lack of resistance on Ōigimi's part alerts Kaoru to the seriousness of her condition, yet he quickly leaves for the capital on grounds of pressing court business. He does, however, leave instructions for priests to be sent, which annoys Ōigimi since they would be stationed near her and possibly catch a glimpse of her wasted form.

We are approaching the finale of the Ōigimi story. The narration of her death counterposes comedy to pathos. It is developed with frequent evocation of the deaths of other heroines, which of course is a maneuver that reveals differences as much as similarities. First, we need Kaoru on the scene, and sure enough, after days of neglect, he rushes over in an access of panic. He finds his lady considerably weaker; he steps up the religious activity (even the abbot has joined the veritable army of priests now encamped in the modest villa) and insists on taking his place at her bedside, to supervise the preparation of medicines, take her hand, and whisper directly in her ear. He implores her to address him that he might hear her voice again, much as the young Yūgiri (now hastening this lady's death by promoting Niou's marriage with his own daughter) wished he could hear the dead Murasaki's voice again. Ōigimi favors him with a reply, that she did indeed have things to say to him, but that she had grown terribly weak: "Since you had been neglecting us lately I feared that I might meet my end without having spoken with you" (5:308; S 862; W 884). The nun Fujitsubo (Murasaki's aunt), who had held Genji at bay for years, also confessed to harboring unspoken words at the moment of her death.

The crucial difference is that unlike the dead Murasaki or the dying Fujitsubo, Ōigimi still has days to go. Yet both she and Kaoru are so conscious of the end that they attempt to shape and even to hasten it, and in the course of this orchestration, to interject numerous discordant notes. Murasaki Shikibu shows herself to be a mistress of comic mistiming, of the inappropriate word and gesture. For instance, Kaoru, gazing upon Ōigimi's frail form, asks himself how he can bear to see it emptied of life. Ōigimi herself, though uncomfortable at being so exposed (she still has the strength and will to cover her face), nevertheless keeps in mind the way in which she would have him remember her and accordingly refrains from rebuffing him for fear of seeming obstinately graceless.

In the meanwhile, Nakanokimi is disconcerted to have Kaoru so close at hand. When she hears him entering behind the curtains, she swiftly backs out, just as her sister once abandoned her, still sleeping, to the intruding Kaoru. Still, with Bennokimi as intermediary, Nakanokimi manages an exchange of poetry with this gentleman whom she had always found austere and remote, but who now reminds her of her absent husband. Kaoru, for his part, finds himself wondering how he could bear to lose this young woman from his life.

The always helpful abbot recounts a recent dream showing the Eighth Prince still unable to achieve salvation. Since the Prince had previously appeared in a dream to Nakanokimi, Ōigimi promptly feels both rejected and culpable, and her condition worsens accordingly. If she herself would only pray to be healed, but no:

> I must contrive to take advantage of this occasion and die. Now that my lord stays with me, and no reserve is left between us, there is no way in which I shall be able to keep my distance. And yet, even with his superior nature [if we were to become familiar], each is likely to disappoint the other, and that would surely be heart-rending. If my life insists on prolonging itself, let me use this illness as a reason for changing my form [i.e., become a nun]. Only then could we hope to perpetuate our feelings forever.
>
> (5:313; S 864; W 886)

The premature spinster is an incurable romantic, and even though she seems to be in little danger of recovering, she requests the administration of vows. No one will hear of it, however, especially out of deference to the attentive Kaoru.

The anorexic Ōigimi's death falls on the day when the emperor partakes of the new fruits and shares them with his subjects as part of the great harvest festival at the Palace. In Uji a raging wind tosses the snow, and day wanes without its ever having grown light. Kaoru, imagining the bustle at the capital, grows forlorn and reproaches Ōigimi for thinking to leave him behind. Ōigimi repeats that she has things to say if only she could be granted a respite from her distress, but that she feels as if she were "fading away" (*kienuru*, 5:316; S 865; W 887)—thus anticipating the wording that will be used to describe her death, as if she were engaging in a linguistic parody of Murasaki's staging of her own death. Kaoru, bitter at the prospect of losing her without ever having been united, wishes he could find something odious about her, signs of the corruption of impending death, that might release him from his attachment. Instead, he finds her as freshly appealing as ever. True, she is terribly thin, but in her white robes, with her hair still lustrous, she offers a vision he knows he will never forget. For some time now she has been unable to attend to her appearance, but just as she is, Kaoru finds her far superior to those who devote themselves to their

looks, all the while maintaining a forbidding air. This "natural-
ness" of manner recalls Yūgiri's appreciation of the dead Murasaki as she lay in repose, unclouded by the distracting gestures
of the living. Ōigimi's last recorded words to Kaoru reproach him
for having rejected Nakanokimi in her stead; Kaoru, in turn,
insists on that extraordinary sincerity of his that precludes such
action but promises to look after Nakanokimi.

Shortly thereafter, Ōigimi "fades completely" (*kiehateta-
mainu*, 5:318; S 867; W 888). Again, like Yūgiri, Kaoru lifts up
the lamp to peer into the dead face and finds it seemingly asleep.
When, in preparation for cremation, the lady's hair is combed,
a sudden fragrance is released, a fragrance unchanged from when
she lived. We had heard nothing about the fragrance of Ōigimi's
hair, however, and the insertion of this detail serves both to reinforce her kinship with Kaoru and to elevate her status by invest-
ing her person with an element of the miraculous. Indeed, she
is at once Kaoru-like and superior, if fragrance at death invokes
sainthood. The supreme Murasaki was pure and even radiant in
death. Since Ōigimi's body, like Murasaki's, obstinately resists
corruption, Kaoru decides that there is no remedy but to proceed
with the cremation. Yet, like Murasaki's, Ōigimi's pyre produces
only the faintest smoke, providing little satisfaction for the bereaved one who had hoped to trace the smoke to the dreary
evening sky and imagine his love among the clouds.[38]

Ōigimi's story has drawn to its close, but the reader may share
some of Kaoru's frustration with her death. She was only twenty-
six. Of course, she starved herself, and there are ready explana-
tions for that, most immediately the humiliation of her sister's
neglect by Niou, culminating the series of indignities inflicted
upon her by life. Yet there is a lingering sense of disproportion,
an extravagant willfulness to her departure that makes it the
equal of Kashiwagi's in dramatic intensity. Drawing on their several similarities, might we not propose that both Ōigimi and
Kashiwagi died because they had been seen? And if so, what
might "being seen" mean in Ōigimi's case?

A survey of the motif of voyeurism (*kaimami*) in early Japanese
literature reveals three types: (1) that in which the object (usually
female) is seen at a moment when it has assumed a degraded,

usually nonhuman form, and the seeing causes a dissolution of the relationship between seer and seen; (2) that in which the seen is a superior (heavenly) being, transformed into an exquisite human, and the seeing results in either union or separation; and (3) that in which the seen is a human superior to the seer, typically a female servant.[39] An example of the first type may be found in the *Kojiki*, in the story of Toyotamabime, daughter of a sea deity, who decides to give birth on land to her child by the deity Hoori no Mikoto; she enjoins her husband from looking in on her during the delivery, but he disobeys, to find that she has turned into a crocodile. Ashamed, Toyotamabime returns to the sea.[40] The famous story of the founding god and goddess, Izanagi and Izanami, offers a variation: Izanagi and Izanami are deities of the same order, but Izanami dies first; Izanagi travels to the land of the dead in hopes of bringing her back. He is told to wait, but in his impatience chances to glimpse her putrefying body, whereupon he retreats in panicked flight.[41] In this case, as with Orpheus and Eurydice or Cupid and Psyche, seeing prevents reunion. The story of the Heavenly Princess in the *Tale of the Bamboo Cutter* is a familiar example of the second type. The princess, originally an inhabitant of the moon, is sent to earth as punishment for an unnamed transgression. Her extraordinary beauty wins her suitors from all over the land, including the emperor himself. She resists them all, however, even turning into a shadow when the emperor approaches. In the end she returns to the moon.[42] As for the third type, there are a number of examples in the *Genji*, including those in the Ukifune story that we shall be taking up.

Now, these various instances of voyeurism share two conditions: (a) the seen is either nonhuman (being superior or inferior) or possesses a nonhuman attribute, and (b) the seer is bound by a taboo from seeing. The great energy contained in voyeurism as *kaimami* finds its source in the tension inherent in these conditions: the more appealing (a) is, the stronger the strictures of (b).[43] Now, with the *Genji*, whose examples fall largely into the second category, both seer and seen are human. Although the seen is endowed with extraordinary beauty often described as exceeding human proportions, nevertheless, the human identity of the seen seems to bring about a shift of interest from the seen to the seer.[44] The *Genji* makes it possible and even useful to speak of subjects and objects on the scene of voyeurism.

Genji beholding the child Murasaki, Yūgiri beholding Murasaki as his lovely stepmother, and Kashiwagi beholding the Third Princess, are all constituted as subjects in the forbidden seeing, thereby acquiring an interiority that makes them aesthetically interesting. Before he chances upon that breathtaking vision of his stepmother in the storm-blown scene, Yūgiri is a prim young man of predictable contours. Because he never translates his gaze into action, he remains so to the public eye (his role in the Uji chapters, with villa on the other side of the river and a daughter to bring misery to the Uji sisters, is consistent with earlier expectations). His double Kashiwagi, on the other hand, stretches Yūgiri's boundaries at both ends: as a young man his sole distinguishing feature is political ambition until he happens to glimpse Genji's young wife the Third Princess. His choosing to embrace a doomed passion transforms him into an intense, brooding figure whose private obsessions are shared with us. In Genji's case, on the other hand, whatever interiority he develops remains sealed, displaced onto his heroines, the objects of his vision. As I have suggested, that is precisely how he maintains his status as solitary archaic hero: he looms larger than life because he remains unrevealed by comparison to lesser figures.

Now, let us turn our attention to the object of vision. What distinguishes the seen of the first category from that of the second? Most examples show that what is seen in the first category is ugliness, in the second, beauty.[45] Yet the more fundamental distinction seems to be one of difference and sameness. Toyotamabime has the form of a crocodile while her husband is a deity with (presumably) human features; she is from the sea, he the land. Izanagi is living, Izanami dead. Another consequence of shifting the objects of vision, of attachment, from the extraterrestrial to this world is that species difference is replaced with sameness.[46] This development joins to reinforce a new interest in the seer, for if the beauty that is seen by the *Genji* heroes is unearthly, it is a beauty that is created in the act of seeing, in short, through longing. Now, this puts us at an enormous remove from the mythic temper of the *Kojiki*, for example, but this longing is still nourished by mythic elements such as the mystery of resemblance, or the irresistible attraction of kingship and all things pertaining to it. Resemblance is the arbitrary product of blood tie, and it inevitably drags with it the specter of incest; the sanctity of kingship is maintained by the strictest of laws, relying on the avowedly natural and consequently arbitrary phenomenon of birth.

In other words, the rules that make possible the demarcation of social categories are summoned to instate difference within the this-worldly homogeneity of the field of vision in the *Genji*. These rules endow many of the acts of seeing with a quasi-magical potency, with emphasis on the *quasi*, for by being placed in the sphere of longing, the rules lose their literalness and their arbitrariness and become metaphors for the arbitrary and the absolute. In this fashion the *Genji* simultaneously upholds and unravels the mysteries of kingship and blood tie, weaves in and out of the adjacent realms of myth and fiction, and shows how each constitutes the other. Again, this is not to say that these domains are symmetrical. The order of difference instated in the field of vision in the *Genji* finally rests on longing, which can never be satisfied. That is the significance of the shift in interest from the seen to the seer; or more accurately, the seen becomes the seer.

For example, if we return to Ōigimi, we recognize that the *Genji* effects transformations in the seen object as well. The chagrin Ōigimi experiences the first time Kaoru intrudes upon her is distinctly rooted in the fact that she is in mourning robes. That she still suffers from the loss of her father and might therefore be unresponsive to the erotic attentions of another man is less pertinent than the specific issue of her dress. Of course, this is thoroughly consistent with her penchant for distinguishing between body and spirit and her fastidiousness about the former camouflaged by explicit valuation of the latter. Her dark sleeves, occasioned by the death of her father, conceal yet suggest the dying flesh within. Her acute self-consciousness is nowhere more evident than in the passage describing the modest efforts made at the Uji villa to acknowledge Nakanokimi's "wedding" to Niou. Of course, nothing could make her more squeamish than such explicit recognition of the third successive occasion of physical union. She is humiliated to be the older sister yet so clearly inexperienced at supervising such festivities, humiliated to be seen in this light by the aging servants, and humiliated to see them festooning themselves:

> She looked about her at all the women past their prime, busily sewing at unsuitably flowery fabrics and primping themselves. None among them offered the slightest excuse for such offenses, she thought; I, too, will soon be past my prime. When I look in the mirror, I see my own form wasting away. None of these women can think herself ugly. Ignorant of how they look from behind, they tug at their bangs and paint their faces diligently. I think that I have not yet descended to their depths, I believe that my nose and eyes are still as they ought to be, but is it not possible that I delude myself?　　　(5:270; S 846; W 869)

Ōigimi attempts to conceal her flesh in her sister's and achieve a disembodied union with Kaoru. She insists upon denying her own material being, and when all efforts to persuade Kaoru to cooperate fail, she has no choice but to die. The goddess Izanami died and became hideous. Her husband's gaze confronted a repulsive otherness. All too unshielded, all too like a woman instead of a distant princess, Ōigimi longs to be other—that is, immaterial. Instead, she is unkindly revealed in her corruptible sameness. Death holds the last promise of achieving otherness. In the *Genji* version of seeing causing separation, what had hitherto been mere object, qualified only by the barest suggestions of "shame" (at being seen a crocodile, or as putrefying flesh), acquires a full-fledged interiority. Murasaki Shikibu's passion for irony finds relentless expression in Ōigimi's incorruptible beauty even after death.

Thus, both seer and seen are constituted as subjects, and death as well as beauty born of longing. What is Kaoru's contribution to these developments? It is true that the first *kaimami* scene makes of him a hero, if only because we have learned how to read this motif. The young man with such unsuitable interests in the religious life becomes rather more promising after that memorable glimpse of lovely princesses by moonlight. Yet there is not even a quasi-magical effectiveness to Kaoru's seeing. He does not act, and he does not recognize what requires recognition. In "Beauty and the Beast" (or less gratifyingly, the "Frog Prince"), the beautiful human subject is able to recognize through imagination (coerced and yet magical in its potency) the sameness of the hideous other and conclude a splendid union. Like the Prince in the "Little Mermaid," Kaoru fails to exercise his mind to recognize who Ōigimi is, just as he cannot recognize the nature of his own self.[47]

Yet, Kaoru's failure is inevitable, or rather his success is inconceivable, for it would require something akin to the secret admission of Ōigimi's, and therefore his own, overvaluation of the flesh—or, for that matter, of kingship. In fact, kingship functions both literally and metaphorically. As a metaphor, it includes attachment to the flesh, to worldly glory—in other words, it is thoroughly identified with the secular side of Kaoru's secular-holy dichotomy. Given this, overvaluation of the secular elements would also have to be apprehended metaphorically, and Kaoru is not the possessor of such imaginative tact. Moreover, the very notion of a modus vivendi for the pair is ludicrous. The taut comedy enacted between them, with its timely evasions and misapprehensions, is the finest accommodation that can be made to profound contradictions.

Mythic seeing (as in the emperor's land survey) entailed magical knowledge, that is, possession. The *Genji* translates seeing into a secular knowledge with a secular, psychological potency. Physical vanquishment is replaced by psychological subjugation, produced by knowledge of another's knowledge. Ōigimi cannot tolerate learning of Kaoru's crass (literal-minded) knowledge of her material being. Kashiwagi takes himself to bed to die when he realizes that Genji knows of his transgression. The best exorcists in the world cannot stop his dying, since he has not been possessed, just as they are powerless before Ōigimi's determined decline: secular knowledge transports such characters beyond the realm of possession.

Ōigimi's death is likened to the "withering away of grass" (5:318; S 867; W 888), and Kashiwagi's to "vanishing foam"

(4:308; S 647; W 689). Murasaki died as the "vanishing dew" and her aunt Fujitsubo as a "flame being extinguished." These are the four most beautiful deaths, enshrouded in the language of poetry, to be found in the *Genji*.[48] To what end this embellishment, and why the summoning of poetry? Are these characters being compensated for, or perhaps rewarded in some way? And if so, is poetry used because it constitutes the highest form of accolade, or because it is the most economical one, being both pointed and wide-ranging through its allusiveness? (And are these possibilities in fact different?) I sense that all these conditions are at work here, and the only point that can be made with certitude is that these characters are identified as a group through their beautiful deaths.

Fujii Sadakazu finds a dividing line in the narrative poems of the *Man'yōshū*, a line marking that point when the other land (*ikyō*) ceases to be visible to mortal eyes.[49] Is it not possible that the line marks the point where the other land loses its sublime simplicity, its unity as otherness? It is this loss that makes subjects of both seer and seen, that makes possible—indeed heralds—the beginning of fiction. Fiction begins when the other land is translated into the landscape of the self.

BETWEEN AUTHENTICITY AND SUBSTITUTION: NAKANOKIMI

In the interim between the death of Ōigimi and the emergence of a new heroine, the hitherto retiring Nakanokimi occupies center stage. Niou's questionable attachment proves sufficient to move her away from Uji to the capital, where she is installed in the Nijōin, bequeathed by Murasaki to her favorite Niou before her death. We should recall that for Murasaki this estate was a private retreat, her refuge from the trials of the Rokujōin, especially after the Third Princess became its official mistress. For Nakanokimi, however, it becomes the site of new unhappiness: Niou cannot, or will not, resist the long-rumored marriage to Yūgiri's daughter, and for all his appreciation of Nakanokimi's beauty and lovely disposition, he is also susceptible to the attractions of a young woman embellished by the resources of the most powerful household in the land, and he begins to spend many of his nights at the Rokujōin. Nakanokimi, who is carrying a child by now, has cause to regret having disobeyed her father's injunction and to admire her sister anew for her resolute rejection of men.

Of course she endures, and endures gracefully; and we seem to be reading a diluted version of the suffering of that idealized heroine Murasaki, whose heir Nakanokimi is by similarity of appearance, manner, and now dwelling. There is one striking difference, however, and that lies in the treatment of her sorrow.[50] When Murasaki helped prepare Genji to leave her for the Third Princess or spent the night putting up a brave front for her attendants, the narrator identified with her and forced us to share in her heartbreaking grief. But a Nakanokimi who sighs, in a poem, that the wind was not so biting even in her mountain village is rebuked for "perhaps having forgotten her past" (5:393; S 899; W 917). When she corrects her ladies for speaking too directly of her plight, the narrator conjectures coolly, "she must have decided, I won't permit any talk about this, let me keep my bitterness to myself—or something of the sort" (5:394; S 899; W 918). The prevailing assessment of Nakanokimi's fate is that she is lucky to get the attention that she does and that it is unreasonable to expect a man in Niou's position to behave otherwise.

Such intimations of the narrator's reserve recur throughout the Nakanokimi interlude, with reference not only to her but to Niou and Kaoru as well. As a result, we as readers are no longer permitted to reexperience innocently the plight of the protagonists: the situation is familiar, but we are evidently not to read it as we read Murasaki's story. This phenomenon is of a piece with the persistent intrusion of comic elements in Ōigimi's unhappy tale. With our emotions in check, we must read on to probe the contours of a new terrain.

The Nakanokimi interlude invokes not only Murasaki's story but Kashiwagi's as well, for it portrays Kaoru's dangerous attentions to Nakanokimi, attentions that cannot escape the watchful Niou (even as he is occupied with his recent marriage) because they are accompanied by that ever troublesome scent. Just as Kashiwagi opportunistically criticized Genji's neglect of the

Third Princess, so Kaoru awaits Niou's absences in order to comfort Nakanokimi—slipping under her curtains, grasping at a sleeve one time, a hand the next. In the process, the erstwhile candidate for sainthood shows himself to be knowledgeable about pregnancy: he recognizes, to her great chagrin, a special sash on Nakanokimi. When she attempts to retire by pleading discomfort, he rebukes her, saying he has heard that pregnant women are not in constant distress.

On that occasion, Kaoru is seated on a cushion reserved for the night priest. After confessing that he has been seeing several women in order to distract himself from the grief of Ōigimi's death but that his heart has never strayed, and that he trusts Nakanokimi to continue to regard him as a friendly supporter since his motives are, as everyone knew, unimpeachable, he proposes the following plan: "near that mountain village, I will have a statue erected, and pictures painted, to remind me of the past, and some sort of hall as well, perhaps not even a formal temple, where I might offer my prayers" (5:437; S 915; W 934). His plan, which he will in fact accomplish with Nakanokimi's "permission," is to tear down the Uji villa, recycle those materials for renovations at the abbot's monastery, and build a new temple on the site of the villa. The object of worship in the temple is to be a statue in the likeness of the Ōigimi who was so prodigal of heart and niggardly of body. In this fashion Kaoru, who now wonders whether his attachment to Ōigimi might not have destroyed his "priestly heart" (*hijiri gokoro*, 5:435; S 915; W 933) for good—Kaoru, as innocent of irony as ever—intends to pursue his original goal: that is, to be at once saintly and secular.

The word translated here as "statue" is *hitogata*, literally, "human form." Before this passage, it has appeared only once, in reference to the figure floated off to sea by the exiled Genji during the purification rites in Suma. It is in this common, voodoolike sense that Nakanokimi interprets Kaoru's use of the word when she replies, "A moving thought, yet it conjures up the images one floats down that unpleasant River Mitarashi, and that would not be very kind . . ." (5:437; S 916; W 934).[51] Where Kaoru intends a devotional image, that is, something to keep and worship, Nakanokimi supposes a disposable scapegoat. What makes this gesture tantalizing is that she proceeds to propose a live human being to fill this role: "speaking of *hitogata*," she begins, then she goes on to disclose to a startled Kaoru the existence of a half sister said to bear an extraordinary resemblance to Ōigimi. It is this young woman, not she, Nakanokimi, who should recall the dead lady for Kaoru. Yet Nakanokimi is sparing of details, and Kaoru correctly attributes her reluctance to a desire to protect the Eighth Prince's memory. But he persists: he would not hesitate to plunge into the sea in search of the dead lady's soul, and although this woman might not be deserving of such strenuous efforts (Nakanokimi has already intimated the inferiority of this half sister), "still, rather than continue in my disconsolate state . . . what could be wrong with including her in my idea of putting up a statue (*hitogata*) to be consecrated in that mountain village?" (5:439; S 917; W 935). Nothing, of course, especially since her mother is at a loss as to what to do with her, but might it not be excessive to "turn her into a Buddha" (5:440; S 917; W 936), demurs Nakanokimi. Kaoru, who began the evening at the night priest's station, concludes it as the recipient of information that will transform his life.

This conversation is repeated again, after Nakanokimi has given birth to a fine son. Kaoru's attentions continue to embarrass her but "being neither rock nor tree," she cannot remain utterly indifferent to his refined pleas. Perhaps out of

> a desire to help him cleanse his heart of such longings, she referred again to that statue (*hitogata*) and hinted, "She has been discreetly brought to these premises." For his part, though stung by no ordinary curiosity, he could not yet bring himself to shift loyalties. "But wait, if the enshrined one should prove able to answer my prayers, it would be a worthy object of devotion indeed; yet, if I am to be troubled from time to time, then the mountain stream would be sullied after all." At this she could not repress a soft laugh— so appealing—as she exclaimed, "O woeful mind of a saint (*hijiri gokoro*)!" (6:46; S 950-51; W 971-72)

At the time of this conversation, Kaoru has in fact spied upon Ukifune and ascertained her resemblance to Ōigimi for himself. Kaoru's appetite has been keenly whetted, but whether out of considerations of propriety or out of genuine reluctance to abandon his pursuit of Nakanokimi or both, he hesitates. Nakanokimi, for her part, is eager to recommend a not unlikable half sister as a substitute not just for Ōigimi but for herself as well.

Finally, Kaoru ventures to request that Nakanokimi speak on his behalf to Ukifune (whom he refers to as *marōto*, the "visitor,") and her mother. The conversation rises to an exchange of poems, with Kaoru the initiator:

Mishi hito no	If she be a copy
katashiro naraba	of the one I used to see,
mi ni soete	I shall place her on my person,
koishiki seze no	a talisman
nademono ni sen	for shoals of longing
	(6:47; S 951; W 972)

"Copy" is a weak rendering of *katashiro*, which is yet another word for human images, typically made of paper, used in purification rites. More than the other terms, *katashiro* makes explicit the process of substitution: by breathing upon or rubbing the form on one's own person, one's ills are transferred onto the image, which is then sent floating down a river. Kaoru, who initially appropriated clear water as a metaphor for the serene heart he could enjoy were it not for his frustrated attachment to Nakanokimi, now shifts to the imagery proposed by Nakanokimi for Ukifune. "Talisman" stands for *nademono*, literally, "thing to be rubbed," which is another term for ritual human forms, this one emphasizing the process of transference. *Seze* is often metaphorically interpreted as "moments" or "occasions," but the literal translation as "shoals" is necessary to preserve the water association, which points to the paradox of Kaoru's desires: water purifies, for example, by removing the tainted surrogate. Kaoru, however, wants to retain the surrogate, precisely because of the shoals of attachment where he founders. He is actually damming the cleansing flow of the water. And of course, we cannot miss the erotic coloring to Kaoru's choice of words.

Nakanokimi responds,

Misogigawa	If it is a talisman
seze ni idasan	you would send

261

nademono o   upon the shoals
mi ni sou kage to   of the cleansing river,
tare ka tanoman   who can trust you to keep it,
                               a shadow on your person?
                                              (Ibid.)

Nakanokimi, alluding to the many women Kaoru has begun
seeing, now professes pity for the figure that will be abandoned
to the shoals. Kaoru deflects the implied accusation by turning
himself into the talisman to be abandoned by an affectionless
Nakanokimi.

What is happening in this skillful conversation? Through their
cooperative interchange the intimacy of Nakanokimi and Kaoru
is verified, indeed, established as it is nowhere else; Nakanokimi,
for the moment her sister's true substitute, turns wordy and
gropes for solutions to her dilemmas through linguistic manipulation—manipulation designed to produce a substitute for herself. No wonder Kaoru prefaces the poetry exchange with the
observation that her ideas are "inauspicious," for the last time a
lady proposed a substitute for herself, she, the original, died. The
memory of their pseudo-intimacy from that night spent together
in Uji by Ōigimi's design awkwardly shadows Kaoru's pursuit of
Nakanokimi.

For all that Nakanokimi is cordial to her half sister, there is
something sinister about her framing Ukifune as a substitute, and
in such doomed terms at that.[52] Indeed, one might say that she
and Kaoru achieve their intimacy by developing another paradoxical formula for the latter's benefit. The cumulative effect of
their conspiratorial word play is simultaneously to make Ukifune
into the expendable (and therefore) cleansing object of Kaoru's
lust and the (presumably) more enduring object of his devotions.
Ukifune is predetermined to serve as a sacrificial figure.

Kaoru's vacillations and contradictions are only too familiar,
but this latest formulation commands our attention because it
draws on a process fundamental to the *Genji* from the beginning:
hitogata, *nademono*, and *katashiro* all refer to the phenomenon
of substitution. With the one exception of *hitogata* appearing in
"Suma," all these words are used only in the Uji chapters and
moreover are introduced by Kaoru. The logic of substitution cul-

minates in its namer Kaoru. Does this make Kaoru the master of substitution? Perhaps. The misbegotten son of a commoner and an unprized princess, Kaoru becomes king of words in the world of the *Genji*. By finding names for the dominant form of action in that world, he manages to substitute for substitution itself.

Drifting Beyond Substitution: Ukifune

We must now consider the latest candidate for substitution, Ukifune. Nakanokimi hesitates to divulge the circumstances of Ukifune's birth because she knows that any disclosure would tarnish her father's memory. Ukifune's mother turns out to be a niece of Ōigimi's and Nakanokimi's mother, a woman known as Chūjō, just like a series of serving women, including the one who enticed Genji in mourning for Murasaki. Ukifune's mother was the niece of the Eighth Prince's wife and also a servant in his household. She gave birth to Ukifune several years after her aunt's death. It was a birth unwelcomed by the Prince, and mother and daughter were, in effect, run out of the household. As we recall, the Prince, bent on the pursuit of the religious life and resentful of any obstacle, refused all suggestions of remarriage after the death of his wife. Even if serving women do not count, the emergence of Ukifune at this juncture demands a certain adjustment in our image of the Prince, somewhat as the Prince's story casts a new view on Genji's youth. (The much reduced time span suggests that myths have become ever more perishable in the Uji story.) This reassessment in itself should not be startling, since we have been rereading the Prince through his heir Kaoru. There is one more preliminary observation to be made: note that Ukifune's mother is a particular kind of substitute, for she is a blood relation to the original wife, but her status in the household is that of a servant and as such, she is subject to her master's casual erotic attentions.[53] It is the issue of such a union who will not only represent the proud family but also reign as undisputed heroine for the closing portions of the *Genji*.

The heroine's mother is worthy of modest scrutiny herself. The man she eventually married becomes governor of the eastern province of Hitachi, a name that should evoke for us another marginal figure, Suetsumuhana, whose late father was known as Prince of Hitachi because of a titular association with that province (note the predictable scaling down from prince to governor). The new household is filled with an assortment of children, some born between the Governor and his first wife, now dead; others born of the new alliance; and Ukifune, who is incomparably superior to the others in appearance and refinement. This is how Ukifune's stepfather is first described:

> The Governor was not a man of mean origins. His family had aristocratic ties, and those with whom he associated would not strike one as vulgar. His fortunes being considerable, he tended to be proud for one of his rank, and he filled his house with splendors amidst which he led a tasteful life. Still, for one who favored elegance, he had a surprisingly crude and rustic bent. Perhaps it was because he had spent the years since his youth buried in the remote east, but his speech had become distorted, and he had acquired an accent. He feared and skirted the houses of wealth and power, and in manner he was always guarded and watchful. Although quite removed from the ways of the flute and the koto, he played the bow interestingly enough.   (6:13; S 937; W 959-60)

The passage goes on to describe the young women whom his wealth has managed to attract to staff his household, and their indulgence in dress and play, hampered only by the fateful fact that they lived in the benighted provinces. As usual, translation but lamely follows the characteristic twists and turns of Murasaki Shikibu's sensibilities. Here, her sociological acuity pins the Governor by juxtaposing praise and criticism without the conjunctions that make for comfortable oppositions in English.

We assume that this view of the Governor overlaps with that of Ukifune's mother, who had witnessed the impoverished, hence all the more pious refinement of the Eighth Prince's household. As a compensatory life's project, this thwarted woman has settled on finding a good match for her lovely daughter, whose stepfather reserves all his affection for his own children. To such an end she selects a young guards lieutenant for a son-in-law who, just before the wedding, learns that Ukifune is but the Governor's stepdaughter, and, with the help of a profit-seeking intermediary, switches from her to an exceedingly young half sister and marries her complete with all the furnishings prepared for Ukifune. Thus a certain spectrum is provided for the phenomenon of substitution, with Ukifune replaced by an altogether uninteresting sibling—scarcely more than a child who, insult compounding injury, is referred to as *himegimi*, "her ladyship."

When Ukifune's mother pours out her frustrations to Ukifune's nurse, she is reminded that Lord Kaoru had expressed an interest in the young woman. The prudent mother brushes aside the suggestion as something fearful, for she has heard that Kaoru, obsessed with thoughts of an unknown lady, had long resisted the most enviable proposals in the land, and now, wedded as he was to the Emperor's Second Princess, there was no room for one such as her daughter—except perhaps in the service of his mother the Third Princess, in which capacity she might occasionally receive his favors:

> However splendid the surroundings may be, surely she will have occasion for heartbreak. I see that even her ladyship whom they call the fortunate one [Nakanokimi] is given to brooding, which shows that in the end, the only way, the only way we can live comfortably is with a man who need not divide his attentions. I'm speaking from my own experience. The late Prince was so feeling, so fine and handsome, but he did not even count me a human, and how I suffered! This man [the Governor] is unspeakably insensitive and his appearance dreadful, but in his dogged way he has never turned his attentions to another woman and so I have passed the years with peace of mind. Of course, when he behaves as he does now, so ungraciously and thoughtlessly, I find him odious, but even when we fight, I have always made clear those points on which I cannot yield. I know there are splendid people among your lords and princes who would put one to shame, but to what good

should we mingle with them if we cannot be counted as
one among them?   (6:30; S 943-44; W 964-65)

This passionately practical view of the possibilities of happiness
in life is new in the *Genji*.[54] We expect that this mother will
attend sensibly to her daughter's interests, but something happens to these hard-won lessons when she travels to the capital to
place Ukifune in her half sister Nakanokimi's care.

There, she has a chance to indulge herself in peeping at her
betters. First, she sees Niou, whom she had been inclined to
judge harshly because of the unhappiness he was causing his wife
Nakanokimi, but such reservations evaporate before the sheer
magnificence of his presence. How gratifying it would be to be
visited by such a person even if it were only once a year, like the
meeting of the Cowherd and Weaver Maid at the Star Festival!
In this surrender to fantasy Ukifune's mother unwittingly anticipates and in effect condemns her daughter to live such a life.
Even this vision is diminished, however, when she has a chance
to observe Kaoru. On that occasion, the Governor's wife, now
called "the visitor's (*marōto*) mother," opines that this lord cannot possibly be the equal of the Prince. Told by the women of
Nakanokimi's household to keep her judgment in reserve, she
watches and, sure enough, succumbs instantly to Kaoru's attractions. The scene that unfolds is the one we have already followed, in which Kaoru and Nakanokimi formulate and exchange
several versions of Ukifune as surrogate. Of course, the well-
meaning mother can only see, not hear.

Yet her education at the peephole in the capital is not incon-
siderable, for she has opportunities to study not only Kaoru and
Niou but Ukifune's original intended as well, the young lieutenant now wedded to one of her daughters by the Governor.
Though he cut a fine figure back in Hitachi, the lieutenant
dwindles to nothing amidst the splendors of the capital. Ukifune's mother's powers of perception, though registering the contrast between him and Niou and Kaoru, are blunted by the magnificence of the latter and unable to discriminate between them.
The negotiations between the lieutenant, his intermediary, and

the Governor of Hitachi laid bare the commodification of women in a fashion never approached by a Tō no Chūjō and certainly not a Genji, who had at their disposal the entire arsenal of aestheticized culture to mask their commerce in daughters. The other not negligible difference between the stories of the Lady of Ōmi, say, and of Ukifune is the absence of humor and frivolity in the latter, which accentuates the starkness of the situation.

Now, an interesting reversal takes place in Ukifune's mother's gazing: it is the men who are reduced to their material contours as potential sons-in-law. This reversal, however interesting, does not signal any triumph for the women, for Ukifune's mother cannot choose judiciously between Niou and Kaoru, just as her daughter will be condemned to vacillate between the two. As we read on, we should keep in mind the hallowed status of the birth mother in tales the world over. According to that logic, Ukifune is more fortunate than Tamakazura, for instance, in having a true mother even though her stepfather is less than desirable. The dubiousness of this assumption becomes clear when this mother concludes her visit with Nakanokimi with the intimation that she would not be averse to a union between her daughter and Kaoru.

Ukifune's mother continues to exercise her tireless eyes upon her return to her provincial home. One day, when that same lieutenant comes calling on her daughter ("her ladyship"), she decides to have a look at the pair. She is especially eager for a glimpse of the lieutenant's comportment in an informal setting. Her opinions fluctuate rather dramatically. When she studies his dress, she is so impressed that she wonders how he could have seemed inferior. As a pair, however, the lieutenant with her still unripe stepdaughter cannot compare with Niou and Nakanokimi. And yet, when she sees him chatting easily with the servants, he does not seem so uninteresting and vulgar as he had in Niou's presence. So much so that she begins to wonder if she had had the wrong party at her peephole in the Nijōin, when the lieutenant obliges by referring to the garden at that estate. The memory of the humiliation inflicted on Ukifune prevents

her from substantially revising her estimate, but Ukifune's
mother cannot resist the temptation to test his cultivation for
herself. She wonders,

Shimeyuishi	Secured with cord,
kohagi ga ue mo	the leaves at the top
mayowanu ni	of the young lespedeza
ika naru tsuyu ni	never stray;
utsuru shitaba zo	what dew could alter
	the color beneath?
	(6:74; S 962; W 984)

The upper leaves, bound in place, not straying from the lower
branches, represent the Ukifune who was engaged to the lieutenant. The dew is the younger half sister who deflected the lieutenant from his pledge. The lieutenant adroitly disarms the challenge by incorporating the images used by Ukifune's mother:

Miyagino no	Had I known her to be
kohagi no moto to	the young lespedeza
shiramaseba	of Miyagi Plain,
tsuyu mo kokoro o	no dew could have led
wakazu zo aramashi	my heart to stray
	(Ibid.)

What a well-matched exchange this is! The parties share a
measure of understanding. Ukifune's mother, though critical,
has extended her original insight that one's worth and possibilities are determined by the social circumstances of birth to include the realization that even the valuation of these circumstances is relative rather than absolute. The lieutenant admits
that there is nothing intrinsic about the two women that governed his choice. The instruments of their shared understanding—the images of the dew, lespedeza, and Miyagi Plain—appeared long ago in a poem sent by the Kiritsubo Emperor via
messenger to Genji's grandmother (1:105; S 9; W 11). There,
the lespedeza referred to the child Genji, the dew to the Emper-
or's lonely tears, and Miyagi Plain to the Palace. Poetic diction
turns promiscuous in the hands of the arch-novelist. The shabbiness of Ukifune's aristocracy and the shameful opportunism of

the lieutenant are equally exposed in the latter's response that makes a mockery of the genteel pretenses of poetic exchange.

Just before trying out her poem on the lieutenant, Ukifune's mother, as we have seen, was busily studying the young man's dress and manner. In formulating her assessment, she conflated two words, *kiyora* and *kiyoge*, that are consistently distinguished in the Uji chapters. *Kiyora*, indicating supreme beauty, often reserved for members of the imperial family, is usually associated with Niou, and *kiyoge*, designating an elevated but less exclusive beauty, is a common adjective for Kaoru.[55] The collapsing of the distinction is a complicated business. On the one hand, their indifferently approbative application to the lowly lieutenant is a tribute to Ukifune's mother's sturdy understanding of the nature of power. On the other, it illustrates a failure to discriminate that is of a piece with her infatuation with both Kaoru and Niou on the basis of their looks and words. We may applaud her faculties of demystification, but it is difficult to dispel a certain sense of impoverishment. The third type of voyeurism, whose subject is a female servant, develops as a species of progress without triumph in the *Genji*. Ukifune's mother's gaze consumes its objects with a peculiar mixture of indiscriminate rapture and practical interest. The adulteration of rapture by sociology is at once a fictional gain and a loss.

It is time to move from mother to daughter. The old mystery is there when Kaoru first catches sight of Ukifune, in a *kaimami* of virtually classic proportions, as if the *Genji* were gathering all its forces to delude us into believing that we will be indulged with one last romance. The scene is perfectly framed but imperfectly sealed from the corrosive elements in the air.

There is, of course, the ever-present matter of Kaoru's status. With great ceremony, he has just been wedded to the Emperor's daughter, the Second Princess. Kaoru himself had always favored her half sister, the prized First Princess, who is the daughter of the Akashi Princess and accordingly Niou's full sister. The public celebration of the nuptials only sharpens Kaoru's private dissatisfaction: in a pointed variation of how Genji, overwrought with longing for Fujitsubo, "spent his days in listless gazing, his nights pressing his demands on the maid Ōmyōbu" (1:305; S 98; W

95), Kaoru "spends the days at home, rising then reclining, gazing out, while by nightfall he hurries out against his will [to the Second Princess's]" (5:463; S 927; W 950).[56] In a flight from this routine, Kaoru makes an expedition to Uji, where he inspects the ongoing work on the conversion of the Prince's villa into a temple where, as we know, he intends to place a statue of Ōigimi for worship. It is then that he spots Ukifune's carriage on the bridge. Initially, he does not know its occupant's identity, but he no sooner finds out than he conceals his men and stations himself discreetly and strategically. Ukifune is on her way home from a second pilgrimage to Hatsuse. The first time, she was accompanied by her mother, but this time, some impediment has left her suitably alone except for the companionship of flighty young attendants. Ukifune on the bridge: we should pause over this innocent creature poised between the sacred, beneficent land of Hatsuse and the ambiguous one of Uji. Her carriage bears her across, unaware of the moment. She is reluctant to descend for fear of being seen and thus passes the initial test Kaoru is administering: she is at least minimally refined. (Her East Country attendants, by contrast, do not hesitate to jump down.) When she finally emerges, the little that Kaoru can discern confirms reports of her resemblance to her late half sister.

Once the party is installed within, Kaoru endures sore muscles in the hopes of gathering more evidence. Although he takes the precaution of removing such garments as might betray him with their rustling (such deliberation augurs ill), his scent cannot escape detection. The young maids speculate loudly, only to conclude by admiring what they take to be the elderly nun's costly incense. So much for Kaoru's fragrance, the sole irreducible presence in the increasingly mundane Uji.

In the end, it is the tears shed by Kaoru that makes this stolen glimpse satisfying to us. They come as he traces Ōigimi in Ukifune's features, just as they came to Genji when he recognized Fujitsubo in the child Murasaki. At last, we think, Kaoru, with both body and soul possessed, has been baptized a hero.

Such hopes are dampened while Kaoru takes his time to abduct Ukifune from her temporary refuge in the capital. He hesitates because he worries about his position and because he is still, albeit ineffectually, pursuing Nakanokimi. When he finally resolves to make his move, it is in the inauspicious Ninth Month. The journey to Uji is for him from beginning to end an elegy for Ōigimi. His yearning finds expression in spite of himself:

Katami zo to   When I see her
miru ni tsukete wa   as a memento
asa tsuyu no   my sleeves grow wet
tokoro seki made   with tears crowded thick
nururu sode kana   as the morning dew.
                        (5:88; S 968; W 991)

The inauspicious words strike a sympathetic chord in the heart of one of his companions, Bennokimi, who took vows at the time of Ōigimi's death.

When the curious party arrive at the villa, Kaoru is so overcome by a sense of Ōigimi's presence that he must leave Ukifune after the most cursory of hostly gestures. Sufficiently collected, he returns to her side to make such observations as "Had you been raised here long ago when everyone was still together, your feelings would no doubt have run deeper. . . . Why did you spend all those years in that [distant] place?" (6:92; S 970; W 993). Efficiently, he proceeds to ascertain that Ukifune (and perforce, her robust maids) is untutored in the ways of Japanese and Chinese poetry, the thirteen-stringed Chinese koto, and even the six-stringed Japanese koto (the wagon). Apart from a single modest but not witless rejoinder, Ukifune's only response is one of shame, whose inevitable consequence, reserve, deepens Kaoru's disappointment. He tells himself that he had anticipated her deficiencies: "Perhaps there were shortcomings, but it is still preferable that her education have been slight. I shall teach her as we go along. Had she come with rustic pretensions, she would have been no use to me as a substitute" (6:91; S 970; W 953). Watching Ukifune toy with her fan, he makes reference to a Chinese poem in which an abandoned lady likens herself to a fan at summer's end—a topic he quickly regrets introducing, even though it cannot be understood by his interlocutors.

When Ōigimi was alive, Kaoru had been in the habit of re-

271

treating from unsatisfactory interviews with her to seek solace from Bennokimi. Now, he sends her the following poem:

Sato no na mo
mukashi nagara ni
mishi hito no
omogawariseru
neya no tsukikage

The name of the village
is still the same,
but the moonlight in the
bedroom
shines upon a face
different from the one I knew.

(6:94; S 971; W 994)

Just as when Kisen wrote his poem about retreating in the mountains of Uji, the name of the village is gloomy, but now, the poet's heart is dark as well. Kaoru, who gave a name to the process of substitution, does not believe in its efficacy. Ukifune cannot become Ōigimi, nor, unlike Murasaki, can she become an object of attachment on her own merits because Kaoru is bent on demonstrating her inadequacy to the destiny he himself has chosen for her. Is it social background that finally emerges as an absolute condition that cannot be overcome? Kaoru with Nakanokimi made a thrust for her sleeve here, a snatch at her hand there. There is no transforming power of desire at work between Kaoru and Ukifune. Is Ukifune's ignorance, her lack of cultivation, sufficient to explain Kaoru's failure of imagination? Yet he is not alone in the damnation of Ukifune. In their not malevolent ways, Nakanokimi and Bennokimi conspire with Kaoru to spell out her doom in slips of the tongue or even modes of dress. Ukifune's fate is, as it were, overdetermined.

What has been observed of Ukifune thus far surely calls to mind the example of Tamakazura. Ukifune is more than any other character heir to Tamakazura's "wandering" (sasurai); like her, she has been long lost to the provinces, to emerge only at the ripe age of twenty. We might also recall that Tamakazura made a pilgrimage to Hatsuse, that she was countrified and deficient in her education, and that she, too, was subject to inappropriate male attention. The great contrast, however, is that where Tamakazura's "wandering" carried her inexorably to the capital, Ukifune's takes her away from it. Whereas Tamakazura was imprisoned in the Rokujōin, Ukifune is immured in the loneliness of Uji. Tamakazura reminded Genji of her mother Yūgao but managed to charm him with her own qualities as well; Ukifune provides the living tissue for the statue of Ōigimi that Kaoru intends to erect in the villa-turned-temple.

Kaoru is reluctant to place Ukifune in his mother's service because there, she would be merely one of the maids available for carnal sport, and he cannot so overtly belittle his own efforts to create an Ōigimi substitute. He means to transport her to the capital in due course, but he is in no hurry, for Uji is convenient enough for her safekeeping. He does not know that he has already been anticipated.

That is to say, during Ukifune's brief stay in her half sister's charge at the Nijōin, she was "discovered" by Niou, who was prowling through the house disgruntled that Nakanokimi was washing her hair and unavailable to him. Guessing that she was a new servant, and finding her uncommonly lovely, Niou lost no time in introducing himself to her. Although spotted by Ukifune's hawkeyed nurse, who registered furious protests with Nakanokimi's maids and passed them on to Nakanokimi herself, Niou was hardly one to be shaken by such objections. Nakanokimi's maids marveled out loud at the fierce devotion of the nurse, who had stationed herself at the couple's side. They wondered if it weren't "too late to be worthwhile" (6:58; S 956; W 997) to convey a message from the Palace that Niou's mother the Empress had fallen ill. In fact, it was not "too late," for the message was too urgent even for Niou to tarry long enough to accomplish the "real thing" (*jitsuji*, in the telling euphemism of the classical commentaries).

Such conversation is extremely unusual in the *Genji*, whose heroines are, as a rule, more gently used. We ought to note that in the above episode, Niou, without any premeditation, was on the verge of accomplishing precisely what Kaoru agonized over endlessly, the project of replacing Nakanokimi with Ukifune. In fact, it was because of this incident that Ukifune's worried mother moved her to a modest house in the capital, from which she was eventually abducted by Kaoru.

The abduction does not, of course cannot, terminate Niou's involvement. Tenacious and resourceful in the pursuit of beautiful women, he manages to trace Ukifune to Uji and braves the way to her temple-prison one night. After peering in on Ukifune with her maids, he easily decides to enter—that was, after all, what he had come prepared for, disguised as Kaoru. Ukifune's maid, unable to distinguish the scent of one from the other, readily admits him. Ukifune is horrified and yet, in the course of the day and a half spent with him, cannot resist the appeal of the extravagantly impetuous Prince. On their first morning together, in contrast to the measured behavior of the sociologically relentless Kaoru, Niou, inspired by the heady democracy of lust, offers her the wash basin first rather than having her wait on his ablutions. True, he does not know her identity, but though he presses her for her name and history, he does not quiz her on her accomplishments. He insists that he cannot bear an instant's separation from her and sketches a scene of a "man and a woman lying together," with the tearful wish they might always be together in that fashion.[57]

What makes this tryst delicious is the familiar but still precious excitement of the forbidden. Since Ukifune was to have been fetched by her diligent mother that day for yet another pilgrimage, so the house must be closed off on the grounds of unexpected defilement—the signs announcing it ironically serving as an innocent marker of the taboo proceedings within. And of course, we recall that the other person who must be kept in the dark, Kaoru converted into a parent figure, had once planned for Niou to impersonate him with Nakanokimi. The next time Kaoru visits Ukifune, he is delighted with her melancholy brooding, which he attributes to the maturing effects of enforced isolation. It cannot occur to him that she is tormented to find herself receiving two men.

Niou makes another visit the following month, this time having contrived to stay away from the capital for two days. He has braved the spring snow in order to see Ukifune. (Niou restores spring to the barren soil of the tale.) He has made plans: he will remove her from Kaoru's domain and cross the river, where they can seclude themselves in the villa of an acquaintance. Before reaching the opposite shore, the boatman pauses at an island in the middle of the river. There, Niou recites a poem that uses the orange trees on the island as a symbol of his unchanging love:

Toshi henu tomo   Though the years pass
kawaran mono kawa   how can it change,
tachibana no   the heart
kojima no saki ni   that plights its troth
chigiru kokoro wa   at the point
    on Mandarin Orange Isle?
    (6:142; S 991; W 1008)

The mandarin orange as a symbol of unchanging attachment evokes the lovely anonymous *Kokinshū* poem that figured in Genji's and Yūgiri's compositions on the late Murasaki:

Satsuki matsu   May-awaiting,
hana tachibana no   the mandarin orange blossom
ka o kageba   bears in its scent
mukashi no hito no   fragrance from the sleeves
sode no ka zo suru   of one bygone.
    (KKS 139, "Summer")[58]

The air is redolent with sweet smells and romance. The hidden identity, the banishment of the world, and above all, the youthful passion, all vividly evoke the tragic escapade of the young Genji with Yūgao. And just as Yūgao, even as she surrendered to Genji, responded to his fervor with dark foreboding (1:234; S 68; W 64), so Ukifune replies in a poem that gives her her name:

Tachibana no   Though the color of the Isle
kojima no iro wa   of the Mandarin Orange
kawaraji o   may not change,
kono ukifune zo   unknowable is the destiny
yukue shirarenu   of this drifting boat.
    (6:142; S 991; W 1018)

The story of Ukifune, the "drifting boat," takes up the stories of Yūgao and her daughter Tamakazura where they left off.

When they disembark, Niou, loath to let anyone lend her a hand, carries her into the house himself, much to the disapproval of the onlookers. On the return trip, too, he will carry her, with the gesture now prefaced by an "as usual" (6:147; S 994; W 1020). Niou and Ukifune are a more carnal pair than any the *Genji* has treated, and the text points to Ukifune's disheveled hair and notes that they "play and cavort" all day long in a manner shameful to behold (ibid.). By now Niou is fairly certain as to who she is: where Kaoru stripped her culturally, he proceeds sartorially. In the chaste prose of this tale, Ukifune is left shivering in but five layers of undergarments, her "slender form" revealed not only to Niou's eyes but to her maid Jijū's as well (6:143; S 992; W 1018). Niou finds her freshly seductive because even the women most familiar to him never appear to him so exposed. He even has her try on her maid's skirt as, this time, she waits on his morning ablutions. Kaoru cherishes, indeed worships, certain women as an exercise in spirituality; Niou admires them all as flesh.

The torrid two days with Niou are the last that Ukifune will spend in the companionship of men. Both Niou and Kaoru make plans to bring her into the city, and each learns of the other's plans. Niou has always been jealous of Kaoru, but Kaoru, though he initially fumes over his captive's unsuspected libidinousness that made her a fit partner for Niou, in the end rejects drastic measures because, as he assures himself, he had never taken her seriously. It is Ukifune who suffers from the knowledge of knowledge, not just of the two men but of her maidservants and potentially, and most seriously, of her mother as well.

She takes to lying abed and listening. It is a posture shared by both Nakanokimi and especially by Ōigimi, but it leads to the most dramatic consequences in the case of Ukifune.[59] Ukifune listens, absorbs, but does not comment, just as she is mute in the scenes with Kaoru and Niou. She dramatizes, indeed makes perceptible, the contrast between, even the shift from, peeping hero to listening heroine as the center of consciousness of the tale. (And, looking back, as usual, we remember how Murasaki endured her maids' chatter; how the grieving Genji exchanged seeing for listening, and desire to see for fear of being seen.) What does Ukifune hear now? Her mother, disturbed by reports of her low spirits, wonders for a moment if she is pregnant but then recalls the canceled pilgrimage (on the occasion of Niou's first visit, when resourceful Ukon pleaded defilement). She prattles about her daughter's improved prospects with Kaoru, refers to the unfortunate incident with Niou, and throws in, for good measure, her refusal to countenance any indiscretions on her daughter's part. Ukifune, growing desperate, begs her mother to take her home for a short visit but is refused: there is no room for her and besides she must make ready to move to the capital. The birth mother's ignorance does not make her abandonment any less cruel. For her part, the maid Ukon is inspired to tell the story of her sister who received two men, a situation remedied only by the murder of one and the banishment of the other. The women exchange their solemn stories with the pride and pleasure that accompany imagined worldliness. The roar of the river may be an appropriate background for the stories, but for Ukifune both are pressingly ominous. She has heard that the boatsman's son fell in just the other day and drowned, and that this river has similarly taken many lives.

The conclusion imposes itself on her: "If my body were to vanish in just that fashion," she thinks, using words almost identical to Murasaki's sorrowful anticipation of death (6:159; S 999; W 1026-27). Ōigimi, wishing to hasten her death, told herself fervently, "I must contrive to take advantage of this occasion to die." In similar yet characteristically simpler terms, Ukifune wonders, "Oh, how can I die!" (6:173; S 1005; W 10034). Unlike her half sister, Ukifune uses the plaintive first-person *maro*.[60] Once the idea enters her mind, it takes hold like a hungry worm and finds food everywhere: stories of women from the remote past—not just unromantic, common creatures like Ukon's sister—faced with a similar dilemma crowd her mind.[61]

The decision is made: Ukifune proceeds to burn or to have tossed into the river her letters from Niou, just as the Emperor burned the Heavenly Princess's message to him after she ascended to the moon, just as Genji burned his and Murasaki's exchanges as he prepared to take vows. She does, however, leave two farewell poems behind: one to her mother, for whom she yearns most desperately, the other to Niou, whose painting she has kept with her to gaze upon tearfully. To Kaoru she leaves

277

not a word, for, she thinks, she would not be seen as fickle after her death. Amidst the bustle of her maids hastening to complete preparations for the move to the capital, Ukifune lies awake wondering how she might steal out undetected. As darkness lifts, she turns her eyes toward the river, and, we are told in an image borrowed from the sutras, she feels "closer to her end than even the slow-paced sheep [being driven to slaughter]" (6:185; S 1010; W 1040). She knows that she commits a grievous sin in preceding a parent in death, but that seems less culpable than bringing about the shame that prolonged existence would surely entail. So, in the sound and the fury of temple bells and roaring river, Ukifune steps out from her prison.

But Ukifune does not die. Just as Chekhov learned to do without the gunshot on center stage, so Murasaki Shikibu, approaching the end of her endeavors, can dispense with a literal death. Instead, since all her characters believe that Ukifune is dead, she can explore a more interesting, less petulant version of the question that we all pose as children: "What if I die . . . what would they do?" "They," in this case, decide to hold a funeral quickly, before people can talk. There is the embarrassment of not having a body, but Ukifune's maids, by now veterans of deception, gather enough of her belongings to hold a cremation. The ultimate substitute is so effaced that she can be buried in absentia. The kaleidoscopic cacaphony is now converted into the wispy smoke of personal effects, and Ukifune has finally become adequate to her sister, that supreme adept in the mortification of the flesh.

What can follow a fictional death? In this case, a parody of rebirth, coming perhaps as a disappointment to hopes that Ukifune might at last have escaped the scripts imposed on her by others. Even if the listening heroine has come to occupy the center of the tale's consciousness, she is hardly a unified, autonomous entity herself. She is discovered unconscious within a dark grove of trees; some say she is a fox or some evil creature in disguise, but a certain Bishop of Yokawa pronounces her a human (the latest in a series of designations conferred upon her by others) and insists that she be cared for accordingly. This worthy prelate, who makes a principle of leaving the lofty heights of Mt. Hiei as little as possible, happens to be on the scene because his elderly mother fell ill on her return from a pilgrimage to Hatsuse in the company of his sister. Both these ladies are nuns; the younger one took vows when she lost her only daughter years ago. Just returning from a pilgrimage, her devout mind can hardly resist construing the mysterious discovery as a miraculous restoration of her child. Late in the day, Hatsuse is to offer something to Ukifune after all: a stepmother.

Ukifune is taken with the nuns to Ono at the foothills of Mt. Hiei, and the Bishop returns to his mountain retreat. When the beautiful creature fails to make any progress after two months (she recovers consciousness only to the extent of asking that she be thrown back into the river), the nuns implore their Bishop to try his exceptional powers on her. With some misgiving, he accedes, overriding the wishes of his prudent disciples, who think it unwise for an august prelate to meddle in affairs concerning young women. The exorcism is a challenging one: it takes one full night for the Bishop and his disciple to force the possessing spirit to speak:

I'm not one who should be brought to this pass by your spells and chants. A long time ago, I was a monk myself, but I had a grudge, so I've had to wander around. In the course of it all, I settled in a place where there were beautiful women. I managed to kill off one of them. This one here was bitter about the world, and all she could think about was how to die. That was useful to me, and so one dark night, when she was all alone, I snatched her away. But the Kannon [a bodhisattva of mercy, here, no doubt the principal object of worship at Hatsuse] seems to have been protecting her along the way. That's why I'm losing out to the Bishop. It's time for me to go.

(6:283; S 1050; W 1091)

Note that this is the first male possessing spirit to be granted speech.[62] In order to understand his words, we must turn to Ukifune, whose mind is revealed to us for the first time. We grope with her to a recollection of what happened:

279

I was so sad, thinking about how unbearable everything was. When everyone was asleep, I opened the shutters: the wind was raging, and I could hear the river rushing by. I was so afraid, all by myself, I couldn't even tell what I was doing. I stepped out on the verandah but didn't know where to go. It seemed weak to turn back. I had decided to be strong, to die to this world. Better be eaten up by a demon than be found in this foolish state, I thought, and called for one to come to me. Then, as I sat there, a beautiful man approached me saying, "Now, come to me." I felt as if he were carrying me in his arms, and I thought he was the one I used to call His Highness the Prince, but then everything was blurred. He took me away and put me down in a strange place and disappeared.

(6:284-85; S 1050; W 1092)

The word Ukifune uses for "beautiful" is *kiyoge*, the adjective reserved for Kaoru. The first time she saw Niou, Ukifune herself had distinguished between the two men in this fashion: "although she had found the Captain so beautiful (*kiyoge*) that it was impossible for anyone else to be like him, this one's [Niou's] refinements and lustrous beauty (*kiyora*) were quite incomparable" (6:124; S 983; W 1009). But here, Ukifune clearly thinks that she was with Niou, for he was the one who held her and carried her about. (Despite the greater length of their acquaintance, there is only one reference to Kaoru's holding her.)[63] Prepared to embrace death, Ukifune embraces Niou: sweet consummation, evidently sweeter than Ōigimi's, but more twisted, with insidious implications for them both. For to introduce a possessing spirit on the scene of Ōigimi's death, when such a presence was flatly denied at the time, has the effect of recoloring the superior, iron-willed sister's end with that of the lesser. It also serves as a subtle reminder of the former's concealed attachment to the flesh.

There is still Ukifune's linguistic conflation of Kaoru and Niou to attend to. It is a gesture that implicates Kaoru (along with Niou) in the enactment of her death. On the most elementary level, Kaoru is summoned to bear responsibility for Ukifune's "death." This also means that Ukifune's conflation (a more interesting version of her mother's and maids' confusion) reflects back and bears witness to the essential ambiguity within Kaoru that was initially suggested by the conflicting interpretations of his fragrance. Kaoru is Niou's double, and Niou's carnality has a secret and all the more potent life in Kaoru: hence, the economy of the possessing spirit taking the form of a defrocked priest.

The possessing spirit seemed to trace a regressive course in Genji's story: the Rokujō Lady's spirit began as sophisticated, neurotic psyche but faded off as primitive demon. Throughout its existence, however, it was unmistakably a dominant agent; that is, our interest was directed to the possessor and not the possessed victim. The scene of possession is different in Uji.

The spirit is no longer active. Whether Ukifune's possessor is construed as the defrocked priest or as Kaoru, he comes in response to her call, to her receptivity to death (for there is still a passive element in the victim: is Uji the site where all active agency fails?) whether in the form of a demon or of Niou. Now, the manifest possessor, the defrocked priest, a newcomer to the tale, is of interest only insofar as he embodies other characters, notably Kaoru. One useful effect is that Kaoru, who had sought to fix Ukifune as a living image of her half sister, is summoned instead to participate in the dissolution of the image. And summoned by her—since it is Ukifune who elects to die, though not, to be sure, with the sureness of Ōigimi. As we read back, we are struck anew by Ōigimi's deliberate parsimony—call it coyness—the controlled reservation and preservation of self until the very end, when she eludes Kaoru altogether as the insubstantial smoke of the funeral pyre. The consummation of Ōigimi and Kaoru is, after all, a mock consummation—a failed union, a failed possession. Had Kaoru witnessed Ukifune's cremation, he would have been even more disappointed.

To speak of Kaoru's "participation" in Ukifune's death is to speak loosely; it is, after all, a participation in absentia. Not only lovers but events, key events at that, begin to elude Kaoru. What do we make of a hero who repeatedly misses the action?

To refocus on the scene of possession: in the earlier instances, we recalled, it was Genji the hero who recognized (identified) the possessor and thus gave her voice. Now, that role is filled by a lesser figure, the Bishop of Yokawa. What are his credentials? Since the *Kakaishō*, readers have eagerly taken this character to be modeled on the celebrated priest Genshin (942-1017), whose work, the *Ōjō Yōshū* ("The Essentials of Salvation") was crucial to the foundations of Jōdo Buddhism. Genshin inspired many accounts, no doubt apocryphal, of his compassion and his humane, flexible interpretation of religious practice. Now, we are indeed shown the Bishop of Yokawa being solicitous to his mother and sister, even to the extent of disrupting his own practice to tend to the former's illness, though her age is so advanced as to discourage decent expectations for recovery. There is a pointed contrast with the abbot-teacher of the Eighth Prince, for whom the letter of the law is utterly unmitigated by sympathetic imagination. He, for example, might have been unwilling, or rather unable, to recognize a human presence in the unconscious Ukifune. Now, when the Bishop is entreated by his sister to descend once more to exorcise the evil spirit from Ukifune, he brushes aside his disciples' objections by observing, "Though the commandments I have broken are many, never has anyone spoken ill of me on account of women, and never have I erred in this respect" (5:282; S 1049; W 1090-91). Many readers, in their haste to applaud the Bishop's generosity of spirit over the narrow-mindedness of the lesser clerics, neglect to attend to this disclaimer. Doesn't he protest too much? Is it really safe for him to save Ukifune?

At the least, "saving" Ukifune proves to be a complicated affair. No sooner is she freed from the possession than she demands to take vows. The Bishop cannot resist her insistency, but not long thereafter, he finds himself in the awkward position of seeming to advise her to renounce her vows. (There is vigorous scholarly disagreement on this point—understandably, since cherished beliefs ride on it.) The reason? He has had yet another occasion to interrupt his austerities, this time to tend to Niou's sister, the First Princess. At her bedside, in the course of a rainy night, the gregarious prelate tells the story of his rescue of a mysterious young woman, which inevitably leads to his learning of Ukifune's identity and of Kaoru's attachment to her. No confidentiality, we might charge. In fact, it had occurred to the Bishop that Ukifune might be the Eighth Prince's lost daughter when he first saw her (and so his humanistic imagination had been helped along). No doubt he was impelled by curiosity, as well as pride in his prowess, to divulge his little story. Like all the religious confidantes in the *Genji*, he finds the burden of knowledge difficult.

At any rate, once he learns of Ukifune's connection to Kaoru, the Bishop suggests to her that she might be performing a worthier service by renouncing her vows, for by making herself accessible to Kaoru again, she would spare him the sin of lust. The Bishop, in other words, exceeds (or falls short of) the pure but humane man of vocation that the Genshin model apparently imposes. Even if we provisionally accept the vexing notion of literary models, there is ample ground to quarrel with the application of this one: although it is entirely possible that Murasaki Shikibu "revered" Genshin (her father may have belonged to his circles, and his disciples—if not Genshin himself—had ties with the potentates whom she served), that by no means rules out the likelihood of her creating a character to expose the tensions within figures such as Genshin rather than reproducing the hagiographies they actually inspired. Exorcism is in part an occasion wherein the exorcist confronts a version of himself: the murky side of the benign Bishop was anticipated in the encounter with the spirit of the defrocked priest.[64] His humanity is at once the bright face of controlled temptation and a mask of spirituality too ready to accede to temporal power.

The scene of possession has changed. The Bishop plays the role not only of the mediating priest but of the identifying hero, who, in this case, is confronted by himself in the fallen priest. Let us duly note the diminishing effect upon Kaoru, the proper (true) hero, who is vicariously fragmented into the three roles of exorcist, hero, and possessing spirit. Lay sainthood offers no luminous unity.

On the other hand, if I have seemed to trace a shift from possessor to possessed paralleling that from seer to seen, it is not to describe a triumphal scenario for the subject of possession. As

283

we know, Ukifune herself takes no pleasure in her recovery. Once she has taken vows, she is condemned to live out the parodic version of the *Tale of the Bamboo Cutter* in the drab surroundings of a country nunnery. Her beautiful hair is miraculously untangled despite her ordeal; the nuns refuse to be shaken from their conviction that a heavenly being has descended into their midst. But like that lunar exile, evening finds her on the verandah gazing out, thereby causing consternation that she, too, could vanish one day. She is even subjected to the attentions (including a *kaimami*) of an unworthy suitor, the former husband of the younger nun's dead daughter.

Like the shrill crescendo that accompanied Ukifune to the river, these passages, in more muted fashion, call attention to her predecessors. Through shared allusion to the Heavenly Princess, Ukifune is elevated to kinship with Murasaki and Ōigimi. Now, the *Bamboo Cutter* allusion served in Murasaki's case to intensify her idealization, and in Ōigimi's case to bestow upon her just that sort of other-worldly beauty she herself might have secretly desired. This is the bright side of the exchange between the *Genji* and the *Bamboo Cutter*. While the earlier tale is squarely situated in this world, it is literally bounded by a celestial other; by transforming the latter into a metaphor, the *Genji* condemns itself to a troubled probing of this-worldly existence: whence, the dark side of the exchange, with the dead Murasaki mercilessly exposed, the dying Ōigimi made to teeter between tragedy and comedy.

Ukifune's case, as it develops, retroactively revises her sisters downwards. Much as their shared possession undermines their claims to autonomous dignity in death, so the unsatisfactory smoke from their pyres is a dismal transformation of the Heavenly Princess's radiant ascent. For Ukifune, "this" world is sociologically shabby. Her suitor is a third-rate aristocrat affecting refined, that is, melancholy, sensibilities. Her household consists of nuns who, sleeping, terrify her with their hideously aged visages and loud snores; awake, they tire her with bad verses and graceless tunes. Yet when invited to take part, Ukifune cannot, not because she deems it beneath her (she has seen and heard better in her "previous life") but because she herself is insufficiently schooled to perform even in such company. She has nevertheless been regarded as the "happy light (*hikari*) of the mountain village" (5:331; S 1071; W 115). The trouble with this radiant creature is that she can neither fly to the moon nor die a simple earthly death, having tried once and failed. And thus the question is posed: how to live on without an other world to flee to. While her adoptive mother is on yet another pilgrimage to Hatsuse to give thanks for the new "light" in her life, Ukifune persuades the Bishop to administer formal vows to cement the effect of the earlier token rite.

Now, Kaoru's mother, the Third Princess, adopted the same solution, but she was always closed to us. Ukifune, who has thus far been mostly seen but hardly heard, becomes invested with language. This is how she presents her case to the Bishop:

> From the time I was a young child, I was always driven to brooding. Even my mother seemed to think of making me a nun and said as much on occasion. Once I was old enough to understand things, my desire deepened, not to be like others, but to strive for a life beyond this one. . . .
> (6:323-24; S 1067; W 1112)

The Bishop listens uncomprehendingly, for she is so beautiful, but nonetheless he accedes to her wishes. Some time hence, faced with a Kaoru who asks him to intercede with her on his behalf, he hesitates, for he has begun to wonder if he might not in fact end up sinning through his involvement in this affair. To allay his anxieties, Kaoru admits,

> It is strange that I should be in the garb of a layman. From the time I was young, I had a deep resolve to take vows, but I was shackled by the lonely Third Princess's depend-ence on my useless self; then, while I attended to various matters, my rank rose of itself, I found that I could no longer dispose of myself as my heart desired. I have had to pass the time longing for but unable to take vows. . . . In my heart I am no different from a holy man.
> (6:367; S 1084; W 1129)

Despite obvious differences, the two statements belong to the same genre: the regretful reflection on one's life. We might recall that Hikaru Genji was also apt to indulge in this exercise, especially after Murasaki's death. What distinguishes Ukifune's plight is that it lacks the contrast between external glory and (titillatingly) tragic loneliness. Yet it manifestly echoes this male heroic mode. Ukifune, who unwittingly dragged her sisters down with her, can also challenge the men.

Her new assertiveness, to put it vulgarly, is apparent in two poems composed the morning after she takes vows:

Naki mono ni	The world I cast away,
mi o mo hito o mo	thinking they and I
omoitsutsu	were finished,
suteteshi yo o zo	I cast away
sara ni sutetsuru	once more
Kagiri zo to	I had thought myself
omoi narinishi	done
yo no naka o	with this world;
kaesu gaesu mo	let me renounce it
somukinuru kana	forever now!

(6:329; S 1069-70; W 1114)

The discovery of language, for Ukifune, takes place in the writing of poetry, for

> she had never been good at telling people what was on her mind, and now more than ever, she had no intimate companions to turn things over with; all she could do when she felt as if she might burst was to turn to her inkstone and struggle to put her thoughts into writing, just as if she were practicing her hand. (Ibid.)

This is just the sort of poetry composition that we saw Murasaki resorting to when Genji married the Third Princess. Now, for Ukifune, who did not grow up turning a verse with every drop of a petal or cry of a cuckoo, this is a far more taxing endeavor, and we must think of the urgency that impels her.

Astonishingly enough, Ukifune has more poems attributed to her than any other heroine in the *Genji*. She has twenty-six to Murasaki's twenty-three, the Akashi Lady's twenty-two, Tamakazura's twenty, Nakanokimi's nineteen, Ōigimi's thirteen, Fujitsubo's twelve, and the Rokujō Lady's eleven. Ukifune, the culturally deprived Ukifune, the carnal one (the two are connected in the minds of scholars), composes more poems than any other heroine.[65] Given this, the traditional appreciation of Ukifune based on her beauty and her pathos is both sentimental and deficient.

Here are some preliminary observations about her poetic output: Ukifune never initiates exchanges with men. Of the four poems that she offers first, three are to her mother and one to her half sister Nakanokimi. Perfectly consistent, we think, with her retiring nature. As for her lovers: Kaoru addresses but four poems to her (in contrast to nine to Ōigimi and seven to Nakanokimi), of which she answers two; Niou addresses six, and Ukifune responds to all six. Untutored though she may be, she has her own means of discriminating. This is her first poem to Kaoru:

Taema nomi	Full of gaps
yo ni wa ayauki	and perilous
Ujibashi o	is the Uji Bridge
kuchisenu mono to	that you would have me trust
nao tanome to ya	never to decay.

(6:137; S 989; W 1015)

The occasion is Kaoru's visit after a long absence, during which Ukifune was visited by Niou. As we recall, Kaoru, sublimely ignorant of what had taken place, attributes her pleasing pensiveness to her loneliness. Perhaps encouraged by her improvement, he recites a poem—the first one he deigns to address to her. She, in the meanwhile, has already responded twice to Niou; does this account for her relative confidence on this occasion? For surely it requires courage for her to expose herself in this fashion to the exacting Kaoru. His poem assures her that their bond will be as lasting as the sturdy Uji Bridge is long and that she need not be anxious. Ukifune skillfully turns his images and sentiments into an expression of her own neglect. She may even be sophisticated enough to be drawing on an anonymous *Kokinshū* poem (6:137, n. 20):

Wasuraruru	I, mournfully forgotten
mi o Ujibashi no	with the Uji Bridge

naka taete	split asunder,
hito mo kayowanu	have passed many years
toshi zo henikeru	without any callers.

(KKS "Love, 5," 825)

With its puns combining the mournfulness (*ushi*) of the forgotten lover with the Uji Bridge, this poem is a plausible description of Ukifune's plight, and Murasaki Shikibu may well have had it in mind as she developed the stories of the Uji sisters. Whether or not Ukifune is alluding to the earlier poem, her composition is a straightforward and capable response to Kaoru's mechanical expression of ardor.

This is Ukifune's second and final poem to Kaoru:

Tsurezure to	Since my kin,
mi o shiru ame no	the dreary rain,
oyamaneba	will not pause for a moment,
sode sae itodo	even my sleeves
mikasa masarite	are flooding over.

(6:152; S 996; W 1023)

"My kin" serves for a phrase borrowed from *Ise* 107, "rain that knows my being [i.e., my plight]." The rain is as familiar as the tears that fall incessantly on the sleeves—a plaintive image made more poignant by the inconclusive ending with a continuative verb in the Japanese. Kaoru had sent on white, rather than more intimate colored paper, a poem that amounted to a greeting of the season, inquiring after her during the long rains. By the time this letter reaches her, Ukifune is quite desperate, yet she manages to recapitulate Kaoru's images and maintain the proper tone. "Proper" (*mamebito*) Kaoru calmly studies her reply and wishes he might see her.

At the same time, Ukifune replies to Niou:

Kakikurashi	Why not make myself,
haresenu mine no	passing rootless
amagumo ni	through the world,
ukite yo o furu	like the dark rain clouds
mi o mo nasaba ya	on the peak that never clears.

(6:152; S 996; W 1023)

288

Niou's response is inconsolable weeping.

We realize, in short, that even before taking vows, Ukifune had found a congenial form in poetry. Particularly in exchanges with Niou, she is able to sketch a sort of identity for herself. We have already considered the mandarin orange poem in which she named herself, so to speak. Here is another poem to Niou:

Furimidare	I shall vanish
migiwa ni kooru	midway—
yuki yori mo	further in the sky
naka zora nite zo	than the wind-tossed snow
ware wa kenubeki	that falls to freeze
	upon the bank.

(6:146; S 993; W 1020)

Niou is annoyed by the "midway" because he takes it to mean that Ukifune is unable to decide between him and Kaoru. Ukifune regrets having been so stupid and tears up her poem, but of course, it is Niou who is shown to be wrongheaded and obtuse about her delicacy.

Conspicuous in Ukifune's poems is the word *mi*, meaning "self," "being," or simply "I," but always with a strong sense of the corporeal, which in turn comes to imply a social reality that is inescapable precisely because it is material.[66] *Mi* occurs in eight of her twenty-two poems, a prominence rivaled only in Genji's poems, where it appears nine times but out of a total of two hundred twenty-one poems. On the other hand, *kokoro* appears but three times in Ukifune's poems. Her poetry reflects the heart-mind/body division maintained by a number of *Genji* characters but especially reiterated in Uji by Kaoru and Ōigimi. Ukifune seems compelled to choose the predictable—predictable, that is, both because of her background and because of Kaoru's unimaginative, cynical assessment of it. But out of being-as-(social)-body Ukifune spins out what ends up as a coherent statement about both her own existence and "fate" in general. We have already looked at a number of her *mi* poems: three to Niou, the second one to Kaoru, and the first one composed after her vows. Here are two preceding her suicide attempt:

Nageki wabi
mi o ba sutsu tomo
naki kage ni
uki na nagasan
koto o koso omoe

If weeping and lamenting
I cast myself away,
still think: a sullied name
will float
upon my shadow.

(6:185; S 1010; W 1040)

Much as Fujitsubo feared long ago, Ukifune understands that eliminating her physical presence will not put an end to her being, that all-important being that exists in the regard of others. The following farewell poem to Niou does not contain the word *mi* but uses the more graphic "shell" (i.e., "remains") in its stead:

Kara o dani
uki yo no naka ni
todomezu wa
izuko o haka to
kimi mo uramin

If I leave behind
not even my shell
in this wretched world,
how will you find
    my tombstone
    to resent?

(6:185-86; S 1010; W 1040)

Haka, "marker," is homophonous for "grave." If the body cannot absorb the total supply of social calumny, it may be the only object of attachment.

Ukifune is not, cannot be, the romantic that Ōigimi was. There is no place in her understanding for an untainted *kokoro*, precious center of being. In one of her few response poems in "At Writing Practice," Ukifune describes the result of taking vows:

Kokoro koso
uki yo no kishi o
hanaruredo
yukue mo shiranu
ama no ukigi o

True, my heart
has left the banks
    of this odious world,
but I am still a drifting
    fisher's boat,
    destiny unknown.

(6:330; S 1070; W 1114)

There is the usual pun of "nun" on *ama*, "fisher." *Uki kishi*, "banks . . . odious," which the heart has ostensibly left behind, is echoed in *ukigi*, the "drifting boat" that Ukifune has become. The world holds no exit for even this modest, insignificant creature.

It should come as no surprise that Ukifune's creator left behind the following three poems in her personal poetry collection:

Kazu naranu
kokoro ni mi o ba
makasenedo
mi ni shitagau wa
kokoro narikeri

I do not entrust
my self
to this lowly heart;
rather, it is my heart
that obeys my self.

Kokoro dani
ikanaru mi ni ka
kanauran
omoishiredomo
omoishirarezu

At least cannot my heart
suit
some sort of self?
I know it cannot be
and yet I would not know.

Mi no usa wa
kokoro no uchi ni
shitai kite
ima kokonoe ni
omoi midaruru

Despair
has followed fondly
into my heart:
and now my thoughts
multiply in disorder.

(*Murasaki Shikibushū*,
55-57)[67]

The heart-mind/body opposition is significant not only in the fictional world of the *Genji* but in the larger world of poetry beginning with the later poems in the *Kokinshū*. It seems to have played a particularly critical role in the poetry of Heian women and, as is evident here, was prominent in both the diary and poetry of Murasaki Shikibu.[68] These three poems by Shikibu, possibly written in succession, are not necessarily reconcilable; at the same time, they resist separation. In the first, number 55, "humble" is an adjective normally accompanying *mi*, as in "humble station."[69] Shikibu's affixing the phrase to *kokoro* demotes the "heart-mind" from the lofty entity one clings to despite one's actual fallen status to an enfeebled creature subject to the whims of external circumstance.[70] Number 56 seems to pursue the argument: if it is the heart-mind that must conform to body-circumstance, what sort of heart-mind should it be? Even to imply a choice belies the resignation of 55, which becomes explicit in the dramatic pairing of the last two lines. In number 57, I have "multiply" making do for *kokonoe*, which literally means "ninefold" but also refers to the Palace. (It is thought that Shikibu entered the service of Shōshi, later to become empress, about this time.) The meaning of this poem is also debated, but what is important is the obstinate pursuit of the dialectic of *mi/kokoro*. The tenaciousness of despair—ironically described as being affectionate—suggests the inescapable constraints of external circumstance, in part, fate as social class. Number 57 surely reminds us of a poem by that *Genji* character who is relentlessly aware of her lesser origins, the Akashi Lady:

Isari seshi	This flare, like the flares
kage wasurarenu	of fishing boats
kagaribi wa	I cannot forget,
mi no ukifune ya	must come from my own
shitai kiniken	vessel of sorrow,
	drifting back fondly.
	(2:456; S 347; W 383)

This poem is difficult, too, with its paradoxical depiction of that which is already-within returning in pursuit. Heart-mind/body-circumstance are split, yet there may be something like a self that is identifiable only because it is inescapable. It has been suggested that the being-brooding compositions of these Heian poets were deliberately minimized in the imperial anthologies.[71] If we follow that suggestion, Ukifune's poetry becomes even richer for harboring a suppressed dimension in the history of Japanese poetry.

Between the author of the above poem, the Akashi Lady, and Ukifune, there exists no blood tie. Instead, they are bound by a sisterhood as tenuous and compelling as a single word, *ukifune*, which appears but twice in the tale, once each in their poems. There is one further observation to be made of the poetry by our heroine of that name. We have already seen how, after her rescue and subsequent removal to the mountain village of Ono, she began to scribble poetry almost as if to practice her calligraphy. Nine of her twelve poems in the "At Writing Practice" chapter lack an addressee. A natural consequence, one might say, of being a nun in an isolated setting. Ukifune, however, could conceivably have been more cordial with the other nuns, or even with her would-be suitor, the third-rate aristocrat. In fact, after taking vows, she evidently feels a certain peace that allows her to play games with the inelegant nuns and to respond to the suitor's poems for the first time. Or, she could just as easily have not written poetry at all.

It is pertinent to recall how, during that lonely year after Murasaki's death, Genji also wrote a number of solitary poems—twelve out of seventeen in "The Wizard" chapter, to be precise. Ukifune, who has been associated with, and usually made to mimic, so many earlier (nobler) characters, is now implicitly compared with Genji. This similarity highlights the most interesting of their differences: whereas Genji's poems, both solitary and exchange, followed the order of the seasonal books of the imperial anthologies, Ukifune's respect no such order. Instead, by insistently dwelling on a fate unmediated by a circular, reassuring temporality, they microcosmically reinforce the truncated, irregular character of the Uji chapters.

What is accomplished by our fictional composer of solitary, nonseasonal poetry? Tracing as she does a course from utter ignorance to idiosyncratic mastery to a refusal of the traditions of the language, does she not move to a place beyond the realm of *aware*—that is, beyond the variety of phenomena expressing or conducive to the experience of that hallowed Japanese aesthetic thought by many to be quintessentially embodied in the *Tale of Genji*? It has been suggested that it is in the imitative shabbiness of Ukifune's new existence that the dissolution of *aware* becomes perceptible, but it is more profoundly revealed in the narrative trajectory describing Ukifune.[72] She is the last of the *Genji* women, undeniably arresting in her own right, but barely recognizable as a heroine according to the earlier terms of the tale.

As if to record a comparable diminution in the hero, we, together with Kaoru, are offered one final stolen glimpse. It comes in "The Drake Fly" chapter, following Ukifune's disappearance. The Akashi Empress has just held a Lotus Sutra ceremony in

293

honor of the memory of her father Genji and Murasaki. (This is
the same ceremony that Murasaki staged shortly before her
death.) After the ceremony, her daughter the First Princess retires to a gallery with her ladies. There, thanks to a servant's
carelessness, Kaoru, who had attended the service, is able to
watch as she and her ladies play with blocks of ice to while away
the summer's day. Kaoru had always been captivated by this
Princess, and, like his father Kashiwagi, had been disappointed
with the offering of the Second Princess (born of a lesser mother)
in marriage. He had seen the First Princess but once as a child,
but that had sufficed to enthrall him for life. Seeing her now, in
their mutual adulthood, he is so overwhelmed that he attributes
the vision to the work of a spirit. Indeed, reflecting upon his
disquiet, he is forced to admit that

> in mind he was almost saintlike, but having strayed once,
> he had become a creature beset by the seeds of brooding. If
> only he had forsaken the world in that distant past, he
> would surely be deep in the mountains by now, he would
> surely not be so distraught.   (6:240; S 1032; W 1069)

The next morning, he is driven to ascertain whether it was
just his fancy, or perhaps mere setting, that had caused the First
Princess to look so superior. He has his wife's ladies sew up a
gossamer robe and urges her to try it on immediately: "Here,
why not put this on? When there are many people around, you
may feel indiscreet in a garment so thin, but it will do for now"
(6:241; S 1032; W 1069). With his own hands he dresses her
exactly like her half sister, and when the results fall short of
expectation, he sends for ice to replicate even that detail. Predictably, he ends up as frustrated as a child disappointed with a
long-anticipated toy and expresses annoyance with the First Princess for having neglected to correspond with her half sister now
that she was wedded to him, a commoner.

The old imperial longing,[73] so grandly expressed by his real
and adoptive fathers, has shriveled into a fetish with Kaoru. As
for his vulgar, literal-minded gesture of dressing his wife in the
hopes of making her into the real thing—is it not here, far more

than in the pathetic playing-at-being-aristocrats of Ukifune's new household, that we sense the irremediable shattering of a world?

Literal-mindedness is the mortal enemy to the practice of *aware*. Ōigimi emerges as Kaoru's sister adept in the cult of sincerity. Prematurely medieval, they are damned by their expectations of language, their insistence on a consistent passage from world to word and back.[74] It is an insistence producing curious results: Ōigimi's overvaluation of the body, Kaoru's graceless philandering. Rigidity leads to excess. It is necessary, on one plane, to distinguish Kaoru's and Ōigimi's puncturing of *aware* from Ukifune's.

Excess, in a sense, characterizes all of Uji. Whether from the wind or the river, the sounds that issue from nature are violent. On one of his earlier expeditions, Kaoru was unable to sleep at night because "with the rough river winds, the sound of falling leaves and the echoing of the water all exceeded the bounds of *aware*, making the place seem both frightful and deserted" (5:148; S 794; W 809-10).[75] If, to check our position, we refer back to the descriptions of the gardens in the wake of the storm in "The Typhoon" chapter, we find that for all the disorder, the passage of the storm was felt to have created its own aesthetic effect.

The four beautiful deaths—of Fujitsubo, Kashiwagi, Murasaki, and Ōigimi—show the usefulness of poetic language in camouflaging excess, for, reading backwards from Ōigimi, all four deaths contain an overstepping, a breach of equilibrium. Through their poeticization, the deaths are both distinguished and domesticated. Hence, the value of Ukifune's not dying, of her ceasing to compose poems.

The closing chapter of the *Genji* contains but one poem, the last of the 759 in the tale. It is addressed by Kaoru to Ukifune:

Nori no shi to	The path I followed
tazuneru michi o	to a teacher of the Law
shirube nite	has led instead
omowanu yama ni	to unexpected hills
fumimadou kana	where now I lose my way.
	(6:378; S 1089; W 1134)

Kaoru, having learned of Ukifune's whereabouts at last, ascends the hills to enlist the Bishop's aid in retrieving her. The final gaze is on him as Ukifune watches his party make its torchlit way down. She knows quite well whom she sees, and she will not even respond when a letter containing the above poem is delivered to her a few days hence by her younger brother. Thus, the tale that began with a question about imperial reign closes, indeterminately, with a suspicion in Kaoru's mind about whether a new lover might not be concealing Ukifune.

Ukifune, not dying, cannot be buried in beautiful verse. She is frozen as a gaze, sublimely undistinguished and arresting. Undistinguished, for example, in terms of any active, moral stance. Though she has taken vows, neither the comfort nor the arrogance of vocation is hers. Sometimes, especially when the plums are out, she thinks back, with longing, to a less arid past. Ukifune is, finally, the homeless one, the one with no place, not even death, to vanish to. Through her, the stepdaughter tale, mere static variant of the story of the traveling hero, bursts through the asymmetric relationship into an undefined beyond. Ukifune undistinguished looms larger than Kaoru.

Ukifune has always been more complex than her adoring readers would have her, such readers as the fiction-addicted Daughter of Takasue, who sighed over the plainness of her features to her diary and hoped for their melioration so that she could fancy herself the Shining Genji's Yūgao or the Uji Captain's Ukifune.[76] Ukifune, at the intersection of melodrama, social realism, and—modernist silence?—reveals the shifting boundaries of the *Tale of Genji*. We could situate one boundary next to the kingdom of myth, another to that of religion (whether as faith or theology). These in turn might be construed as historical demarcations, separating the *Genji* from the archaic on the one hand, the medieval on the other. The borders are perennially in flux and will be for as long as this novel is read, for there will always be found terra previously incognita, even as other lands, once known, slip from the surface of our recognition.

Postscript

IT HAS BEEN OBSERVED to me that my reading of the *Tale of Genji* suggests a very different novel from one the reader might expect. I hope in the course of these pages to have made abundantly evident the extent to which "my" reading is thoroughly permeated by the readings of other contemporary Japanese scholars of the *Genji* as well as by the thought of writers of various disciplines on either side of the Pacific. Let me reiterate, then, my indebtedness.

Beyond that, let me address the question of that shadowy yet all the more substantive "other" *Genji* that readers might expect. I take it that this *Genji* would have the contours of a beautiful sad story populated by languorous princes and princesses who console themselves for unrequited and perhaps even tragic love by refining their already exquisite sensibilities vis-à-vis the affectingly mutable manifestations of nature. This, of course, is a caricature, but I believe it only mildly exaggerates the image held by most readers in Japan as well as the West—by readers who have actually read the tale as well as those who think they might some day read it and those who have no interest in seeing such contours filled out. Countless elements have contributed to the formation of this image, which, I should hasten to emphasize, is not the only popular understanding of the *Genji* to have crystallized over the centuries; for modern readers, however, Motoori Norinaga's reading of the tale and Arthur Waley's translation have functioned as dominant influences. It is perhaps not even Norinaga's criticism or Waley's translation in itself that has so ineradicably stamped the tale, but the reputation of Waley's Bloomsburyite associations and of Norinaga's aesthetics of *aware*. What follows is a brief consideration of the concept of *aware* as manipulated by Norinaga.

The work of Motoori Norinaga (1730-1801) is perhaps the most broadly and enduringly influential of the eighteenth- and nineteenth-century nativist thinkers. Among other distinctions, Norinaga can be considered the first modern critic of the *Genji*.

297

He has been acclaimed for his efforts to free the appreciation of fiction from the strictures of unimaginative, narrow-minded, and above all wrongheaded Buddhist and Confucian thought. In militating to elevate the status of fiction, he enlisted the service of poetry—a gesture anticipated, as we have seen, in the "Fireflies" chapter of the *Genji* itself. In so doing, he colored the whole of the *Genji* with *aware*, the essential quality he believed the work possessed in common with Japanese poetry. The *Genji* for so many Japanese readers means *mono no aware* (loosely, very loosely, the "affectingness—the pathos—of things"), and Norinaga is the man responsible for this. I offer here a selection of his descriptions of *aware* from his *Genji Monogatari Tama no Ogushi*, completed two years before his death at the age of seventy-one, in the hope that even this glimpse at the complexity of Norinaga's thought should make clear that it exceeds the bounds of such elementary if striking responsibility. Here are the examples:

1. *Aware* is not limited to pathos. That which is joyous, interesting, pleasing, or attractive—if it is felt to be *aware*, then it is. . . .[1]

2. In popular usage it seems that *aware* is reserved for that which is good, but this is not so. As the dictionaries say, emotion is movement. If the heart is moved, whether by good things or bad, then that movement causes one to think he has experienced *aware*. . . .[2]

3. In this tale [the *Genji*] there is made manifest in writing the various things that people must feel, thus causing them to experience *aware*. First of all, there are things both public and private, the best of things interesting, splendid, or awesome; there are also such things as flowers, birds, the moon, and the snow, appealingly described according to the season, whether spring, summer, winter, or fall. All of these things move the human heart and make it experience *aware*. When the heart is heavy, then especially do the sight of the sky, the colors of the trees and grass, act to produce *aware*.[3]

4. Nothing is felt more deeply by the human heart than love.

Therefore, *aware* is experienced particularly profoundly, indeed unendurably, most often in love.[4]

5. As in the life of Genji, in the matter of Utsusemi, Oborozukiyo, and Fujitsubo, there is to be found in love that is impermissible yet inevitable *aware* that is even more profound than usual. This is why a point is made of depicting illicit love, to show the deep *aware* to be found therein.[5]

Although the selection necessarily simplifies, it reflects the range of work demanded by Norinaga of the term *aware*. There is a shift in levels as well as in content from (1) to (5); or, to put it another way, *aware* is used to designate both a general affective experience or a capacity for such experience and a content for that experience, which content is itself inconstant. The denial in (1) is significant because "pathos" is the meaning most readily ascribed to *aware*, with the result that the *Genji* is reduced to elegant lachrymosity. (It must also be admitted that it is not difficult to see, from Norinaga's specific examples, how readers would slip into such a reading.) In addition to those phenomena that produce pathos, joy, interest, or pleasure, (3) proposes nature, especially nature as it is aestheticized in the imperial anthologies of poetry, and (4) love, and (5) illicit love as sources of *aware*. This immediately calls to mind the classificatory scheme of the imperial anthologies—surely an appropriate evocation since Norinaga himself holds Japanese poetry to be paradigmatic. In the *Shibun Yōryō*, a work thought to be an early version (by some thirty-six years) of the *Tama no Ogushi*, he tirelessly repeats that the point of the fifty-four chapters of the *Genji* is to enable the reader to know *aware*. He then gives the following description of *mono no aware*:

> To spell it out: with all the variety of things in this world, to savor myriad deeds in one's heart, to absorb the essence of myriad deeds in one's heart according to what one sees with the eye, hears with the ear, touches with one's being— that is to know the essence of deeds, to know the essence of things, to know the *aware* of things.[6]

Even the rhythms recall the *Kokinshū* Preface.

Now, as we have seen, in the imperial anthologies six books on seasonal poetry and five on love head two sections of ten books each. Nature and love are opposed; the first is circular and orderly, the second, linear and disruptive. The first easily symbolizes propitious rule, for it is the reproductive character of nature, not the romantic and unpredictable manifestation of erotic attachment, that is required for the maintenance of power. As suggested in the discussion of the Rokujōin, the books on the seasons and those on love, by cohabiting the genre of the imperial anthology, contaminate each other: that is, the seasons acquire a certain linearity (from spring as beginning to winter as end), and love, the circularity of the predictable. Still, a tension persists, must persist, between the two for as long as the imperial anthology is to remain interesting.

In this perspective, the above series shows Norinaga ascribing a general content to the phenomenon of *aware*, then designating as the essence of that phenomenon something antithetical to it. (Even in the third example above, love is insinuated into the dominant position through the implication that aestheticized nature and naturalized ritual are most effective in producing *aware* where love has already done its work, that is, caused heavy-heartedness.)

In Genji's discussion of fiction with Tamakazura in the "Fireflies" chapter, the word *aware* appears but once, after Genji concedes that the old romances are useful in whiling away the time. From among all those lies (*itsuwaridomo*), those plausible descriptions of brooding princesses and the like that "show *aware*" would move at least part of one's heart (3:203; S 437; W 503). Norinaga, in showing the "concealed intent" (*shimo no kokoro*, an expression he repeatedly uses in his annotations) of this passage, argues that the purpose of the *Genji* is thus shown to be to "cause *mono no aware* to be known."[7] Now, it should be apparent that there is a certain willfulness in Norinaga's insistence on the essential relation of *aware* to the *Genji*. As arbitrary as Norinaga seems, however, we must acknowledge his uncanny grasp of both a literary strategy and the central problem of Heian culture—an understanding, moreover, that is transparently buried in his maneuvers. His logic strikingly reflects the *Genji*'s valuation of taboo breaking, its inversion of values—

practices crucial to the production of fiction. Such a practice presupposes the necessity of tensions, including oppositions of the sort implicit in the imperial anthologies. In a sense, Norinaga's meditation on *aware* makes of it a name for such oppositions.

This is hardly to suggest that Norinaga thought to argue for oppositions, still less for outright contradictions, as a principle of fiction writing and reading. (He would certainly not have admitted it in poetry.) Indeed, the principal consequence of his monochromatic drenching of the *Genji* in *aware* is the effacement of animating tensions.[8]

The muting of tensions and the conversion of *aware* into a name are part of the same gesture. It is as if, from a distance of seven centuries, Norinaga gave a name to something that Heian writers must have known only too well, but which their art and lives depended on their not naming. I refer to the unsettling and fruitful disjunctions between such aspects of life as power and love, mind and body, thought and action, words and things. Look at the poetry of the editors of the *Kokinshū*—the exuberant punning, the relentless wordplay. These were people who understood the ways in which reality (including the content of Norinaga's *aware*) at once constituted and was constituted by language—by botanical, musical, sartorial, and above all, verbal codes. They were the inhabitants of a postmythic world. The aestheticization of life, so evident in the writings of the Heian period, bears witness to this. The gap between word and world was not so much disguised as exploited through embellishment. Norinaga recognized the gap and sealed it over as *aware*, the name for a supreme unitary aesthetic and ethic.

Names endow the abstract with a pseudo-material reality. It was helpful to Norinaga in developing an apology for fiction to find a shared characteristic with poetry, namely, *aware*. In invoking the assistance of Japanese poetry, however, he inevitably invoked its historic ideological role, which included belief in a special access to meaning and truth. Reconciling fiction and Japanese poetry by equating the two, Norinaga sacrificed *aware* as a dynamic process in favor of *aware* as a static presence, a name. The discussion on fiction in the "Fireflies" chapter never accommodated Japanese poetry in this way. There, fiction was not robbed of its negativity: its lowly status as a collection of "lies" was recognized to be essential to its critical truthfulness. (One might even observe of the *Genji* that it liberated Japanese poetry itself by submitting it to the methods of fiction.) It is this crucial negativity of fiction that Norinaga's *mono no aware* as basis for a general epistemology threatens to obscure.[9]

THE *Tale of Genji* is an exemplary novel, at once embodying a mode of thought, of cognition, and of being. The emigre Czech writer Milan Kundera has observed of the novel, "You have only to open *Being and Time* to realize that all the existential themes analyzed by Heidegger had already been uncovered, demonstrated, studied by four centuries of novel-writing." Kundera's essay is titled "The Novel and Europe," and it closes on this note: "I am attached to nothing apart from the European novel, that unrecognized inheritance that comes to us from Cervantes."[10] Will that inheritance ever acknowledge as one of its crown jewels a Japanese novel written by a woman at the dawn of the eleventh century?

It will not do so without our labor. I was recently reminded of the fable of Shakespeare's sister with which Virginia Woolf concludes *A Room of One's Own*. It was in a classroom, and the student who brought it up exclaimed, rapping on her copy of Waley, "Here is Shakespeare's sister." Of that "poet who never wrote a word and was buried at the crossroads," Woolf wrote, "But she lives; for great poets do not die; they are continuing presences; they need only the opportunity to walk among us in the flesh."[11] Woolf goes on to discuss the conditions necessary for Shakespeare's sister to be born. Murasaki Shikibu was indeed born and the *Tale of Genji* was written, but neither being born nor writing a great work is sufficient in itself. This is where the labor of generations of readers must be invoked: to read the *Genji* into a general inheritance of novels that it might benefit not only the European male or the Japanese idolator of *aware* but constitute a legacy to be perpetually transformed by our acknowledgment of the unlooked-for similarities as well as the provocative differences posited in time and space.

Appendix

Chapter Titles in the *Tale of Genji*

Seidensticker *Translation*	*Waley* *Translation*	*Japanese*
1. The Paulownia Court	Kiritsubo	Kiritsubo
2. The Broom Tree	The Broom-Tree	Hahakigi
3. The Shell of the Locust	Utsusemi	Utsusemi
4. Evening Faces	Yugao	Yūgao
5. Lavender	Murasaki	Waka Murasaki
6. The Safflower	The Saffron-Flower	Suetsumuhana
7. An Autumn Excursion	The Festival of Leaves	Momiji no Ga
8. The Festival of the Cherry Blossoms	The Flower Feast	Hana no En
9. Heartvine	Aoi	Aoi
10. The Sacred Tree	The Sacred Tree	Sakaki
11. The Orange Blossoms	The Village of Falling Flowers	Hana Chiru Sato
12. Suma	Exile at Suma	Suma
13. Akashi	Akashi	Akashi
14. Channel Buoys	The Flood Gauge	Miotsukushi
15. The Wormwood Patch	The Palace in the Tangled Woods	Yomogiu
16. The Gatehouse	A Meeting at the Frontier	Sekiya
17. A Picture Contest	The Picture Competition	Eawase
18. The Wind in the Pines	The Wind in the Pine Trees	Matsukaze
19. A Rack of Cloud	A Wreath of Cloud	Usugumo
20. The Morning Glory	Asagao	Asagao
21. The Maiden	The Maiden	Otome
22. The Jeweled Chaplet	Tamakatsura	Tamakazura
23. The First Warbler	The First Song of the Year	Hatsune

Seidensticker *Translation*	*Waley* *Translation*	*Japanese*
24. Butterflies	The Butterflies	Kochō
25. Fireflies	The Glow-Worm	Hotaru
26. Wild Carnations	A Bed of Carnations	Tokonatsu
27. Flares	The Flares	Kagaribi
28. The Typhoon	The Typhoon	Nowaki
29. The Royal Outing	The Royal Visit	Miyuki
30. Purple Trousers	Blue Trousers	Fujibakama
31. The Cypress Pillar	Makibashira	Makibashira
32. A Branch of Plum	The Spray of Plum-Blossom	Ume ga E
33. Wisteria Leaves	Fuji no Uraba	Fuji no Uraba
34. New Herbs, Part One	Wakana, Part I	Wakana Jō
35. New Herbs, Part Two	Wakana, Part II	Wakana Ge
36. The Oak Tree	Kashiwagi	Kashiwagi
37. The Flute	The Flute	Yokobue
38. Bell Cricket	[Omitted]	Suzumushi
39. Evening Mist	Yugiri	Yūgiri
40. The Rite	The Law	Minori
41. The Wizard	Mirage	Maboroshi
42. His Perfumed Highness	Niou	Niou Miya
43. The Rose Plum	Kobai	Kōbai
44. Bamboo River	'Bamboo River'	Takekawa
45. The Lady at the Bridge	The Bridge Maiden	Hashihime
46. Beneath the Oak	At the Foot of the Oak-Tree	Shii ga Moto
47. Trefoil Knots	Agemaki	Agemaki
48. Early Ferns	Fern-Shoots	Sawarabi
49. The Ivy	The Mistletoe	Yadorigi
50. The Eastern Cottage	The Eastern House	Azumaya
51. A Boat Upon the Waters	Ukifune	Ukifune
52. The Drake Fly	The Gossamer-Fly	Kagerō
53. At Writing Practice	Writing-Practice	Tenarai

Seidensticker Translation	*Waley Translation*	*Japanese*
54. The Floating Bridge of Dreams	The Bridge of Dreams	Yume no Ukihashi

Abbreviations

The following abbreviations have been used in the Notes and Works Cited:

GMH *Genji Monogatari Hyōshaku.* 14 vols. Edited and annotated by Tamagami Takuya. Kadokawa Shoten, 1964-1969.

KGMS *Kōza Genji Monogatari no Sekai.* 9 vols. Edited by Akiyama Ken, Kimura Masanori, and Shimizu Yoshiko. Yūhikaku, 1980-1984.

NKBT *Nihon Koten Bungaku Taikei.* 102 vols. Iwanami Shoten, 1957-1968.

NKBZ *Nihon Koten Bungaku Zenshū.* 51 vols. Shōgakkan, 1970-1978.

NST *Nihon Shisō Taikei.* 67 vols. Iwanami Shoten, 1970-1982.

SNKS *Shinchō Nihon Koten Shūsei.* 85+ vols. Shinchōsha, 1976—.

Notes

1. For these and other details from the diary see Richard Bowring's translation, *Murasaki Shikibu: Her Diary and Poetic Memoirs* (Princeton, N.J.: Princeton University Press, 1982).

2. Takasue's Daughter's father's surname was Sugawara. He was a descendant of the famous ninth-century scholar-statesman Michizane. The Daughter's fancy for Yūgao and Ukifune may be followed in an English translation by Ivan Morris in *As I Crossed the Bridge of Dreams: Recollections of a Woman in Eleventh-Century Japan* (New York: Dial Press, 1971), pp. 56-57. The works traditionally ascribed to her are also available in English: Thomas H. Rohlich, trans., *A Tale of Eleventh-Century Japan: Hamamatsu Chūnagon Monogatari* (Princeton, N.J.: Princeton University Press, 1983) and Carol Hochstedler, trans., *The Tale of Nezame: Part Three of Yowa no Nezame Monogatari* (Ithaca, N.Y.: Cornell University, China-Japan Program, 1979). Edward Seidensticker has translated Michitsuna's Mother's diary as *The Gossamer Years: The Diary of a Noblewoman of Heian Japan* (Tokyo and Rutland, Vt.: Charles E. Tuttle Co., 1964). The theme of women readers becoming heroines is given spirited discussion in Rachel Brownstein's *Becoming a Heroine: Reading About Women in Novels* (New York: Viking Press, 1982). This topic will be taken up in Chapter 2.

3. The currently available text was revised and edited by Mitani Eiichi and published in three volumes by the Meicho Fukyūkai in 1979 and in a reasonably priced paperback edition by Kodansha in 1982.

4. From *Kokubungakushi Jukkō*, quoted by Mitani Kuniaki, "Meijiki no *Genji Monogatari*," *Kokubungaku Kaishaku to Kanshō* 48 (July 1983): 54. Mitani describes Haga's work as an attempt to suppress the newly asserted autonomy of the modern subject. In this same article (pp. 54-55) Mitani points to the bias against women implicit in the work of many scholars of the late Meiji and Taishō periods, including the eminent intellectual historian Watsuji Tetsurō (1889-1960), whose interest in unearthing an ur-*Genji* presumed the unlikeliness of female authorship. To my knowledge Mitani is the only scholar to have made such an observation.

5. The information on Masamune Hakuchō and Hori Tatsuo comes from Tsunoda Bun'ei and Nakamura Shin'ichirō, *Omoshiroku Genji o*

Yomu: Genji Monogatari Kōgi (Asahi Shuppansha, 1980), pp. 160-61. Waley himself referred to the possibility of Proustian comparisons in "Murasaki's Affinities As a Writer," his 1933 introduction to *The Bridge of Dreams*, the last volume of his translation, reprinted in Ivan Morris, ed., *Madly Singing in the Mountains: An Appreciation and Anthology of Arthur Waley* (London: George Allen & Unwin, 1970), pp. 331-32. This may be the place to mention the principal current translations of the *Genji* of which I am aware into languages other than English: Oscar Benl's *Die Geschichte vom Prinzen Genji: Altjapanischer Liebesroman aus dem 11. Jahrhundert, verfasst von der Hofdame Murasaki,* 2 vols. (Zurich: Manesse Verlag, 1966); Lin Wen-yüeh's *Yüan Shih Wu Yü,* 5 vols. (Taipei: Chung Wai Wen Hsüeh Yüeh K'an She, 1974-1978); and René Sieffert's *Le Dit du Genji,* 2+ vols. (Paris: Publications Orientalistes de France, 1978—).

6. In *Oeuvres Romanesques* (Paris: Gallimard, 1982), pp. 1176-77.

7. Aileen Gatten delivered a paper titled "Supplementary Narratives to *The Tale of Genji*: 'Yamaji no Tsuyu,' 'Kumogakure Rokujō,' and 'Tamakura' " at "The World of Genji: Perspectives on the *Genji Monogatari*" (the 8th Conference on Oriental-Western Literary Cultural Relations, Bloomington, Indiana, August 1982).

8. Yosano Akiko, *Gendaigoyaku Genji Monogatari,* 2 vols. (Nihon Shobō, 1961); Tanizaki Jun'ichirō, *Jun'ichirō Shinshinyaku Genji Monogatari,* 6 vols. (Chūō Kōronsha, 1966); and Enchi Fumiko, *Genji Monogatari,* 10 vols. (Shinchōsha, 1972-1973). The first two are recent editions of much-revised translations. I should add that there are perhaps a dozen other modern-language translations prepared by scholars.

9. The first passage comes from p. 130, the second from p. 131, of the essay collected in *In Praise of What Persists,* ed. Stephen Berg (New York: Harper and Row, 1983).

10. For information on Murasaki Shikibu herself, the best place to go is Richard Bowring's translation of her diary and poetic memoirs. His introductory essay makes clear why there is so little to be said about her—in standard biographical terms. As for other material in English, the reader may wish to pick and choose among the following works, which vary in their literary and historical emphases: John Hall and Jeffrey Mass, eds., *Medieval Japan: Essays in Institutional History* (New Haven, Conn.: Yale University Press, 1974); Cameron Hurst, *Insei: Abdicated Sovereigns in the Politics of Late Heian Japan* (New York: Columbia University Press, 1976); Helen McCullough, *Ōkagami, The Great Mirror: Fujiwara Michinaga (966-1027) and His Times; A Study and Translation* (Princeton, N.J.: Princeton University Press, 1980); Helen and William McCullough, *A Tale of Flowering Fortunes: Annals*

of Japanese Aristocratic Life in the Heian Period, 2 vols. (Stanford, Calif: Stanford University Press, 1980); and Ivan Morris, *The World of the Shining Prince* (Oxford and New York: Oxford University Press, 1964); and George Sansom, *A History of Japan to 1334* (Stanford, Calif.: Stanford University Press, 1958). There is also a volume of critical essays on the last third of the *Genji* edited by Andrew Pekarik, *Ukifune: Love in the Tale of Genji* (New York: Columbia University Press, 1982).

11. David Pollack has written an essay on the place of China in the *Genji*: "The Informing Image: 'China' in the *Genji Monogatari*," in *The Fracture of Meaning: Japan's Synthesis of China from the Eighth through the Eighteenth Centuries* (Princeton, N.J.: Princeton University Press, 1986).

12. Mitani Kuniaki's formulation, offered in lectures and conversation.

13. Translated by Ivan Morris, *The Pillow Book of Sei Shōnagon*, 2 vols. (New York: Columbia University Press, 1967).

14. Also associated with Izumi Shikibu is a diary-like piece, translated by Edwin Cranston, *The Izumi Shikibu Diary* (Cambridge, Mass.: Harvard University Press, 1969) and Earl Miner in his *Japanese Poetic Diaries* (Berkeley, Calif.: University of California Press, 1969).

15. See passages 66 and 71 in the Bowring translation of the diary.

16. Lecture delivered at Waseda University, Tokyo, in May 1982.

17. The reader will undoubtedly detect the encouragement I have taken in Bakhtin's thought. See especially the essays "Epic and Novel" and "Forms of Time and Chronotope in the Novel" in the *Dialogic Imagination: Four Essays by M. M. Bakhtin*, ed. Michael Holquist and trans. Holquist and Caryl Emerson (Austin: University of Texas Press, 1981). I am also grateful to James Shields for introducing me to the arguments of A. D. Nuttall in *A New Mimesis: Shakespeare and the Representation of Reality* (London and New York: Methuen, 1983). Nuttall characterizes fictional knowledge as "hypothetical/experiential" and proposes that it is cast "in the form of a noun, not a proposition" (pp. 76-77). Although the opposition of nominal to propositional is appealing in thinking about the novel, the implied alignment of nominal with experiential, provoking as it does the flight of time, is unsatisfactory.

CHAPTER 1

1. For information on court rank, residences, and many other matters, the reader is advised to consult the *Princeton Companion to Clas-*

sical Japanese Literature, by Earl Miner, Hiroko Odagiri, and Robert E. Morrell (Princeton, N.J.: Princeton University Press, 1986).

2. This useful observation is made by Shimizu Yoshiko in her *Genji no Onnagimi* (Hanawa Shobō, 1967), p. 19.

3. All ages are by oriental count, which makes the characters one to two years older than they would be by western count.

4. Koto is the generic name for a group of stringed instruments. The sō no koto has thirteen strings, the kin no koto (often associated with royalty), seven, and the wagon, or Yamatogoto, a native version, six. Each instrument is associated with one or more characters, and music is frequently used to suggest empathy or its absence. Kokiden's music-making during the nights following the Kiritsubo Lady's death is an egregious display of her character. The Suzaku Emperor, wishing to make amends to Genji, proposes music to him upon his return from exile but is rebuffed. On the positive side it is the Akashi Lady's musical interest that attracts Genji and leads to the conception of the Akashi Empress. (Painting, on the other hand, figures in barren relationships: Genji and Murasaki, Reizei and Akikonomu.) A minor nicety about the Genji-Fujitsubo music-making is that although Genji is presumably a consummate performer on all instruments, he is seldom associated with the flute, which is the instrument of Kashiwagi, who will cuckold him many years hence.

5. Gotō Shōko, "Fujitsubo no Eichi," in kgms 3 (1981): 165. Commentators are fond of this passage (1) as evidence of Fujitsubo's learning and (2) for the plot resemblance of the Chinese example to the *Genji.* The skeletal similarities, however, serve more to emphasize the differences. No matter how shrill or malicious Kokiden can be, it is impossible to imagine such grotesque behavior in the *Genji.* At most, the extravagance of the comparison suggests an unexpectedly melodramatic turn to Fujitsubo's mind.

6. At the time the *Genji* was written, only one woman in history had received such honors. Known as Higashi Sanjōin (961-1000), she was the daughter of Fujiwara no Kaneie (an eminent statesman and the neglectful husband of the author of the *Gossamer Years* and the mother of Emperor Ichijō (r. 986-1011), whose consort Shōshi was Murasaki Shikibu's mistress. Higashi Sanjōin was the older sister of Fujiwara no Michinaga and is thought to have been exceedingly influential with this consummate politician.

7. In this respect she is most similar to the Rokujō Lady with her eleven poems, nine addressed to Genji. The Akashi Lady has twenty-two, thirteen to Genji; Murasaki twenty-three, seventeen to Genji; and Tamakazura twenty, nine to Genji. I am relying on Suzuki Hideo's

valuable catalogue of poems listed by character and classified as to *do-kuei* (solitary composition), *zōka* or *tōka* (an initiating or responding poem in an exchange between two characters), or *shōwa* (in this case, one of at least three poems composed by as many characters in one setting), to be found in vol. 6 of the Shōgakkan edition of the *Genji*, pp. 517-49. Of the two poems by Fujitsubo not addressed to Genji, one belongs to a *shōwa* composed with other ladies on "her" side in the Picture Contest. The other poem, listed by Suzuki as a *dokuei*, actually harmonizes with a poem in the preceding chapter by Genji.

8. A centuries-old dispute surrounds the question of whether the meeting in which Reizei was conceived was the first for Genji and Fujitsubo. The hypothetical "Her Shining Highness" (Kagayaku Hi no Miya) chapter has been adduced to fill this gap among others. There is, however, only one reference to such a chapter (by the poet Fujiwara no Teika, 1162-1241), which only denies its existence. For a recent evaluation of this once lively topic, see Ikeda Tsutomu's " 'Kagayaku Hi no Miya'-ron: Gen-Kiritsubo no Maki no Seiritsu," in KGMS 1 (1980): 85-94. There are fifteenth- and sixteenth-century commentaries that support the view that Genji and Fujitsubo had earlier, unrecounted meetings. See Kitamura Kigin's *Kogetsushō*, 1:275-76. Mitani Kuniaki presents an updated version of this argument in "Fujitsubo Jiken no Hyōgen Kōzō: 'Waka Murasaki' no Hōhō Aruiwa 'Pure-tekisuto' to Shite no *Ise Monogatari*," in *(Imai Takuya Hakushi Koki Kinen) Monogatari, Nikki Bungaku to Sono Shūhen* (Ōfūsha, 1980), pp. 288-89.

9. The Shōgakkan text reads as follows: "Miya mo asamashikari*shi* o omoiizuru dani, yo to tomo no onmonoomoi naru o, [I] *sate dani yaminan*, to fukō oboshitaru ni, ito ukute, imijiki onkeshiki naru [a] *mono kara*, natsukashū rōtage ni, [b] *sari tote* uchitokezu, kokoro fukō hazukashige naru onmotenashi nado no, nao hito ni nisasetamawanu o, [II] *nadoka nanome naru koto dani uchimajiritamawazariken*, to, tsurō sae obosaruru." To describe this as beginning in Fujitsubo's mind and ending in Genji's is to oversimplify, of course: strictly speaking, only [I] and [II] are representations of Fujitsubo's and Genji's thoughts within the narrator's discourse. Phrases such as [a] *mono kara* and [b] *sari tote* are favorite tools in the Shikibu arsenal for producing serial clauses whose contents are not precisely antithetical but are contradictory enough to create a strong tension. The perfective *shi* in asamashi-kari*shi* is often used to bolster the argument that there was at least one previous encounter between Genji and Fujitsubo.

10. Andrew Plaks, *Archetype and Allegory in the Dream of the Red Chamber* (Princeton, N.J.: Princeton University Press, 1976), p. 44.

11. Mircea Eliade, *The Sacred and the Profane: The Nature of Re-*

ligion, trans. Willard Trask (New York: Harcourt Brace Jovanovich, 1959), p. 14.

12. I am putting aside the important topic of ruling empresses (as distinguished from consorts) as well as the even more problematic subject of near-legendary female rulers such as Himiko. The imperial succession reflected (perhaps promoted) the progressive erosion of the matrilineal tradition even though property continued to be inherited through the mother. See, however, Takamure Itsue's account "Tennō no Katei" in her *Nihon Kon'inshi* (Shibundō, 1963), pp. 57-66, in which she asserts the essentially matrilineal character of the imperial family until the Meiji period.

13. This description is of course greatly indebted to current discussions of the effect of supplementarity stimulated by the work of Jacques Derrida. The topic recurs in various manifestations in his writing, but see, for example, *Of Grammatology,* trans. Gayatri Chakravorty Spivak (Baltimore, Md.: Johns Hopkins University Press, 1976).

14. The point is made by Fujii Sadakazu in the seminal *Genji Monogatari: Shigen to Genzai* (Tōjusha, 1980), pp. 144-45, where he goes on to argue that we must see the logic of resemblance not as a mere relic of myth in the fictional narratives called *monogatari* but as an active presence, the sign of a stance the fictional narrative assumes toward myth. Of course, the logic of identity survives in fiction as well, in all those plots that involve lost kinship, concealed ethnic origins, and so forth. The attraction of the mystery of birth is perennial, and it can be fairly called the attraction of the mythic, which survives in fiction as in life.

15. Oka's views are contained in his *Genji Monogatari no Kisoteki Kenkyū* (Tōyōdō Shuppan, 1966). Fujii's influential study is contained in the chapter "Tabū to Kekkon" in his *Shigen to Genzai,* pp. 233-51.

16. Nomura Seiichi, "Fujitsubo no 'Tsumi' ni Tsuite," *Genji Monogatari no Sōzō* (Ōfūsha, 1969), pp. 164-80.

17. Fujii Sadakazu, *Shigen to Genzai,* pp. 246-47.

18. For readers who like to trace genealogical tangles: Murasaki is the niece of Fujitsubo, the daughter of her brother Prince Hyōbu; Kashiwagi's violation of the Third Princess is all but absurdly overdetermined, since she, too, is a niece of Fujitsubo, and the daughter of Genji's older brother and weak rival Suzaku. Genji prevents Suzaku from obtaining Akikonomu and presents her to his own son Reizei instead. In the case of Tamakazura, he prevents her from making herself known to her true father, his friend and figurative brother Tō no Chūjō, and dangles her before his own brother, Prince Hotaru, as well as her brother Kashiwagi.

19. One might say that Genji and Fujitsubo represent a mildly parodic version of brother-sister rule (*hikohimesei*) since such ruling sisters were priestesses to the tutelary deities of the clan and Fujitsubo by that time was a Buddhist nun. For a discussion as to whether such ties were incestuous, as well as for numerous examples of such relationships, see Kuratsuka Akiko's *Fujo no Bunka* (Heibonsha, 1979), especially the chapter "Ani to Imōto no Monogatari," pp. 190-221, as well as her article, "Kōtōfu ni Okeru 'Imōto': Kodai Joseishi Josetsu," *Bungaku* 36 (June 1968): 61-73. See also Takamure, *Nihon Kon'inshi*, pp. 58-59.

20. Ōmyōbu's identity is suggested by Saigō Nobutsuna in his *Genji Monogatari o Yomu Tame Ni* (Heibonsha, 1983), pp. 69-76, where he discusses the special relationship between masters and mistresses and their wet nurses' children.

21. The motif of a night spent together unconsummated recurs with several variations. In "Evening Mist," Genji's son loses his head over Ochiba no Miya, his friend Kashiwagi's widow. Despite her obdurate resistance (she is another princess, one of Suzaku's daughters, whose marriage to a commoner brought only misfortune), Yūgiri manages to move her back to the city from her mountain retreat and prepare for nuptials. As a last resort, the princess locks herself into a closet, and Yūgiri is left to spend the night alone outside. In "Trefoil Knots," Kaoru and Ōigimi reenact this scene with intensified refinement.

22. The weak Suzaku continues to be attached to Oborozukiyo even when her preference for his brother is made plain. Is there an unconscious element of revenge in his insistence many years later that Genji marry his immature daughter, the Third Princess?

23. Orikuchi Shinobu, "Nihon Bungaku no Naiyō," *Orikuchi Shinobu Zenshū* (Chūō Kōronsha, 1955), 7:344.

24. See Mircea Eliade, *Rites and Symbols of Initiation: The Mysteries of Birth and Rebirth*, trans. Willard Trask (New York: Harper Colophon Books, 1975), and Mitani Eiichi, "Monogatari no Genryū to Sono Sekai," *Monogatarishi no Kenkyū* (Yūseidō, 1967), pp. 25-93. Should *kishu ryūritan* be translated as "quest myth," the term Northrop Frye uses for the "central myth of literature" (*Fables of Identity: Studies in Poetic Mythology* [New York: Harcourt Brace Jovanovich, 1963], p. 18)? There is probably little harm in doing so, though "quest" implies an object or goal that is absent in *ryūri* ("wandering").

25. The exploits of these heroes are to be found in W. G. Aston's translation, *Nihongi: Chronicles of Japan from the Earliest Times to A.D. 697*, 2 vols. in one (Rutland, Vt. and Tokyo: Charles E. Tuttle Co., 1972) and in Donald Philippi's translation, *Kojiki* (Tokyo: Univer-

sity of Tokyo Press, 1968). For the *Ise Monogatari*, see Helen Mc-Cullough's translation, *Tales of Ise: Lyrical Episodes from Tenth-Century Japan* (Stanford, Calif.: Stanford University Press, 1968).

26. See Mitani Eiichi, *Monogatarishi no Kenkyū*, pp. 384-94, for a related account with differing emphases and conclusions.

27. All citations are my own translations based on the *Ise Monogatari* ed. Fukui Teisuke, in Katagiri Yōichi et al., eds., *Taketori Monogatari, Ise Monogatari, Yamato Monogatari, Heichū Monogatari*, NKBZ 8 (1972). Future references will be to *Ise* followed by episode number, as in *Ise* 125.

28. Ozawa Masao, ed., *Kokinwakashū*, NKBZ 7 (1971): 292. Future references will be abbreviated as KKS followed by the name of the book (e.g., "Summer") and the poem number. There are two recent translations of the *Kokinshū* into English. The first is by Laurel Rasplica Rodd with Mary Catherine Henkenius, *Kokinshū: A Collection of Poems Ancient and Modern, Including a Study of Chinese Influences on the* Kokinshū *Prefaces by John Timothy Wixted and an Annotated Translation of the Chinese Preface by Leonard Grzanka* (Princeton, N.J.: Princeton University Press, 1984). The second is by Helen Mc-Cullough, *Kokin Wakashū: The First Imperial Anthology of Japanese Poetry with "Tosa Nikki" and "Shinsen Waka"* (Stanford, Calif.: Stanford University Press, 1985).

29. *Mumyōzōshi*, ed. Kitagawa Tadahiko, in *Kodai Chūsei Geijutsuron*, NST 23 (1973): 389. A recent translation in three parts by Michele Marra may be found in *Monumenta Nipponica* 39, nos. 2-4 (1984).

30. A thorough discussion in English may be found in Konishi Jin'ichi's "Association and Progression: Principles of Integration in Anthologies and Sequences of Japanese Court Poetry, A.D. 900-1350," trans. Robert Brower and Earl Miner, *Harvard Journal of Asiatic Studies* 21 (1958): 67-127. The durability of the essentialist categories of Japanese poetry is attested to in Earl Miner's *Japanese Linked Poetry* (Princeton, N.J.: Princeton University Press, 1978).

31. For two recent discussions, see Watanabe Minoru's afterword to his edition of the *Ise Monogatari*, SNKS 2 (1976), and "Ichihayaki Tōtatsu—*Ise Monogatari*" in his *Heianchō Bunshōshi* (Tokyo Daigaku Shuppankai, 1981), pp. 22-24.

32. For a succinct discussion see n. 10, p. 110, *Shimpan Ise Monogatari*, ed. Ishida Jōji (Kadokawa Shoten, 1979).

33. The Hellenic term for fiction, *erōtika pathēmata*, or "a story of erotic sufferings," is an acknowledgment from centuries and continents removed of the crucial importance of the erotic to storytelling. See Ar-

thur Heiserman, *The Novel Before the Novel: Essays and Discussions about the Beginnings of Prose Fiction in the West* (Chicago, Ill.: University of Chicago Press, 1977), pp. 4-10. I should point to one early Japanese example in which transgression has clear erotic and political dimensions. It is popularly known as the "Kagehime Monogatari," and it appears in the *Nihon Shoki* (for a translation see Aston, *Nihongi*, 1:399-403). A version significant for its differences appears in the *Kojiki*. See Philippi, *Kojiki*, pp. 373-76. The importance of this episode in the development of Japanese prose fiction is discussed in Mitani Kuniaki's "Kagai no Uta (Seineiki)," in *Kiki Kayō*, ed. Yamaji Heishirō and Kubota Shōichirō (Waseda Daigaku Shuppanbu, 1976), pp. 145-59.

34. Saigō, *Genji Monogatari o Yomu Tame Ni*, pp. 48-49, 139. I must take responsibility, however, for linking art and play here.

35. This is an example of polarities converging in a shared third term. I have benefited from Sissela Bok's *Secrets: On the Ethics of Concealment and Revelation* (New York: Pantheon Books, 1982). The introductory chapter, "Approaches to Secrecy," pp. 3-14, is especially useful. Although it is not secretive about erotic transgression involving the imperial family, the *Ise* makes the topic available to the *Genji* as a literary theme—or such is the consequence of the latter's aggressive reading of the earlier text, according to Mitani Kuniaki's argument in "Fujitsubo Jiken."

36. This idea was suggested to me, though to different effect, by an observation made by Fujii Sadakazu in "Orikuchi Shinobu no Kokubungaku," in *Orikuchi Shinobu o "Yomu"* (Gendai Kikakusha, 1981), p. 84.

37. Fujii Sadakazu, "Ariwara no Narihira no Ryūri," *Dentō to Gendai* 16 (March 1972): 35.

38. Donald Keene's translation, *"Taketori Monogatari* (The Tale of the Bamboo Cutter)," is appended to Thomas Rimer's *Modern Japanese Fiction and Its Traditions: An Introduction* (Princeton, N.J.: Princeton University Press, 1978), pp. 275-305. The heroine of the *Bamboo Cutter* ascends to the moon at the end.

39. For a comparison with historical precedents, see Kawasaki Noboru, "Rokujō Miyasudokoro no Shinkōteki Haikei," *Kokugakuin Zasshi* 68 (September 1967): 13-23.

40. The morning glory is also associated with Genji's staunch resister, Princess Asagao, the other lady never referred to as "the woman." *Yūgao* appears in no. 276 in the *Shinkokinwakashū*, an imperial anthology compiled in 1205. See the comments of Kubota Jun, ed., *Shinkokinwakashū Zenhyōshaku* (Kodansha, 1976), 2:186.

41. For a useful introduction to folk-tale motifs in Heian fiction, see Mitani Eiichi's *Monogatarishi no Kenkyū*, especially pp. 76-95. Mitani discusses the same subject with specific reference to Yūgao in his "Yūgao Monogatari to Kodenshō," in KGMS 1:198-219. Takahashi Tōru undertakes a comprehensive discussion of the fabrication of the "Yūgao" chapter in his "Yūgao no Maki no Hyōgen: Tekusuto, Katari, Kōzō," *Bungaku* 50 (November 1982): 77-98.

42. The debate is summarized by Takahashi, "Yūgao no Maki," pp. 84-86.

43. Saigō Nobutsuna, "*Genji Monogatari* no Mononoke ni Tsuite," *Shi no Hassei: Bungaku ni Okeru Genshi, Kodai no Imi*, rev. ed. (Miraisha, 1964), p. 300.

44. Ibid., p. 302.

45. The account appears in "Yamashiro no Kuni," *Fudoki*, ed. Akimoto Kichirō, NKBT 2 (1960): 414. The *Fudoki* is an early eighth-century compilation of such items as the products, poetry, and legends (including place-name etymology) of the various provinces. I am grateful to Mitani Kuniaki for pointing out this passage to me. In "Maboroshi," the last chapter in which Genji appears, the only erotic encounter takes place during the Aoi Festival.

46. Mitani Kuniaki, "Gen no Naishi no Monogatari," in KGMS 2 (1980): 212-33.

47. Hirota Osamu, in "*Genji Monogatari* ni Okeru Waka no Denshōsei: Rokujō Miyasudokoro no Mononoke no Baai," *Nihon Bungaku* 31 (May 1982): 54-63, points out the following tendencies in the Rokujō Lady's poems: (1) reiteration of the speaker's misery; (2) the use of imperatives, including the negative imperative, to call attention to the speaker; and (3) the relative absence of natural objects (p. 58). From my point of view these reflect the psychological (hence, so-called modern) aspect of the Rokujō Lady's characterization. As Hirota observes, however, her poems also incorporate folk-magical traditional compositions.

48. Each of the three, however, has but one example. The study is Murone Kyōko's, as presented in Suzuki Hideo's seminar at Seijō University in the fall of 1980. Subsequent figures are from the same study. The *Yamato Monogatari* is available in English translation by Mildred Tahara: *Tales of Yamato: A Tenth-Century Poem-Tale* (Honolulu: University of Hawaii Press, 1980). Wayne Lammers has translated an important part of the *Tale of the Hollow Tree* as "The Succession: Kuniyuzuri, A Translation from the *Utsuho Monogatari*," *Monumenta Nipponica* 37 (1982): 139-78.

49. The *Eiga Monogatari* is translated into English as *A Tale of*

Flowering Fortunes: Annals of Japanese Aristocratic Life in the Heian Period by William H. and Helen Craig McCullough. Ōasa Yūji, in "Rokujō Miyasudokoro no Kunō," in KGMS 3:24, suggests that the portrayal of the Rokujō Lady's spirit influenced the depiction of the possessing spirit in the *Flowering Fortunes*.

50. Fujii Sadakazu suggests that the Heian *mono* had clearly moved in the direction of "vagueness." The "ineffable" is suggested by the *Iwanami Kogo Jiten* (1974) in its entry for *mono*, which is criticized by Mitani Kuniaki in "Monogatari to 'Kaku Koto': Monogatari Bungaku no Imi Sayō Aruiwa Fuzai no Bungaku," *Nihon Bungaku* 26 (October 1976): 10-11. An introduction to these complexities may be found in Mitani Eiichi's *Monogatarishi no Kenkyū*, pp. 11-13.

51. The account that follows relies heavily on Saigō's "*Genji Monogatari* no Mononoke ni Tsuite," *Shi no Hassei*, particularly the section called "Yūrikon," pp. 302-308.

52. The *tama/kokoro* distinction is Saigō's (ibid., p. 304). Others draw different distinctions, as between *mono* and *tama*. The imprecise phrasing "heart-mind" for *kokoro* reflects the intractable complexity of the concept. In answer to the question, "Where do we look for our mark of distinction?" the physicist Eric Harth, who has devoted himself to the study of the brain, writes as follows: "There was a time when we believed our bodies were inhabited by spirits and humors. People had souls. Our hearts were capable of generating love, and we could hate with our guts. But science has taught us that a heart is just a pump and our guts a chemical factory. And so the spirits have been exorcised, from one part of our bodies after another, 'from whence,' in the words of Warren McCulloch, the late MIT psychiatrist-cybernetician, 'they went straight to our heads, like bats to the belfry' " (*Windows on the Mind* [New York: William Morrow and Co., 1982], p. 14).

53. Saigō, "*Genji Monogatari* no Mononoke ni Tsuite," *Shi no Hassei*, p. 307.

54. Suzuki Hideo, "Kuruma Arasoi Zengo no Rokujō Miyasudokoro: *Genji Monogatari* Hyōgenron Oboegaki," *Seijō Bungei* 91 (March 1980): 4. On *ushi* versus *tsurashi* see also Suzuki, "Hikaru Genji no Onnagimitachi," in *Genji Monogatari to Sono Eikyō: Kenkyū to Shiryō*, vol. 6 of *Kodai Bungakuronsō*, ed. the Murasaki Shikibu Gakkai (Musashino Shoin, 1978), p. 108. Note Fujitsubo's use of *ushi* in contrast to Genji's *tsurashi* in their dream poems.

55. Sakamoto Kazuko, "Rokujō Miyasudokoro no Ise Gekō to On'ryō Shutsugen," *Bungaku Gogaku*, no. 88 (August 1974): 90-100.

56. The efforts of one historical father, Fujiwara no Michinaga, to

assure his daughter's ascendancy in court are documented in Murasaki Shikibu's diary, a substantial portion of which concerns the period when she was in the service of this daughter. See the Bowring translation.

57. On the development of the office of the Ise Priestess and its implications for the declining role of women in archaic Japan, see Kuratsuka's "Kōtōfu ni Okeru 'Imōto,' " pp. 72-73.

58. Fujii, "Hikaru Genji Monogatari Shudairon," *Shigen to Genzai*, pp. 158-59.

59. Sakamoto Kazuko, "Hikaru Genji no Keifu," *Kokugakuin Zasshi* 76 (December 1975): 33-43.

60. Hijikata Yōichi, "*Genji Monogatari*: Yukari no Onnagimi no Keifu" (Presentation at the meeting of the Monogatari Kenkyūkai, Tokyo, December 12, 1981).

61. Fukazawa Michio, "Rokujō Miyasudokoro Akuryō Jiken no Shudaisei ni Tsuite," in *Genji Monogatari to Sono Eikyō: Kenkyū to Shiryō*, p. 85.

62. Saigō Nobutsuna, "*Genji Monogatari* no Mononoke ni Tsuite," *Shi no Hassei*, p. 306.

63. This is included as her "Poetic Memoirs" in Richard Bowring's translation of the *Diary*. See p. 231 for the relevant passage. Here, I have used as a text a recent version published in the October 1982 issue of *Kokubungaku* devoted to Murasaki Shikibu. The annotations for the pair of poems under discussion were prepared by Suzuki Hideo ("Murasaki Shikibu Zenka Hyōshaku," pp. 110-12).

64. The provocative suggestion is attributed to Kimura Masanori by Suzuki in his discussion, which I should add differs in interpretation from mine.

65. From the class of such governors came a number of accomplished young women who entered the service of one or another imperial consort. Because the author of the *Genji* was herself a member of this class, many readers have been encouraged to identify the Akashi Lady with her creator. See Abe Akio, "Zuryō no Ishiki" and "Zuryō no Musume," *Genji Monogatari Kenkyū Josetsu* (Tokyo Daigaku Shuppankai, 1959), pp. 905-18. Much of this important work is devoted to the Akashi story. For details on the Akashi Priest as ex-provincial governor as well as other aspects of his portrayal, see Akiyama Ken's "Harima Zenshi, Akashi no Nyūdō," KGMS 3: 276-90.

66. The episode can be found in Aston's *Nihongi*, 1:14-21. See also Additional Note 4 in the Appendix to Philippi's *Kojiki*, p. 399.

67. For this and other details of the mythological aspects of Genji's

exile in Suma and Akashi, see Ishihara Shōhei's "Hiru no Ko to Su-
miyoshi no Kami: *Genji Monogatari* 'Suma' 'Akashi' no Shinwasei," in
*(Nishio Kōichi Kyōju Teinen Kinen Ronshū) Ronshū Setsuwa to Setsuwa
Bungaku* (Kasama Shoin, 1979), pp. 71-87.

68. Aston, *Nihongi*, 1:20.

69. Ishihara, "Hiru no Ko," p. 75.

70. Suzuki, "Hikaru Genji no Onnagimitachi," pp. 130-42.

71. Fujii Sadakazu, "Uta no Zasetsu," in *Genji Monogatari Oyobi
Igo no Monogatari: Kenkyū to Shiryō*, vol. 7 of *Kodai Bungakuronsō*,
ed. the Murasaki Shikibu Gakkai (Musashino Shoin, 1979), p. 83.

72. This pronouncement is recorded in the linked-verse poet Ichijō
Kanera's *Kachō Yosei* (1472), from which it has found its way to various
texts. See Kitamura Kigin, *Kogetsushō*, 1:670.

73. Mitani Kuniaki, "*Genji Monogatari* ni Okeru Eiga to Tsumi no
Ishiki: Yasoshima Matsuri to *Sumiyoshi Monogatari* no Eikyō o Tsūjite," *Heianchō Bungaku Kenkyū* 2 (May 1965): 125-40.

74. Kuwabara Hiroshi, "Akashi Kara Ōi E," in KGMS 4 (1980): 128-
40.

75. Nevertheless, the form of marriage represented by the Eastern
Pavilion and the Rokujōin, which housed veritable colonies of wives,
apparently diverges from historical practice. See Takamure, "Zen-Mu-
kotorikon no Sho Mondai," *Nihon Kon'inshi*, pp. 83-97.

76. Kuwabara, "Akashi Kara Ōi E," p. 138. There is a tradition
among readers, however, that refers to her as *ue*.

77. In an age when property was inherited matrilineally, children
were also raised by their mothers' families. This tended to be particularly true of sons. The example of Fujiwara no Kaneie suggests that
daughters who were intended for court careers were at times raised in
their fathers' homes (Takamure, *Nihon Kon'inshi*, p. 88). See also William H. McCullough, "Japanese Marriage Institutions in the Heian
Period," *Harvard Journal of Asiatic Studies* 27 (1967): 103-67.

78. This point is spelled out by Takahashi Tōru in "Kanōtai no Monogatari no Kōzō: Rokujōin Monogatari no Hansekai," *Genji Monogatari no Taiihō* (Tokyo Daigaku Shuppankai, 1982), pp. 48-50.

79. Kimura Masanori, "Waka Miya Tanjō: Akashi Ichizoku no Shukuun, 1" in KGMS 6 (1981): 136-56.

80. Some sources attribute the second poem, purportedly by the
mother, to the Akashi Lady, perhaps because of the strength of this
expectation. See Kimura Masanori, "Sumiyoshi Mōde: Akashi Ichizoku
no Shukuun, 2" in KGMS 6:196.

CHAPTER 2

1. The translation of "jeweled garland" for *tamakazura* captures only several of the aspects of the word that are active in the context. The *Iwanami Kogo Jiten* designates it first as a general term for vines, with *tama* serving as an ornamental prefix. The long, creeping form of vines explains why *tamakazura* serves as a *makurakotoba*, a "stylized semi-imagistic epithet" (Robert Brower and Earl Miner, *Japanese Court Poetry* [Stanford, Calif.: Stanford University Press, 1961], p. 12) for constancy, continuity, or distance; for lines of relationship; and for the act of crawling. Vines, like thread or twine, can be reeled in or wound up (*kuru*), which produces a link with "coming," also *kuru*. Vines were used to garland the head: *tamakazura* becomes a beaded hair ornament and metonymically, beautiful hair itself. This, in turn, generates additional *makurakotoba* uses. Such propagation of meaning is of course not unusual. The vines-ornaments relationship with all its ramifications is actively exploited throughout the Tamakazura chapters. Here, Genji uses *suji* (line 4), "line," and *kitsuran* (line 5), a form of *kuru*, and substitutes *wataru* (line 1), an auxiliary of duration, for *taezu*, "ceaselessly."

2. Speculation on the order of composition of the chapters and the original form of the *Genji* has a venerable history, traceable to the twelfth century. For modern examples of this school, see Kazamaki Keijirō, *Nihon Bungakushi no Kenkyū, Ge* (Kadokawa Shoten, 1961) or Takeda Sōjun, *Genji Monogatari no Kenkyū* (Iwanami Shoten, 1954). A discussion in English is available in Aileen Gatten's dissertation, "The Secluded Forest: Textual Problems in the *Genji Monogatari*" (University of Michigan, 1977).

3. Suzuki Hideo's "Kago Shūshū: *Kokin Rokujō*," *Kokugo Tsūshin* 232 (December 1980): 8-16, offers a selective study of this development of poetic diction, with specific reference to *nadeshiko*. For a discussion of Tamakazura's various appellations and their significance, see Yoshikai Naoto, "Tamakazura Monogatariron: Yūgao no Yukari no Monogatari," *Kokugakuin Daigaku Kiyō* 11 (1979): 84-110.

4. The guards officer's parodic account of women's tales calls to mind the life of the author of the *Gossamer Years*. It is possible that this passage satirizes that long-suffering lady's penchant for melodrama. (Mitani Kuniaki, seminar discussion at the Yokohama Municipal University, Spring 1982.) It should also be noted that the guards officer's disquisition is thought to borrow the structure of a Buddhist sermon. This view was proposed by Ichijō Kanera in his *Kachō Yosei*. See Abe

Notes to Chapter 2

Akio, "Sakusha no Bukkyō Shisō no Keitō," *Genji Monogatari Kenkyū Josetsu*, pp. 517-46.

5. The example of Suetsumuhana illustrates the suppleness with which the notion of class (based on birth) is manipulated, since, as the daughter of a prince, she is literally of the highest class. Not only is she fallen economically, however, but her physical and aesthetic defects make her ludicrous and therefore saintly.

6. For example, in 1:243, n. 18. The comment on the use of ōke-nashi in the *Genji* was made by Suzuki Hideo in a seminar at Seijō University, Fall 1980.

7. Takahashi Kazuo, "*Genji Monogatari* 'Rokujōin' no Gensen ni Tsuite," in his *Genji Monogatari no Shudai to Kōsō* (Ōfūsha, 1971), pp. 299-319.

8. In the economy of the *Genji* such a detail is never wasted. Uki-fune, the last and lowliest incarnation of all the heroines, is the step-daughter of a governor of the same province.

9. For this detail, as well as for an explication of the issues in the "Jeweled Chaplet" chapter, I am indebted to Mitani Kuniaki's "Tama-kazura Jūjō no Hōhō: Tamakazura no Ryūri Aruiwa Jojutsu to Jimbutsu Zōkei no Kōzō," *Genji Monogatari no Hyōgen to Kōzō*, ed. the Chūko Bungaku Kenkyūkai (Kasama Shoin, 1977), pp. 83-123.

10. Tamagami Takuya, GMH 3 (1965): 411.

11. Perhaps, in a sense, this class of women is the most powerful in the *Genji*: it is from among them that the narrators are drawn. In this chapter Yūgao's wet nurse's daughter, Ukon, must be summoned to duty to reintroduce Tamakazura into the tale. The opening and transitional portions of the chapter are recounted from Ukon's point of view, and the Tsukushi episode is shaped by the nurse's vision. It is in the Uji chapters that the voices of the serving women become distinctly audible. For a study of servants as surrogates for their mistresses, see Mitamura Masako's "*Genji Monogatari* ni Okeru Katashiro no Mondai: Meshūdo o Kiten ni Shite," *Heianchō Bungaku Kenkyū* 3, no. 7 (December 1970): 11-21.

12. See Robert Borgen, *Sugawara no Michizane and the Early Heian Court* (Cambridge, Mass.: Harvard University Press, 1986). Ivan Morris has a chapter on Michizane in *The Nobility of Failure: Tragic Heroes in the History of Japan* (New York: Holt, Rinehart and Winston, 1975), pp. 41-66.

13. One other reference to the leech child in the *Genji* occurs in "The Wind in the Pines" chapter (2:413; S 330; W 357), when Genji is busy at work placating Murasaki for his ties with the Akashi Lady.

Genji's true concern is to have his daughter, the future Akashi Empress, raised by Murasaki. The little girl is said to have reached the age of the leech child. She and Tamakazura are two distinct centers of interest in the Rokujōin.

14. The list comes from Hasegawa Masaharu's "*Genji Monogatari no Sasurai no Keifu*," *Nihon Bungaku Ronkyū* 14 (November 1980): 34-35. It is as follows: Yūgao, 2; Genji, 3; Murasaki, 1; "numerous ladies," 1; Tamakazura, 2; Higekuro's first wife, 1; the Third Princess, 1; Kaoru, 1; the Uji Princesses, 3; people without protectors (implicitly, Ōigimi), 1; Ukifune, 4.

15. Ibid., p. 34.

16. The Akashi Lady, by comparison, spends four years at her father's estate in Ōi before moving in to the Rokujōin. Fujii Sadakazu reads Tamakazura's six months at the outskirts of the city as a religious retreat in "Tamakazura," *Genji Monogatari Kōza*, ed. Yamagishi Tokuhei and Oka Kazuo (Yūseidō, 1971), 3:223-24. Hasegawa Masaharu emphasizes the boundary location of such retreats in "Sasurai no Himegimi," KGMS 5 (1981): 55-56. The concept of the boundary becomes particularly useful in the Uji chapters. Yamaguchi Masao has been influential in introducing the concepts of center and periphery into these discussions. See his "Shōchōteki Uchū to Shūenteki Genjitsu," *Bunka to Ryōgisei* (Iwanami Shoten, 1975), pp. 201-44. Tamakazura herself is a boundary character, being of age but uninitiated, pure but erotic (*nadeshiko* and *tokonatsu*), rustic yet refined.

17. Ukon had been praying on behalf of one "Fujiwara no Rurigimi," or "Lady Ruri of the Fujiwara" (3:106; S 398; W 450). This is the only instance when Tamakazura is referred to in this fashion. Just as she is about to make her debut in Genji's fictional world as his daughter, we are reminded of her actual identity as a Fujiwara.

18. See Keene, *Taketori Monogatari*, p. 276.

19. Mitani Eiichi touches on the difference between the male pattern and its female variant in his *Monogatarishi no Kenkyū*, p. 95. Seki Keigo's "Kon'intan to Shite no *Sumiyoshi Monogatari*: Bungaku to Mukashi Banashi," *Kokugo to Kokubungaku* 49 (October 1972): 79-95, studies variant motifs in the stepdaughter tale and speculates on the significance of the prevailing structure. Needless to say, neither the tale of masculine exile nor its stepsister is exclusively Japanese. The elements in Seki's lists, though less comprehensive than Vladimir Propp's, may be compared with those in the latter's *Morphology of the Folktale*, trans. Laurence Scott, 2d ed., rev. and ed. Louis A. Wagner (Austin: University of Texas Press, 1968).

20. Seki, "Kon'intan," p. 80.

21. On the heroines and readers of stepdaughter tales, see Mitani Kuniaki's "Heianchō ni Okeru Mamakoijime Monogatari no Keifu: Ko-Sumiyoshi Monogatari Kara Kaiawase Made," *Waseda Daigaku Kōtō-gakuin Kenkyū Nenshi* 15 (January 1971): 14-33. The benign view of stepmother cruelty may be found in Seki, "Kon'intan," p. 92.

22. One exception is the heroine of the *Tale of Ochikubo*. Seki, "Kon'intan," pp. 86-87, 91-92. For an English translation of the *Ochikubo*, see Wilfrid Whitehouse and Eizō Yanagisawa, *Ochikubo Monogatari, or The Tale of the Lady Ochikubo: A Tenth-Century Japanese Novel* (London: Peter Owen, 1965).

23. The *Sumiyoshi* exists only in widely varying Kamakura texts. There are apparently enough consistent features, however, to argue for a thematic and structural relation with the Tamakazura chapters. See Mitani Kuniaki, "Tamakazura Jūjō no Hōhō," pp. 99-103, 118.

24. Seki, "Kon'intan," p. 91. For examples of isolation as an element of female initiation in other societies, see Eliade, *Rites and Symbols of Initiation*, pp. 41-47. The literary implications of menstruation as a time of retreat for women (the taboo against blood pollution meant, for example, that women in court service had to leave the Palace during their periods and were thus relieved of their duties) are receiving increasing attention. See, for example, Fujii Sadakazu's *Monogatari no Kekkon* (Sōjusha, 1985).

25. In a provocative essay Takahashi Tōru considers the range of meanings implied by the designation "Ochikubo no Kimi" for the heroine of the *Tale of Ochikubo*: " 'Ochikubo' no Imi o Megutte: Monogatari Tekusuto no Hyōsō to Shinsō," *Nihon Bungaku* 31 (June 1982): 89-94. Bruno Bettelheim's chapter on Cinderella in *The Uses of Enchantment: The Meaning and Importance of Fairy Tales* (New York: Vintage Books, 1977), pp. 236-77, offers interesting points of comparison.

26. Mitani Eiichi, *Monogatarishi no Kenkyū*, p. 95.

27. This suggestion comes from Fujii Sadakazu in his "Monogatari no Shinwa Kōzō: Ikyōronfū Ni," *Shinsō no Kodai* (Kokubunsha, 1978), pp. 86-87. Fujii, who has imaginatively developed the concept of the other land in contemporary literary and folklorical discussions, suggests that stepdaughters come from the other land and therefore incur the jealousy of their earthly stepmothers ("Ikyōron no Kokoromi," *Shigen to Genzai*, pp. 98-100)—an interpretation that keeps the stepdaughter confined to a primary relationship with her stepmother.

28. Mitani Kuniaki, "Tamakazura Jūjō no Hōhō," p. 105.

29. Tamakazura's entry into the Rokujōin marks the end of the con-

ventional stepdaughter tale, as indicated by the rewarding of the helpers: Yūgao's nurse's family is comfortably installed in Tamakazura's new household.

30. Sandra M. Gilbert and Susan Gubar, *The Madwoman in the Attic: The Woman Writer and the Nineteenth-Century Literary Imagination* (New Haven, Conn.: Yale University Press, 1979), pp. 38-39.

31. Fujii Sadakazu, "Tabū to Kekkon," *Shigen to Genzai*, p. 235.

32. Mitani Kuniaki, "Heianchō ni Okeru Mamakoijime Monogatari," pp. 26-27.

33. This is the second woman Genji snatches from his half brother, the first being Oborozukiyo. It was, of course, the Oborozukiyo incident that ostensibly necessitated Genji's removal to Suma. The youthful Genji rashly bespoiled the Emperor's fruits.

34. Hirota Osamu, linking the Akashi Lady and Fujitsubo from this chapter, foresees a logic for the former's becoming the lady of winter in the Rokujōin. He is of course correct to point out the seasonal associations of events from the opening of the tale (e.g., Genji's mother dies an autumnal death); indeed, the production of events by a nature that exceeds the bounds of decor (or sentimental reflection, as in pathetic fallacy) constitutes the reversal characteristic of the *Genji's Kokinshū* legacy. Still, we cannot ignore the heightened concentration of such imagination in the creation of the Rokujōin. See Hirota's "Rokujōin no Kōzō: Hikaru Genji Monogatari no Keisei to Tenkan," *Shinwa, Kinki, Hyōhaku: Monogatari to Setsuwa no Sekai*, ed. Hirokawa Katsumi (Ōfūsha, 1976), pp. 124-25.

35. Genji's entreaty for pity (*aware to dani notamawasezu wa*, 2:450-51; S 344; W 380) stunningly anticipates Kashiwagi's repeated pleas to the Third Princess (4:214, 216, 219, or 281; S 613—two examples, 615 and 637; W 657, 659-60, and 679). See Suzuki Hideo, "*Genji Monogatari* no Waka," *Genji Monogatari no Tankyū* (Kazama Shobō, 1980), 5:393-95.

36. Note the power of the social conventions surrounding *waka* poetry. To refuse to respond to a poetic overture from an unwanted suitor or at an improperly early stage in a courtship is a customary means for a lady to check advances. Here, Akikonomu understands that refusal to respond in a purportedly social context would be construed as "poetic" and therefore amorous.

37. See Harimoto Masayuki, "Shunjū Arasoi," KGMS 5:120-30.

38. Saigō Nobutsuna, "Chinkonron," *Shi no Hassei*, pp. 243-94. See also Carmen Blacker, *The Catalpa Bow: A Study of Shamanistic Practices in Japan* (London: George Allen & Unwin, 1975), p. 43.

39. At the time of change in reign, the Niinamesai, the harvest festival, is replaced by the Daijōe, the ascension ceremony. Here we have an exemplary intersection of the cyclical time of nature with linear human time. If the Niinamesai marks the ritual death and rebirth of nature, enacted in the person of its representative, the emperor, then the Daijōe, or ascension ceremony, is an initiatory rite for a particular emperor, whose reign is finite. The annually repeated imperial rites, the *nenjū gyōji*, mimic the annual rites of an agrarian society. The latter, too, are intersected by the rites of passage associated with the birth, coming of age, marriage, and death of its individual members. Both the cyclical and the linear series have at their core the opposition of birth and death.

40. Fukazawa Michio, *Genji Monogatari no Keisei* (Ōfūsha, 1972), pp. 10-12.

41. Kikuchi Yasuaki, "Kodai no Tennō," *Kodai Kokka*, vol. 1 of *Kōza Nihonshi*, ed. the Rekishigaku Kenkyūkai and the Nihonshi Kenkyūkai (Tokyo Daigaku Shuppankai, 1970), pp. 181-216.

42. From the Introduction to Ian Levy's *The Ten Thousand Leaves: A Translation of the Man'yōshū, Japan's Premier Anthology of Classical Poetry* (Princeton, N.J.: Princeton University Press, 1981), 1:14.

43. For example, Hitomaro's laments composed at the deaths of various members of the imperial family combine what Levy calls "iconic images" expressing the divinity of imperial rule with grief for the dead individual (ibid., pp. 14-19).

44. Ibid., p. 46.

45. This is a somewhat cynical version of an argument developed by Suzuki Hideo in his "Rokujōin no Sōsetsu," *Chūko Bungaku* 14 (October 1974): 30-39.

46. Johan Huizinga, *Homo Ludens: A Study of the Play-Element in Culture* (Boston: Beacon Press, 1955), p. 22.

47. Eliade, *The Sacred and the Profane*, p. 85. My indebtedness to Huizinga and Eliade extends far beyond these brief citations. Other works that I have found especially helpful in this context are Emile Durkheim's "The Principal Ritual Attitudes" in *The Elementary Forms of the Religious Life*, trans. Joseph Ward Swain (New York: Free Press, 1965), pp. 337-65; Saigō Nobutsuna's *Shi no Hassei* and *Nihon Kodai Bungakushi* (rev. ed., Iwanami Shoten, 1963); Nagafuji Yasushi's *Kodai Nihonjin to Jikan Ishiki* (Miraisha, 1979); and Mitani Kuniaki's "Ibukuro to Bungaku, Shiron: Nihon Kodai Bungaku to 'Ajiwau' Koto," *Bungei to Hihyō*, Part 1, 3 (June 1969): 76-88, and Part 2, 3 (October 1969): 87-99. Mitani's "Kodai Chimei Kigen Densetsu no Hōhō," *Ni-*

hon Bungaku 30 (October 1981): 41-49, uses a dualism analogous to that of sacred/profane to spell out a political history in the text of the *Fudoki*.

48. Eliade's useful definition of myth as "sacred history" that "tells how, through the deeds of Supernatural Beings, a reality came into existence, be it the whole of reality, the Cosmos, or only a fragment of human behavior, an institution" (*Myth and Reality*, trans. Willard Trask [New York: Harper and Row, 1963], pp. 5-6), and Robert Scholes and Robert Kellog's decidedly secular designation of myth as a "traditional plot which can be transmitted" (*The Nature of Narrative* [London: Oxford University Press, 1966], p. 12), are both noncontextual in this sense. Saigō Nobutsuna's definition of myth provides an interesting alternative: "Needless to say, the original function of myth was not the explanation of origins. It was at once the form and the content of the recited parts of festivals, but as the two [words and gestures] became separate, myth developed into an explanation of origins, and, as the example of the *Kojiki* shows, myth began to turn into history. . . . Whereas ritual had formerly shown [the relation] of the magical to the economic, it now began to show that the magical was religious and to render as sacred autocratic rule through the use of symbol and mystery . . . ." (*Shi no Hassei*, p. 264). Of course, to pose the "form and content" of ritual as the original form of myth is problematic as well.

49. Yamaguchi Masao handles this paradox neatly by identifying the emperor with the center (i.e., order and authority) and the prince with the periphery, or chaos. Extending this reasoning, one would say that only princes can generate tales. See his "Tennōsei no Shōchōteki Kūkan," *Chi no Enkinhō* (Iwanami Shoten, 1978), pp. 369-98, or his "*Genji Monogatari*: Bunka Kigōron no Shiten Kara Mita," *Kigōgaku Kenkyū* 1 (1981): 119-39. See also Hirokawa Katsumi, "Hikaru Genji Monogatari: Han-shinwaronteki Shihatsu, Kinki Haihan no Keifu," in his *Shinwa, Kinki, Hyōhaku: Monogatari to Setsuwa no Sekai* (Ōfūsha, 1976), pp. 96-104.

50. The artificiality of the spring-autumn debate, as well as of the Rokujōin itself, is interpreted by Ishizu Harumi to be part of Genji's strategy for imposing self-control in the wake of his loss of Fujitsubo. See her "Tamakazura Jūjō no Hashi o Megutte," *Murasaki* 14 (June 1977): 47-56.

51. For a convenient list of appellations deriving from the Rokujōin for all four ladies, see Mitani Eiichi, *Monogatarishi no Kenkyū*, pp. 407-408.

52. Nomura Seiichi, perhaps the leading practitioner of the "rhetor-

ical" view, describes the various approaches at the beginning of his essay, "Rokujōin no Shiki no Machi," KGMS 5:36-47. Nomura has other helpful essays such as "Rokujōin no Kisetsuteki Jikū no Motsu Imi wa Nani Ka," *Kokubungaku* 25 (May 1980): 100-105. Mitani Eiichi is largely responsible for cultivating the religious-folklorical terrain: "Inu-i no Onkata," *Nihon Bungaku no Minzokugakuteki Kenkyū* (Yūseidō, 1960), pp. 118-30; "*Genji Monogatari* to Minkan Shinkō," *Monogatarishi no Kenkyū*, pp. 404-26. Other important approaches are exemplified by Takahashi Kazuo, "*Genji Monogatari* 'Rokujōin' no Gensen ni Tsuite," *Genji Monogatari no Shudai to Kōsō*, pp. 290-319; Fujii Sadakazu, "Hikaru Genji Monogatari Shudairon," *Shigen to Genzai*, pp. 156-79; and Takahashi Tōru, "Gyaku Mandarateki Ryūshutsu: *Genji Monogatari* no 'Katari,' " *Genji Monogatari no Taiihō*, pp. 31-46.

53. Among numerous examples, Mitani Eiichi cites one from a medieval text, the *Hokiden*, which appears to be a composite of earlier images from Chinese and Indian as well as domestic sources: it is the palace of a dragon king built upon directional axes with seasonal associations and a wife in each section (*Monogatarishi no Kenkyū*, pp. 424-25). There are, however, five wives. The superfluous wife raises the much-debated issue of the relation of the Rokujōin to the Chinese Five Elements theory.

54. On the *Tale of the Hollow Tree* and the Akashi Lady's directional connotations, see Takahashi Tōru, "Gyaku Mandarateki Ryūshutsu," *Genji Monogatari no Taiihō*, pp. 38-42. On Akashi and the dragon king, see Nomura, "Rokujōin no Kisetsuteki Jikū," pp. 102-103.

55. Hirota Osamu, "Rokujōin no Kōzō," p. 121.

56. Yamanaka Yutaka, "Rokujōin to Nenjū Gyōji," KGMS 5:106-109.

57. Nomura Seiichi, "Rokujōin no Shiki no Machi," p. 41.

58. The effects of the calendar imported from China in the seventh century are traced in Nagafuji Yasushi's absorbing *Kodai Nihonbungaku to Jikan Ishiki*. The *Kokinshū* is overly credited or blamed for the development of an "artificial nature," for it is as much a result, a summation, as it is a model. See "The Early Classical Period" in Brower and Miner's *Japanese Court Poetry*, pp. 157-230, for a discussion of the *Kokinshū* aesthetic.

59. A substantial portion of Noguchi Takehiko's *Hana no Shigaku* (Asahi Shimbunsha, 1978) is devoted to the metaphoric flora of the *Genji*.

60. Brower and Miner, *Japanese Court Poetry*, pp. 393-94.

61. It may be mildly surprising to the reader that the imperial anthologies make room for books titled "Miscellany." Kojima Naoko spec-

ulates on the concept of miscellany in these anthologies in relation to the Uji chapters of the *Genji* in "*Genji Monogatari* to Waka: *Kokinshū*, Zō, Ge, no Kōzō Kara*," Monogatari Kenkyū* 3 (1981): 13-26.

62. In the Shōgakkan edition of the *Kokinshū*, p. 49. On the Chinese influences on the Prefaces, see John Timothy Wixted's essay as well as Leonard Grzanka's translation of the Chinese Preface in the Rodd translation.

63. This is related to, perhaps underlies, what Nuttall calls "experiential knowledge." I suspect that the ideology of the imperial anthology is realized by its communication of propositional knowledge under the presumably innocent, emotional guise of the experiential. See n. 17 to the Introduction.

64. On the significance of "leaves of words," I have been educated by Takahashi Tōru's essay on the development of rhetoricity in the Heian period, "Koto no Ha o Kazareru Tama no Eda: Monogatari Gengo no Seisei," *Kokugo to Kokubungaku* 61 (May 1984): pp. 1-13.

65. See Tamagami Takuya, "Byōbue to Utamonogatari: *Yamato Monogatari*," *Monogatari Bungakuron* (Hanawa Shobō, 1960), pp. 101-21. See also Richard Bowring, "The Aesthetics of Opposition: Reflections on the 'Eawase' Chapter of the *Tale of Genji*" (Paper delivered at the 8th Conference on Oriental-Western Literary and Cultural Relations, Bloomington, Indiana, August 1982).

66. Masuda Katsumi, "Teiō no Ikikata: Kodai Kizoku Seikatsu to Seishinshi no Kyōkaiiki Kara," *Kokubungaku Kaishaku to Kanshō* 31 (November 1966): 218-20.

67. Yanagimachi Tokitoshi relates Genji's disquisitions on various topics to his shifting position in the tale: authoritative talk and power stand in inverse relation to each other. "Ronja to Shite no Hikaru Genji: Hikaru Genjiron no Tame no Danshō," *Murasaki* 17 (July 1980): 23-32.

68. The intrusion of Buddhism, with its own chronologies, anticipates future developments. Murasaki and Buddhism have a specific interest that will be taken up in Chapter 3.

69. Fujii Sadakazu, "Natsu to Josei," *Koten o Yomu Hon* (Nihon Buritanika, 1980), pp. 80-84. Fujii does not develop his argument, but it may be supplemented by Hayashida Takakazu's "Nagame Bungaku no Tenkai," *Genji Monogatari no Hassō* (Ōfūsha, 1980), pp. 61-68. Hayashida, starting out from Orikuchi's work, shows how the Fifth and the Nine Months, critical times for the rice culture, were periods of abstinence.

70. For a translation of Jomei's poem, see Levy, *Ten Thousand Leaves*, p. 38.

71. Kurahashi Masaji, *Kyōen no Kenkyū, Bungakuhen* (Ōfūsha, 1969), p. 694.

72. Shirakawa Shizuka, *Shoki Man'yōron* (Chūō Kōronsha, 1979), p. 141. This phenomenon is discussed in a number of sources. In Kurahashi's *Kyōen no Kenkyū*, see "Kunimi to Chōga," pp. 6 and 92-96. Mitani Eiichi has a chapter called "Kunimi to Bungaku Seiritsu no Kiban," in his *Nihon Bungaku no Minzokugakuteki Kenkyū*, pp. 269-352. For a discussion of the literary significance of verbs meaning "to eat," see Mitani Kuniaki's "Ibukuro to Bungaku," in two parts.

73. Kurahashi, *Kyōen no Kenkyū*, p. 696.

74. Fujii Sadakazu, "Suetsumuhana no Maki no Hōhō," KGMS 2:139-40.

75. Yamanaka Yutaka, "Rokujōin to Nenjū Gyōji," pp. 111-12.

76. The *Tale of the Hollow Tree* passage is to be found in the "Naishi no Kami" chapter, *Utsuho Monogatari*, ed. the *Utsuho Monogatari Kenkyūkai* (Kasama Shoin, 1973-1975), 1:216-17. The *Ise* passage is n. 139.

77. Fujii, *Shigen to Genzai*, pp. 20-21.

78. The literature on the *monogatariron* is voluminous. Modern discussion stems from Motoori Norinaga's celebrated assertion that this passage contains the heart (or in his idiom, the eye) of the tale (*Genji Monogatari Tama no Ogushi*, in *Motoori Norinaga Zenshū*, ed. Ōno Susumu [Chikuma Shobō, 1969] 4:187). Norinaga's impassioned efforts to extract from this passage the essence of the entire work, if not of literary experience in general, understandably pose interesting problems. Some of them are treated by Abe Akio in "Hotaru no Maki no Monogatariron," now readily available in *Genji Monogatari* [ed. Takahashi Tōru], *Nihon Bungaku Kenkyū Shiryō Sōsho* (Yūseidō, 1982), 4:285-99. This essay contains other valuable material on the *monogatariron* and will be referred to further. Norinaga and the *Genji* are discussed in English by Thomas Harper in his Ph.D. dissertation, "Motoori Norinaga's Criticism of the *Genji Monogatari*: A Study of the Background and Critical Content of his *Genji Monogatari Tama no Ogushi*" (University of Michigan, 1971). Other important studies include Fuchie Fumiya's "Hotaru," *Genji Monogatari Kōza*, ed. Yamagishi Tokuhei and Oka Kazuo (Yūseidō, 1971), 3:245-63; Nomura Seiichi, "Kyokō no Ronri: Monogatari Hihyō no Rekishi, Josetsu," *Genji Monogatari no Sōzō* (Ōfūsha, 1969), pp. 210-24; and Takahashi Tōru, "Monogatariron no Hassei to Shite no *Genji Monogatari*: Monogatarishi Oboegaki," *Nagoya Daigaku Kyōikugakubu Kiyō*, A22 (1978): 205-68. Takahashi's essay is useful both for its textual study (covering virtually each line of the original) and for the range of its theoretical speculations.

79. Genji's shift of attitude here is one of Waley's famous omissions.

80. Rachel Brownstein, *Becoming a Heroine*, p. 150. This is a striking study of the centrality of novels to women's lives and of women to novels.

81. Translation from Harper, "Motoori Norinaga's Criticism," p. 27.

82. In addition to Fujii's account in *Shigen to Genzai*, pp. 14-26, I am indebted to Mitani Kuniaki's "Monogatari to 'Kaku Koto,' " as well as Mitani Eiichi's "Josetsu Monogatari to wa Nanika: Hasseiteki Shiten Kara," *Monogatari Bungaku no Sekai* (Yūseidō, 1975), pp. 1-17, which is also helpful in situating the contributions of Orikuchi and Yanagita Kunio to this discussion. As Mitani Kuniaki suggests in his essay, the relevant entries in the *Iwanami Kogo Jiten* are also useful.

83. My own liberal interpretation of Mitani Kuniaki's argument in ibid., pp. 4-7. Mitani gives "event," "communication," and "mimesis" as the three elements of *katari* (p. 4).

84. The infant is Kaoru (4:310; S 648; W [689]). Noted in Fujii, *Shigen to Genzai*, p. 18.

85. The distinction is adapted from Abe Akio's "Hotaru no Maki no Monogatariron," pp. 291-94. Clara, the heroine in Margaret Drabble's novel *Jerusalem the Golden* (Harmondsworth, Middlesex, England: Penguin Books, 1969), is described in a quandary strikingly similar to Tamakazura's. She also sought, of course, the more usual and natural means of escape and fantasy, such as the watching of advertisements, the reading of fiction, and the spinning of self-indulgent romances, but her experience of life as a child was so narrow that she had no way of telling the possible from the absurd (pp. 32-33).

86. Fujii Sadakazu, "Monogatariron," KGMS 5:163.

87. Fujii Sadakazu, "Amayo no Shinasadame Kara 'Hotaru' no Maki no 'Monogatariron' E," *Kyōritsu Joshi Daigaku Tanki Daigaku (Bunka) Kiyō* 18 (1974), quoted in Takahashi, "Monogatariron no Hassei to Shite no *Genji Monogatari*," p. 234.

88. Kawaguchi Hisao, ed., *Kagerō Nikki* in *Tosa Nikki, Kagerō Nikki, Izumi Shikibu Nikki, Sarashina Nikki* NKBT 20 (1957): 109; see Seiden-sticker, *Gossamer Years*, p. 33.

89. Shōgakkan edition, p. 49.

90. Brownstein, *Becoming a Heroine*, p. 202, apropos of George Meredith's *Diana of the Crossways*.

91. Shoshana Felman, *The Literary Speech Act: Don Juan with J. L. Austin, or Seduction in Two Languages*, trans. Catherine Porter (Ithaca, N.Y.: Cornell University Press, 1983), p. 40. Emphases in the original.

92. Brownstein, *Becoming a Heroine*, p. xvi.

Notes to Chapter 2

93. In a slightly different vein, Kawazoe Fusae contrasts the women of Tō no Chūjō's household with those of Genji's by showing that the former, with the exception of the daughter defeated by Akikonomu, do not generate floral metaphors. See her "Genji, Nezame no Hana no Yu: Sono Hyōgenshiteki Gyakushutsu," Nihon Bungaku 31 (September 1982): 72-73.

94. For a study of aspects of this relationship, see Nomura Seiichi, "Suetsumuhana to Ōmi no Kimi," Genji Monogatari no Sōzō, pp. 97-112. Ōmi no Kimi herself is treated at length by Mushakōji Tatsuko in "Ōmi no Kimi," Genji Monogatari no Joseizō (Kadokawa Shoten, 1966), pp. 101-40. Akiyama Ken's "Ōmi no Kimi to Sono Shūhen," Genji Monogatari no Sekai (Tokyo Daigaku Shuppankai, 1964), pp. 135-49, succinctly examines her function with respect to the Rokujōin world.

95. This exchange is discussed by Kubukihara Rei in her study of the history of the magical element (often taking comical, grotesque, or obscene form) in waka. This element was banished from the mainstream of Heian waka and confined to particular books in the anthologies or transformed so as to be more acceptable. Kubukihara suggests that the Lady of Ōmi's nonsensical stringing of nouns is a late parodic expression of such a magical tradition. See her "Hikaika Kara Waka E: Wakashi Kōsō no Tame Ni," Kokugo to Kokubungaku 60 (January 1983): 14-30. I would like to take this poem nonparodically as well, as suggesting the "sacred" aspect of the Lady of Ōmi. Her absurd speech, like Suetsumuhana's nose or even Kaoru's scent, is an emblem of remote kinship with praiseworthy Folly.

96. Therefore, when Genji begins to divide his time equally between Murasaki and the Third Princess in "New Herbs, Part Two," he is mimicking in advance Yūgiri's characteristic solution to the problem of two wives.

97. When nowaki is used in "Purple Trousers," it refers to Yūgiri's glimpse of Tamakazura in that chapter. One unrelated instance in "The Wormwood Patch" refers to the autumn devastation of Suetsumuhana's estate.

98. This translation of Naishi no Kami is adopted from McCullough and McCullough, Tale of Flowering Fortunes. See pp. 121-22.

99. Allusion to a Gosenshū poem, "Winter," anonymous [Kokka Taikan, ed. Matsushita Daizaburō and Watanabe Fumio (Kyōbunsha, 1903), 1:482]:

Omoitsutsu
nenaku ni akuru

From these sleeves
of winter's night,

333

fuyu no yo no   spent in thought,
sode no kōri wa   and ending sleepless,
tokezu mo aru kana   the ice never melts.

100. Hasewaga Masaharu, "Sasurai no Himegimi," p. 57.

101. Translation by Helen Craig McCullough from *Ōkagami, The Great Mirror: Fujiwara Michinaga (966-1027) and His Times; A Study and Translation* (p. 96). Copyright © 1980 by Princeton University Press. Reprinted by permission.

102. Ibid., p. 97. Reprinted by permission.

103. Sadabumi is also the protagonist of a mid-tenth-century "poem-tale," the *Heichū Monogatari*. An edition may be found in Katagiri et al., NKBZ 8.

CHAPTER 3

1. Maeda Yukichika, *Murasaki Kusa* (Kawade Shobō, 1956), p. 4. I am grateful to Kawazoe Fusae for bringing this and the following two items in the text to my attention.

2. Itō Aki, *Heianchō Bungaku no Shikisō* (Kasama Shoin, 1965), pp. 162-63.

3. Hirota Osamu, "*Genji Monogatari* no Hyōshō Kōzō—Shikisō to Shinshō," in Hirokawa Katsumi, ed., *Genji Monogatari no Shokubutsu* (Kasama Shoin, 1978), p. 279. KKS 867 is generally thought to have been read metaphorically from the Heian period on. KKS 868, by Ariwara no Narihira (also appearing in *Ise* 41), uses 867 to describe the effect of love on one's perception of the beloved's kin. See comments in KKS, p. 330, as well as Katagiri Yōichi's comments in his *Zen Taiyaku Kokinwakashū* (Sōeisha, 1980), p. 344.

4. I am taking Kanera's citation of the *Ise* in his *Kachō Yosei* from Kitamura Kigin's *Kogetsushō*, 1:307.

5. For the *Ise* serving to impart a sense of "sin," see Mitani Kuniaki, "Fujitsubo Jiken."

6. Adapted from the *Iwanami Kogo Jiten* and the *Ōbunsha Kogo Jiten* (1965).

7. I have used the text prepared and annotated by Nakanishi Susumu, *Man'yōshū* (Kodansha, 1978), 1:58-59.

8. The Akashi Princess (Genji's biological daughter) is only eleven when she is sent off to the Crown Prince, twelve when she conceives, and thirteen at delivery. Shimizu Yoshiko compares these ages to those of historical consorts and concludes that Murasaki Shikibu, knowing

full well that the Akashi Princess was underage, attempted to deflect criticism by having Genji and other characters express concern for her youth and slight figure. "Wakana Jō, Gekan no Shudai to Hōhō," *Genji Monogatari no Buntai to Hōhō* (Tokyo Daigaku Shuppankai, 1980), pp. 181-83.

9. Thus there is a horizontal, sibling-like aspect to the Genji-Murasaki relationship just as with the Genji-Fujitsubo relationship. Vertically, the latter pair become mother and son, the former father and daughter.

10. Of course, the reciprocity of the surrogate-original relationship must not be overlooked. The "original" comes into existence only because of the surrogate, who reifies the original. It is the second or third link on the chain that makes the first visible.

11. For a discussion of the semantic development of the *yo* in *yozukazu*—its spatial, temporal, social, and erotic dimensions—see Nagafuji Yasushi's *Kodai Nihonbungaku to Jikan Ishiki*, pp. 59-77. It is interesting to note that *yo* as "sexual relations" is the last of the definitions given in the *Iwanami Kogo Jiten*. In Heian poetry and prose, at least, the narrowest and newest function of *yo* virtually obliterates all others, so that often, if the wider world is being signified, it is by a reversed metaphoric extension of male-female relations.

12. Akiyama Ken, "Murasaki no Ue no Henbō," *Genji Monogatari no Sekai*, pp. 100-101. Akiyama argues in this essay that Murasaki changes after the "A Rack of Cloud" chapter. See also Akiyama's preceding chapter, "Murasaki no Ue no Shoki ni Tsuite," pp. 75-92, on her idealized depiction.

13. Akiyama, "Murasaki no Ue no Henbō," pp. 100-101.

14. In the case of the third, Niou, the affection exceeds the bounds of cliche. Murasaki makes him heir to the Nijōin and bids him take special care, in her memory, of a plum tree and a cherry tree.

15. The exchanges between the reluctant Princess and her eager attendants recall those of Suetsumuhana with her aging ladies and anticipate those of Ochiba no Miya (the Second Princess) and the Uji sisters, especially Ōigimi, with their servants. What is exposed is the luxury of proud chastity: the highborn, wishing to cling to their prerogative of refusing sexual overtures, are pressured by their attendants, who see no merit in rejecting offers of shelter, clothing, and food.

16. I have been persuaded by Lewis Cook, in personal correspondence, that the one explicitly said to lie wakeful is Genji rather than Murasaki, which makes for a smooth transition to the "lonely awakening poem." This is the interpretation of Ishida Jōji and Shimizu Yo-

shiko's annotated *Genji Monogatari* (Shinchōsha, 1978), 3:213, n. 9, contrary to Shōgakkan 2:485, Seidensticker 359, and Waley 397, though the last omits the poem (these differences are of course not new but, one might say, traditional).

17. The description in the Japanese runs as follows: "ito onzogachi ni, mi mo naku aeka nari" (4:66; S 558; W 632). *Onzogachi* is used but once in the *Genji*. *Onzo* is "clothing" with an honorific prefix, and *-gachi* means "tending to," as in *nagamegachi*, "tending to gaze," and is often preceded by verbs and adjectives as well as by nouns as is the case here. (Two examples each of both uses of *-gachi* are given in the *Iwanami Kogo Jiten*, all from the *Genji*.) It is more than literal translation that makes "tending toward clothing" unusual. *Onzogachi* is a good example of the way Murasaki Shikibu stretches the boundaries of available vocabulary. In the latter part of this line, *mi mo naku aeka nari*, "fragile, having no body (flesh)," in which *mi mo naku* also suggests having no content, the Third Princess is reduced to her royal paraphernalia.

18. Mitani Kuniaki, in conversation. Not all women who take vows, however, have partaken of illicit love. Princess Asagao, for example, must make amends for her years as the Kamo Shrine Priestess.

19. To argue that Murasaki never takes vows because she is a bodhisattva figure who postpones her own salvation for the sake of Genji's is to fail to understand the use of religion as metaphor. Fukazawa Michio, for example, suggests that Murasaki is compelled to linger in this world for the same reason that the Bishop of Yokawa urges Ukifune to renounce her own vows: to spare Kaoru the sin of lust! ("Murasaki no Ue: Higekiteki Risōzō no Keisei," *Genji Monogatari no Keisei*, pp. 217-321).

20. I owe this information to Mitani Kuniaki. Haraoka (Kamono) Fumiko, in her "Bukkyōteki Shiten Nado," *Kokubungaku Kaishaku to Kanshō* 40 (April 1975): 102, points out that the *Mingo Nisso*, Nakanoin Michikatsu's *Genji* commentary of 1598, calls Murasaki's Hoke Hakkō a *gyakushu*.

21. Haraoka (Kamono) Fumiko, in making this point, contrasts Murasaki's Hoke Hakkō with the Third Princess's dedication of holy figures for her chapel in the "Suzumushi" chapter (ibid., pp. 101-102). That is a curious affair indeed, with Murasaki attending to the sewing and Genji arranging everything else, from the selection of the sutra to the care of the child Kaoru so that he would not disrupt the proceedings.

22. See Tamagami's useful summary in his GMH 9:50-53.

23. This is an odd synecdoche for "the seasons." There is no indi-

cation of a parting with Akikonomu who, however, sends Genji a condolence poem referring to the spring-autumn rivalry.

24. *Yukue shirazu* appears thirty-five times in the *Genji*. Suzuki Hideo, "Murasaki no Ue no Zetsubō: 'Minori' no Maki no Hōhō," *Bungaku Gogaku* 49 (1968): 61-64.

25. Pointed out by Fujii Sadakazu in "Hikaru Genji Shudairon," *Shigen to Genzai*, p. 173. Fujii takes this to be evidence of Murasaki's salvation.

26. The latter is the interpretation of the folklorist and biologist Minakata Kumakusu, quoted by Mitani Kuniaki, "Yūgiri no Kaimami,' in KGMS 5:221-22.

27. Kawazoe Fusae in "*Genji Monogatari* no Uchi Naru *Taketori Monogatari*: 'Minori,' 'Maboroshi' o Kiten to Shite," *Kokugo to Kokubungaku* 61 (July 1984): 1-15, pursues the complex uses of the *Bamboo Cutter* made by the *Genji*. Apropos of Murasaki's death, she argues that the speedy cremation and burial together with her beauty create the sense of "heavenly ascent" (p. 5). See also Sekine Kenji's "Kaguyahime to Sono Sue," *Monogatari Bungakuron: Genji Monogatari to Sono Zengo* (Ōfūsha, 1980), pp. 22-39, which emphasizes the otherworldly underpinnings of the *monogatari*.

28. Mitamura Masako, "Baika no Bi," in KGMS 6:1-6.

29. Lewis Cook has suggested to me that women were always able to see—that is, to look through and out. That presumably depends on the conditions of lighting and the quality of the screens and shades on hand. We have all had the experience of being able to see through shades or curtains without ourselves being seen as long as it was darker inside than out. As for men being seen, Mitani Kuniaki has suggested, also in conversation, that kingship is exercised in part by the ruled being compelled to gaze upon their ruler or his image, as in ceremonial processions or upon coins. It is tantalizing to consider the overlap between the conditions of kingship and of femininity.

30. For an example from her diary, see section 7, p. 49, in Richard Bowring's translation.

31. *Satsuki* is of course the Fifth Month, but that rendition will hardly serve. The euphonious *hana tachibana*, with its noble reversal of word order, blooms from late April on.

32. See Konishi Jin'ichi, "Association and Progression: Principles of Integration in Anthologies and Sequences of Japanese Court Poetry, A.D. 900-1350."

33. For a list of the conventional seasonal items to be found in this chapter, see Suzuki Hideo's "Hikaru Genji no Saibannen: *Genji Mo-*

nogatari no Hōhō ni Tsuite no Danshō," *Gakugei Kokugo Kokubungaku* 8 (June 1973): 7-16. Komachiya Teruhiko's " 'Maboroshi' no Hōhō ni Tsuite no Shiron," *Nihon Bungaku* 14 (June 1965): 56-63, is a pioneering effort to discuss the poetic structure of this chapter.

34. Suzuki, "Hikaru Genji no Saibannen," pp. 15-16.

35. Keene, *Taketori Monogatari*, pp. 304-305.

36. Fujii Sadakazu, "Hikaru Genji Shudairon," *Shigen to Genzai*, pp. 178-79. Suzuki Hideo and Komachiya Teruhiko in their previously cited articles appear to share these assumptions.

CHAPTER 4

1. Mitani Kuniaki discusses the nuances of the opening to "The Bamboo River" as well as other features of the apparently marginal Niou chapters by relating them to the *Genji* as a whole in "Tamakazura no Sono Go," KGMS 7 (1983): 267-77, and "*Genji Monogatari* Daisanbu no Hōhō: Chūshin no Sōshitsu Aruiwa Fuzai no Monogatari," *Bungaku* 50 (August 1982): 76-104.

2. The history of the city of Uji is lavishly chronicled by a municipal publication in six volumes. My account owes much to the first volume, *Ujishishi: Kodai no Rekishi to Keikan*, ed. Hayashiya Tatsusaburō and Fujioka Kenjirō (Ujishi: Ujishiyakusho, 1973). See also Ishihara Shōhei, "Uji no Denshō," KGMS 8 (1983): 14-32.

3. See the interpretation by Akiyama Ken in *Kokinwakashū, Ōchō Shūkashū*, ed. Akiyama and Kubota Jun (Shōgaku Tosho, 1982), pp. 131-32.

4. See Philippi, *Kojiki*, pp. 274-90; Aston, *Nihongi* 1:270-77.

5. Inoue Mitsurō and Yamada Ryōzō, "Rekishi Denshō to Kofun," *Ujishishi*, p. 210.

6. I have used the text in *Kojiki Jōdaikayō*, ed. Ogihara Asao and Kōnosu Hayao, NKBZ 1 (1973): 259.

7. See the absorbing account in *Ujishishi*, pp. 213-20.

8. See Kitagawa Tadahiko, "Ōchō no Bungaku to Uji," *Ujishishi*, pp. 518-28.

9. *Hijiri* is a complicated term variously used in the *Genji*. The *Iwanami Kogo Jiten* gives some indication of its range, from one who has supernatural powers (the exemplary figure being the Emperor, who is "sun knowing"—*hi-jiri*), and by extension, one exceptionally gifted in a given endeavor (Hitomaro as the *hijiri* of poetry), to a distinguished priest, a hermit, or lay ascetic. *Hijiri* covers both those who are insti-

tutionally sanctioned and those who are not, the common characteristic apparently being the possession of extraordinary powers. *Saint* as a fixed translation for this word is problematic. As lugubriously solemn about himself as the Eighth Prince is, it is unlikely he would call himself a "saint." On the other hand, when others refer to him as a *hijiri*, they may well intend a saintly resonance out of deference to his high birth. "Ascetic," the alternative candidate, cannot double as a term of praise.

10. See "Parable," especially pp. 64-71, of the *Scripture of the Lotus Blossom of the Fine Dharma (The Lotus Sutra)*, Translated from the Chinese of *Kumarajiva* by Leon Hurvitz (New York: Columbia University Press, 1976).

11. The *Hōjōki* has been translated by A. L. Sadler in *The Ten Foot Square Hut and The Tale of the Heike, Being Two Thirteenth Century Japanese Classics: "The Hojoki" and Selections from "The Heike Monogatari"* (Westport, Conn.: Greenwood Press, 1970), and by Donald Keene, "An Account of My Hut," included in his *Anthology of Japanese Literature, Earliest Era to the Mid-Nineteenth Century* (Rutland, Vt. and Tokyo: Charles E. Tuttle Co., 1956), pp. 197-212.

12. The Japanese phrase is *zoku hijiri*. For this and other observations regarding the term *zoku hijiri*, I am indebted to Mitani Kuniaki's "*Genji Monogatari* Daisanbu no Hōhō," pp. 86-93.

13. I have followed Tamagami's account in his GMH 9:218.

14. Fujii Sadakazu contrasts the "riddle, or the unanswered question" of Genji's story to the "unasked-for answer" given at the opening of the Uji chapters. See his "Ōken Kyūzai Chinmoku" in *Shigen to Genzai*, p. 199.

15. On the bifurcated structure of the Uji world, I am indebted to the following: Mitamura Masako's presentation, "Uji Jūjō no Kūkan," and subsequent discussion at the annual convention of the Monogatari Kenkyūkai (Shizuoka City, Japan, August 1983); Takahashi Tōru's "Uji Jikūron" in his *Genji Monogatari no Taiihō*, pp. 168-93; and Mitani Kuniaki's "*Genji Monogatari* Daisanbu no Hōhō."

16. The first interpretation belongs to none other than the editor of the prestigious Iwanami edition (in the NKBT series of classical literature) of the *Genji*, Yamagishi Tokuhei; the second is the view of Okada Shachihiko, author of the provocatively titled *Genji Monogatari Satsujinjiken* (Murder in the *Genji Monogatari*); and the third is Fujii's view, based on examples from the *Nihon Ryōiki* (translated by Kyōko Motomochi Nakamura as *Miraculous Stories from the Japanese Buddhist Tradition: The Nihon Ryōiki of the Monk Kyōkai* [Cambridge, Mass.: Harvard University Press, 1973]) and the *Nihon Shoki*. The translation of

time into space is my extension of Fujii's interpretation of the highly secularized game of incense-matching as it is depicted in the "Branch of Plum" chapter of the *Genji*. Fujii's decidedly serious essay, "Ka Kaori Kaoru Kō: *Genji Monogatari* no Seiritsu to Kōzō," appears in a magazine published by a cosmetics firm (Pōla): *is* 8 (March 1980): 20-23.

17. Ibid. The view that *nioi* initially referred to a visual phenomenon and only secondarily to an olfactory one is standard. See, for example, the entry in the *Iwanami Kogo Jiten* or Fujita Kayo's *"Niou" to "Kaoru"*: *Genji Monogatari ni Okeru Jimbutsu Zōkei no Shuhō to Sono Hyōgen* (Kazama Shobō, 1980). Fujita's book, especially pages 27-71, offers a fine scrutiny of these terms as they pertain to the *Genji*.

18. Fujita, *"Niou" to "Kaoru,"* p. 25.

19. Ibid., pp. 55-67, and Fujii, "Ka Kaori Kaoru," p. 22.

20. The traces of what I have called a shift might be compared with, for example, what Leo Spitzer calls the "polyonomasia" or the "polyetymologia" in *Don Quixote*. Certainly the *Genji* is replete with examples of these phenomena, but their effect is never theologically or, as in Rabelais, intellectually cumulative but rather differential. I am grateful to Peter Chemery for directing me to Spitzer's essay, "Perspectivism in *Don Quixote*," *Linguistics and Literary Theory: Essays in Stylistics* (Princeton, N.J.: Princeton University Press, 1948), pp. 91-185.

21. Identified in Takahashi Tōru's "Uji Monogatari Jikūron," *Genji Monogatari no Taiihō*, pp. 176-77.

22. I cannot resist citing Roland Barthes' observation that the Eiffel Tower is distinctive because "the world ordinarily produces either purely functional organisms (camera or eye) intended to see things but which then afford nothing to sight, what *sees* being mystically linked to what remains *hidden* (this is the theme of the voyeur), or else spectacles which themselves are blind and are left in the pure passivity of the Visible. The Tower (and this is one of its mythic powers) transgresses this separation, this habitual divorce of *seeing* and *being seen* . . . it is a complete object which has, if one may say so, both sexes of sight" ("The Eiffel Tower," in *The Eiffel Tower and Other Mythologies*, trans. Richard Howard [New York: Hill and Wang, 1979], p. 5).

23. Hasegawa Masaharu, "Hashihime," *Kokubungaku* 19 (September 1974): 134.

24. Princesses of the blood were a historic problem, too. Before the ascent of the Fujiwara clan, most of the imperial consorts were princesses of the blood. When the Fujiwara consolidated their power by making their daughters consorts, the princesses of the blood had nowhere to go. They presented the same problem that Elizabeth I claimed

was the intractable obstacle to any marriage for her. One solution was to appoint the princesses Shrine Priestess of Ise, but that disposed of only one per reign. Things became easier when it was decided that they could be married to commoners, which is precisely what happened with the Third Princess and Genji. Between 781 and 986, only fifteen percent of the princesses of the blood were married (4:23, n. 25).

25. The poem, included in Book 4 of the *Kokin Rokujō*, is no. 18136 in the *Zoku Kokka Taikan*, ed. Matsushita Daizaburō, 2 vols. (Kigensha, 1925-1926).

26. Extant texts of this poem do not show the wording the sisters use.

27. See Tamagami, GMH 10:311.

28. Shinohara Shōji explains refusal of marriage by such characters as Ōigimi or Princess Asagao as being a variation in the pattern of the stepdaughter tale: that is, the absence of their birth mothers causes them to turn their backs upon love. See his "Kekkon Kyohi no Monogatari Josetsu: Asagao no Himegimi o Megutte," in [Takahashi Tōru, ed.] *Genji Monogatari*, vol. 4. This view is criticized by Mitani Eiichi, who proposes that "refusal of marriage" is a motif with two sources, one being the tale of the adopted child and the other, the narrative of siblings' mutual ceding of marriage (*Monogatari Bungaku no Sekai*, pp. 136-37).

29. The episode with Genji and Fujitsubo is to be found in "The Sacred Tree" (2:100-104; S 196-98; W 203-205), and that with Yūgiri and the Second Princess in "Evening Mist" (4:453; S 703-705; W 721).

30. See, for example, Hasegawa Masaharu's "Uji Jūjō no Sekai: Hachi no Miya no Yuigon no Jubakusei," in [Takahashi Tōru, ed.] *Genji Monogatari*, vol. 4.

31. Shimizu Yoshiko regards this as the one rupture in Kaoru's otherwise idealized portrayal. "Kaoru Sōzō," *Bungaku* 25 (February 1957): 223.

32. Commentators attribute this comparison of Ōigimi to the cricket to the *Book of Rites*, in which the passage on the "third month of summer" states that the "cricket takes its place in the walls." *Li Chi. Book of Rites: An Encyclopedia of Ancient Ceremonial Usages, Religious Creeds, and Social Institutions*, trans. James Legge (New Hyde Park, N.Y.: University Books, 1967), 1:276-77.

33. See Orikuchi Shinobu, "*Ise Monogatari* Shiki," *Orikuchi Shinobu Zenshū* (Chūō Kōronsha, 1956), 10:35-127; and "*Ise Monogatari*," *Orikuchi Shinobu Zenshū Nōtohen*, vol. 13, ed. the Orikuchi Hakushu Kinen Kodai Kenkyūsho (Chūō Kōronsha, 1969).

34. According to the official genealogy, Kaoru is Genji's son and

brother to the Akashi Empress and therefore Niou's uncle. As the son of the Third Princess, sister to the Crown Prince who is Niou's father, Kaoru is Niou's cousin. Note the irrelevance of Kashiwagi, Kaoru's birth father. Note, too, that the principal difference between Kaoru and Niou in terms of blood tie is the absence of the Akashi element in Kaoru's genealogy. Through his mother, the Third Princess, Kaoru is linked to the sad fortunes of the descendants of "the previous Emperor."

35. Takahashi Tōru spells out the intricacies of *akegure* in his "*Genji Monogatari* no Uchi Naru Monogatarishi," in *Genji Monogatari no Taiihō*, pp. 155-63. Takahashi points out that *akegure*, which appeared only sporadically in earlier poetry, appears twelve times in the *Genji* (p. 160). In other words, it is a time made literarily significant by the *Genji*, and in so saying, we should bear in mind that prior to the *Genji*, the creation of literary significance was the prerogative of poetry. We have seen some of the subtle ways in which Murasaki Shikibu contests the prose-poetry relation she inherited; her use of *akegure* includes a choice morsel in which Yūgiri takes the word from the preceding prose passage and inserts it in his poem. The technique of poetic allusions in prose, of course, customarily assumes the priority of poetry (pp. 161-62).

36. Ibid.

37. Noted by Shimauchi Keiji, "*Genji Monogatari* ni Okeru Hyōgen to Sono Kiban: Niou Miya, Utsusemi, Ōigimi o Megutte," *Kokugo to Kokubungaku* 58 (July 1981): 46.

38. Takahashi (*Genji Monogatari no Taiihō*, pp. 150-54) traces an imagistic evolution beginning with the "morning clouds" and "evening rain" to which the goddess compared herself as she left the King of Ch'u's erotic dream. The paired image becomes a "euphemism for sexual intercourse, but with strong associations of the impermanence of sensual pleasure" in Chinese poetry (Stephen Owen, *The Poetry of the Early T'ang* [New Haven, Conn.: Yale University Press, 1977], p. 137). The *Genji* adopts the "evening rain" half of the pair, attaches it to actually dead rather than magically inaccessible lovers, and turns the image (nourished by other sources along the way) into a marker for evening as a time of contemplative longing.

39. These categories come from Shinohara Yoshihiko's survey of voyeurism in early Japanese literature, "*Genji Monogatari* ni Itaru Nozokimi no Keifu," *Bungaku Gogaku* 68 (August 1973): 56-67.

40. Philippi, *Kojiki*, pp. 156-58.

41. Ibid., pp. 61-67.

42. Keene, *Taketori Monogatari*.

43. Shinohara, "Nozokimi no Keifu," p. 66.

44. Ibid.; Amanda Stinchecum, "Narrative Voice in the *Genji Monogatari*" (Ph.D. dissertation, Columbia University, 1980), p. 92.

45. This is how Shinohara distinguishes between the categories ("Nozokimi no Keifu," p. 66).

46. The *Tale of the Hollow Tree*, in having human heroines either taken to be celestial or compared to celestial beings, may conceivably have prepared the ground for the *Genji*, but it reserves an important place for the fantastic construed literally.

47. Roger Sale, in his *Fairy Tales and After: From Snow White to E. B. White*, writes that "Hans Christian Andersen wrote what he called fairy tales, what were accepted by his audience as fairy tales, but which show on almost every page how much a break had been made, with the oral as well as the written tradition" (Cambridge, Mass.: Harvard University Press, 1978), p. 64. In the perspective of our discussion, the Prince's heartbreaking failure to recognize his adoring savior in "The Little Mermaid," Andersen's most popular tale, emerges as particularly symptomatic.

48. Ishida Jōji discusses the sources for the language used in these depictions in "Genji Monogatari ni Okeru Yottsu no Shi: Kago no Koto Nado," *Genji Monogatarironshū* (Ōfūsha, 1961), pp. 308-21.

49. Fujii Sadakazu, *Shigen to Genzai*, pp. 79-82.

50. For this observation with examples on narrative distancing, I am indebted to Haraoka Fumiko's "Saiwaibito Naka no Kimi," KGMS 8:252-56, and to Ikeda Kazuomi's "Ukifune Tōjō no Hōhō o Megutte: Genji Monogatari ni Yoru Genji Monogataridori," *Kokugo to Kokubungaku* 54 (November 1977): 84-85.

51. For a detailed discussion of Kaoru's and Nakanokimi's repartee and its implications for Ukifune, see Fujii Sadakazu, "Katashiro Ukifune," KGMS 8:279-82.

52. Takahashi Tōru offers an absorbing discussion on the implications of the imagery associated with Ukifune in his "Uji Monogatari Jikūron," *Genji Monogatari no Taihō*, pp. 168-93. Fujii Sadakazu deems Ōigimi to be the active agent in the latest substitution: her soul, as he provocatively puts it, "hungers for Ukifune's flesh" so that she might at last be joined with Kaoru. See his "Katashiro Ukifune," p. 284.

53. According to Tamagami (GMH 9:155), even unburdensome relations with women of the servant class were forbidden to men after they had taken vows. The contradictions in the Eighth Prince's desire to be a secular monk are betrayed once more.

54. Monogamy as the condition for female happiness is a strong

theme in the roughly contemporaneous *Ochikubo Monogatari* or *The Tale of the Lady Ochikubo*.

55. *Iwanami Kogo Jiten, Shōgakkan Kokugo Daijiten,* and Ikeda Kazuomi, "Tenarai Maki Mononoke Kō," *Genji Monogatari no Jimbutsu to Kōzō,* ed. the Chūko Bungaku Kenkyūkai (Kasama Shoin, 1982), pp. 172-73.

56. Suzuki Hideo pairs the two descriptions as "somewhat typified" depictions of overwhelming love ("Eiga to Yūshū: Kaoruron 4," KGMS 8:264-65), but Kaoru clearly, and necessarily, suffers from a deficiency of passion. The two heroes, in their strategically contrasting ways, seem to be mimicking the listless lover in *Tales of Ise,*

Oki mo sede	Neither rising nor sleeping
ne mo sede yoru o	I gaze
akashite wa	at the slow drizzle
haru no mono tote	and pass
nagame kurashitsu	the spring night

(IM 2)

57. It is unclear whether this painting belongs to the pornographic genre known as *osokuzu* (6:124, n. 7). Does Niou's shedding tears provide a clue? How can we guess at the "normal" sentiments provoked by such art in the Heian period?

58. I follow 6:142, n. 8, in reading the shadow of the *Kokinshū* poem here.

59. Examples were noted in Mitamura Masako's presentation, "Uji Jūjō no Kūkan": 5:299 and 301; S 858-59; W 880-81; or 6:170-73; S 1003-1004; W 1032-33. Ukifune is depicted as reclining to listen far more frequently than her sisters.

60. Ōigimi's words are *nao kakaru tsuide ni ikade usenan* (5:313; S 864; W 886), Ukifune's, a much more succinct and simple *maro wa ikade shinaba ya*. Although there is an implicit sense of the first person in the assertiveness of the verbal ending *nan* in Ōigimi's phrasing, it lacks the distinctive appeal of Ukifune's first-person pronoun. *Maro,* with its poignant, intimate ring, is used only thirty-seven times in the entire *Genji,* in contrast to, for example, another first-person pronoun, *ware,* which appears nearly ten times as frequently from a cursory count of the entries in Ikeda Kikan's indispensable concordance in his *Genji Monogatari Taisei* (Chūō Kōronsha, 1953), vols. 4 and 5.

61. Women who are beset by two lovers and take their lives, often by drowning, appear in the *Man'yōshū* (Unai Otome, 9:1801-1802, 1809-1810; and 19:4211-12; Sakurako, 16:3786-87; Kazurako, 16:3788-90)

and the *Yamato Monogatari*, no. 147. Orikuchi Shinobu has written a provocative essay on the associations of women with water: "Mizu no Onna," *Orikuchi Shinobu Zenshū* (Chūō Kōronsha, 1955), 2:80-109. Hayashida Takakazu pursues this theme in "Jusuitan no Hassei: Ukifune Monogatari Zenshi," *Genji Monogatari no Hassō*, pp. 257-82.

62. Long ago, when Genji's first wife Aoi suffered from a possession, it was rumored that the Rokujō Lady's father, the late Minister, was among the vengeful spirits. The dead Kashiwagi also appeared in a dream to Yūgiri to request that his flute be bequeathed to his descendants. These examples, however, are of a different order.

63. Kaoru carried Ukifune when crossing a rough part on the road to Uji (6:87; S 967; W 990); pointed out by Ikeda, "Tenarai Maki Mononoke Kō," p. 171.

64. Mitani Kuniaki states outright that the defrocked priest is a projection of the Bishop (*"Genji Monogatari* Daisanbu no Hōhō," p. 101). The assumption that Murasaki Shikibu "revered" Genshin appears in a guide to the *Genji*, in the entry "Yokawa no Sōzu," by Yanai Shigeshi in *Genji Monogatari Hikkei, II, Bessatsu Kokubungaku* 13 (1982): 133, though I should add that Yanai's article as a whole does not necessarily support the Genshin-model thesis.

65. Examples of this syndrome can be found in Ikeda's article (see n. 55 above) or in Shimizu Yoshiko's *Genji no Onnagimi*, in which she blames both Ukifune's unseemly plight (of being sought by two lovers) and her violent solution on her unaristocratic background. Shimizu goes on to say that Ukifune is of a "lowly status, sensitive only to her desires" (pp. 142-43).

66. Richard Bowring's translation of *mi* in Murasaki Shikibu's own poems as "fate" brings out these dimensions. See his *Murasaki Shikibu, Her Diary and Poetic Memoirs*, pp. 214-15, 234-35. Fujita Kayo distinguishes between characters who refer primarily to *yo* (in this case, "world") and those who refer to *mi*, finding that the former are largely male and the latter female with the important exception of Kashiwagi. Here *yo* suggests the public arena of action, *mi* a more abstract "existence" (*"Niou"* to *"Kaoru,"* pp. 234-49). The opposition *mi/yo* naturally highlights different qualities from the opposition *mi/kokoro*.

67. Text from *Kokubungaku* 27 (October 1982): 115-16; annotations by Gotō Shōko. See also the Bowring translation, pp. 234-35.

68. Nomura Seiichi, " 'Mi' to 'Kokoro' to no Sōkoku: Sakaretaru Sonzai ni Tsuite," *Kokubungaku* 23 (July 1978): 64. Nomura finds that the compositions of women poets pursue a complex opposition between the two terms such that each term is itself split into several layers. (He

qualifies this complexity by asserting that as "actual" entities, *mi* and *kokoro* are unities: p. 68.)

69. Akiyama Ken, "Murasaki Shikibu no Uta, Izumi Shikibu no Uta," *Kokubungaku* 23 (July 1978): 104-105.

70. Nevertheless, the poem does not make a comfortable whole. Akiyama suggests that we must interpolate a thought such as "nevertheless, it is only this heart to which I can turn" between the third and fourth lines (ibid., p. 106). If so, the heart-mind acquires an importance denied by the surface argument.

71. Nomura (" 'Mi' to 'Kokoro' no Sōkoku," p. 70, n. 6) makes the provocative suggestion that these poems were avoided in the imperial anthologies because of their "hidden" sense of class difference. It would also seem that such a radical sundering of the subject is in itself contrary to the ideology of the imperial anthologies.

72. Haraoka (Kamono) Fumiko, " 'Aware' no Sekai no Sōtaika to Ukifune no Monogatari," *Kokugo to Kokubungaku* 52 (March 1975): 13-27.

73. Readers have been baffled by Kaoru's apparent callousness as revealed in this scene following upon Ukifune's "death"; the First Princess episode used to be interpreted as part of a plot line that had been abandoned. For a more sensible view, see Kojima Naoko's "Onna Ichinomiya Monogatari no Kanata E: *Genji Monogatari* 'Fu' no Jikan," *Kokugo to Kokubungaku* 58 (August 1981): 23-37.

74. I am referring to the view expressed in the phrase *kyōgen kigo*, rendered as "fictive phrases and floating utterances" by William LaFleur in a chapter title in his *The Karma of Words: Buddhism and the Literary Arts in Medieval Japan* (Berkeley: University of California Press, 1983). Although this assessment of language, especially the language of fiction, as hopelessly wedded to untruth becomes dominant in the medieval period, it can readily be traced back to Heian Buddhist texts, as Takahashi Tōru does in his provocative "Koto no Ha o Kazareru Tama no Eda: Monogatari Gengo no Seisei."

75. Many examples were given by Mitamura in her presentation, "Uji Jūjō no Kūkan." As in the passage cited, the adjective *aramashi*, "rough," is repeatedly used for Uji's natural elements (e.g., 5:124, S 782, W 798; 5:269, S 845, W 868; 5:393, S 899, W 917; and 6:128, S 985, W 1010-11).

76. The *Sarashina Nikki*, ed. Akiyama Ken. sNKS 39 (1980):36. Morris, *As I Crossed the Bridge of Dreams*, pp. 56-57.

POSTSCRIPT

1. Motoori Norinaga, *Tama no Ogushi*, p. 202.
2. Ibid.
3. Ibid., p. 203.
4. Ibid., p. 215.
5. Ibid., p. 217.
6. Vol. 60 in SNKS, ed. Hino Tatsuo (Shinchōsha, 1983), p. 125.
7. Motoori Norinaga, *Tama no Ogushi*, p. 187.
8. For contemporary criticism of Norinaga's discussion of *aware*, see Noguchi Takehiko's "Motoori Norinaga to Murasaki Shikibu: *Genji Monogatari Tama no Ogushi* Shōron," *Kokubungaku Kaishaku to Kanshō* 40 (April 1975): 121-29. Abe Akio's essay, "Hotaru no Maki no Monogatariron," magisterially traces Norinaga's forcible containment of the *Genji* within the notion of *aware*. He shows, for example, how few of Norinaga's illustrations of *aware* are actually drawn from the *Genji* itself. He also points out (p. 297) Norinaga's intriguing failure or unwillingness to distinguish between the simple term *aware* and the phrase *mono no aware*; the longer term tends to appear at the culmination of a series of examples illustrating *aware*—a suggestive rhetorical gesture.
9. See Yoshikawa Kōjirō's thoughtful essay, "Bunjaku no Kachi: 'Mono no Aware o Shiru' Hokō," *Motoori Norinaga*, ed. Yoshikawa, Satake Akihiro, and Hino Tatsuo, vol. 40 in NST (Iwanami Shoten, 1978), pp. 593-625. Naoki Sakai translates *mono no aware* as the "Meaningfulness of Mono" in "Voices of the Past: The Discourse On Language in Eighteenth Century Japan" (Ph.D. dissertation, University of Chicago, 1983).
10. Translated by David Bellos, *The New York Review of Books* (July 19, 1984), pp. 15 and 19.
11. Virginia Woolf, *A Room of One's Own* (San Diego, Calif.: Harcourt Brace Jovanovich, 1957), p. 117. My thanks to Carol Kimmel for seizing upon the identification of "Shakespeare's sister" with Shikibu.

Works Cited

The place of publication is Tokyo for all works in Japanese.

Abe Akio. *Genji Monogatari Kenkyū Josetsu.* Tokyo Daigaku Shuppan-kai, 1959.

———. "Hotaru no Maki no Monogatariron." *Genji Monogatari.* [Edited by Takahashi Tōru.] Vol. 4. *Nihon Bungaku Kenkyū Shiryō Sōsho.* Yūseidō, 1982.

———, Akiyama Ken, and Imai Gen'e, eds. *Genji Monogatari.* NKBZ 12-17 (1970-1976).

Akimoto Kichirō, ed. *Fudoki.* NKBT 2 (1960).

Akiyama Ken. *Genji Monogatari no Sekai.* Tokyo Daigaku Shuppankai, 1964.

———. "Harima Zenshi, Akashi no Nyūdō." KGMS 3 (1981).

———. "Murasaki Shikibu no Uta, Izumi Shikibu no Uta." *Kokubungaku* 23 (July 1978): 104-108.

———, ed. *Sarashina Nikki.* SNKS 39 (1980).

———, and Kubota Jun, eds. *Kokinwakashū, Ōchō Shūkasen.* Shōgaku Tosho, 1982.

Aston, W. G., trans. *Nihongi: Chronicles of Japan from the Earliest Times to A.D. 697.* 2 vols. in one. Rutland, Vt. and Tokyo: Charles E. Tuttle Co., 1972.

Barthes, Roland. *The Eiffel Tower and Other Mythologies.* Translated by Richard Howard. New York: Hill and Wang, 1979.

Benl, Oscar. *Die Geschichte vom Prinzen Genji: Altjapanischer Liebesroman aus dem 11. Jahrhundert verfasst von der Hofdame Murasaki.* 2 vols. Zurich: Manesse Verlag, 1966.

Bettelheim, Bruno. *The Uses of Enchantment: The Meaning and Importance of Fairy Tales.* New York: Vintage Books, 1977.

Blacker, Carmen. *The Catalpa Bow: A Study of Shamanistic Practices in Japan.* London: George Allen & Unwin, 1975.

Bok, Sissela. *Secrets: On the Ethics of Concealment and Revelation.* New York: Pantheon Books, 1982.

Borgen, Robert. *Sugawara no Michizane and the Early Heian Court.* Cambridge, Mass.: Harvard University Press, 1986.

Bowring, Richard. "The Aesthetics of Opposition: Reflections on the 'Eawase' Chapter of the *Tale of Genji.*" Paper delivered at the 8th Conference on Oriental-Western Literary and Cultural Relations, Bloomington, Indiana, August 1982.

Bowring, Richard, trans. *Murasaki Shikibu: Her Diary and Poetic Memoirs*. Princeton, N.J.: Princeton University Press, 1982.

Brower, Robert H., and Earl Miner. *Japanese Court Poetry*. Stanford, Calif.: Stanford University Press, 1961.

Brownstein, Rachel. *Becoming a Heroine: Reading About Women in Novels*. New York: Viking Press, 1982.

Cranston, Edwin. *The Izumi Shikibu Diary*. Cambridge, Mass.: Harvard University Press, 1969.

Derrida, Jacques. *Of Grammatology*. Translated by Gayatri Chakravorty Spivak. Baltimore, Md.: Johns Hopkins University Press, 1976.

Drabble, Margaret. *Jerusalem the Golden*. Harmondsworth, Middlesex, England: Penguin Books, 1969.

Durkheim, Emile. *The Elementary Forms of the Religious Life*. Translated by Joseph Ward Swain. New York: Free Press, 1965.

Eliade, Mircea. *Myth and Reality*. Translated by Willard Trask. New York: Harper and Row, 1963.

———. *Rites and Symbols of Initiation: The Mysteries of Birth and Rebirth*. Translated by Willard Trask. New York: Harper Colophon Books, 1975.

———. *The Sacred and the Profane: The Nature of Religion*. Translated by Willard Trask. New York: Harcourt Brace Jovanovich, 1959.

Enchi Fumiko. *Genji Monogatari*. 10 vols. Shinchōsha, 1972-1973.

Felman, Shoshana. *The Literary Speech Act: Don Juan with J. L. Austin, or Seduction in Two Languages*. Translated by Catherine Porter. Ithaca, N.Y.: Cornell University Press, 1983.

Frye, Northrop. *Fables of Identity: Studies in Poetic Mythology*. New York: Harcourt Brace Jovanovich, 1963.

Fuchie Fumiya. "Hotaru." *Genji Monogatari Kōza*. Edited by Yamagishi Tokuhei and Oka Kazuo. Vol. 3. Yūseidō, 1971.

Fujii Sadakazu. "Ariwara no Narihira no Ryūri." *Dentō to Gendai* 16 (March 1972): 33-39.

———. *Genji Monogatari: Shigen to Genzai*. Tōjusha, 1980.

———. "Ka Kaori Kaoru Kō: *Genji Monogatari* no Seiritsu to Kōzō." *is* 8 (March 1980): 20-23.

———. "Katashiro Ukifune." KGMS 8 (1983).

———. *Koten o Yomu Hon*. Nihon Buritanika, 1980.

———. *Monogatari no Kekkon*. Sōjusha, 1985.

———. "Monogatariron." KGMS 5 (1981).

———. "Orikuchi Shinobu no Kokubungaku." *Orikuchi Shinobu o "Yomu."* Gendai Kikakusha, 1981.

———. *Shinsō no Kodai*. Kokubunsha, 1978.

Works Cited

————. "Suetsumuhana no Maki no Hōhō." KGMS 2 (1980).

————. "Tamakazura." *Genji Monogatari Kōza*. Edited by Yamagishi Tokuhei and Oka Kazuo. Vol. 3. Yūseidō, 1971.

————. "Uta no Zasetsu." *Genji Monogatari Oyobi Igo no Monogatari: Kenkyū to Shiryō*. Edited by the Murasaki Shikibu Gakkai. Musashino Shoin, 1979.

Fujita Kayo. *"Niou" to "Kaoru": Genji Monogatari ni Okeru Jimbutsu Zōkei no Shuhō to Sono Hyōgen*. Kazama Shobō, 1980.

Fukazawa Michio. *Genji Monogatari no Keisei*. Ōfūsha, 1972.

————. "Rokujō Miyasudokoro Akuryō Jiken no Shudaisei ni Tsuite." *Genji Monogatari to Sono Eikyō: Kenkyū to Shiryō*. Edited by the Murasaki Shikibu Gakkai. Musashino Shoin, 1978.

Gardner, John. "Cartoons." *In Praise of What Persists*. Edited by Stephen Berg. New York: Harper and Row, 1983.

Gatten, Aileen. "The Secluded Forest: Textual Problems in the *Genji Monogatari*." Ph.D. dissertation, University of Michigan, 1977.

————. "Supplementary Narratives to the *Tale of Genji*: 'Yamaji no Tsuyu,' 'Kumogakure Rokujō,' and 'Tamakura.' " Paper delivered at the 8th Conference on Oriental-Western Literary Cultural Relations, Bloomington, Indiana, August 1982.

Gilbert, Sandra M., and Susan Gubar. *The Madwoman in the Attic: The Woman Writer and the Nineteenth-Century Literary Imagination*. New Haven, Conn.: Yale University Press, 1979.

Gotō Shōko. "Fujitsubo no Eichi." KGMS 3 (1981).

Hall, John, and Jeffrey Mass, eds. *Medieval Japan: Essays in Institutional History*. New Haven, Conn.: Yale University Press, 1974.

Haraoka Fumiko. "Saiwaibito Naka no Kimi." KGMS 8 (1983).

Haraoka (Kamono) Fumiko. " 'Aware' no Sekai no Sōtaika to Ukifune no Monogatari." *Kokugo to Kokubungaku* 52 (March 1975): 13-17.

————. "Bukkyōteki Shiten Nado." *Kokubungaku Kaishaku to Kanshō* 40 (April 1975): 102-107.

Harimoto Masayuki. "Shunjū Arasoi." KGMS 5 (1981).

Harper, Thomas James. "Motoori Norinaga's Criticism of the *Genji Monogatari*: A Study of the Background and Critical Content of his *Genji Monogatari Tama no Ogushi*." Ph.D. dissertation, University of Michigan, 1971.

Harth, Eric. *Windows on the Mind*. New York: William Morrow and Co., 1982.

Hasegawa Masaharu. "*Genji Monogatari* no Sasurai no Keifu." *Nihon Bungaku Ronkyū* 14 (November 1980): 33-41.

Works Cited

Hasegawa Masaharu. "Hashihime." *Kokubungaku* 19 (September 1974): 130-32.

———. "Sasurai no Himegimi." KGMS 5 (1981).

———. "Uji Jūjō no Sekai: Hachi no Miya no Yuigon no Jubakusei." *Genji Monogatari.* [Edited by Takahashi Tōru.] Vol. 4. *Nihon Bungaku Kenkyū Shiryō Sōsho.* Yūseidō, 1982.

Hayashida Takakazu. *Genji Monogatari no Hassō.* Ōfūsha, 1980.

Hayashiya Tatsusaburō and Fujioka Kenjirō, eds. *Ujishishi: Kodai no Rekishi to Keikan.* Ujishi: Ujishiyakusho, 1973.

Heiserman, Arthur. *The Novel Before the Novel: Essays and Discussions about the Beginnings of Prose Fiction in the West.* Chicago, Ill.: University of Chicago Press, 1977.

Hijikata Yōichi. "*Genji Monogatari*: Yukari no Onnagimi no Keifu." Presentation at the meeting of the Monogatari Kenkyūkai, Tokyo, December 12, 1981.

Hirokawa Katsumi. "Hikaru Genji Monogatari: Han-shinwaronteki Shihatsu, Kinki Haihan no Keifu." *Shinwa, Kinki, Hyōhaku: Monogatari to Setsuwa no Sekai.* Edited by Hirokawa Katsumi. Ōfūsha, 1976.

Hirota Osamu. "*Genji Monogatari* ni Okeru Waka no Denshōsei: Rokujō Miyasudokoro no Mononoke no Baai." *Nihon Bungaku* 31 (May 1982): 54-63.

———. "*Genji Monogatari* no Hyōshō Kōzō—Shikisō to Shinsō." *Genji Monogatari no Shokubutsu.* Edited by Hirokawa Katsumi. Kasama Shoin, 1978.

———. "Rokujōin no Kōzō: Hikaru Genji Monogatari no Keisei to Tenkan." *Shinwa, Kinki, Hyōhaku: Monogatari to Setsuwa no Sekai.* Edited by Hirokawa Katsumi. Ōfūsha, 1976.

Hochstedler, Carol. *The Tale of Nezame: Part Three of Yowa no Nezame Monogatari.* Ithaca, N.Y.: Cornell University, China-Japan Program, 1979.

Huizinga, Johan. *Homo Ludens: A Study of the Play-Element in Culture.* Boston: Beacon Press, 1955.

Hurst, Cameron. *Insei: Abdicated Sovereigns in the Politics of Late Heian Japan.* New York: Columbia University Press, 1976.

Hurvitz, Leon, trans. *Scripture of the Lotus Blossom of the Fine Dharma (The Lotus Sutra), Translated from the Chinese of Kumarajiva.* New York: Columbia University Press, 1976.

Ikeda Kazuomi. "Ukifune Tōjō no Hōhō o Megutte: *Genji Monogatari* ni Yoru *Genji Monogataridori.*" *Kokugo to Kokubungaku* 54 (November 1977): 72-86.

———. "Tenarai Maki Mononoke Kō." *Genji Monogatari no Jimbutsu*

Works Cited

to Kōzō. Edited by the Chūko Bungaku Kenkyūkai. Kasama Shoin, 1982.

Ikeda Kikan. *Genji Monogatari Taisei.* 8 vols. Chūō Kōronsha, 1953.

Ikeda Tsutomu. "'Kagayaku Hi no Miya'-ron: Gen-Kiritsubo no Maki no Seiritsu." KGMS 1 (1980): 85-94.

Ishida Jōji. *Genji Monogatarironshū.* Ōfūsha, 1961.

———, ed. *Shimpan Ise Monogatari.* Kadokawa Shoten, 1979.

———, and Shimizu Yoshiko, eds. *Genji Monogatari.* SNKS. 8 vols. (1976-1983).

Ishihara Shōhei. "Hiru no Ko to Sumiyoshi no Kami: *Genji Monogatari* 'Suma' 'Akashi' no Shinwasei." (*Nishio Kōichi Kyōju Teinen Kinen Ronshū*) *Ronshū Setsuwa to Setsuwa Bungaku.* Kasama Shoin, 1979.

———. "Uji no Denshō." KGMS 8 (1983).

Ishizu Harumi. "Tamakazura Jūjō no Hashi o Megutte." *Murasaki* 14 (June 1977): 47-56.

Itō Aki. *Heianchō Bungaku no Shikisō.* Kasama Shoin, 1965.

Katagiri Yōichi, ed. *Zen Taiyaku Kokinwakashū.* Sōeisha, 1980.

———, Fukui Teisuke, Takahashi Shōji, and Shimizu Yoshiko, eds. *Taketori Monogatari, Ise Monogatari, Yamato Monogatari, Heichū Monogatari.* NKBZ 8 (1972).

Kawaguchi Hisao, ed. *Kagerō Nikki* in *Tosa Nikki, Kagerō Nikki, Izumi Shikibu Nikki, Sarashina Nikki.* NKBT 20 (1957).

Kawasaki Noboru. "Rokujō Miyasudokoro no Shinkōteki Haikei." *Kokugakuin Zasshi* 68 (September 1967): 13-23.

Kawazoe Fusae. "*Genji Monogatari* no Uchi Naru *Taketori Monogatari*: 'Minori,' 'Maboroshi,' o Kiten to Shite." *Kokugo to Kokubungaku* 61 (July 1984): 1-15.

———. "*Genji, Nezame* no Hana no Yu: Sono Hyōgenshiteki Gyakushutsu." *Nihon Bungaku* 31 (September 1982): 71-78.

Kazamaki Keijirō. *Nihon Bungakushi no Kenkyū, Ge.* Kadokawa Shoten, 1961.

Keene, Donald, trans. "An Account of My Hut." *Anthology of Japanese Literature, Earliest Era to the Mid-Nineteenth Century.* Rutland, Vt. and Tokyo: Charles E. Tuttle Co., 1956.

———. "*Taketori Monogatari* (The Tale of the Bamboo Cutter)." In Thomas Rimer's *Modern Japanese Fiction and Its Traditions: An Introduction.* Princeton, N.J.: Princeton University Press, 1978.

Kikuchi Yasuaki. "Kodai no Tennō." *Kodai Kokka.* Vol. 1 of *Kōza Nihonshi.* Edited by the Rekishigaku Kenkyūkai and the Nihonshi Kenkyūkai. Tokyo Daigaku Shuppankai, 1970.

Works Cited

Kimura Masanori. "Sumiyoshi Mōde: Akashi Ichizoku no Shukuun, 2." KGMS 6 (1981).

————. "Waka Miya Tanjō: Akashi Ichizoku no Shukuun, 1." KGMS 6 (1981).

Kitamura Kigin. *Kogetsushō*. 3 vols. Revised and edited by Mitani Eiichi. Meicho Fukyūkai, 1979.

Kojima Naoko. "*Genji Monogatari* to Waka: *Kokinshū*, Zō, Ge, no Kōzō Kara." *Monogatari Kenkyū* 3 (1981): 13-26.

————. "Onna Ichinomiya Monogatari no Kanata E: *Genji Monogatari* 'Fu' no Jikan." *Kokugo to Kokubungaku* 58 (August 1981): 23-37.

Komachiya Teruhiko. " 'Maboroshi' no Hōhō ni Tsuite no Shiron." *Nihon Bungaku* 14 (June 1965): 56-63.

Konishi Jin'ichi. "Association and Progression: Principles of Integration in Anthologies and Sequences of Japanese Court Poetry, A.D. 900-1350." Translated by Robert H. Brower and Earl Miner. *Harvard Journal of Asiatic Studies* 21 (1958): 67-127.

Kubota Jun, ed. *Shinkokinwakashū Zenhyōshaku*. 9 vols. Kodansha, 1976-1977.

Kubukihara Rei. "Hikaika Kara Waka E: Wakashi Kōsō no Tame Ni." *Kokugo to Kokubungaku* 60 (January 1983): 14-30.

Kundera, Milan. "The Novel and Europe." Translated by David Bellos. *The New York Review of Books*, July 19, 1984, 15-19.

Kurahashi Masaji. *Kyōen no Kenkyū, Bungakuhen*. Ōfūsha, 1969.

Kuratsuka Akiko. *Fujo no Bunka*. Heibonsha, 1979.

————. "Kōtōfu ni Okeru 'Imōto': Kodai Joseishi Josetsu." *Bungaku* 36 (June 1968): 61-73.

Kuwabara Hiroshi. "Akashi Kara Ōi E." KGMS 4 (1980).

LaFleur, William. *The Karma of Words: Buddhism and the Literary Arts in Medieval Japan*. Berkeley: University of California Press, 1983.

Lammers, Wayne. "The Succession: Kuniyuzuri, A Translation from the *Utsuho Monogatari*." *Monumenta Nipponica* 37 (1982): 139-78.

Legge, James, trans. *Li Chi. Book of Rites: An Encyclopedia of Ancient Ceremonial Usages, Religious Creeds, and Social Institutions*. Vol. 1. New Hyde Park, N.Y.: University Books, 1967.

Levy, Ian H. *The Ten Thousand Leaves: A Translation of the Man'yōshū, Japan's Premier Anthology of Classical Poetry*. Vol. 1. Princeton, N.J.: Princeton University Press, 1981.

Lin, Wen-yüeh. *Yüan Shih Wu Yü*. 5 vols. Taipei: Chung Wai Wen Hsüeh Yüeh K'an She, 1974-1978.

Works Cited

McCullough, Helen Craig, trans. *Kokin Wakashū: The First Imperial Anthology of Japanese Poetry with "Tosa Nikki" and "Shinsen Waka."* Stanford, Calif.: Stanford University Press, 1985.

———. *Ōkagami, The Great Mirror: Fujiwara Michinaga (966-1027) and His Times; A Study and Translation.* Princeton, N.J.: Princeton University Press, 1980.

———. *Tales of Ise: Lyrical Episodes from Tenth-Century Japan.* Stanford, Calif.: Stanford University Press, 1968.

———, and William H. McCullough. *A Tale of Flowering Fortunes: Annals of Japanese Aristocratic Life in the Heian Period.* 2 vols. Stanford, Calif.: Stanford University Press, 1980.

McCullough, William H. "Japanese Marriage Institutions in the Heian Period." *Harvard Journal of Asiatic Studies* 27 (1967): 103-67.

Maeda Yukichika. *Murasaki Kusa.* Kawade Shobō, 1956.

Marra, Michele, trans. "Mumyōzōshi" (Parts 1-3). *Monumenta Nipponica* 39, nos. 2-4 (1984).

Masuda Katsumi. "Teiō no Ikikata: Kodai Kizoku Seikatsu to Seishinshi no Kyōkaiiki Kara." *Kokubungaku Kaishaku to Kanshō* 31 (November 1966): 218-22.

Matsushita Daizaburō, ed. *Zoku Kokka Taikan.* 2 vols. Kigensha, 1925-1926.

———, and Watanabe Fumio, eds. *Kokka Taikan.* 2 vols. Kyōbunsha, 1903.

Miner, Earl. *Japanese Linked Poetry.* Princeton, N.J.: Princeton University Press, 1978.

———, Odagiri Hiroko, and Morrell, Robert E. *The Princeton Companion to Classical Japanese Literature.* Princeton, N.J.: Princeton University Press, 1986.

———, trans. *Japanese Poetic Diaries.* Berkeley: University of California Press, 1969.

Mitamura Masako. "Baika no Bi." KGMS 6 (1981).

———. "Genji Monogatari ni Okeru Katashiro no Mondai: Meshūdo o Kiten ni Shite." *Heianchō Bungaku Kenkyū* 3, no. 7 (December 1970): 11-21.

———. "Uji Jūjō no Kūkan." Presentation at the annual meeting of the Monogatari Kenkyūkai, Shizuoka City, Japan, August 1983.

Mitani Eiichi. *Monogatari Bungaku no Sekai.* Yūseidō, 1975.

———. *Monogatarishi no Kenkyū.* Yūseidō, 1967.

———. *Nihon Bungaku no Minzokugakuteki Kenkyū.* Yūseidō, 1960.

———. "Yūgao Monogatari to Kodenshō." KGMS 1 (1980).

Mitani Kuniaki. "Fujitsubo Jiken no Hyōgen Kōzō: 'Waka Murasaki' no Hōhō Aruiwa 'Pure-tekisuto' to Shite no *Ise Monogatari.*" *(Imai*

Works Cited

Takuya Hakushi Koki Kinen) Monogatari, Nikki Bungaku to Sono Shūhen. Ōfūsha, 1980.

―――. "Gen no Naishi no Monogatari." KGMS 2 (1980).

―――. "*Genji Monogatari* Daisanbu no Hōhō: Chūshin no Sōshitsu Aruiwa Fuzai no Monogatari." *Bungaku* 50 (August 1982): 76-104.

―――. "*Genji Monogatari* ni Okeru Eiga to Tsumi no Ishiki: Yaso-shima Matsuri to *Sumiyoshi Monogatari* no Eikyō o Tsūjite." *Heianchō Bungaku Kenkyū* 2 (May 1965): 125-40.

―――. "Heianchō ni Okeru Mamakoijime Monogatari no Keifu: Ko-*Sumiyoshi Monogatari* Kara *Kaiawase* Made." *Waseda Daigaku Kōtōgakuin Kenkyū Nenshi* 15 (January 1971): 14-33.

―――. "Ibukuro to Bungaku, Shiron: Nihon Kodai Bungaku to 'Aji-wau' Koto." *Bungei to Hihyō,* Part 1, 3 (June 1969): 76-88, and Part 2, 3 (October 1969): 87-99.

―――. "Kagai no Uta (Seineiki)." *Kiki Kayō.* Edited by Yamaji Hei-shirō and Kubota Shōichirō. Waseda Daigaku Shuppanbu, 1976.

―――. "Kodai Chimei Kigen Densetsu no Hōhō." *Nihon Bungaku* 30 (October 1981): 41-49.

―――. "Meijiki no *Genji Monogatari.*" *Kokubungaku Kaishaku to Kanshō* 48 (July 1983): 52-57.

―――. "Monogatari to 'Kaku Koto': Monogatari Bungaku no Imi Sayō Aruiwa Fuzai no Bungaku." *Nihon Bungaku* 26 (October 1976): 1-21.

―――. "Tamakazura Jūjō no Hōhō: Tamakazura no Ryūri Aruiwa Jojutsu to Jimbutsu Zōkei no Kōzō." *Genji Monogatari no Hyōgen to Kōzō.* Edited by the Chūko Bungaku Kenkyūkai. Kasama Shoin, 1977.

―――. "Tamakazura no Sono Go." KGMS 7 (1983): 267-97.

―――. "Yūgiri no Kaimami." KGMS 5 (1981).

Morris, Ivan. *The Nobility of Failure: Tragic Heroes in the History of Japan.* New York: Holt, Rinehart and Winston, 1975.

―――. *The World of the Shining Prince.* Oxford and New York: Oxford University Press, 1964.

―――, ed. *Madly Singing in the Mountains: An Appreciation and Anthology of Arthur Waley.* London: George Allen & Unwin, 1970.

―――, trans. *As I Crossed the Bridge of Dreams: Recollections of a Woman in Eleventh-Century Japan.* New York: Dial Press, 1971.

―――, trans. *The Pillow Book of Sei Shōnagon.* 2 vols. New York: Columbia University Press, 1967.

Motoori Norinaga. *Genji Monogatari Tama no Ogushi.* Motoori

Works Cited

Norinaga Zenshū. Edited by Ōno Susumu. Vol. 4. Chikuma Shobō, 1969.

―――. "Shibun Yōryō." *Motoori Norinaga.* Edited by Hino Tatsuo. SNKS 60 (1983).

Mumyōzōshi. Edited by Kitagawa Tadahiko. *Kodai Chūsei Geijutsuron.* NST 23 (1973).

Murone Kyōko. "Mononoke no Kenkyū." Presentation in Suzuki Hideo's seminar at Seijō University, Tokyo, November 1980.

Mushakōji Tatsuko. *Genji Monogatari no Joseizō.* Kadokawa Shoten, 1966.

Nagafuji Yasushi. *Kodai Nihonbungaku to Jikan Ishiki.* Miraisha, 1979.

Nakamura, Kyōko Motomochi. *Miraculous Stories from the Japanese Buddhist Tradition: The Nihon Ryōiki of the Monk Kyōkai.* Cambridge, Mass.: Harvard University Press, 1973.

Nakanishi Susumu, ed. *Man'yōshū.* 4 vols. Kodansha, 1978-1983.

Noguchi Takehiko. *Hana no Shigaku.* Asahi Shimbunsha, 1978.

―――. "Motoori Norinaga to Murasaki Shikibu: *Genji Monogatari Tama no Ogushi* Shōron." *Kokubungaku Kaishaku to Kanshō* 40 (April 1975): 121-29.

Nomura Seiichi. *Genji Monogatari no Sōzō.* Ōfūsha, 1969.

―――. " 'Mi' to 'Kokoro' no Sōkoku: Sakaretaru Sonzai ni Tsuite." *Kokubungaku* 23 (July 1978): 64-70.

―――. "Rokujōin no Kisetsuteki Jikū no Motsu Imi wa Nani Ka." *Kokubungaku* 25 (May 1980): 100-105.

―――. "Rokujōin no Shiki no Machi." KGMS 5 (1981).

Nuttall, A. D. *A New Mimesis: Shakespeare and the Representation of Reality.* London and New York: Methuen, 1983.

Ōasa Yūji. "Rokujō Miyasudokoro no Kunō." KGMS 3 (1981).

Ogihara Asao and Kōnosu Hayao, eds. *Kojiki Jōdaikayō,* NKBZ 1 (1973).

Oka Kazuo. *Genji Monogatari no Kisoteki Kenkyū.* Tōyōdō Shuppan, 1966.

Okada Shachihiko. *Genji Monogatari Satsujin Jiken.* Ōbunsha, 1980.

Orikuchi Shinobu. "Ise Monogatari." *Orikuchi Shinobu Zenshū Nōtohen.* Edited by the Orikuchi Hakushu Kinen Kodai Kenkyūsho. Vol. 13. Chūō Kōronsha, 1969.

―――. "Ise Monogatari Shiki." *Orikuchi Shinobu Zenshū.* Vol. 10. Chūō Kōronsha, 1956.

―――. "Mizu no Onna." *Orikuchi Shinobu Zenshū.* Vol. 2. Chūō Kōronsha, 1955.

―――. "Nihon Bungaku no Naiyō." *Orikuchi Shinobu Zenshū.* Vol. 7. Chūō Kōronsha, 1955.

Works Cited

Owen, Stephen. *The Poetry of the Early T'ang*. New Haven, Conn.: Yale University Press, 1977.

Ozawa Masao, ed. *Kokinwakashū*. NKBZ 7 (1971).

Pekarik, Andrew, ed. *Ukifune: Love in the Tale of Genji*. New York: Columbia University Press, 1982.

Philippi, Donald L., trans. *Kojiki*. Tokyo: University of Tokyo Press, 1968.

Plaks, Andrew. *Archetype and Allegory in the Dream of the Red Chamber*. Princeton, N.J.: Princeton University Press, 1976.

Pollack, David. "The Informing Image: 'China' in the *Genji Monogatari*." *The Fracture of Meaning: Japan's Synthesis of China from the Eighth through the Eighteenth Centuries*. Princeton, N.J.: Princeton University Press, 1986.

Propp, Vladimir. *Morphology of the Folktale*. Translated by Laurence Scott. 2d ed. Revised and edited by Louis A. Wagner. Austin: University of Texas Press, 1968.

Rodd, Laurel Rasplica, and Mary Catherine Henkenius, trans. *Kokinshū: A Collection of Poems Ancient and Modern, Including a Study of Chinese Influences on the* Kokinshū *Prefaces by John Timothy Wixted and an Annotated Translation of the Chinese Preface by Leonard Grzanka*. Princeton, N.J.: Princeton University Press, 1984.

Rohlich, Thomas H., trans. *A Tale of Eleventh-Century Japan: Hamamatsu Chūnagon Monogatari*. Princeton, N.J.: Princeton University Press, 1983.

Sadler, A. L., trans. *The Ten Foot Square Hut and The Tale of the Heike, Being Two Thirteenth Century Japanese Classics. "The Hojoki" and Selections from "The Heike Monogatari."* Westport, Conn.: Greenwood Press, 1970.

Saigō Nobutsuna. *Genji Monogatari o Yomu Tame Ni*. Heibonsha, 1983.

———. *Nihon Kodai Bungakushi*. Rev. ed. Iwanami Shoten, 1963.

———. *Shi no Hassei: Bungaku ni Okeru Genshi, Kodai no Imi*. Rev. ed. Miraisha, 1964.

Sakai, Naoki. "Voices of the Past: The Discourse on Language in Eighteenth Century Japan." Ph.D. dissertation, University of Chicago, 1983.

Sakamoto Kazuko. "Hikaru Genji no Keifu." *Kokugakuin Zasshi* 76 (December 1975): 33-43.

———. "Rokujō Miyasudokoro no Ise Gekō to On'ryō Shutsugen." *Bungaku Gogaku*, no. 88 (August 1974): 90-100.

Works Cited

Sale, Roger. *Fairy Tales and After: From Snow White to E. B. White.* Cambridge, Mass.: Harvard University Press, 1978.

Sansom, George. *A History of Japan to 1334.* Stanford, Calif.: Stanford University Press, 1958.

Scholes, Robert, and Robert Kellog. *The Nature of Narrative.* London: Oxford University Press, 1966.

Seidensticker, Edward, trans. *The Gossamer Years: The Diary of a Noblewoman of Heian Japan.* Tokyo and Rutland, Vt.: Charles E. Tuttle Co., 1964.

———. *The Tale of Genji.* New York: Alfred A. Knopf, 1976.

Seki Keigo. "Kon'intan to Shite no *Sumiyoshi Monogatari*: Bungaku to Mukashi Banashi." *Kokugo to Kokubungaku* 49 (October 1972): 79-95.

Sekine Kenji. *Monogatari Bungakuron: Genji Monogatari to Sono Zengo.* Ōfūsha, 1980.

Shimauchi Keiji. "*Genji Monogatari* ni Okeru Hyōgen to Sono Kiban: Niou Miya, Utsusemi, Ōigimi o Megutte." *Kokugo to Kokubungaku* 58 (July 1981): 44-57.

Shimizu Yoshiko. *Genji Monogatari no Buntai to Hōhō.* Tokyo Daigaku Shuppankai, 1980.

———. *Genji no Onnagimi.* Hanawa Shobō, 1967.

———. "Kaoru Sōzō." *Bungaku* 25 (February 1957): 88-97.

Shinohara Shōji. "Kekkon Kyohi no Monogatari Josetsu: Asagao no Himegimi o Megutte." [Edited by Takahashi Tōru.] *Genji Monogatari.* Vol. 4. *Nihon Bungaku Kenkyū Shiryō Sōsho.* Yūseidō, 1975.

Shinohara Yoshihiko. "*Genji Monogatari* ni Itaru Nozokimi no Keifu." *Bungaku Gogaku* 68 (August 1973): 56-67.

Shirakawa Shizuka. *Shoki Man'yōron.* Chūō Kōronsha, 1979.

Sieffert, René. *Le Dit du Genji.* 2+ vols. Paris: Publications Orientalistes de France, 1978—.

Spitzer, Leo. *Linguistics and Literary Theory: Essays in Stylistics.* Princeton, N.J.: Princeton University Press, 1948.

Stinchecum, Amanda. "Narrative Voice in the *Genji Monogatari.*" Ph.D. dissertation, Columbia University, 1980.

Suzuki Hideo. "Eiga to Yūshū: Kaoruron 4." KGMS 8 (1983).

———. "*Genji Monogatari* no Waka." *Genji Monogatari no Tankyū.* Vol. 5. Kazama Shobō, 1980.

———. "Hikaru Genji no Onnagimitachi." *Genji Monogatari to Sono Eikyō: Kenkyū to Shiryō.* Edited by the Murasaki Shikibu Gakkai. Musashino Shoin, 1978.

Works Cited

Suzuki Hideo. "Hikaru Genji no Saibannen: *Genji Monogatari* no Hōhō ni Tsuite no Danshō." *Gakugei Kokugo Kokubungaku* 8 (June 1973): 7-16.

———. "Kago Shūshū: *Kokin Rokujō*." *Kokugo Tsūshin* 232 (December 1980): 8-16.

———. "Kuruma Arasoi Zengo no Rokujō Miyasudokoro: *Genji Monogatari* Hyōgenron Oboegaki." *Seijō Bungei* 91 (March 1980): 1-20.

———. "Murasaki no Ue no Zetsubō: 'Minori' no Maki no Hōhō." *Bungaku Gogaku* 49 (1968): 59-68.

———. "Rokujōin no Sōsetsu." *Chūko Bungaku* 14 (October 1974): 30-39.

——— et al., eds. "Murasaki Shikibu Zenka Hyōshaku." *Kokubungaku* 27 (October 1982): 96-132.

Tahara, Mildred, trans. *Tales of Yamato: A Tenth-Century Poem-Tale.* Honolulu: University of Hawaii Press, 1980.

Takahashi Kazuo. *Genji Monogatari no Shudai to Kōsō.* Ōfūsha, 1971.

Takahashi Tōru. *Genji Monogatari no Taiihō.* Tokyo Daigaku Shuppankai, 1982.

———. "Koto no Ha o Kazareru Tama no Eda: Monogatari Gengo no Seisei." *Kokugo to Kokubungaku* 61 (May 1984): 1-13.

———. "Monogatariron no Hassei to Shite no *Genji Monogatari*: Monogatarishi Oboegaki." *Nagoya Daigaku Kyōikugakubu Kiyō*, A22 (1978): 205-68.

———. " 'Ochikubo' no Imi o Megutte: Monogatari Tekusuto no Hyōsō to Shinsō." *Nihon Bungaku* 31 (June 1982): 89-94.

———. "Yūgao no Maki no Hyōgen: Tekusuto, Katari, Kōzō." *Bungaku* 50 (November 1982): 77-98.

Takamure Itsue. *Nihon Kon'inshi.* Shibundō, 1963.

Takeda Sōjun. *Genji Monogatari no Kenkyū.* Iwanami Shoten, 1954.

Tamagami Takuya. *Genji Monogatari Hyōshaku.* 14 vols. Kadokawa Shoten, 1964-1966.

———. *Monogatari Bungakuron.* Hanawa Shobō, 1960.

Tanizaki Jun'ichirō. *Jun'ichirō Shinshinyaku Genji Monogatari.* 6 vols. Chūō Kōronsha, 1966.

Tsunoda Bun'ei, and Nakamura Shin'ichirō. *Omoshiroku Genji o Yomu: Genji Monogatari Kōgi.* Asahi Shuppansha, 1980.

Uesaka Nobuo. *Genji Monogatari: Sono Shinshō Josetsu.* Kasama Shoin, 1974.

Utsuho Monogatari. 2 vols. Edited by the *Utsuho Monogatari* Kenkyūkai. Kasama Shoin, 1973-1975.

Works Cited

Waley, Arthur, trans. *The Tale of Genji*. New York: Random House, 1960.

Watanabe Minoru. *Heianchō Bunshōshi*. Tokyo Daigaku Shuppankai, 1981.

———, ed. *Ise Monogatari*. SNKS 2 (1976).

Whitehouse, Wilfrid, and Eizō Yanagisawa, trans. *Ochikubo Monogatari, or The Tale of the Lady Ochikubo: A Tenth-Century Japanese Novel*. London: Peter Owen, 1965.

Woolf, Virginia. *A Room of One's Own*. San Diego, Calif.: Harcourt Brace Jovanovich, 1957.

Yamagishi Tokuhei, ed. *Genji Monogatari*. 5 vols. NKBT (1958-1963).

Yamaguchi Masao. *Bunka to Ryōgisei*. Iwanami Shoten, 1975.

———. *Chi no Enkinhō*. Iwanami Shoten, 1978.

———. "*Genji Monogatari*: Bunka Kigōron no Shiten Kara Mita." *Kigōgaku Kenkyū* 1 (1981): 119-39.

Yamanaka Yutaka. "Rokujōin to Nenjū Gyōji." KGMS 5 (1981).

Yanagimachi Tokitoshi. "Ronja to Shite no Hikaru Genji: Hikaru Genjiron no Tame no Danshō." *Murasaki* 17 (July 1980): 23-32.

Yanai Shigeshi. "Yokawa no Sozu." *Genji Monogatari Hikkei, II. Bessatsu Kokubungaku* 13 (1982): 133-35.

Yosano Akiko. *Gendaigoyaku Genji Monogatari*. 2 vols. Nihon Shobō, 1961.

Yourcenar, Marguerite. "Le Dernier Amour du Prince Genghi." *Nouvelles Orientales* in *Oeuvres Romanesques*. Paris: Gallimard, 1982.

Yoshikai Naoto. "Tamakazura Monogatariron: Yūgao no Yukari no Monogatari." *Kokugakuin Daigaku Daigakuin Kiyō* 11 (1979): 84-110.

Yoshikawa Kōjirō. "Bunjaku no Kachi: 'Mono no Aware o Shiru' Hokō." *Motoori Norinaga*. Edited by Yoshikawa, Satake Akihiro, and Hino Tatsuo. NST 40. Iwanami Shoten, 1978.

Index

abbot, the, 235, 249
Agemaki. *See* Ōigimi
Akashi, exile to, 93, 97, 102
Akashi Empress / Akashi Princess,
105; and the Akashi Lady, 75-82,
129, 242; and the Akashi Priest,
82-83; and Genji, 78, 81, 84-85,
101, 104-106, 117-18, 120, 135,
158, 202, 293-94; and the Hoke
Hakkō, 162; and the Kiritsubo
Lady, 78-80; and Murasaki, 44,
82, 176, 185, 188, 195-96, 293-94;
and the old nun, 78-80; and Prince
Hotaru, 200; and Tamakazura,
124-25; and the Third Princess,
78, 187
Akashi family, 64; and Genji, 66, 68-
69, 75, 79, 191; pilgrimage to the
Sumiyoshi Shrine, 84-85; and the
Rokujō Lady, 60-61
Akashi Lady, 105; and the Akashi
Empress / Akashi Princess, 75-82,
129, 242; and the Akashi Priest,
81; and Akikonomu, 61; and
Genji, 64-85, 101, 104, 121-22,
124, 173, 177-78, 202-204, 208-
209, 214, 222; and Murasaki, 78,
84, 175-76, 182, 188, 193-94, 242;
poetry of, 72-73, 185, 213, 286,
292-93; and the reading and writing of fiction, 129; and the Rokujō
Lady, 61, 64; and the Rokujōin,
111, 113, 117; and Ukifune, 292-
93
Akashi Priest, 64-65; and the Akashi
Empress / Akashi Princess, 82-83;
and the Akashi family, 84; and the
Akashi Lady, 81; and class in
Genji, 89; and Genji, 66-70, 72,
84; religious vows of, 189
Akikonomu, 136, 146; and the Akashi Empress / Akashi Princess, 106;

and the Akashi Lady, 61; and Fujitsubo, 21, 109-10; and Genji, 28,
81, 101-102, 104-11, 124-25, 141,
158, 168, 179, 199-200; and Murasaki, 106-107, 144, 175, 182-84,
190-91, 199-200; naming of, 104-
11; as Priestess of Ise, 47; and the
Reizei Emperor, 105, 168; and the
Rokujō Lady, 45, 56-57, 104; and
the Rokujōin, 111, 117; and the
Suzaku Emperor, 30; and Tamakazura, 145; and Tō no Chūjō's
daughter, 105; and Yūgiri, 142
Amaterasu, 67
Aoi: and Genji, 47, 49-50, 58-59,
74, 103, 170, 197; and Princess
Ōmiya, 205; and the Rokujō Lady,
46, 48, 50-51, 54-56, 62, 170; and
Tō no Chūjō, 198
Aoi Matsuri, 48, 204
Ariwara no Motokata, 119
Ariwara no Narihira, 35, 37-38
Ariwara no Yukihira, 93
As I Crossed the Bridge of Dreams, 4,
75, 296
Asagao, Princess: and dichotomies
and substitutions in *Genji*, 18-19;
and Genji, 102, 176-79; and Murasaki, 175-77; and Prince Shikibu,
176-77
aware, concept of, 297-302

Ben. *See* Bennokimi
Bennokimi; and Genji, 32; and
Kaoru, 231, 237, 242-43, 272; and
Nakanokimi, 249; and Ōigimi, 271
Bennomoto, 145
Bishop of Yokawa. *See* Yokawa,
Bishop of
Buddhism, 54, 190, 226, 282
Buddhist interpretations of *Genji*, 5-7
Byōdōin Temple, 221, 226

363

Index

Index

Index

Library of Congress Cataloging-in-Publication Data

Field, Norma, 1947-
The splendor of longing in the Tale of Genji.

Bibliography: p.   Includes index.
1. Murasaki Shikibu, b. 978? Genji monogatari. I. Title.
PL788.4.G43F5 1987   895.6'31   86-21224
ISBN 0-691-06691-4   ISBN 0-691-01436-1 (pbk.)